THE HUMANIST MOVEMENT IN MODERN BRITAIN

THE HUMANIST MOVEMENT IN MODERN BRITAIN

A History of Ethicists, Rationalists and Humanists

Callum G. Brown, David Nash and Charlie Lynch

With

Jessica Douthwaite and Linda Fleming

BLOOMSBURY ACADEMIC
LONDON • NEW YORK • OXFORD • NEW DELHI • SYDNEY

BLOOMSBURY ACADEMIC
Bloomsbury Publishing Plc
50 Bedford Square, London, WC1B 3DP, UK
1385 Broadway, New York, NY 10018, USA
29 Earlsfort Terrace, Dublin 2, Ireland

BLOOMSBURY, BLOOMSBURY ACADEMIC and the Diana logo are trademarks of
Bloomsbury Publishing Plc

First published in Great Britain 2023

Copyright © Callum G. Brown, David Nash and Charlie Lynch, 2023

Callum G. Brown, David Nash and Charlie Lynch have asserted their right under
the Copyright, Designs and Patents Act, 1988, to be identified as Author of this work.

Cover design by Akihiro Nakayama

Bloomsbury Publishing Plc does not have any control over, or responsibility for,
any third-party websites referred to or in this book. All internet addresses given in this
book were correct at the time of going to press. The author and publisher regret any
inconvenience caused if addresses have changed or sites have ceased to exist, but can
accept no responsibility for any such changes.

Every effort has been made to trace the copyright holders and obtain permission
to reproduce the copyright material. Please do get in touch with any enquiries or any
information relating to such material or the rights holder. We would be pleased to
rectify any omissions in subsequent editions of this publication should they be drawn
to our attention.

A catalogue record for this book is available from the British Library.

A catalog record for this book is available from the Library of Congress.

ISBN: PB: 978-1-3501-3660-1
HB: 978-1-3501-3661-8
ePDF: 978-1-3501-3662-5
eBook: 978-1-3501-3663-2

Typeset by Deanta Global Publishing Services, Chennai, India
Printed and bound in Great Britain

To find out more about our authors and books visit www.bloomsbury.com and sign up for
our newsletters.

CONTENTS

BIOGRAPHICAL SIDE PANELS

FIGURES

CONTRIBUTORS

Callum G Brown is Professor of Late Modern European History at the University of Glasgow, UK.

David Nash is Professor of History at the Oxford Brookes University, UK.

Charlie Lynch is Research Associate in History at Ulster University, Belfast, UK.

Jessica Douthwaite is Postdoctoral Research Fellow in History and Museology at University of Stirling, Scotland, UK.

Linda Fleming is a research affiliate at the University of Glasgow, UK

PREFACE

Humanism is still in the process of coming of age. From the inception of the Ethical Union in 1896, it comprised quite small numbers of members – a few thousand at most, and often fewer – combining a cerebral philosophical bent with what previous historians described as a quasi-religion including ethical 'worship'. Now, in the twenty-first century, the successor body, Humanists UK, is becoming close to a mass movement with a six-figure following, and a new assessment of earlier treatments is long overdue. We here recount this transition and the advance of the movement into new spheres of moral activism, influence in British society and government, and the digital age.

The book is intended to fill two gaps. One is in the library on the history of the nonreligion movement in Britain, where freethought, secularism and rationalism have been well served, but in which – most curiously – humanism has been rather neglected. A second gap is in the academic history of nonreligionism, to which this book likewise introduces humanism as the leading feature of a movement once held to be mainly secularist. By the 1950s humanism absorbed (and some would argue reduced) freethought, secularism and rationalism, evolving values and moral causes which now in the 2020s have become in many regards the ethical values of British society. With so many forms of heritage and objectives, tensions of expectation swirl in the humanist movement, but the enterprise here is to provide a coherent analytical narrative of its history.

Straddling from the 1890s to the 2020s, the sources used for this book are diverse. But researching the period 2000–21, the work has exposed the historian's new problems: the fading of hard-copy sources, the transience of websites, emails and attachments, and the greater reliance on recollection. Even digital newsletters and journals were hard to locate. We have footnoted our sources in every case, but some are not in any archive but came into our hands direct; we shall be depositing wherever we can in Bishopsgate Archive. But, despite the fickleness of the modern historical record – and indeed of the very 'archive-in-waiting' in the digital cloud – historians have no option but to rely on what they can see.

The book has been a team effort. Callum Brown has been mainly responsible for Chapters 1, 2, 4 (a), (c), and (e), most of 5, 6, 7, 8, two-thirds of 9, 10,

11 and 12, and most of 13; most biographical panels; copyediting, image selection, sources and index, preparation of the manuscript, financial control and project management at Glasgow and overall. David Nash has been mainly responsible for Chapters 3 (a), (b); 4 (b), (d); entries on blasphemy, secularism and moral education in Chapters 9(c), 10(b) and 12(d); copyediting, index and project management at Oxford Brookes. Charlie Lynch has been responsible for archival research forays in London and Edinburgh during Covid-19, considerable Zoom interviewing, and writing about one-third of Chapters 9, 10, 11 and 12; he also undertook spot research on demand and drafted several biographical panels.

Jessica Douthwaite, the project's first assistant, conducted research in archives and in-person oral-history interviews in the London area, digital data collection and finalised ethical approval. Linda Fleming conducted research in archives in Edinburgh and London, digital data collection, in-person oral-history interviews in the London area, and research and writing on education and several biographical side panels. Everybody contributed tracing of data and illustrations. Covid-19 forced vulnerable members of the team to self-isolate for long stretches, extending the period of the project. Unusually beset by circumstances (including Covid-19 and a severe illness afflicting Linda), the project has not been unaffected by the times in which it was produced. But with everybody pulling in the same direction, the project was completed.

FOREWORD

*P*rofessor Alice Roberts, president of Humanists UK 2019–22
    Though there's a very long history of humanistic thought, going right back to ancient Greek and Indian schools of philosophy, there's also a more recent history, from the twentieth century to the present day, which shows how humanism – as a movement – grew in confidence, and has had a real impact on philosophies, values and morals in wider society. In the nineteenth century, many started to see moral progress and social reform as something which could be pursued quite separately from religion and ethical societies formed in Britain, fusing in 1896 to form the Union of Ethical Societies which, by 2018, had evolved into a major organisation, Humanists UK.

I have been privileged to be president of Humanists UK. As a humanist 'in public', I am often asked the question by religious people – how can I have morals, without religion? It's a question that I think – perhaps even more than the belief or nonbelief in divinity – gets right to the heart of the real difference between a humanist and a religious worldview, and comes with a tacit suggestion that, as a nonreligious person, you must be somehow adrift when it comes to possessing a moral compass: amoral – perhaps even, immoral. My local vicar once asked me over a cup of tea at the vicarage: where do morals come from, if not religion? She didn't intend it as an insult – it was a genuine, if somewhat surprising, enquiry. I suggested that the fundamental difference between us was possibly this: she believed that morality came from *outside* humans, and I thought it came from *inside* us.

It was a question tackled by Margaret Knight, a psychology lecturer at Aberdeen University, in a pair of radio essays on *Morals without Religion* broadcast in 1955 on the BBC's Home Service. Her focus was education and the teaching of morals to children. 'Parents are repeatedly told', she said, 'that there can be no sound character-training that is not based on religion.' She then demolished that proposal, making the case for humanism. 'Why should I consider others?' she posed rhetorically. 'These ultimate moral questions, like all ultimate questions, can be desperately difficult to answer . . . [but] I think the only possible answer to this question is the humanist one – because we are naturally social beings; we live in communities; and life in any community, from the family outwards, is much happier, and fuller, and richer if the members are friendly and cooperative than if they are hostile and resentful.' And she added: 'I have never yet met the child – and I have met very few adults – to whom it has ever occurred to raise the question: "Why should I consider others?"'

Margaret Knight's essays sound so measured and reasonable to most of us today, testament to just how far humanist influence spread through the later twentieth century. Because, at the time, her broadcasts resulted in a storm of antipathy, provoking thousands of letters to Knight herself, the BBC and to newspapers. Knight was hounded and vilified in the press for several weeks, accused of being anti-Christian, unpatriotic and dangerous. But then a significant proportion of letter writers to the BBC were also responding in a positive way: 'At last someone is saying these things we have felt for so long', wrote one listener. We can now see Margaret Knight's broadcasts as a turning point – not only a marker on the journey towards secularism in Britain but also as the moment when a theological question was transformed into a philosophical one and opened up for public debate. Though Knight was criticised for not knowing enough theology, her argument was not dumbed down. Instead, it was devastatingly simple. Her really dangerous idea was not that morals could be taught without religion, but that these things could be open for *everyone* to debate. She reduced the argument down to basic principles and made it understandable and accessible. Ordinary people could dare to think for themselves.

The history of humanism in Britain throughout the twentieth and into the twenty-first century is a truly extraordinary one. It's here, within these pages. And we've come a long way in just a century and a quarter.

Alice Roberts

ACKNOWLEDGEMENTS

The idea for this book came from David Pollock, a long-time trustee at Humanists UK and office bearer in various capacities over six decades at the Oxford University Humanist Group, Ethical Union, British Humanist Association, Rationalist Press Association and their successors. He lived through almost half the period covered and was a leading committee member and chair across the organisations. He has also been an assiduous collector of the movement's paperwork, forming an unmatched personal archive to which he allowed us free access. He was interviewed by us repeatedly on events to which he was witness and ensured that the authors had access to as much accurate detail as was feasible to include.

The authors are indebted to the generous funding from the trustees of Humanists UK, and to the liaison work of David Pollock which facilitated access to information and interviewees. The funding enabled us to employ three research assistants in succession from October 2018 to September 2021 – Jessica Douthwaite, Linda Fleming and Charlie Lynch – who each undertook considerable archival research, most of the interviews and administration. Linda was sadly forced to retire completely from work in mid-project after suffering a cerebral haemorrhage in January 2020 and then, thankfully, recovering. Charlie joined the research and writing team in April 2020.

Thanks go to the present and former humanists, staff and office-bearers who gave generously of their time, allowing us to interview them (live or via Zoom), sometimes repeatedly. A full list appears in the sources. Special commendation for transcription at an impressive speed and quality goes to Jessica Douthwaite, Linda Fleming, Charlie Lynch and, for the greater number of interviews, Ben Boswell Jones.

A wide variety of archives, archivists and librarians have been unfailingly helpful. These have been led by Stefan Dickers and his staff at Bishopsgate Archive, Sophie Hawkey-Edwards late of Conway Hall Library and Archive and Richard Bapty at Glasgow University Library who set up online sources during Covid-19 and sorted broken hyperlinks. Great assistance also came from the Institute of Education, London; National Library of Scotland, Edinburgh; Bodleian Library,

Oxford; and Hertfordshire Archives. Several people provided generous access to their personal archives: David Pollock (whose material is now in Bishopsgate Archive), John Leeson and Nigel Collins. Additionally, we are grateful to David Pollock, our interviewees and Humanists UK staff for locating digital materials.

Grateful thanks for permission to use unpublished research goes to Jessica Beck (for her PhD on the musical women of Conway Hall), and Jessica Roper (for her MA dissertation on British humanism 1945–58).

The Covid-19 emergency from February 2020 to September 2021 delayed the project, principally because of archival closure. Pre-Covid-19 oral-history interviews were conducted in-person, the remainder by Zoom, all with transcription 'by hand'. Noteworthy and brave service was rendered by Charlie Lynch who made two archival trips to London during relative lulls in the pandemic (and who memorably described the atmosphere on the Glasgow-bound sleeper train departing London during the first lockdown as like the last helicopter out of Saigon). Thanks are due to Deborah Mills, Tom Sutcliffe and Richard Whittle for providing Charlie with accommodation, hospitality and assistance in London. Special acknowledgement for workaround solutions go to Stefan Dickers and his staff at Bishopsgate Institute, and, at Conway Hall Ethical Society, Carl Harrison (who found SPES data for us), Jim Walsh and Liz Lutgendorff (chair, CEO and former chair, respectively).

Thanks also to Fraser Sutherland, CEO of Humanist Society Scotland, for the supply of a Survation 2018 poll and advice; Rhian Beynon, adoption manager, for advice on the evolution of adoption procedure; Patsy Wallace for advice about the Funeral Tribute Archive; Clive Field for settling a query on the *Puzzled People* report; and Daryl Leeworthy of Swansea University for insights into the humanist heritage of the Labour Party in Wales. At the University of Glasgow, our special gratitude goes to Elaine Wilson for financial supervision in trying times, Trish MacLaren for extensive HR assistance, Jenny Hutchison for her support, and Michael Brady, Catherine Steel and Roibeard Ó Maolalaigh for being there during the project's emergency.

Images come from a variety of sources. The greater number are from Bishopsgate Archive, and thanks go to Stefan Dickers for supplying these. Other photographs were supplied by National Picture Gallery, Matthew Horwood, Andrew West/Humanists UK and the Rationalist Association. Photograph credits appear beneath each.

Lastly, thanks for assiduous reading of drafts go to Lynn Abrams, Andrew Copson, Bert Gasenbeek, Madeleine Goodall, Gary McLelland, David Pollock and Jim Tomlinson, who all saved us from making errors of omission and commission, and pointed us to new perspectives. The remaining shortcomings are the responsibility of the authors. Our partners and significant others played their customary supportive parts, for which we are grateful and, where relevant, sorry.

ABBREVIATIONS

AAS (IAS)	Agnostics Adoption Society (from 1969, Independent Adoption Society)
AGM	annual general meeting
ALRA	Abortion Law Reform Association
BA	Bishopsgate Archive
BHA	British Humanist Association
C100	Committee of 100 (nuclear disarmament)
CND	Campaign for Nuclear Disarmament
CHES	Conway Hall Ethical Society (2012–)
CHLA	Conway Hall Library and Archive
DPA	David Pollock Archive (in BA)
DPP	Director of Public Prosecutions
CO	conscientious objector
CUP	Cambridge University Press
EGM	extraordinary general meeting
EU	Ethical Union 1920–65
FPSI	Federation of Progressive Societies and Individuals
GALHA	Gay and Lesbian Humanist Association
HCMRE	Humanist Committee on Moral and Religious Education
HET	Hets Utrechts Archief (Utrecht Municipal Archive)
HLRS	Homosexual Law Reform Society
HO	Home Office
HPG	Humanist Parliamentary Group
HSS	Humanist Society Scotland
JLA	John Leeson Archive
IEU/IUES	International Ethical Union/International Union of Ethical Societies
IHEU	International Humanist and Ethical Union (1952-2018)
ILEA	Inner London Education Authority
LEA	Local Education Authority

LGBTQ+	Lesbian Gay Bisexual Transgender Queer and inclusion of others
LPA	Lambeth Palace Archive
LSS	Leicester Secular Society
MIL	Moral Instruction League
NCCL	National Council for Civil Liberties
NGO	non-governmental organisation
NLS	National Library of Scotland
NSS	National Secular Society
ODNB	*Oxford Dictionary of National Biography*
OUHG	Oxford University Humanist Group
OUHGA	Oxford University Humanist Group online archive
OUP	Oxford University Press
PHG	Parliamentary Humanist Group
PL	Progressive League
PMC	Public Morality Council (1899-1965)
RA	Rationalist Association (2003-)
RE	religious education
RPA	Rationalist Press Association (1899-2003)
RPS	Rationalist Peace Society
SACRE	Standing Advisory Committee on Religious Education
SHF	Student Humanist Federation 1968-77
SMC	Social Morality Council (1965-)
SPES	South Place Ethical Society (-2012)
TNA	The National Archive
UDC	Union for Democratic Control
UES	Union of Ethical Societies 1896-1920
UDHR	Universal Declaration of Human Rights
UHF	University Humanist Federation 1959-1968
UN	United Nations
UNESCO	United Nations Economic, Social and Cultural Organisation
VES	Voluntary Euthanasia Society
WA	Wellcome Archive
WSPU	Women's Social and Political Union

1 INTRODUCTION

On Thursday, 30 April 1896, the Union of Ethical Societies (UES) was formed as the first national organisation in Britain professing what we now call humanism. Emerging in 2018 as Humanists UK, the humanist movement developed over 125 years as a significant philosophical, moral and social-reform cause whose mixture of utopianism with practical social activism appealed to British intellectuals, elite scientists, middle-class professionals and idealistic young people as they sought to conjure a progressive future for humankind. Relatively small in scale until the twenty-first century, the movement has been much overlooked, dismissed by some historians as the fading legacy of a once-mighty Victorian secularism, and too often elided in wider cultural histories. For most of the period, the numbers in the formal membership of the humanist movement were small, fewer than five or six thousand. But from 2010, members and supporters grew at a blistering pace, reaching in 2021 around 100,000. Yet, as this book shows, the significance of the humanist movement has been underrated. In the midst of secularisation, its mixture of science, rationality and an evolving ethical standpoint offered an alternative to the moral power of the churches, achieving an astonishing, for some bewildering, influence in international affairs and domestic social policy. Prone to intermittent decline and internal rancour, it started to blossom as a mass movement by championing a distinctive ethical approach to human rights, sexual liberty and the autonomy of the individual. Using extensive archival research and oral-history interviews, this book offers the first full assessment of the humanist movement's impact on modern Britain, and how the major organisation, Humanists UK, came to be by 2021 the central organisation of British nonreligionism.

In this chapter, we look first at how historians have perceived the British humanist movement and introduce the ways in which we will offer a distinctive scholarly revisionism. In the second section, we introduce the central building in London and its role since 1929 in conferring much unity to a movement of many kindred bodies.

(a) What is at stake: this book's interventions

Humanism is to be found in most nations of the world, especially of the West. But it is a movement diverse in its international configuration, foundations and influence. In nations such as Belgium, the Netherlands, Germany and Norway, humanist bodies have gained large-scale membership within so-called pillared societies, in which each major religious and political tradition (or pillar), including humanism, has been allowed a degree of state funding to create separate civil institutions (ranging from hospitals, schools and newspapers to broadcasting and cooperative ventures). In the United States, which figured large in the origins of organised British humanism, religious freedom and a constitution with a secularist First Amendment endowed ethicist and humanist organisations with a vigorous patriotic attachment – to uphold legal freedoms in the courts, and to combat the country's Cold War rhetoric of 'godless communism'. In India, humanism has been erected on the back of early atheistic materialist thought like Lokāyata, J. S. Mill liberalism and a modern Marxist tradition within the anti-colonial movement. And adjacent movements to humanism, such as secularism and freethought, enjoyed vigorous influence in many nations including Marxist regimes.

In Britain, though, the twentieth-century experience of the humanist movement has seemed at best erratic and perhaps overall diminishing. Much of the time it has been one of the smallest of nonreligious movements in Europe, but adorned by a variety of organisations with different currents, each offering an alternative to church and faith. Its activists drew upon a long tradition of freedom of thought, radicalism and philosophical innovation in public meetings, demonstrations and publications to pursue a broad agenda of moral change and freedom. By the 1890s, this was signalled in the various names by which its supporters identified themselves or were known: freethinkers, secularists, atheists, agnostics, rationalists, sceptics (now most often rendered as skeptics), un- or non-believers, nonreligionists, apostates, infidels, progressives (though a much-contested word), ethicists and, rarer at that time, humanists. It was the last of these that was to become by the 1950s the moniker of choice to identify the moral turn of modern nonbelief – the positive purpose of social reconstruction beyond mere atheism and separation of church from state. Secularist and other organisations aligned and affiliated with humanist organisations to create a movement which, on the outside, seemed divided and fractured but which, from the inside, was diverse yet strongly unified behind core values and campaigns. This book is concerned with the emerging stature of the humanist movement in Britain, from its coming of age on the formation of the Union of Ethical Societies in 1896 (renamed the Ethical Union in 1920, becoming known from 1963 as the British Humanist Association and then formally reconstituted as such in 1967), and its journey until the 2010s when the main organisation became known as Humanists UK; meanwhile, the ethical brand survived in the influential South Place Ethical Society (renamed the Conway Hall Ethical Society in 2012), and a plethora of affiliated local and special interest groups and a sister organisation in Scotland. So, this is a history of a movement, not a history of ideas. The task here is to follow the character and campaigns, successes and failures, and strengths and weaknesses, to expose the influence of an organised cause with many interests in national and international affairs.

The work of humanism has a longer history than the use of the word itself, which has disputed origins. Some place the term's roots in the fifteenth or sixteenth centuries, some in early-nineteenth-century educational theory and then from 1841 among historians *describing* the Renaissance, and in the 1870s to 1900s for modern usage in a secular and ethicist context.[1] Though a term claimed by Christian traditions, modern humanist scholars emphasise its emergence as always carrying implications contrary to religion, bearing upon humanity as possessing history, evolution and morality independent of a deity. It is in the ancient world that that argument still reigns regarding the origins of what became known as humanism. Historians of philosophy have looked to the city-states of classical Greece and the tradition (and more especially the reputation) established by Socrates as when essential ingredients of humanism emerged within a civil polity: individual responsibility, consciousness, freedom of the will, freedom of belief, and the possibility of atheism (on which he was charged). Other things have been assigned to classical origins – democracy (though Socrates experienced the populist danger of a jury of 300 assigning him to death by suicide as a scapegoat for Athenian civil problems); and atheism (though Socrates denied he adhered, if his *Apology* is to be believed as his own sentiments). Taken up, some have argued, by ancient Rome, the course of unbelief and humanism over the medieval and early modern periods has in recent years been undergoing a rediscovery, with the result that what is emerging from the scholarship is the long-term existence of religious unbelief, of protest against religious hegemony too, but yet victimisation of nonreligionists and the stifling of nonreligious morality.[2] Despite this, nonbelief and an argued atheism were emerging in Western society in the eighteenth century, fostered partly by science, philosophy and the Enlightenment, but partly by political jolts like the American Constitution of 1788 and the French Revolution of 1789, each bearing witness to secularist ideas. Those ideas rocked Britain too, but less strongly than in most of Europe as, between the 1770s and 1900, it was industrialisation and the fight for workers' rights that constituted the main venue for the struggle cultivated by freethought and secularist traditions.

With the rise of secularism in Victorian Britain, ethicism emerged as a rival moral position to religions, culminating in 1896 in the formation of the UES where this book starts to chart the movement's development. Though some regional ethical societies remain untraced, the movement came to appeal disproportionately to a London and South-East secular elite, and by the 1930s and 1940s it acquired considerable intellectual influence, literary cachet and social policy and internationalist impact. In the mid-twentieth century, the movement did much to change the law and moral compass of the nation, leading the way also in framing internationalism in the postcolonial world. Yet, it remained a small movement of fewer than a thousand paid-up activists until the boom years of the 1960s when it caught the zeitgeist among students. As this book chronicles, there then followed a spectacular decline from 1970 until the mid-1990s, which only started to fully reverse after 2000, leading ten years later to an explosion of joining. This is a roller coaster of fortunes, with changing demographics, diverging moral positions and contested machinations of political ideology, leading to instability, internal ructions and competing external associations. It was an irony that the secularist movement in its broadest sense enjoyed far greater numbers and commitment, especially from the working classes, in the late Georgian and Victorian era of strong churches and religious growth than it did amid the church decline and fading personal faith of the twentieth century.

The almost constant crisis of scale – the failure of membership drives – puzzled humanist leaders, no more so than in the 1950s when, no matter what it did, the movement could not attract the young man and woman. Yet, as we will show in this book, the young did come to the movement but in two different generations. The first surge came with the expansion in university students in the 1960s, the so-called 'me generation' – a breakaway cohort fleeing the fusty morality and academic subjects of bourgeois respectability, and many young women, grasping new social-science subjects and the moral turn towards autonomy and individualism, who joined student humanist societies. The second surge occurred after 2000, again perhaps mostly students or the young graduates of the millennial digital cohort who seemed, in the main, to join the humanist movement online via social media rather than campus societies. The savvy humanist activists, reorientating the movement into vibrant campaigning meetings, found it easy to harvest the young to the new moral concerns – LGBTQ+, anti-racism and the desire to be free from religion. The 'social-media' medium that did so much to transmit humanist morality in the 2010s became, in a sense, part of the message.

We spend time in this book examining the demographics of the movement. If the young became humanists with really very marked inconsistency, certain groups joined in large numbers – teachers, intellectuals and elite research scientists. We look in some detail at the gilded age between 1930 and 1970 when, under the utopian inspiration of H. G. Wells and the canny leadership of Harold J. Blackham, the British humanist cause led not just world humanists but some global institutions. Much was achieved in those decades as humanism was positioned as a brand of moral thinking that would endure well into the twenty-first century – to undergird modern knowledge, learning, social campaigning and international peace with human rights. This is why a history of British ethicism and humanism is important. The humanist movement did not achieve scale until recent years, but, before it did, it had already assisted much to crafting the moral foundations of the modern world.

(b) The place and approach of this book

Until now, the history of the humanist movement in modern Britain has been served mainly by two types of study.

There have been in-house books, each focussing customarily on one organisation or cause, in which the internal developments, policies and politics of adjacent movements to humanism have been examined in detail: the movements of freethought, secularism and rationalism. Written by long-term members of the movement – enthusiasts 'who were there' – they contributed an institutional history evoking a sense of the passion, service, achievement and, occasionally, the disputes, with much focus on the role of leading men and women. Books by Horace J. Bridges, Gustav Spiller, A. Gowans Whyte, David Tribe, Jim Herrick and Bill Cooke provide much contemporaneous as well as historical observation.[3] Most usefully, despite often focussing on one organisation, these authors displayed the elements of unity and the collective mentality of the nonreligious movement, in which diverse humanist and secularist organisations have long held strong cross-membership, a phenomenon we shall observe repeatedly. This offers a sharp contrast to the historiography of the Christian religion in late modern Britain, most of which is organised by denomination, written by denominational adherents and sometimes published by denominational series or imprints. Additionally, church historians are frequently employed as lecturers in university theology, religious studies or history departments; none of the in-house historiography of nonreligion has shared the same academic privilege.

There has been a limited academic literature on the history of humanism – including monographs, doctoral theses and many articles, most of it published since the 1960s, and seemingly the entirety of it conducted within the walls of history, sociology and sometimes philosophy departments rather than religious studies units. The history of humanist thought, both in Britain and internationally, has been absorbed into a wider history of philosophy and secularism and has a strong reputation for scholarship. Ian McKillop's *The British Ethical Societies* (1986) is an important study stretching from the 1790s to the 1970s that focusses mainly on the philosophical history of the societies, based on a close and informed reading of the writers, speakers and their publications, and gives a powerful sense of the evolutionary intellectual momentum from ethicism to humanism. However, McKillop's approach is lighter on the movement's outreach into social reform, international causes and parliament, changing fortunes and internal disputes.[4]

In the realm of social, cultural and organisational history of the humanist movement, previous literature has focussed upon the eighteenth and nineteenth centuries, with a recent surge of approaches to the early twentieth century and including some sociological studies of the 1950s and 1970s. Led by publications by Edward Royle, they include Susan Budd's leading treatment of the twentieth century, David Nash's many books and articles, and Liz Lutgendorf's recent contribution.[5] The post-1950 period has been poorly treated by historians, largely because social historians like Callum Brown have hitherto adopted a religious-history approach to humanists – on the history of atheists and humanists, their social experience of losing religion, and on the contest between the humanist movement and the British churches for a place in civil society.[6] Likewise, in sociology and anthropology of religion, there have been key works on the composition and approaches to humanism developed by sociologist Colin Campbell in the 1960s (whose work we study in Chapter 2) and more recently by a range of scholars including Matthew Engelke, but in much of which there has remained a lingering anchorage to religious-history concepts.[7] New work has grown, specifically feminist history, with Laura Schwartz's major study of Victorian 'infidel women' in the freethought movement, Jessica Beck's study of women and music in the South Place Ethical Society, and Madeleine Goodall's authorship in the Humanist Heritage project.[8]

But the field is still underdeveloped, and this book aims to supply some important new approaches and challenges. At its heart, the volume seeks to lay down key narrative innovations which locate the humanist cause – numerically small as its membership might imply – as at the heart of the developing British and, more broadly, Western values of the twentieth- and twenty-first centuries.

First, there is no overview of the development of the movement from the foundation in 1896 of the Union of Ethical Societies to the present. There were tortuous struggles about disunity, failed organisational mergers, attempts at administrative union of headquarters and efforts at increasing cooperation both within the movement and beyond its borders. But we explore in this book the extent to which the surface disunity might have been a strength, efficiently distributing tasks in an often-hostile civil society. When the Union of Ethical Societies was formed in 1896, modern Christianity was in many ways at its peak in Britain, and nonbelief organisations were exposed to much hostility and contempt. Church membership per capita was at its peak between 1890 and 1914, with Christian denominations enjoying a supremacy of social institutions: weekly churchgoing marked family and individual respectability, whilst alignment to Christian faith and social values was required for acceptance in most strata of society. In comparison to the millions who went to church weekly, organised atheism and secularism had rather low support. Among the late-Victorian and early-twentieth-century intellectual bohemians, those who became the Bloomsbury Group and its regional equivalents, a more cavalier irreligious attitude prevailed.[9] So too in parts of the trade unions and the left of the Labour Movement – though it is important to recall that British working-class movements were far more Christian-based than their European counterparts which aligned to Marxism and laicity.[10] Within a monopolistic Christian culture, the British ethical movement was overwhelmingly congregated in London and the south east, and much weaker in places, notably Leicester, where secularism had been firmly established in the mid-nineteenth century.[11] The uneven geographical development of the humanist movement will be examined in this book, as too will its very uneven chronological progress, resulting in periods of stasis, decline and then most rapid growth.

Second, from this synoptic account the authors will re-examine some key academic arguments. One is the accepted narrative that secularism and adjacent movements including ethicism and humanism were at a low ebb from the 1890s to at least the 1930s, and then, in some accounts, declined further. In various guises in separate studies by Edward Royle and Susan Budd, the case has been allowed that secularism was a movement of the nineteenth century that essentially withered, albeit gradually, to form in the twentieth century an honourable but largely inconsequential presence in British society. Royle's version of this 'declinist' argument begins in the mid-1880s when, he says, 'Secularism sank into the background' and its support slipped away, the victim of secularisation as much as religion. Though rationalism fared better, Royle considers it lacked the credentials of a 'religio-political organisation', whilst ethicism, he claims, peaked in 1906 with the Ethical Union, falling into decline after 1918, with most societies closing, and only the South Place Ethical Society remaining by the 1990s as 'an active participant in various agitations for freedom of thought and expression'.[12] Yet, we show in this book that ethicism was broader and more resilient than this, much of it transforming into the humanist movement, including the Hampstead Ethical Institute as late as till 2015. Nowhere in Royle's narrative does he identify the significance of the evolution from ethicism to humanism. In Susan Budd's similar declinist narrative, what she characterises as 'militant secularism' crashed in the inter-war years due to the dominance of social Darwinism and eugenics – which then, she argues, imploded under the intellectual weight of a new Christian-based science elite, fear of communist influence and incessant intellectual disquiet within the Rationalist Press Association; this led, she says, to a 'contemporary mood of ennui' and 'the emotional residue of the falling apart of the intellectual universe of knowledge itself'.[13] This declinist gloss, focussed on philosophical intellectualism, has recently been challenged effectively by Liz Lutgendorf's study of secularist and ethical writing down to 1930.[14] But in the main, the reason why Budd's declinist narrative has prevailed for so long is because of her concentration on elite science and philosophy debates, with insufficient attention being paid to the *changing nature* of the nonreligious movement. One shift she understated was that from an overwhelmingly working-class-backed cause, founded on Victorian worker organisations mainly of the Midlands, north of England and Scotland, marshalled in radical *secularist* societies and groups still marked by a timbre of grassroots activism, to an ethical, *humanist* movement with a rising middle-class component located strongly in London, the south east and the south coast. Though worker atheism did not disappear, this social and geographical shift gave the cause a new and well-ventilated voice, one in which modern intellectualism, science and a literary brand of social utopianism flourished in the second quarter of the twentieth century. The ethical movement and its moral causes did not gain the prominence under Budd's recounting that it deserved. She presented secularism as the signal ideology of the movement as a whole until quite late, really the 1960s, focussing her readers' attention on how it 'attempted to destroy Christianity or replace it by reason or by religions of socialism or ethics'.[15] She arrives at this presentation by mistakenly projecting the movement's character of the mid-nineteenth century forward into the very different world of the mid-twentieth century, one which we assess closely in this book.

A third issue is a case, long advanced, that the nonreligious movement has been a religion and should be treated as such by the historian. Susan Budd asserted in 1967 that 'Humanist groups have the character of a sect in that they reject or oppose much of the wider society, [and] are composed of converts' – two statements, carefully deploying the language of religions, neither of which were justified or fully correct even in the decade when written, and which became almost wholly incorrect as declining proportions of supporters belonged to any religion prior to atheism.[16] Ten years later, Budd wrote that the nonreligious movement was an example 'of "advanced" religious groups', perceived by Durkheim as a seamless web characterised by '[t]heology, eschatology, metaphysics, ritual practices' that are 'all bound together by the cake of custom'. She based this, again, on projecting forward her initial reading of the movement in the 1810s when the future South Place Ethical Society was still a Unitarian chapel.[17] Yet, Budd went further to assert that the humanist 'movement does not have value-systems which are clearly defined', but is over-ridden by a 'belief in argument and discussion' in which being 'anti-Christian' was, alone, a unifier: 'The antipathy to religion can be invoked in a group setting to reunite an otherwise dissident group.' The lack of agreement across the movement, Budd averred, caused endemic division, undermining the unity of this 'religion', and did not dent the fact that 'the majority of Humanists have previously been strongly religious'.[18]

That mistaken contention that nonreligion was in fact a religion was to be found expressed by two further scholars. Shirley Mullen approached what she called 'the religion of unbelief' via research on six freethought journals between 1841 and 1872, arguing that freethinkers regarded learned metaphysical and theological thinking as a prerequisite to being a secularist.[19] In the most considered and oft-repeated case of all, Edward Royle proposed across several publications that secularism in the nineteenth century had been, and should be, likened to a religion, and proceeded to apply that test across all the periods of his studies. In characteristics and membership, he argued secularism overlapped with movements cut from a similar cloth – the Positivists, the ethicists and the rationalists – 'which co-existed with Secularist societies like separate denominations within a parallel – or indeed parody – of the Christian world'. He went on that, despite defining themselves as a large collective group, secularists also gave much time to debating activities within their organisations, just as Christian denominations did. Even atheist history mirrored religious history, Royle postulated, using religious terms and rhetoric – apostles, missionaries, gospel – existing within a 'freethought denominationalism' adorned with the birthdays of Paine and Owen being marked akin to Christmas day; so, 'celebrations enjoyed by Christians were not denied to atheists'. Royle emphasised the evidence of secularists observing religious festivals, and Sabbath observance with lessons, socialist hymn singing and study of the bible's errors. In Royle's rhetoric, we see a movement opposed to religion that could not define itself separately from a religious model and deployed religious terminology. Radical freethought, he wrote, 'can best be understood as an anti-religious sect, an extreme form of Nonconformity' with similar 'emotional and social satisfactions of the religious life', whilst secularism 'served a quasi-religious function'. Royle contrasts secularism as 'the freethought of the chapel' with the ethical movement as 'the freethought of the Church – even the High Church'. He applied the religious barometer to organised nonreligionism so seriously that he dismissed the Rationalist Press Association as having 'more in common with a book club than with a church', whilst the National Secular Society of the twentieth century should be 'compared to a campaigning charity'. Add to this Royle's regard for the movement's rituals (including readings) and you have 'services' seemingly mirroring those of the churches continuing as late as the 1960s.[20] Moreover, it is indicative of how many scholars persisted in thinking that nonreligionism needed assessment by secularist and rationalist criteria, rather than by ethicist and humanist measures.

Contrastingly, in this book we emphasise the transition from ethicism to humanism in the twentieth century, in a changing character in which 'religion', as conventionally understood, did not apply, and in which legacies of religious-like ritual were gradually abandoned; what remained was *human* ritual. Reorientating understanding of humanism as different from religion has been broached by anthropologist Matthew Engelke in studies of a local humanist group in the London area and of a Humanists UK management meeting. He emphasised the *difference* between religion and nonreligion, observing that humanists help to define how Christianity and belief are different, just as Christians have over a long period tried to define what atheists are – to such an extent, it might be added, that humanists are busily undoing much of that legacy of mistaken definition.[21] But in a further study, Engelke exposed how the de-sacralisation of the crematorium prior to humanist funerals, to remove 'the religion' as it were from church-like spaces, was yet accompanied by complex negotiation between the 'mere' materiality of the coffin and its symbolism – between the rationalist's view of the absent deceased (with no life after death) to their unavoidable presence for the grieving attendees, notably at the emotive committal.[22] In a third study, he showed how the humanist conception of happiness was constructed as both a pleasure and a purpose – something thoroughly secular, this-worldly, similar to the Enlightenment thought of Kant and Hume, but, for most humanists, not acquired through the reading of those, but rather through their celebration at Humanists UK-organised annual lectures (now broadcast online), events and publications.[23] In this book, we move further in argument to embrace humanist action. Four main elements of the humanist moral campaigning can be identified in the period 1896–2021: freedom of thought and expression based on rationalism; humanitarianism; the individual's autonomy over their own body; and internationalism of 'one world' government and the equality of human rights. Within each of these, we will come across numerous nonreligious moral campaigns which conferred both identity for individual humanists and for the movement.

There is a last, more conceptual, historiographical context to be contemplated for humanism. The most lauded magnum opus of recent faith-based historical scholarship has been Charles Taylor's *A Secular Age* of 2007 in which he acknowledged, though berated, the weakness of modern secularism's intellectualism and the failure of its morality. His narrative follows Christianity's (Western) 'descent' through three stages of secularity: Secularity 1 in which religion was divorced from politics; Secularity 2 the decline of religious belief, practice and churchgoing; and finally Secularity 3 in which there was a slide from a position (in 1500 CE) when belief was unchallengeable and unbelief 'virtually impossible' to a position (after the 1960s, in Taylor's account) when belief emerged no longer axiomatic, was hard to sustain, and sometimes 'never even seems an eligible possibility'.[24] Extolled by faith scholars for its complexity and admixture of philosophical and social history, *Secular Age* has attracted considerable criticism from broadly secular scholars, not least for the weakness of its command of recent research. One criticism offered by Callum Brown has been Taylor's failure to acknowledge that the endpoint of this decline is not his supposed transformation of faith into a brand of spirituality, but is atheism – comprehensive nonbelief – constituting a stage beyond the hard-to-sustain belief of Secularity 3: in other words, a 'Secularity 4' requires recognition.[25] To grasp this stage fully in the twentieth century is to accept the evidence that secularism did not progress alone into atheism, but was escorted by an increasingly humanistic moral order. In this volume, we will see how ethicism translated into a complex, multi-dimensional campaigning humanism that itself became a hugely influential marker of modern Western ethics.

So, in this book, we present the humanist movement historically – as a consequential outcome of secularism, freethought and ethicism, but in which the humanist activist emerges as a policy progressive committed to undoing the legacy of a religion deeply embedded in social organisation and the self. The reformation of society and self becomes a story that started in nineteenth-century secularism but flourished in twentieth-century ethical social policy, re-worked as an expanding pursuit of human rights. In this process, we consider that the ritual in humanism should not be taken to be a synonym for religion. The ritual that the movement cultivated in the late twentieth century took the form of humanist weddings, funerals and baby namings, but these were not equivalent to *religious* rituals; *rites de passage* are a feature of all humanity, antecedent to and surviving organised religion.[26] In any event, as we shall see, the meaning of 'religion' has been contested by some humanists, claiming it as something bigger than merely conventional religions.

This leads to an observation concerning the steadily-spreading vocabulary of humanism in British daily life. A trend has been identified by religious studies scholars of the infusion since 1970 of the vocabulary and ideology of New Age religions, ornamented by the word 'spiritual', into mainstream religion, popular culture, advertising and capitalism.[27] By the same token, we point to the 'humanist turn' of Western culture since the 1940s: the conjunction of social policy with humanist ideas, science, comprehensive humanitarianism and secular rationalism, accompanied by leisurely secularism and contraction of the supernatural in everyday life. This has had epistemological consequence. Historians of charities and the 'third sector' have noted of modern non-governmental organisations (NGOs) that they constituted locations for creating new meanings in politics, which challenged for dominance, becoming part of an expanded notion of 'the political' entering late modern culture. One such was 'human rights', in which, as we shall see, the British humanist movement played a major part from the 1940s to the 2020s. Chris Moores notes recently how the vocabulary of NGOs spread, extending into other organisations: peace organisations (Peace Pledge Union and the Campaign for Nuclear Disarmament), science ethics (like the 'Pugwash' organisation, which we approach in Part 2) and human rights (like the National Council for Civil Liberties, now called Liberty).[28] It has been insufficiently recognised how much the humanist movement was a hub for new vocabularies and their meanings being projected into British public spaces, legal reform, campaign zones and internationalism. Humanist claims to success have not been complete by any means; opponents resisted this 'turn' in areas like school education and assisted dying where, as we shall see, change emerged less well advanced by 2021 than humanists hoped. All the same, the 'humanist turn' in culture was evident in changing speech and sentiment – in areas such as health care and sexual freedoms in which humanist sexologists were especially active from the 1940s to the 1970s, in religious and nonreligious rights, in the rights of the individual over their body, and over their own death. The process, seemingly subtle, helped entrench secularisation, contributing also to the process that altered the dominant radical rhetoric of the left – from class struggle to human rights, and from community to the individual.[29] It may have contributed, too, to the changing rhetoric of the churches – from sin, grace and redemption to justice, equality and rights. Even the ecclesiastical recourse to 'the spiritual' – as a way in the early twenty-first century to re-establish faith in secular discourse – gets confused when some atheists also lay claim to it. Rhetoric was disputed, no longer signaling a hegemonic discourse. But the trend over the period 1900–2020 has remained indisputably in the direction of the secular.

The development path for the humanist movement has never been straightforward. The rebellious and protesting edge to the cause, and the will to fight establishments, were inherited from freethought and secularism. Yet, humanists had practical schemes to be achieved by negotiation and persuasion, including with churches, even if humanists seldom agreed among themselves on such tactics. The opportunities for making great strides in numbers and influence required some tolerance of compromise with opposing, invariably religious, camps. Such tensions within the humanist movement have never, and may never, fade entirely, but actually achieving those strides persuades doubters of the merits of becoming part of a reforming civil society rather than perennially shouting at it from outside. Part of the cause here were the demographics of British humanists, explored in Chapter 2, in which we expose over 125 years the changing population composition and shifting modes of developing the humanist self. One innovation we note as a tactical success of the movement was the identification of an external constituency of people – those who did not formally join a humanist organisation did not necessarily call themselves humanists, and who in some cases continued to associate with a church, but who, notwithstanding, must properly be recognised as an attachment to the humanist movement. These we call 'proto-humanists', including atheists recognised as humanitarians, men and women who came to the humanist feast of ethical reflection, many of whom frequented Conway Hall in London giving lectures at humanist and progressive conferences. They demonstrate how the *reach* of humanism into British civil society went beyond humanist membership to influence science, policy and moral sensibilities, and thence into government and even church circles. To exert influence, humanists had to attest to their moral beliefs, but they inclined others to attest too. From the 1910s particularly, humanists populated the committee rooms, the parliamentary benches, the diplomatic legations and the international conferences of the emerging 'global village', bringing an agenda of postcolonial change, rights and justice, and transnational cooperation.

HAROLD J. BLACKHAM 1903–2009

FIGURE 1 Harold J. Blackham. Photo: Bert Verhoeff / Anefo, (Dutch) Nationaal Archief, CCO.

Harold Blackham (HJ to his friends) is widely regarded as the father of British humanism and the leading figure in its international growth. In the early 1930s, he responded to an advertisement in the *TLS* from Stanton Coit, becoming his successor as the leader of the West London Ethical Society (Ethical Church). Blackham eroded the ritualistic element in meetings and planned the sale of the building in 1953 for a new office in Kensington. More broadly, from 1934 he planned the modernisation of humanism as the first chairman, then secretary, of the Ethical Union. Acting as an organiser in 1938 of the World Congress of Freethinkers at Conway Hall, and, thinking in 1945 to revitalise it, Blackham changed his mind to join Dutch humanist leader Jaap van Praag in 1952 to found and be first secretary of the International Humanist and Ethical Union. He taught philosophy most of his life, tutoring and writing, organising a branch of the League of Nations Union for a period, working then as a philosophy lecturer for London County Council and by the 1960s for the WEA. He founded and edited for over twenty years the quarterly humanistic philosophy magazine, *The Plain View*, attracting to his advisory panel leading humanist writers Bertrand Russell, Barbara Wootton, Lord Chorley and Gilbert Murray. As the first director of the BHA from 1963, he advocated compromise and kindness in dealings with churches and turned attention to the 'open society' idea and to moral education which he promoted as chair of the Social Morality Council. His lectures were sometimes complex, yet his writings became more accessible, leading people to describe him as charismatic and inspirational, demonstrating that a humanist should be a humanitarian, concerned for people, and once expressing disappointment with how much the BHA had become a talking shop rather than a pastoral organisation.

In the process of invoking these themes, we shall observe the role of key humanist figures. Some of these are featured in Biographical Side Panels, but others are dealt with quite prominently in the main text. They come in various roles, starting with key humanist organisers, of whom by far the most important was Harold J. Blackham, a man rightly regarded as the father of modern British humanism and the midwife of international humanism. Other organisers, many of them writers and editors, included Stanton Coit, J. M. Robertson, Gustav Spiller and Hector Hawton. Key utopians, most often scientists or philosophers, brought optimism and strategic vision, and represented the *crème de la crème* of British thinkers: individuals like H. G. Wells, Bertrand Russell, A. J. Ayer, Julian Huxley, John Boyd Orr, Barbara Wootton, Joseph Rotblat, Peter Ritchie Calder and several more. A third group were specialist advisers, led by the key lawyer Glanville Williams who drafted several parliamentary reform bills for abortion reformers, and sexual campaigners Diane Munday, Madeleine Simms and Eustace Chesser. And lastly, there was the generalist campaigner, like Barbara Smoker, who, for almost seven decades, turned up at demonstrations and marches, events and talks, to promote the cause of humanism through thick and thin.

Through these various themes and approaches, we seek to shift the popular and scholarly gaze. The 'humanist turn' in modern British civil society was a swerve from faith to morality that grafted ethical regeneration to the secularising nation. Success in these fields varied across the century and a quarter we cover, and we will highlight causes of failure as much as causes of success. We narrate how, though repeatedly rejected in some corridors of power, humanist influence grew as that of other institutions, notably the churches and their agencies, faltered. Small in number, humanists slowly inherited Christianity's fading moral mantle.

(c) The movement's home

The humanist movement, from the outset, has been organisationally splintered. The National Secular Society was formed in 1866, and is one of the world's oldest surviving secularist bodies, fighting religious discrimination of all sorts, and for the separation of church and state. If there was shouting to be done, the NSS has tended to be in the vanguard, yet in recent decades it has emerged as an exponent of humanist causes. Notwithstanding that recent humanistic impulse, for reasons we outline in Chapter 3, we exclude the NSS from close study in this book as it did not evolve into the breadth of humanist concerns characteristic of the ethical and humanist organisations. The Union of Ethical Societies was formed in 1896 as a federal body to represent ethical humanism as a positive philosophy, consisting at birth of the North, South, East and West London Ethical Societies which had existed individually for up to a decade. By 1927, a total of at least seventy-four ethical societies had existed around the UK, forty-six of which joined the Union, but at most only a few hundred individuals held direct membership; going through further name changes to emerge in 2017 to Humanists UK, this is now the largest of all the organisations. Alongside that strand of development, there existed from 1899 the Rationalist Press Association (from 2000 known as the Rationalist Association), created from a range of late-Victorian secularist publishing houses to act as the publication, print and propaganda arm of British organised nonreligion, and through its publications it became the greatest mouthpiece of humanist causes. Country organisations also sprang up – with the Scottish Humanist Council from 1978 (resuscitating an earlier organisation) which changed in 1987 into the Humanist Society of Scotland,[30] whilst Welsh and Northern Ireland Humanists emerged as sections of Humanists UK, and other local and smaller organisations with names like the Progressive League and the Personalists adorned the movement in the mid-twentieth century.

With such a plethora of bodies, can a single humanist movement be said to have existed since 1896? The answer is both yes and no. Efforts to merge some or all of the national organisations into one have come and gone (as we shall record), leaving the impression to some outsiders that the movement has been hopelessly fragmented and disunited. But the movement has acted as close to one on many combined activities, sharing outlooks, joint campaigns and heroes – all of which has brought the cause together. Activists are routinely members of more than one organisation, and there was a tradition of leaders taking executive posts of more than one body in turn. Likewise, by the 2010s humanism was known to many Britons as a source of celebrants for funerals, weddings and baby namings, whilst its campaigns in recent decades for gay, religious and racial equality have been prominent and, in almost all regards, successful. In these activities, all the organisations have participated, and all have been at one time or another members of the international organisation called the International Humanist and Ethical

Union (IHEU) founded in 1952 and renamed in 2019 as Humanists International. So, in such ways and others we shall explore, it is not merely justified but necessary to develop a movement-wide analysis of humanism.

In the nineteenth century, the typical locus of the secularist and freethought movement was the debating hall – scores of venues in London and major cities where secularists lectured and often debated with religious evangelists. Many of these seem to have been private enterprise halls, rented out day and evening, but some were dedicated operations – the hall of the Leicester Secular Society, or the Hall of Science in Old Street in London which features in many accounts as a place of secularist learning. Private homes also played host to circles of supporters. But another version of the debating locus was the open air. By the end of the nineteenth century, there were many public places for public speaking and debating in British cities: Hyde Park Corner and Victoria Park in London, the Mound in Edinburgh, but also many back-street spots which, notably on Sundays, became free of traffic and tolerated open-air debates. Listed weekly in ethical and secularist journals, the contest of issues in public, whether roofed or not, was the home of the secularist cause. But come the ethical movement from the 1870s, things started to change, with groups meeting to discuss a rather different, less confrontational cause, hiring or buying premises where they could meet free from critics. Ethicists came to congregate for less debate and more for fellowship and moral discussion. Leading the way was South Place.

For the last ninety years, these many organisations have shared a common meeting place. Conway Hall in Red Lion Square in central London was opened in 1929 as the premises of the South Place Ethical Society (SPES, renamed in 2012 as the Conway Hall Ethical Society) which had originated as a nonconformist chapel in the City of London that, in 1787, rejected the doctrine of eternal damnation. The congregation moved its premises thrice after 1793, and slowly transformed its religious alignment and its principles towards first ethicism then to humanism, and even more slowly discarded the semblance of religious ritual. Some families built up strong inter-generational links with the South Place congregation, whilst others held to a fellowship placed somewhere on a religion–nonreligion spectrum. Notwithstanding that SPES was and remains a relatively small organisation of some 500 members, the building and its resident society are held with affection as the landlords of the movement's home (Figure 2).

Conway Hall became the major place of identification for humanists in London and the South East of England, but more broadly in Britain and, indeed, with a standing in the world of humanism. Until the 2000s there was an Annual Reunion of Kindred Societies hosted by SPES – a morning, afternoon or evening of speeches and refreshments for the BHA, RPA, NSS, the Progressive League and other nonreligion organisations. Humanists of all organisations have felt comfortable here, both in its large hall and adjacent smaller meeting rooms, even in its corridors where there are plaques, notices and works of art collected from the movement's origins. The main hall has been a venue for thousands of meetings since 1929, at which famous speakers from around the world have come to be applauded in relation to both the

FIGURE 2 Conway Hall. Set in the secluded Red Lion Square, this has been the home since 1929 of the South Place Ethical Society, renamed Conway Hall E.S., and the common meeting place for all British humanists, rationalists and secularists. Photo: By User: Geni CC-BY-SA 4.0.

direct work of the organisations but also radical and progressive groups in general. It is also the place where concerts have been held and continue to be so. SPES was the principal injector of an artistic dimension into the nonreligion movement, led by classical music which developed as a distinctive feature of humanist societies drawn in part from Unitarian origins. In the United States, the Ethical Society of Boston and the New York Society for Ethical Culture incorporated short classical pieces during their Sunday morning meetings; so too Conway Hall had the Sunday morning meeting opened with a secular hymn, a singer and accompanist, or solo pianist, and still hosts long-running Sunday-evening classical concerts. This aesthetic heritage may be weakening somewhat, but music and art illustrate how the Hall is a place combining different sentiments and ways of being humanist, from outdoor rambles and mass meetings to lectures by academics, scientists and intellectuals. This has been a citadel of reason with art, and there is a pride in this conjunction.

Conway Hall, however, delivers more. It is a Grade II listed building erected 1927–9, designed by South Place member F. Herbert Mansford (1871–1946), and described by Historic England as 'particularly handsome with its grand classical entrance bay and stone urns along the parapet'.[31] Its style has a cathedralic serenity conferred by its location in the small and generally peaceable Red Lion Square.[32] The main hall originally seated 325 on the ground floor and 178 in the gallery, with pilasters flanking the proscenium containing bas-relief panels of man, woman and child with a light on one side and a mirror on the other adorned by a motto 'To thine own self be true' to complete a theme of self-knowledge. The serenity is best evoked not in its meeting rooms – most of which, if truth be told, are quite drab in places – but in the Conway Hall Library and Archive on the first floor. On some days, this room is quite empty and quiet, with a book collection dedicated to the reading tastes of rationalists, atheists and humanists, but on others can be populated by a children's group or visiting guests. There is a large collection of books on humanism, atheism, agnosticism and freethinking – in disciplines like philosophy, history, psychology and sociology. It is home also to a significant archive of material, including that of SPES, the National Secular Society and papers of humanist leader Harold Blackham. This is the central chapel of reason in British atheism, a place where god only intrudes in many books of skepticism. Part of its glory comes from its busts and portraits of leading lights erected high around the room. For many, it is the beating heart of the British humanist movement.

The library contains the history of its own building, where lots of interesting things happened. The 1938 Congress of World Freethought met here, watched by Special Branch and MI5 agents alerted to the possibility of Soviets, communists and anarchists being in attendance. The building has been almost continuously an object of interest to the security service since many humanists had left-wing sympathies, a small number being communist and suspected (though rarely evidenced) of having links to Soviet intelligence. But non-humanist organisations and radical causes have regarded Conway Hall as the meeting place of choice for rallies and lectures. There is a frisson of subterfuge and ideological collision to be felt entering this building. More mundanely, there are files stored here about controversial meetings, including those of progressive causes. One was the premiere in 1971 of the sex education film *Growing Up* whose audience was watched entering the building by police and the Crown Office looking out for children being admitted to 'obscene' viewing. Beyond the nonreligious sector, it is a building that has for decades been hired by other organisations – left-wing, right-wing, communist and fascist – admitted on the principle that freethought demands free speech, and prompting the press attention and the paraphernalia of the modern media: TV cameras, satellite dishes and communication vans. Conway Hall has thus been a home to causes, some linking to the progressivism of the resident ethical society.

In the library there are the records of hundreds of lectures delivered here by some considered the greatest minds of the twentieth century – philosophers, linguists, politicians and many scientists. Indeed, outside of buildings dedicated to science, there can be few structures to have heard more talks on scientific, intellectual and moral issues than Conway Hall. But the library has also a distinctive and learned aesthetic. Though not the only archive of the British humanist movement (the main one being the Bishopsgate Institute archive in central London), Conway Hall retains a special ambience and place in the hearts of many of the leading humanists, no matter to which organisation they owe allegiance. One such was Barbara Smoker who spoke to us of feeling more at home here than in her own home, patrolling the corridors, chairing a Sunday morning or midweek evening meeting, and urging the attenders to greater dedication to the various causes she espoused. Conway Hall has been a gathering place and a hangout, a location for committee meetings, planning and celebration, though also the venue for debate and dispute. The great intellectuals of the cause, and many proto-humanists, gave lectures here.

But the building has in its time had a wider public role. Until 1977 it was the location of nonreligious weddings, in the main hall and also on occasion in the library, conducted because SPES originated in a Unitarian congregation and under English law retained its rights to marry – until the authorities concluded in the 1960s (and enforced in 1977) that because of the absence of god worship it did not meet legal requirements.[33] But non-legal humanist weddings, as well as baby namings, funerals and life celebration ceremonies are held. In the middle decades of the twentieth century, the building played host to the myriad of leisure activities

FIGURE 3 Conway Hall Library. Containing SPES and Rationalist Association book collections and NSS and SPES archives, and adorned with busts of leading figures of the movement, the library draws a special affection from humanists. Photo: JWSLubbock Creative Commons Attribution-Share Alike 4.0 International.

that the ethical society hosted. It was from here that Sunday walks started, and where in the 1940s and 1950s the table tennis club met one evening a week in the library. A huge variety of organisations hire it for events – concerts, orchestral rehearsals, companies holding courses, training events and public meetings. For some years until 2020 it was the site for Britain's largest auction of pianos, when scores of the instruments occupied every room and corridor space, with the clever pianists ringing a cacophony of overlapping sounds around the building.[34] The hall was even used in 1958 by the leading skiffle musician Lonnie Donegan to record a live album.[35]

Seeing the instant success of Conway Hall, the Rationalist Press Association in 1947 determined to match it with something of their own – 'a commodious building' with lecture hall, library, reading room, restaurant and club amenities, and sought to raise £100,000 (£3.9 million at 2020 prices) to pay for it.[36] This was never realised. Conway Hall remained unique, a custom-built home to the movement. It resonates with the present and the past of the humanist and allied causes, nestling at the corner of Red Lion Square overlooking a relatively quiet small public garden that has been partly absorbed by the movement with a life-size statue to Fenner Brockway and a bust to Bertrand Russell, both leading disarmament campaigners and humanists. In this way, the building spills out into public space, including into the village community of the adjacent Lamb's Conduit Passage and Street. The structure symbolises in part the openness of the movement – its democracy, its absence of rules and regulation, its sense of common ownership by the members – and is nothing akin to the feel of either a cathedral like St Paul's or Westminster Abbey or of a church headquarters like Lambeth Palace. Its doors are open, no bouncer meets you there, no displays or literature evangelise you on entry, and no questions are asked of you or your faith as happens at some churches. The building provides the movement as a whole with its meeting place of first choice. But it was only opened in 1929. It was two miles to the east of Red Lion Square that the ethical movement in Britain really started.

2 THE DEMOGRAPHY OF HUMANISTS, 1896–2021

Across its history, the identity of those in the various branches of the humanist and secularist movement has changed. We can follow this better from the mid-twentieth century than before because of the growing volume of data about nonreligionists. This chapter presents an analysis of the demography of humanists, in the first section collating information on numbers, in the second analysing their profile, and in the third examining the personal accounts of movement leaders in their approach to humanism.

(a) The number of humanists

The various organisations of British humanism have published the numbers of their members with varying degrees of diligence. In many cases, there has been a reluctance to broadcast such data, and the annual reports often contain no published numbers. In other cases, the numbers have been presented in magazines and are sometimes hard to locate. It is certainly the case that the numbers belonging to such organisations have been smaller compared to the numbers of the Victorian secularist bodies. In the nineteenth century the numbers probably reached well into five figures, whereas in the twentieth century they are unlikely to have exceeded four figures. Indeed, for much of the twentieth century, the ethicist and humanist organisations – thus excluding the National Secular Society – for most decades had individual memberships of under 1,000 each. These were modest scales. However, there have been two periods – the 1960s and after 2000 – when the numbers rose markedly (Figure 4).

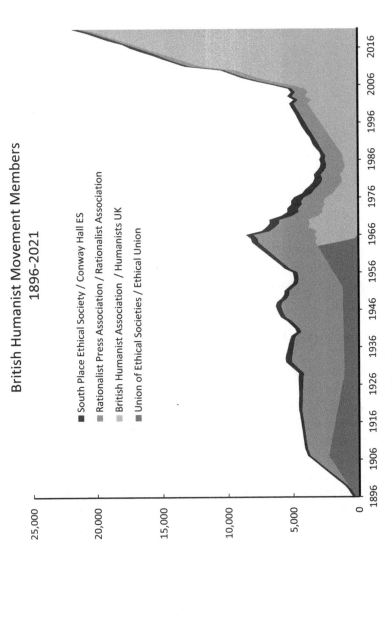

FIGURE 4 British Humanist Movement Members 1896–2021.

Technical note to graph

In this stacked graph, data from annual reports, committee minutes, in-house journals and organisation databases, recorded in the year concerned, create a tabulation for every year between 1896 and 2021 inclusive. The early decades presented problems. Some ethical societies did not affiliate either permanently or at all with the Union of Ethical Societies from 1896, whilst some smaller organisations did not regularly record numbers of members. The data were rare in the early years. From available figures, estimates have been produced for gap years before 1965, based mainly on the number of affiliated UK ethical/humanist societies recorded by Gustav Spiller or by intermittent annual reports: 26 societies in 1905–6, between 10 and 18 in 1934, 19 in 1956 and 34 in 1964, which have been translated into estimated individual members in the order of 272 in 1896, 2,116 in 1906, 1,008 in 1930, 1,880 in 1956 and 3,071 in 1963. (The numbers of affiliated ethical societies are estimated from (sometimes contradictory) data in Gustav Spiller, *The Ethical Movement in Great Britain* (London, Farleigh Press, 1934), 114–16; BA,BHA/1/5/1 EU Annual Report 1956, 1–3; BA,BHA/1/5/1 *Annual Reports* 1964 and 1965.) The remainder of the data are based on published organisation annual membership figures, often erratic (principally because recording occurred at different months, exacerbated by failures in sending out membership reminders and by office-bearers openly offering estimates). SPES membership data include a notional 200 members each year 1896–1918, after which data are mostly annual. The graph is unable to allow for individuals being members of more than one organisation. For discussion of subscriber and associate membership numbers, see main text.

The graph displays the known membership numbers (excluding subscribers and associate members who paid reduced fees) for the four main organisations – the UES/EU and its successor the BHA/Humanists UK, SPES including its successor CHES, and RPA including its successor RA. Despite some issues attending accuracy, this graph provides a good indication of the changing and relative strengths of the different branches of the movement. This is a stacked graph, in which the number of members in each year are added accumulatively so that the top line is an estimate of the size of the whole movement. Several organisations have not been included, especially the once-large National Secular Society; though it came to be a major supporter of humanist causes in Britain in the post-1945 period, its main focus was on secularism rather than humanism. In addition, some other elements of humanism have been omitted largely due to the absence of clear data. (More information is given in the Technical Note.)

The graph shows that in the early decades, the humanist movement was gathering pace rather slowly, and suffered periods of likely setback, partly due to economic circumstances (such as the depression years of the 1920s and 1930s, noted by humanist leaders) and some significant volatility to membership.[1] Most disappointing for the organisations was the lack of major growth in the more prosperous times of the late 1940s and 1950s when full employment prevailed and there seemed to be an alignment of civil fortunes (including the Labour government of 1945–51) favouring radical causes in which humanists thought they would feel the beneficial backwash. It was only in the late 1950s and early 1960s that circumstances started to change. The membership of the BHA, RPA and SPES each attained surge peaks at the same time, in the 1965–70 period, and then shared an enduring decline. In the twentieth century overall, the steadiest membership was at the Conway Hall, less so in the RPA, and most volatile in the Ethical Union/BHA. After attaining membership of 4,700 in the late 1960s, the BHA suffered an almost catastrophic decline until the 1980s when it bottomed out at under a thousand – meaning a loss of over 75 per cent of its members. During the 1990s there was a slow and hard-won recovery for the BHA to some 3,000 in the early 2000s, which was sustained at a strong rate into the 2010s when there followed very high growth.

However, the fortunes of the Rationalist Press Association declined steadily from the 1950s onwards, partly due to publishing loss-making books, partly in acknowledgement that the printed word was going out of fashion, but partly because readers could just as easily buy the main magazine, the *New Humanist*, without joining; even it lost readers, contracting in stages from monthly to quarterly. One notable feature of the humanist movement since the 1890s was the two levels of association permitted in many organisations. Members (what in the early twentieth century were called subscribers) paid an annual fee (for BHA members in 2014 it was £38 per annum) whilst supporters paid a reduced fee or nothing. To an extent, this twin-track membership mirrored arrangements in some churches, offering access to less-connected adherents but without the right to vote at annual general meetings. The supporter role rarely reached the popularity of the main subscriber track; the earliest it did seems to be in the RPA in 1972. But in the 2010s, interestingly, the popularity has been resoundingly reversed. Levels of supporters have risen to more than twice the level of members, certainly in the BHA/Humanists UK, facilitated by the digital age which has encouraged enrolment via social media on the whim of a mouse click or tap of a finger; indeed, it seems likely that the vast majority of supporters never attend a meeting. We have been unable to obtain detailed demographics, or the circumstances of commitment, involvement and longevity of association of the supporter as distinguished from the member, and how readily the supporter becomes a member. One of the benefits for organisation managers, similar to the churches, is being able to use the supporter figures (oftentimes added to the members figure) to perceive a larger constituency and to expand support in campaigns and online petitions.[2]

In the 1960s some humanist managers had allowed themselves to dream of a six-figure following. It was only in the 2010s that such a scale of adherence was attained by adding a paying membership to mostly non-paying supporters. But, as we shall see in the course of this book, the number of humanists was never the primary factor affecting the movement's impact upon British society.

(b) Who were the humanists?

What demographic characteristics can we discern about humanists? The composition of those in the humanist movement has been estimated and examined intermittently by academic studies. Of course, those being examined initially labelled themselves before 1900 as belonging to ethical societies, but from the 1900s to the 1950s the term 'humanist' grew in favour until it was dominant in the 1960s. We need to contextualise the humanists across the range of terms and organisational names – people who counted themselves as atheists, freethinkers, rationalists, secularists and nonreligious. We have no conclusive way of deciphering over the period whether the change of term signified a demographic shift. Moreover, scholars have used 'irreligious' as a collective term, and until the 1970s tended to regard those in whatever part of the movement as being actively against religion.[3] But this no longer is the case. Towards the end of the twentieth century, as the proportions of people without a religion or religious belief increased, it became necessary to conceptually accommodate the drop in anti-religion and the rise in religious disinterest or apathy. Further, the presumption of the earlier studies that those without religion had been almost universally in some sense prior religious (often by being raised in a religion) has to be discarded as large numbers of the young came of age from the 1970s to the 2010s without counting themselves as in any meaningful extent 'religious' in the first place. In short, after the 1970s atheists and humanists were no longer mainly *losers* of religion, but were born and grew up de facto atheist (sometimes referred to as 'practical atheist'). We must regard them as largely never-churched.

Against that background of shifting scholarly perceptions, we can still make some important observations. The social composition of the nonreligious in the early nineteenth century and before has to rely largely on impressionistic judgement. Edward Royle shows that, notwithstanding secularist and rationalist activity in London and Edinburgh, the movement had strongholds among working people of the industrial north-west of England, midlands and industrial central Scotland: Lancashire, Cheshire, the West Riding, Birmingham, Leicester and Lanarkshire, especially in light industries like textiles and shoes. The movement shadowed the radicalism of the hour – including Owenism, Chartism and socialism – and drew its support from artisans and working men of militant action as well as thought.[4] Royle first meaningfully estimated social composition for 661 people outwith London cited in freethought and secularist journals and directories from 1837 to 1858, judging the movement comprised 7 per cent men of the higher social classes, 29 per cent lower middle classes (shopkeepers and booksellers predominating), 26 per cent upper working classes (mostly craftsmen) and 38 per cent other working classes.[5] In the mid-nineteenth century, Royle noted that the shift from freethought to secularism retained the geographical criticality of the industrial midlands and north.[6] Contemporaries agreed that members of the secularist movement were largely 'respectable' working classes, and this persisted. In 1888 *The Freethinker* journal noted that 'Freethought gains the elite of the working class', whilst commentators in the 1890s and 1900s referred to the movement's respectable mechanics, clerks and lower middle classes. Susan Budd's analysis of 263 secularist obituaries stretched out from 1852 to 1965 found that 40 per cent were semi- or unskilled, 20 per cent skilled workers, 20 per cent white collar, 15 per cent small business owners and 2 per cent from the professions.[7] Royle's study of obituaries of ninety-seven local members (for dates not specified, but which must run between 1866 and 1915) found 26 per cent semi- and unskilled, 23 per cent craft and skilled, 16 per cent white collar, 32 per cent small business owners and 3 per cent professions.[8] Among Leicester Secular Society members during 1881–1901, David Nash found large manufacturers and proprietors constituting 13 per cent, smaller proprietors 14 per cent, professions 2 per cent, white collar 7 per cent, and semi- and unskilled workers 4 per cent, with 36 per cent no occupation and 24 per cent untraceable suggesting more unskilled workers; he concluded this was a mainly working-class organisation, likely with increasing numbers of women.[9] Though

Laura Schwartz has drawn attention to the distinctive secularism of around forty Victorian women,[10] and whilst there were prominent women leaders, the movement as a whole was majority male, drawing its supporters mainly from the early nineteenth to the early twentieth centuries from industrial districts and from the commercial small businessmen, skilled and unskilled workers. In age terms, the movement has always been adult-dominated though there were between the 1880s and 1940s Sunday schools for quite small numbers of children – many likely of adult members, though some organisations like South Place in Finsbury, the Leicester Secular Society and the Oldham society attracted children of working-class families.

Even though secularism was to survive, the nonreligion movement developed from the 1880s the new and vigorous brand of ethicism and its successor form humanism, and in that transition there was a substantial change to both the movement's geography and demography. By the time of the next major study of its composition in 1962–5, Colin Campbell showed from a gross sample of 2,390 returned questionnaires that London, the south east and southern England accounted for 48 per cent of UK humanist members (well above the 27 per cent of population who lived in those parts), with all other regions equal to or, most often, lower than their proportions of UK population. This was a very significant shift in the nonreligious movement as a whole – from broadly the north to broadly the south and south-east. The members were 73 per cent male, possibly showing a significant fall since 1900 in the proportion of women among ethicists (to which we return in Chapter 4), though likely representative of secularists. Both the age distribution above twenty years of age and the marital status distribution were broadly representative of the population as a whole. Occupationally, the retired comprised 14 per cent (compared to 5 per cent of the population), and students 8 per cent (2 per cent in the UK). But the clearest skewing of the membership occurred with considerable occupational change, where professionals, technicians, artists, administrators and managers made up 69 per cent (cf. 8 per cent of the UK population). The lower middle classes and skilled manual workers who had so dominated the nineteenth-century movement had all but evaporated; clerical workers made up 11 per cent (compared to 10 per cent in the population), whilst the remainder, mostly manual workers, made up a mere 20 per cent (compared to 82 per cent of the UK population). The largest occupational group were teachers, where about 20 per cent of the membership were in the profession or retired.[11] In short, by the 1960s UK humanists were overwhelmingly male, middle and upper-middle class from the south and south-east, leading Colin Campbell to entitle his thesis 'Humanism and the culture of the professions'.

If embourgeoisement of the movement dominated change between 1900 and 1964, change between 1964 and 2014 was more complex. Down to the mid-1980s, these trends were little altered with internal surveys and commentaries at BHA arriving at roughly the same profile of the average member as found by Campbell; a survey run by the executive committee in 1985 found 72 per cent male, 53 per cent living in south-east England, 53 per cent over 60 years of age, and 57 per cent being members for more than ten years.[12] Most changes occurred in the following thirty years. An in-house BHA survey of 2001 of its total membership of 3,803 found the proportion of women was 39 per cent; a full-scale survey (of 1,097 humanists) undertaken in 2014 by Gareth Longden produced a figure of 35 per cent women; but by 2020, when Humanists UK were undertaking annual demographic surveys of supporters in England and Wales, the figure seemed to have fallen back to 27 per cent women. However, the proportion of women in other categories by 2020 was significantly higher: 44 per cent of humanist volunteers, 42 per cent of staff and, most notably, 72 per cent of humanist celebrants. A second observation was a decrease in the proportion of the young. By 2014, there had been a 27 per cent reduction in the proportion of members under 50 years compared to 1964 (higher than the 21 per cent reduction in the population at large), and a halving of the proportion of students from 8 per cent to 4 per cent (at a time when the proportion of people at university, notably women, was rising rapidly). By 2020, the proportion of supporters under fifty-four years of age stood at 25 per cent (as compared with 72 per cent of the population as a whole); those aged fifty-five to seventy-four made up 53 per cent of Humanists UK's support, partly the product of an aging population. However, a notable change between the 1980s and 2020 was a rising regional distribution of supporters. London and the southeast accounted for only 32 per cent of Humanists UK's support in 2020, with the midlands making up 34 per cent and the north of England a further 20 per cent, revealing the first significant repivoting northwards of British-organised nonreligionism since the secularist age of the Victorian period.

But, in stark contrast to the overwhelmingly working-class Victorian secularists, there was a noticeable increase in the qualifications and wealth of humanists in the second half of the twentieth century. The proportion of humanists with university degrees was 34 per cent in 1964 but rose sharply to 72 per cent in 2014 (against 22 per cent in the population at large). The previous dominance of school teachers faltered (reduced from 20 per cent to 12 per cent of members), displaced by a varied range of middle-class occupations including IT and HE teaching by the 2010s. Accompanying this was an increased proportion of retirees – up from 14 per cent to 37 per cent and a very large proportion (83 per cent) owning their own homes. On the aging of the community into the twenty-first century, Engelke and Longden separately noted that members typically take a long time to decide to join an organisation – in the latter's survey, fifteen years was the average gap between becoming a humanist and joining the BHA. Callum Brown stretched the length of delay, observing from his large-scale oral-history interviewing during 2009–16 that very large numbers lost religion between seven and eighteen years of age in the 1960s and 1970s but didn't join a nonreligion organisation until their fifties or sixties – a point helping to explain the membership surge among older groups between 2000 and 2020.[13] The humanist community by the 2010s was not only markedly older and more financially classic middle class but was also dominated by highly qualified professionals. Meanwhile, the ethnic composition of humanism seemed to change little until the 2010s. In the 2011 census, British no religionists were 94 per cent white (confirmed at 95 per cent in the British Social Attitudes survey), and, though there has been no wide survey of humanists, it is likely the proportion has been low. However, there are indicators of change. The rising importance of work by Humanists UK among those experiencing the trauma of losing faith has brought heightened awareness of those departing non-Christian religions dominated by ethnic South Asians and Africans, with notable donor support after 2018 for charitable work in that field. At the same time, ethnic minority participation in humanist work in Britain has risen; by 2020, the trustees of Humanists UK had become 18 per cent Pakistani, Bangladeshi and mixed-race (compared to 4 per cent of the population at large). The diversity of humanism seems likely to strengthen considerably in the 2020s.

During the demographic and geographic transformation of the nonreligion movement between the nineteenth and twenty-first centuries – from proletarian to bourgeois, largely self-taught to degree-holding, young to old, and, though less pronounced, male to mixed-gender – the politics shifted. Radical and working class in origins in the early- and mid-nineteenth century, it had been overwhelmingly siding with Owenites, Chartists and socialists, posing a near-revolutionary challenge to the status quo. By the period's end, the bulk of the membership remained left of centre but more distant from political activism. In a survey in 1971, 63 per cent said they voted Labour and 9 per cent Conservative (with the balance likely Liberal, in which the movement had originated), and many of its new recruits were attracted by advertisements in the middle-class left-of-centre Sunday newspaper *The Observer*.[14] In part, the Labour movement itself had shifted demographically and nonreligionists reflected that. Though there was a strong Liberal legacy in London as late as the 1980s, many by the 2020s had embraced a more consumerist, prosperous and digital-enabled popular culture with values that found resonance in modern humanism. Specialist groups emerged – notably the UK Armed Forces Humanist Association, formed in 2014 and renamed Defence Humanists, which by 2021 had over 400 members and supporters among serving and retired service personnel and civil servants.[15] But, the movement's attractions were diversifying – in the 2000s to include lectures and debates by superstars of popular 'new atheism', but ten years later to include ebullient youthful events like the Sunday Assembly which started in London in 2013 and formed its largest meeting in Conway Hall with nineteen other British meetings and forty-eight in total around the world.[16] In Humanists UK and elsewhere, a 'digital' membership was thriving by the early 2010s among many who seem rarely to have had a physical encounter with humanist events. The humanists now included the young, the 'woke' and – dare it be said – the trendy, but also those who had a less radical outlook than many of the earlier secularists and ethicists.

(c) Coming to humanism

How did individuals become humanists? Using autobiographical, biographical and oral-history sources, we explore how leading humanists in the British movement – prominent organisers, campaigners and intellectuals – lost religion and found their humanism. On the face of it, atheism preceded humanism, but, if inspected carefully, this was often only because they knew the 'a' word (sometimes using 'agnostic') but not the 'h' word. A very significant proportion of prominent humanists have had religious backgrounds, and atheism invariably came as a recoil from an adverse experience of church and faith. Despite there being many young ethicists in the 1880s and 1890s, most humanists discovered later in life that they were already humanists – often after hearing a talk or seeing a poster in a public place, and finding a name for how they felt and lived. That pattern tended to be foreshortened for those who became leaders of the humanist movement. And these stages start to shorten for all in the late twentieth and twenty-first centuries as more and more people came to nonreligion without having been religious in the first place.

Frederick James (F. J.) Gould (1855–1938), Ethical Union vice-president 1918–23 and one of the most noteworthy of early ethicists who as early as 1909 was referring to 'us Humanists',[17] was deeply entwined with religion when young. Born into a 'shabby-genteel home', his mother found him a place at age ten in the choir of St George's Chapel in Windsor Castle, where he lived a life of ritual though, he recalled, never 'really prayed' and 'felt little penetration from the ghostly sphere'. Being settled in a village school, at sixteen years he experienced a conversion, sitting in the church among the village choir when he seemed to hear a voice: 'How wonderful is the love of God!' Becoming an avid bible reader and an 'insatiable explorer' in faith, he became a puritan in the time of Moody and Sankey revivalism, but his hunger for theology was 'intimately joined' to that for education and teaching methods, advocating at a parish meeting teaching by parables without moralising. '[U]nderneath these outward conformities', he wrote later in life, 'heretical sparks got kindled – I know not how – and at length blew up into vivid doubts and challenges'. By twenty years of age he started to argue sceptically to a few friends and to his diary, attending lectures of theistic scepticism – one on the 'Mental Epidemics' of revivalism by Florence Fenwick Miller (1854–1935), a feminist journalist who, barred from being awarded a medical degree at Edinburgh University in 1871, became a midwife and a lecturer at the Sunday Lecture Society where, likely, Gould heard her in Langham Place in January 1876.[18] Gould wrote of her in his diary: 'these Secularists cut asunder Christ and Truth, or they attempt it'. Becoming a head teacher of a village school at Great Missenden in his early twenties, he found 'the old Evangelical spirit indulged in a spasmodic flare', but led soon to 'the Revivalist flame' being extinguished within him. By twenty-four years of age he had abandoned prayer and communion, and, with religious doubt mounting, he became a teacher at a board (state) school in Bethnal Green, hearing Charles Bradlaugh lecture at the Hall of Science in London in October 1879. There, his by-then 'thin and feeble Deism . . . diminished and soon died'.[19] His career then followed the intellectual hurly-burly of late-Victorian London including encounters with freethought, Positivism and secularism, followed by his ethicist and humanist career in Leicester, then to London again where he emerged as a pioneer in moral education.

Gould offers the paradigm of the religion-tracked childhood encountering the combined power of the inquisitive mind, secular reading and hearing lectures from freethinkers. But he benefited from the absence of overbearing parents. Edmund Gosse (1849–1928), poet and literary biographer, and later ethicist, did not have it so easy. Through his autobiography, Edmund made famous the impact of Darwinism upon his father Philip, an evangelical scientist, who worked strenuously in the 1860s to develop a compromise between the theory of evolution and Christianity, only to have his work humiliatingly rejected by scientists. Edmund's own journey to atheism in his teens was difficult, as his father enforced churchgoing and baptism. In his celebrated auto/biography *Father and Son*, Gosse the son seemed, academic Martin A. Danahay opines, to be depicting individual autonomy as 'subjected sovereignty' under his father's power, and was using the book as a site of resistance to him, fitting Michel Foucault's dictum that 'humanism is everything in Western civilization that restricts the desire for power'.[20] Atheism could feature as resistance to the intellectual parental autocracy of Victorian Christianity and its dreaded respectability.

Resisting his father's faith was hard for Edmund Gosse until adulthood, but Bertrand Russell reveals an early precocity. In his autobiographical account, he rejected faith with mathematical certainty at the age of fifteen and adopted atheism in its entirety at eighteen – a decision taken, irrevocable, unarguable. Yet, Russell had to contend with some religious interference. On his death, his father decreed that Bertrand be passed to other relatives on the proviso that he be brought up without superstition and appointed two freethinkers as guardians. The courts set aside these instructions and ordered him educated in the Christian faith. Yet, raised without Sabbatarianism and eternal punishment, Russell nonetheless recalled that 'in other respects morals were austere, and it was held to be certain that conscience which is the voice of God, is an infallible guide in all practical perplexities'.[21] His Scottish presbyterian grandmother dominated his childhood, her morality 'extremely strict', making him as he put it 'unusually prone to a sense of sin'. At eleven, he discovered his love of mathematics through reading Euclid, remaining his chief interest until he co-wrote *Principia Mathematica* at age thirty-eight. In his adolescence, '[my] interests were divided between sex, religion, and mathematics', the first of these, he recorded candidly, met by 'moderate' masturbation until the age of twenty. For the second, he was taken alternate weeks to Anglican and presbyterian churches, whilst at home he was taught Unitarianism. His faith held until dissolving in intellectual stages, writing in Greek in a jotter to conceal his doubt: dismissing free will at fifteen, no life after death (though still a god because of the 'First Cause' argument) at seventeen; then, at eighteen, he read a question in John Stuart Mill's *Autobiography* that could not be answered, 'Who made me?', since it suggested a second question 'Who made God?'. 'This', Russell concluded succinctly, 'led me to abandon the "First Cause" argument, and to become an atheist.'[22]

Other humanist leaders lost their faith with increasing speed. The novelist E.M. Forster (1879–1970), BHA vice-president 1957–70, told how in his second year at Cambridge: 'I moved into college where my Christianity quietly and quickly disappeared . . . And by the end of my third year I disbelieved much as I do now.'[23] The classicist scholar and staunch internationalist Gilbert Murray (1866–1957), Ethical Union president 1929–30 and intellectual buddy to so many British humanists, had a greater youthful choice in faith, being born to an Irish Catholic father and Anglican mother in Australia, and found humanist principles early. Because his father abhorred sectarianism and distrusted priests, '[r]eligious orthodoxy had never meant much to me'. But on removal to London and Merchant Taylors' school in the 1880s, he began to 'think very seriously about religion', reading widely in the atheism and agnosticism of Mill, Spencer, Shelley, Godwin and above all Auguste Comte, going with his Aunt Fanny to Richard Congreve's Positivist service in Lamb's Conduit Street (in what is now Rugby Street, a skip from Conway Hall). Though never a 'card-carrying' Positivist, as an agnostic he found 'under these guides an escape from cruel superstition and at the same time a fairly clear explanation and justification of the moral law and the ultimate duty of man' – an underlying humanist principle to his lifework of helping to build first the League of Nations then the United Nations as a prelude to benign world government.[24]

Gilbert Murray explains something of how his graduation towards rationalism and humanism might have a wider impact on public life, but Leslie Stephen (1832–1904), president of the West London Ethical Society, was the quintessential Victorian agnostic who, according to his biographer, 'would have been the last to claim that the secularisation of public life was brought about by intellectuals such as himself'. He showed how not to be Christian yet live a virtuous life: 'I now believe in nothing, to put it shortly', he wrote after becoming an agnostic; 'but I do not the less believe in morality etc. etc. I mean to live and die like a gentleman if possible.' Stephen inherited from his father a strict evangelicalism of the Clapham sect, but it was a faith of worldly activism – of talking, acting and evangelising for transformation. He transferred his agnosticism to the same evangelical mould of moral action – in oneself, one's family and in society around. His anti-religious revolt was thus moral as well as intellectual, and far more startling. Joining what became later known as the Bloomsbury circle, he trained as a mathematician, becoming moulded in the 1850s by reading the moral history of Thomas Carlyle and thereby welcoming a secularising model of human evolution alongside translating Christian morality into a secular variety. The religion of humanity, Comtean in origin, would become with Stephen a scientific ethicism, like Herbert Spencer though with more vigour, governed by evolution like life itself. This made morality an evolving and improving entity, not a static relic.[25]

Bertrand Russell's journey from atheism to humanism, like that of many intellectuals, seems less easy to place or date. One element was his critique of idealism that elevated him as a major turn of the century anti-idealist, a second the simultaneous emergence of his opposition to utilitarianism, and a third his disdain for the Christian ethical legacy. He explained this in correspondence in 1902–3 with Gilbert Murray. He wrote:

> The notion that general [ethical] maxims are to be found in conscience seems to me to be a mistake fostered by the Decalogue. I should rather regard the true method of Ethics as inference from empirically ascertained facts, to be obtained in that moral laboratory which life offers to those whose eyes are open to it. Thus the principles I should now advocate are all inferences from such immediate concrete moral experiences.

Russell was playing with philosophy to magnify his ethical reason, but became contemptuous in the later stages: 'Although I denied it when [humanist] Leonard Hobhouse said so, philosophy seems to me on the whole a rather hopeless business. I do not know how to state the value that at moments I am inclined to give it.' Two years later, in a correspondence in 1904 with humanist political scientist and philosopher Goldie Lowes Dickinson, Russell reveals a shift in his sentiments from philosophy to the nature of experience: 'it is a sudden realisation, or perhaps a gradual one, of ethical values which one had formerly doubted or taken on trust; and this realisation seems to be caused, as a rule, by a situation containing the things one realises to be good or bad.'[26] Humanism was a doing, not a mere philosophy. So, in 1950, Russell saw the necessity to acknowledge a fourth component, adopting as his 'guiding thought' the principle that ethics is derived from passions. He accepted David Hume's maxim: 'Reason is, and ought only to be, the slave of the passions', partly to counterbalance his critics' fondness for charging him with being wholly rational.[27]

There could be an element of machismo in reasoned arguments for atheism, whilst for many women Christian puritanism presented a burden less easy to jettison. As late as the 1960s, Hanne Stinson (b.1948), BHA chief executive 2001–9, reported that there was an attraction in the positive quality to calling oneself a humanist compared to the stubbornly negative connotations of the term atheist.[28] This was clearly partly a gendered issue; men might gain kudos for arguing their way out of religion, but for generations of women it might confer social stigma to be without a church.[29] Yvonne Stevenson, born in 1915, recounted the 'relentless religious conditioning' of her childhood education, reporting at four years of age that 'the wonders of God suffused me'; she talked to Jesus and prayed to God, and when 'sometimes Jesus and I got tired of talking' they would play hide-and-seek in the graveyard. At the age of seven, she went riding on a pony on her holidays with Jesus at her side. Between the ages of eight and thirteen, she attended a Clergy Daughters' Boarding School where all the children 'thought exactly as I did. We all believed in God, Jesus and Heaven, and such concepts were discussed freely.' From thirteen she was preoccupied with 'my inner reformation' and attempted to be perfect in the image of Jesus. At fifteen she was faint with the strain when kneeling at confirmation, deciding at seventeen to become a missionary. At eighteen, Yvonne was intensely absorbed with Christ, especially on the cross, deciding to drive a nail through her hand; at the point of hitting, she heard the voice of God which told her to desist. She became concerned with sex, though she still did not know the facts of life (her mother promised to tell her on the eve of marriage). Absorbed with morality and Christianity, at nineteen she was a student at a university college, arguing incessantly with a young socialist woman about Christianity, Marxism and sex, but her science let her down. Intellectually bored at a domestic science college, she read in Marxist writers and Freud, going to a redbrick university where she excelled in mathematics. There it was, finally, she lost her innocence and her religion together. Her autobiography is a classic woman's story of how childhood Christianity was entwined with ignorance of sex, the body and anything outside the narrow social circle of vicarage tea parties. Through her later teens and early twenties, she worried that her religious hallucinations and swing from Christianity to socialism were evidence of being 'mad'. But in the 1940s she lost this view doing war work at Cambridge University, then until the 1960s she became a clinical psychologist applying her reading in the research literature to understand breakdown and identity crisis. She concluded: 'If our education . . . were less full of idiotic and psychotic material we wouldn't need either violent or slow mental upheavals to bring on the road to sanity.'[30] Yvonne Stevenson's account is a trope that emphasises the psychological terrors of a religious upbringing, and that dwells on the peculiarly strong, close to horrific impact upon women. The move from passivity to activity, from powerlessness to autonomy, allowed her feminism to secure her humanism.

ANNIE BESANT 1847–1933

FIGURE 5 Annie Besant. Photo: ©NPG.

The most prominent of woman secularists, Annie Besant was a charismatic and forceful speaker who attracted wide public attention for a myriad of causes for the weakest in society, starting with contraception and reproductive rights for women. She had already been married and separated with two children when she met fellow atheist Charles Bradlaugh, together forming a publishing concern to keep Charles Knowlton's 1832 pamphlet *The Fruits of Philosophy* in print, resulting in 1877 in their blasphemous libel trial and their ultimate acquittal. Besant promoted a women's right to control over her own body, helping to found what became the Family Planning Association, maintaining the long history of connections between secularism and sexual rights. In the 1880s and 1890s Besant became an ardent socialist, joining the Fabians and fighting work insecurity and poverty. She pioneered trade unionism for the unskilled – first for the poorest of the poor, the London match girls, in their 1888 strike, and then for the daily-hired male dockworkers in their strike of 1889–90 that spread around Britain's ports – in both cases arousing middle-class moral sympathies for the first time for the 'social question' of how to help the nation's weakest workers. By 1890 she was interested in 'Madame' Blavatsky and Theosophy, widely regarded as the first 'New Age' religion and deeply influential in the West's twentieth-century obsession with the East. Following this spiritual path and her-term criticism of Christianity, she became leader of the Theosophical Society in 1907, moved to India where she became equally famous for her socialism and support for trade unions, and for her Indian nationalism, in 1916 launching her own Home Rule League and becoming briefly the president of the Indian National Congress Party. Though scatter-gun in good causes, Besant's approach to labour relations was consistent with supporting the victims of religious subjugation, patriarchy and imperialism, conjuring an ethical path that touched secularism, socialism and spirituality.

Annie Besant was another woman whose prolonged process of losing her Christian faith mixed deep emotion, family tribulation and reading.[31] So too Barbara Wootton (1897–1988), the eminent Cambridge polymath, Ethical Union and BHA vice-president 1954–68 and stalwart of the RPA, who in her early twenties was 'troubled by doubts about the truth of the Christian doctrines which I had been taught at school and in church, and which I had never heard questioned at home'. She held her doubts in check during engagement and marriage, but the grief at widowhood six weeks after her wedding unleashed her intellectual doubts. 'I was not disposed either to seek the comforts of religion or alternatively to thumb my nose at the Deity for what he had done'. Yet, she found the whole gospel story simply 'too improbable to be true'. She persisted attending church and pursuing her studies in theology. 'But it was no good. As I saw it, either one believed literally in the Incarnation and all its supernatural consequences as described in the gospels, or one did not'. This intellectual process was attended by 'much emotional disturbance': 'I did not part easily with belief in a comfortably-settled, divinely managed universe'. Eventually, her disquiet evaporated, never to return.[32] Another Cambridge intellectual, Frances Partridge (1900–2004), lost Christianity after deciding at twelve years of age: 'if there were no ghosts, no angels and no Holy Ghost, then there could surely be no God either?' Belief in God 'finally dropped out of my universe' after a breakfast conversation among non-believers when absence of evidence led to 'an immense sense of liberation which was purely pleasant, nor did I ever feel the least temptation to believe in God again'. After Cambridge, she fell in with what became known later as the Bloomsbury Group in the aftermath of the First World War, what she described as 'left-wing, atheists, pacifists', and held to her atheism for the rest of her life.[33] More recently but in a similar vein, the pioneer of humanist celebrancy, Jane Wynne Willson (b.1933) – father a Quaker, mother a second-generation agnostic – had no significant religious dimension to her childhood; even RE lessons at grammar school she reports had no influence at all. Being born into no religion, she reported: 'I always think, when I'm meeting loads of humanists and they've all thought their way out of religion, I always feel a bit sort of feeble.'[34] Women's rising autonomy was making their humanism easier.

But repercussions remained specially reserved for many women who adopted atheism. Perhaps regarded as easy targets, they were selected by Christians for different treatment from men. Novelist and Anglo-Catholic Dorothy L. Sayers thrived on heaping scorn publicly upon atheists male and female – like astronomer Sir Fred Hoyle, 'lecturing him through spiritual pince-nez' (as Kathleen Nott put it) for having criticised the Christian dogma of immortality on BBC radio in 1950. Sayers then did the same in 1955 to Margaret Knight after her controversial broadcasts on humanist morality.[35] Knight had been uneasy about religion during her adolescence but only changed when at Cambridge, reading Russell and other philosophers: 'A fresh, cleansing wind swept through my stuffy room that contained the relics of my religious beliefs. I let them go with a profound sense of relief, and ever since I have lived happily without them.'[36] She became one of the most vilified women of British humanism in any period, hounded by the press in the midst of early Cold War paranoia for speaking on BBC radio about teaching morality to children without religion. Kathleen Nott fired back on her behalf, undermining the anti-rationalist arguments of Sayers, T. S. Eliot, C. S Lewis and others, describing them as 'fundamentalists' in whom 'may be discerned again and again a wish to discredit scientific thinking which springs from a profounder wish to make theology paramount again'. Another call to the same line of atheist defence from the 1950s to the 2010s came from Barbara Smoker (1923–2020), who told us that she always preferred to call herself atheist rather than humanist, seeing it in more need of proclamation. She realised her loss of Catholic faith whilst in the philosophy section of a public library at noon on 5 November 1949, later describing this recognition as 'like an enormous orgasm'.[37] The culmination of much reading and reflection, she recalled 'the conclusive battle' in her autobiography as something exhilarating.[38]

But there was a classic troublesome woman's route from faith to humanism. Diane Munday (b.1931) pointed to three incidents that locate her decisive childhood move from religion. Raised in a liberal Jewish household, Diane found it odd that her mother supplied an uncle with a ham sandwich once a month. This struck her, then aged seven or eight, as 'utterly ridiculous, the illogicality; either you believed all this, what I now call nonsense, and stuck with it, or you didn't'. In a second incident, her brother was ill and messed his bedclothes, her mother washed and hung them out on a Sunday, to be accosted by a Christian neighbour remonstrating at this sabbath breach; Diane roared back at the woman's hypocrisy for hanging *her* clothes out on the Jewish sabbath. These two incidents 'really stick with me, and I think they were the beginning of the end of having any truck with religion'.

As a teenager, she attended churches and 'listened with incredulity to the words', reading T.H. Huxley which 'opened a door, a ray of light not because of what it said only, but because . . . . I was no longer alone, I was no longer in my own mind an oddity'. Married with several young children and living on the Yorkshire moors, she called herself an agnostic initially 'because it was polite – atheist was a wicked word'. Seeing a newspaper advertisement in about 1956, she joined the Ethical Union, her views sharpening with an insurance claim for damage to her car from falling church masonry (that almost killed her son), and then with her son being told by a schoolteacher to read the bible to classmates wearing a dunce's hat. Diane withdrew her son to another school, fought the rebuilding of the church school, and won a village vote to construct a nonreligious school. Moving to London, she found 'the tipping point for everything' was joining the pro-abortion campaign in 1961, partly because of the denial of abortion to thalidomide mothers, leading her in the mid-sixties to staunch support for the pro-abortion British Humanist Association.[39]

Many coming to humanism from the 1890s to the 1970s were characterised by tethering to ethical passions which humanists as individuals, and as an emerging collective, felt impelled to pursue. For some people, the key was internationalism beginning in the anti-imperialist movement and broadening into a succession of causes: the anti-war movement of the First World War, the nationalist movements of the British colonies in the 1920s and 1930s, the world government movement in the 1930s and 1940s, in the early human rights cause of the 1940s and then nuclear disarmament in the 1950s and 1960s. Numerous and diverse protest causes shaped modern humanism, but the ethical impulse befalling the individual supporter was intense.

An individual's route to humanism often involved more than one moral cause. Peter Tatchell (b.1952) was raised in a strongly evangelical household in Australia, and, via re-reading the New Testament for its social message, he steered himself into the American Civil Rights cause and humanitarian issues of the 1960s and 1970s – as he put it to us, 'to fulfil Christ's message of peace, social justice, kindness and goodwill to others'. At the age of fifteen, he campaigned from a religious approach for the reprieve of a convict, Ronald Ryan, sentenced to death in Melbourne for the murder of a prison warder, satisfying himself by his own research that the man was innocent; Ryan was executed, but the public outcry made his judicial execution the country's last. This drew Tatchell as an organiser into serial campaigning for justice and human rights issues, against the Vietnam War and to self-discovery of being gay. This finally indicated to Tatchell that the bible was wrong, leading to rejecting religion at age twenty, migrating to Britain to avoid Australian military conscription, and becoming quickly involved in the Gay Liberation Front. He became aware in the mid-1970s of the Gay Humanist Group as well as the RPA and NSS, and, being drawn into campaigning directly against religious intolerance and bigotry, felt compelled to become involved in the humanist movement.[40]

A section of the humanist movement, though difficult to isolate but yet significant, were those we have called proto-humanists. Though not full-fledged atheistic humanists, these were men and women magnetically attracted to humanist causes, equivocal about their beliefs, sometimes Christian and humanist at the same time, but characteristically embedded in the humanist network. Here are three notable examples. The first was Joseph Needham (1900–95) a Cambridge biochemist and specialist in Chinese science history, and the head of science at UNESCO under his humanist friend Julian Huxley in the late 1940s. Needham was a regular lecturer at SPES and RPA meetings, but he was an intermittent Anglican, eventually receiving a Christian burial; for his work on China, MI5 suspected him a communist.[41] The second was Cecil R. Hewitt (1901–94), who wrote under the pseudonym C.H. Rolph, and lived a double life for several decades as a police inspector with the City of London Police and as a writer for the *New Statesman*, the BBC and other publications. Hewitt was a man of considerable learning, though not of formal education; he remarks how he and his brother 'argued [their father] out of his none-too-confident religious faith'.[42] He was one of a number of proto-humanists who had identified as atheists (certainly to his own children) and mixed with many humanists – including Kingsley Martin, editor of the *New Statesman* (Hewitt wrote his biography), and with humanist reformers in the human rights, penal reform, nuclear disarmament and freedom of speech movements. A third proto-humanist was Richard Doll (1912–2005), a BHA member and atheist epidemiologist who contributed much to the discovery that smoking causes lung cancer, and who, with his wife Joan, developed and part-funded the idea of an Agnostics Adoption Society.[43] Doll, Hewitt and Needham were to varying degrees deeply embedded in the network of progressive humanists in the UK – in Hewitt's case, organising campaigns against capital punishment and censorship, and writing the 'official' Penguin book of the censorship trial of *Lady Chatterley's Lover*. They represent a type of activist who worked with humanist organisations, even joining some, but who thrived on independent action.

Cambridge – both university and town – features in the autobiographical narratives of many prominent British atheists and humanists. Kingsley Martin (1897–1969) was a pivotal figure in the mid-twentieth century, referring in his life story to how '[c]onversation, argument, the search for answer, were the stuff of Cambridge life'. He reported that the best part of students' education lay in all-night discussion: 'We talked to one, two, or three in the morning, mostly about God, Freud, and Marx. I dismissed God in my first year.' He rejected 'an anthropomorphic deity' and the philosophers' 'other God', whilst a creator God 'explained nothing and seemed improbable'. In his twenties, he wrote his father: 'My religion is to have none and to doubt always.'[44] The passage to atheism was just as easy forty years later for the Hitchens brothers. Christopher Hitchens (1949–2011) tells his journey in terms of school days in Cambridge, his awareness of the university and its 'great libraries and quadrangles', and his generation, 'restlessly modern as we aspired to be in the early 1960s', passing the Cavendish Laboratories where the atom was split and The Eagle pub into which 'Crick and Watson had strolled with exaggerated nonchalance one lunchtime to announce that with the double helix they had uncovered "the secret of existence". Shifting culture, he then scrolls to the summer of 1966 at a concert for masters and boys on the cricket ground of his Methodist school, when a pupils' pop group played a 'passably potent' version of *House of the Rising Sun* that triggered a ground invasion by a mass of youngsters from the town, crossing 'a social and geographic boundary that they had never transgressed before'; only later did Hitchens appreciate 'what had just happened to old Britain in front of my very eyes'. He continued the sixties context, as a student at Oxford and as an activist, as a tale of the radical and *soixante huitard*, communicating all that is required to understand a New Atheist famous for excoriating religion but talking remarkably little about it in his own life.[45] Christopher's brother Peter (to excuse the appearance of a non-humanist in this narrative) tells almost exactly the same story – the same school and the same destruction of the dominant Christian culture of Britain. He opened his memoir: 'I set fire to my Bible on the playing fields of my Cambridge boarding school one bright, windy spring afternoon in 1967.' He showed a deep comprehension of what becoming an atheist from the age of twelve is like for those, like himself, who in his thirties found God again and left atheism. He identified the young's dislike for submission to authority in regard to personal thoughts, loyalties and duties as defined by establishments and enforced by older generations. 'When I am in church nowadays', Peter Hitchens wrote in 2010, 'I notice that it is people of around my generation (I was born in 1951) who are mostly absent.' Turning his back on the sixties' manifesto, this Hitchens pours scorn on the moral effrontery of reforms like abortion and Barbara Wootton's proposal for tolerance of cannabis – 'the shared pleasure, the unholy communion and the initiation rite, of the post-1968 cultural and moral revolutionaries'. Peter Hitchens came to detest atheism because of the version he practised himself – 'noisily, arrogantly atheist' – and embraced the patriotic virtues of returning to a church as 'entering my inheritance, as a Christian Englishman, as a man, and as a human being'.[46]

Despite the secularisation of British society, routes from religion to humanism in the later twentieth century remained varied. 'I was brought up as an Anglican sort of Christian', reported Alice Roberts, anatomist, biological anthropologist, broadcaster and professor of Public Engagement in Science at Birmingham University. Her family went almost every Sunday not to their village church but to the cathedral-sized St Mary Redcliffe in central Bristol: 'an awe-inspiring building, with soaring vaulting, shimmering stained glass and a booming organ.' After Sunday school in the damp crypt, she would join her family in a pew near the front for a quite 'high church' service with 'plenty of ritual and mystery'.

> I loved the smell of the candles, the lowest notes of the organ that shook the tiled floor and vibrated under my sternum, the embroidered chasubles and altar cloths. During particularly boring sermons, I would tip my head back and scrutinise the gilded roof bosses, each one different, unique. I liked the mermaid best. I did pay attention though; I knew the prayers of intercession by heart. And I think I could still chant the Nicene Creed, if the need arose.

But in her teens she started to question these beliefs. Her favourite subjects at school were 'science, especially biology, and the idea that the world was a natural, understandable place seemed to me to stand in opposition to ideas about virgin births, life after death, and even the very existence of a deity'. She liked history too, and started to see the bible 'as just another historical text – a collection of historical texts, indeed – written by humans, a very long time ago'. The result was that 'Divinity disappeared from my world. With each new question I asked, the religious ideas I'd been brought up with receded'. Roberts was left looking for a word to describe her worldview.

> 'Atheist' was too negative for defining something by absence. I needed something which would encapsulate all of this: a scientific, rational approach to the world; a need to find or create my own meaning of my own life; a morality that was reflective; a firm idea of human equality. It wasn't until much later that I would find the answer, and that the word which perfectly described my adult worldview was 'humanism'.

She emerged in 2019 as president of Humanists UK.[47]

After the sixties, many Britons and Irish continued to experience troublesome issues concerning religion. Comedian and actor Jo Brand (b.1957) held her socialist mother in high esteem as a 'pre-feminist' and a woman with 'a big brain' who had already rejected Catholicism as a schoolgirl, and though Jo still chummed a childhood friend to church and did some bell-ringing, she found many Christians hypocrites and had later 'to create my own emotional disturbance' for her comic material.[48] Fellow comic Shappi Khorsandi (b.1973), Humanists UK president 2016–19, was born in Iran and immigrated to Britain, and, though raised without religion, she was painfully aware of its potential power. Her father constantly received phone calls threatening death; oftentimes racially profiled, she was 'branded' Muslim by both whites and a Muslim cab driver.[49] But among humanist leaders of the late twentieth and twenty-first centuries, religious experience, if any, tended to become shorter, less traumatic and easier to jettison. Claire Rayner (1931–2010), BHA president (1999–2004), tried very hard as a young child to be a religious believer: 'I wanted very much to believe there was a kindly God who cared about me, personally'. She argued a lot – even at infant school, where she asked the teacher if Jesus watched her in the lavatory, getting a walloping that made her so angry 'I told her there wasn't any Jesus anyway'. The religious issue 'was put to death for ever' after she fell down a hole on a bombsite as she sped for a shelter: 'whoever else this God was interested in it certainly wasn't me, so I wasn't interested in him.'[50] Many were coming to have lengthening family traditions of nonreligion. Polly Toynbee (b.1946), BHA president during 2007–12, was brought up in a family with no religion at all – though her mother had been Catholic when young and her father (Gilbert Murray's son) converted late in life from atheism to religion.[51] Chris Butterworth, BHA chair from 1999 to 2004, described herself as a fourth-generation atheist who had 'a Humanist-centred childhood' with a powerful socialist slant; though she went to Sunday school so she could join the Brownies, she and her sister had started to reject religious ideas at a young age, later joining the BHA ceremonies network in part to officiate at uncles' and aunts' funerals.[52]

Though second-generation immigrant children, notably from Catholic Ireland and Europe, were secularising rapidly in the late twentieth century, such trends segued rapidly into what became a notable feature of coming to atheism and humanism: emerging from families without practising religion. BHA's chair in the mid-1990s, Richard Paterson's (b.1945) parents were passive Anglicans, but he 'had a sort of instinct towards religion' as he thought 'it was the right thing to be religious and to believe and so forth'. At his parents' instigation, he went to Sunday school and started attending a local Wesleyan chapel, to make 'an attempt to try to get a hold of and cement some sort of religious belief. But the more I tried the more disaffected I became, and I felt that religion was just a massive ridiculous absurdity.' A few years later, a girlfriend at university took him to a church service, and that just made his decision fixed. And he 'vaguely thought: that means I am one of these humanist people'. But it was not until his late thirties that he joined BHA, then, after retiring from the civil service, became the director of Cruse Bereavement Care in Wales, then a celebrant and on to leadership work in BHA.

Among nonreligionist leaders, being never-churched was rare until the late twentieth century. One of the few was Chapman Cohen (1868–1954), who had 'no pains in giving up religion' because '[i]n sober truth I cannot recall a time when I had any religion to give up'. Instead, he claimed 'a clear right' to the title of being 'a born atheist'.[53] Among later generations, Graham Kingsley (b.1939) joined the Cambridge Humanists as a student after being raised by very traditional parents but 'totally devoid of any religious affiliation'.[54] The CEO of Humanists UK since 2010, Andrew Copson, recalled that by the 1980s the working class of his Midlands upbringing 'was quite a secular demographic', whilst his own mother and grandparents were paid-up humanists. Though Copson joined the British Humanist Association at age twenty-two for its campaign against faith schools, becoming within three years its education officer and director of public affairs,[55] this growing trend of atheistic upbringing fed into the character of the movement. Many humanist joiners from the 1970s to the 2020s found it ever-more congenial to make the transition to living a life as if there is no god. Consequently, the emotions surrounding religion became milder, and the pressure from within the humanist movement for aggressive postures towards the churches and religious privilege was much reduced. To be losers of religion, to experience obstacles and oftentimes trauma in the leaving, became less common: as Copson told us: 'It's not a burning outrage that propelled me towards humanism.' The twenty-first century has thrown up a new normal – maybe not a universal, but now a much-shared experience – of the potential atheist and humanist requiring neither lengthy secular philosophical education nor emotional suffering. In the post-1990 era of intensifying personal autonomy, atheism was more accessible and humanism more cheerily adoptable as the matching moral position.

PART I

THE ETHICAL MOVEMENT 1896–1930

3 ORIGINS AND EVOLUTION OF MODERN HUMANISM

The early decades of the ethicist movement in Britain were preoccupied with articulating the theory and principles of the cause, together with the development of organisation and cultivation of international contacts. From the 1880s to the 1920s, the movement had both organisational and intellectual leadership, the latter mainly from the classics and humanities (notably philosophy and history) and of a Liberal bent revered by a mostly middle-class following. A starting point of the movement was the tension in the late-Victorian period between religious and nonreligious positions concerning the source and content of morality. The so-called Victorian crisis of faith has been much debated by historians, with a 'crisis of doubt' being advocated in which would-be atheists and agnostics were supposedly tempted to re-join Christianity.[1] But David Nash has responded that the religious landscape was fluid, in which Christian culture was still strong but with numerous trends spreading between faith and doubt, including Annie Besant's experience of secularism followed by theosophy, meaning that things were often less polarised than many historians think.[2] Religious affairs were intellectually unsettled by a number of developments: Charles Darwin's *The Origin of Species* (1859), the rise of historical research into the context of biblical narrative (known as the Higher Criticism in biblical studies), the 'death of hell' in much popular preaching, and the late-Victorian stasis in church growth. Much religious argument held that without the bible and faith, there would be no morality. The emergence from the 1870s of the philosophical challenge to the origins of moral behaviour realigned the whole nonreligious cause, and with time was joined by a comprehensive secular challenge. This chapter focusses on the first of these – the philosophical emergence of humanism.

(a) Precursors

Humanism emerged into a general currency applied to the achievements of ancient Greece and, to a lesser extent, Rome. In the search for their own past, humanist movement historians of the 1950s and 1960s saw this as a serviceable description of how the deities played a secondary ethical role to human philosophy as an episodically tolerant approach to private religious devotions and politicised public spaces. Margaret Knight laboriously traced humanism from Greece to Bertrand Russell, noting that the humanist 'holds that man must face his problems with his own intellectual and moral resources, without invoking supernatural aid', whilst David Tribe from within the secularist movement argued that humanism could see its first progenitor in Protagoras who had argued: 'Man is the measure of all things, of things that are that they are, and of things that are not that they are not.'[3] Tim Whitmarsh has recently expanded our understanding of the Greek and Roman 'battle with the gods' at the foundations of Europe, invested with a moral intellectualism with which the modern humanist movement would comfortably align.[4] Humanism in the Renaissance revisited both original Christian texts and a number of rediscovered non-Christian ones, including Lucretius, which inspired the artists and visionaries such as Erasmus intent on a more secular focus than on a universe created with a divine purpose by an all-seeing god. New outlooks and forms of knowledge developed, carrying a preoccupation with humankind and the universe. Yet humanism was not accepted as a way of elaborating a nonreligious world view or explanation of the universe, and singularly failed to offer an outwardly visible challenge to religion. The Enlightenment notwithstanding, the atheist struggled to be heard or read without self-endangerment, though recently Michael Hunter has brilliantly shown him (less often her) to be a more common presence in early modern Britain than was formerly allowed.[5]

Despite the humanist urge to seek early antecedents, a recognisably modern humanist movement is a product of the nineteenth century, assisted by the first stirrings of modern political radicalism which challenged the status of the ruling classes of Britain, and the arrival of a modern state powered more by industry than land. Political life changed as the landed class control of the beliefs and morals of the populace, as vested in the established churches of England, Wales and Scotland, and enshrined in the legal system and the constitution, was superseded. Early-nineteenth-century radicalism embraced the fierce anticlericalism of the French Revolution, an attitude which simultaneously rejected the powers of kings and prelates, and led loudly by ideologue and supreme publicist Thomas Paine. His ideas, much like the church-state link, fused religion with politics which, at least for a time, meant that religious scepticism was closely aligned with dangerous political activities that smacked of treason.[6]

Although not universally influential, the French Revolution gave impetus to campaigns in the British Isles for forms of freedom that had been routinely suppressed by church and state. But scepticism about religion which had circulated in polite circles under the radar of official scrutiny began to spread and eventually broke the surface. In England and Scotland, early-eighteenth-century atheist discourse was followed by an underworld of freethinkers from the 1820s.[7] This went hand in hand with the circulation of the printed word which had become a significant tool of radical thought, something which criticised a variety of ideas from politics and religion to the 'dangerous' arrival of the new police force.[8] Those who stepped back from religion, for political or philosophical reasons, became known to the public as infidels – initially embraced by some as a token of pride in breaking away from religion's shackles, but later something which they would shun and seek to transcend. This was largely because infidel became regarded as a marker of disloyalty to the truth. In the 1830s and later 1840s, movements inspired by their ideals would have their moments in the spotlight. Richard Carlile brought them notoriety in the 1830s with his campaigns against censorship and the laws of blasphemy.[9] Robert Owen's utopian vision, which included pledges to help the world transcend religion's limiting influence, also had a brief moment in the spotlight before fading from view.

(b) Victorian developments

The last third of the nineteenth century saw what had been termed infidelity reach a new stage of maturity. By now it had coalesced into two, sometimes entwined and sometimes antagonist, lines of thought. The first of these focussed upon transforming the experience of being an atheist in Victorian England into one which could resemble that of other citizens. By the end of the century a range of disabilities and prohibitions which excluded atheists from society was questioned and many overturned. The right to affirm in court proceedings was granted in 1869–70 and, over the last half of the century, the English Common Law of blasphemy retreated, allowing a controlled measure of criticism of religion to be now protected by law.[10] From being pariahs denied suitable access to many churchyards to bury their dead with their own order of service, secularists had, within the last quarter of the nineteenth century, acquired burial rights and were consciously developing a powerful counterculture that would resist deathbed conversions. From here they worked diligently into the twentieth century to provide viable funerary rites for themselves.[11]

This campaigning wing of infidelity was effectively led by the man who became the most notorious atheist in Victorian England. Charles Bradlaugh's reaction to religion was quite visceral, and he envisaged a time soon when religion would be destroyed and superseded. The culmination of his quest to open up British society to the influence of its secularist population came in his attempts to enter parliament which, after a number of barriers were broken, happened eventually in 1886.[12] All of this impetus had been aided by Bradlaugh's creation in 1866 of the National Secular Society (NSS) which publicised these campaigns and had its own newspaper the *National Reformer* avidly consumed by adherents in the provinces. This often represented their only contact with such ideas and imagined communities. But all these things, taken together, demonstrate the emerging problem with this wing of secular ideology. It relied very heavily on the campaigning impetus, and too much of its ideological capital was sunk into the persona of Bradlaugh himself. Thus, it could satisfy only a limited array of needs and priorities and these were themselves compromised by Bradlaugh's death in 1891. By then, too, secularism had developed a strongly metropolitan air, gravitating to the secular halls of London. The NSS was also not dedicated to ethicism and humanism. It was, and to a great extent remains, the bulldog of the nonreligious movement, much of its campaigning and rhetoric anti-religious in a character reminiscent of European anticlericalism, and not afraid to confront clergy and religionists by loud and vigorous propagandising.[13] NSS challenges to religion were invariably with the more conservative Christian speakers, each side becoming well trained in the capital's many debating houses and grounds. Before his transition to a quieter mode, F. J. Gould, who features strongly in the story, learned his trade as a 'raging and tearing Radical' in those places: Old Street (the Hall of Science), Camberwell (the Secular Hall), Langham Place (St George's Hall), Piccadilly (Prince's Hall), West End (Willis's Rooms) and in the open air on Sundays at Oxford Street (Mortimer Street), Victoria Park and Hyde Park (Speaker's Corner).[14] Religious organisations considered these meetings vital; from 1899 the ecumenical Public Morality Council appointed Sunday lecturers to attend at Hyde Park to confront equally the gay men and infidel speakers gathering there.[15] Meanwhile, the same roaring battles were going on in print, led by *The Freethinker*, the NSS's mouthpiece from 1881 to the present, where satirical commentary and cartoons (a speciality) attacked church clergy, notably though not exclusively of the Church of England as the state church in England and (until 1920) Wales. The NSS did tangle with humanist concerns: anti-imperialism, war and pacifism, sex and birth control and what in the late-Victorian period was known as 'free love' (the legitimation of human relationships outside Christian marriage and shorn of state interference). But these issues divided members of the NSS, and until the last quarter of the twentieth century there were outbreaks of internal dispute over social-reform matters which blunted and, in some cases, entirely muted progressive voices in secularist rhetoric. It also opposed any significant treating with the churches and liberal Christians who might share humanist views on certain causes and who were judged by humanist leaders as good allies against what many in ethicism and humanism regarded as the real 'enemy' – conservative religion. The NSS drew less distinction in imagining the opposition. Yet the NSS was an important wing of the overall nonreligious movement, invariably leading the charge against religion, but quite willing to disagree with humanist organisations on whether to get involved in social reform as well as constantly challenging the modus operandi of humanist work.[16]

There was, however, an alternative wing of secular organisational culture. Coming from the generation before Charles Bradlaugh, the co-operator and former follower of Robert Owen, George Jacob Holyoake, represented a different heritage. Where Bradlaugh saw evil in religion, Holyoake wanted to avoid conflict with it and defined an ideology he called 'secularism' in the early 1850s. This claimed not to be certain of a god's existence or of a future life and contested the claims of Christianity to have intellectual sovereignty over humankind. His criticism was eclectic and designed to create spaces for the sceptical to explore the meaning of freedom and the right to pursue ideas – however close to, or distant from, religion they might appear to be. But this was an exploration to be conducted within this life, and secularism emphatically desired to concentrate upon the knowable universe.[17]

We might now consider this as a form of agnosticism, but its ambivalent character was important at its inception because it allowed local secular societies to develop in the provinces and create their own culture of reading and philosophical discussion. This involved them sifting their way through social and political ideas as they arose, and, because of this open-mindedness, these came before an incisive, inquisitive readership and audience. Such an approach opened up a considerable range of wider philosophical and scientific enquiry, discernible in the secular periodicals of the final third of the nineteenth century.[18] Campaigning periodicals like the *National Reformer* and *The Freethinker* would contain angry anticlerical copy which fed the indignation of its readers. Yet, this was countered by more thoughtful periodicals like the *Secular Review* and the *Agnostic* which contained articles covering deeper debates in science, psychology, politics, literature and social issues of the day. If pushed, the readers of the campaigning periodicals characterised the readers of their counterparts as erudite and perhaps armchair unbelievers and sceptics, whilst the readers of the thoughtful periodicals saw the campaigning ones as well-meaning but occasionally over-enthusiastic.

Consequently, by 1900 secularist ideas were largely polarised into these two camps – the angry and the thoughtful – becoming an enduring and tiresome legacy for many manifestations of secularism and humanism into the next century and beyond. On the one side, the NSS survives today as a robust campaigning organisation, fighting religious privilege and institutions, whilst, on the other side, the secularism of Holyoake continues as the foundation for new ethical and moral codes and some degree of liaison with other religions on issues of mutual concern. One alternative strand to emerge was the philosophy of Positivism, sometimes referred to as the 'Religion of Humanity', linked to the French philosopher and eventual so-called 'father of Sociology', August Comte. This moved away from the materialism that acted as an article of faith for hard-line atheists in the movement, and instead sought to embrace religious influences as indicative of a higher purpose for a human race evolving towards a state beyond religious and social conflict. Adherents of Positivism created a pantheon of human achievement, with quasi-religious services putting humans instead of god as objects of reverence, if not entirely outright worship. Strangely perhaps, this appealed to a range of contemporary thinkers such as George Jacob Holyoake, John Stuart Mill, Harriet Martineau, Henry Lewes and George Eliot. All these sought to merge positive freethought with a direction towards human reverence, and even a genuine humanist of later decades like Gilbert Murray initially made his name embracing Positivist ideas.[19] Additionally, the Positivists innovated in adopting a stronger link with Labour and communist politics than other secularists like Bradlaugh, who had notably walked out of the First International soon after it had convened. The philosopher and barrister Ernest Belfort Bax (1854–1926) associated himself with the Positivists because they unequivocally supported the Paris Commune of 1870, and were some distance from the individualist Liberals in the NSS – people he considered 'steeped in Manchester School economic prejudices'.[20]

Running parallel but disjoined from this in the last quarter of the nineteenth century were those starting from the religious end who sought merging the religious with the secular. One of the ethical societies, known until 1886 as the South Place Religious Society (in Finsbury), traced its origins to a Nonconformist congregation that in 1787–93 became Universalist (adhering to the universal offer of redemption) which by the 1820s was Unitarian. This eventually lost its traditional religious character to become an ethical society of the 1880s, but retained as its constitution: 'The object of the Society is the cultivation of a rational religious sentiment, the study of ethical principles, and the promotion of human welfare, in harmony with advancing knowledge.'[21] The first aim of the Union of Ethical Societies (UES) adopted in 1896 was: 'By purely natural and human means to assist individual and social efforts after right living', with the addition in 1906 of: 'The moral life involves neither acceptance nor rejection of belief in any deity, personal or impersonal or in a life after death.' With time, the position against the existence of a deity was to harden in British humanism.[22] In this manner, 'religion' remained in the air of ethicism as it turned into humanism.

One of the key issues was not religion as such but concerned the origins of morality. The modern humanists, in the guise of Humanists UK, date their foundation to 1896, but the philosophical origins date to the previous decade. Alongside Positivism, one other current of thought sought to organise a response to religion which highlighted the desirability and power of ethics and ethical teaching. James Martineau (1805–1900), brother of well-known freethinker Harriet and the principal of Manchester New College London, lectured in 1881 on the link between religion and ethics, seeing the exploration of the latter as the clearest method of encountering the mind of God.[23] Another philosopher Sylvan Drey's investigation of Herbert Spencer's views on religion and morality reached conclusions that took morality beyond the expectation of divine punishment for transgression. Instead, moral perfection became a guarantor of 'social happiness' and wrongdoers would be made to pay for their transgressions by either an organised society or a developed conscience which would instil 'pangs of remorse'.[24] Certainly, the 1880s in Britain was characterised by widespread discussion of the nature of morality, largely inspired by a perceived inadequacy of religious explanations. This had significantly occurred through the impact of the biblical 'Higher Criticism' and developments within the natural sciences.

The transition from the religious to the ethical was most obvious in a 'catechism' compiled in 1895 by American Stanton Coit (1857–1944), formerly of South Place and by then leader of the West London Ethical Society. It contained a range of titles resonant of an eighteenth-century Anglican catechism, albeit with a slight evangelical fervour: bristling with admonitions like 'We must be born again', 'spiritual life is a constant growth', and 'I will lift mine eyes unto the hills'. Themed chapters with verses evoked the Christian, whilst secular moral sentiments pushed through: those converted 'are ever merciful, ready to assist, without regard to their own advantage', whilst 'lifting mine eyes to the hills' no longer begged theistic help but encouraged ethicists to proclaim that 'The dreary intercourse of daily life, shall e'er prevail against us, or disturb Our cheerful faith, that all which we behold Is full of blessings'.[25] Despite its Christian echoes, the portrayal here was of secular moral messages that power, responsibility and redemption came solely on earth. However, closely observed, this was a hybrid and perhaps a compromise measure. Some secularists were sceptical about this slant in late-Victorian secular thought, seeing the term 'humanism' to be too vague, lacking in constancy, definition and strength, and well into the third quarter of the twentieth century regarded it as the inheritor of a high-minded idealism that heralded the potential downfall of Positivism in England.[26] Secularists were sometimes reluctant but resigned bedfellows with those with their heads stuck in the clouds. Religious language might still function as means of expression and communication, and, though leaving a clash in need of resolution, it was to linger for some time in early humanist thought.

Despite somewhat waspish criticism from previous-generation sceptics who had endured struggles to reach beyond religion, many individuals were being inspired by new and thoughtful teaching. T. H. Green (1836–82) from Oxford and Edward Caird (1835–1908) from Glasgow had sought direction and organisational framework to provide impetus to their progressive thinking – perhaps intellectually dispossessed seekers, yet they had challenged philosophical and theological positions for many decades, and followers espoused a more idealised form of politics shaped by ethics, one which would ensure that individuals should treat humanity 'in thine own person and the person of others always as an end and never as a means only'.[27] At a meeting likely to have happened in the summer of 1886 at University Hall, Gordon Square, London, it was decided to found an ethical society borrowing from the existing American model, initially led by J. H. Muirhead, Bernard Bosanquet, James Bonar and J. S. Mackenzie. Their first meaningful statement of principles indicates the transition in moral authority they were mapping:

> The members of this Society agree in believing that the moral and religious life of Man is capable of a rational justification and explanation, apart from Authority and Tradition. They believe that there is at present great need for the teaching of a reasoned out doctrine on this subject, especially where old sanctions and principles have lost their hold.[28]

The society's first Annual Report showed some ambiguity of purpose, recognising its temporary bridging from theology to rational morality; there was a contemporary 'widely felt need for the intelligent study of the basis of morality' with established moral explanations questioned whilst ethical claims 'rest upon the rational nature of man as a member of an organic spiritual community'.[29] With the exception of Positivism, other secular movements of the nineteenth century would have baulked at the juxtaposition of the words 'rational' and 'spiritual', regarding the first as the antithesis of the latter. The 1886 Ethical Society's members wanted to move beyond cruder materialism to promote what they saw as 'good and noble' behaviour: 'moral life is not a bondage imposed from without, but is only another name for man's proper freedom.'[30] The society's aims were 'directed toward the purification and elevation of the ideal of Human Life'.[31] This caused friction. Stanton Coit in 1887 put on record his regret that humankind had ended its relationship with a personal God and would potentially be left with 'the awful blank of atheism'; this situation could only be solved by replacing God in the human heart with 'man'.[32] Meantime, unlike other secular organisations, the 1886 Society's stated intentions were to be constructive and not combative and saw the pressing need for lectures and instruction promoting this message. In these early years, the society's membership grew from forty to 137 by 1889,[33] and by 1891 it was effectively in charge of a series of University Extension Lectures which took place at London's Essex Hall, commencing an association with wider philosophical education that was to both deepen and expand. Lectures on literary subjects and philosophers such as Dante, Milton and Nietzsche, as well as on contemporary ethical issues like 'Secondary Education', 'Democracy', 'The Ethical Function of Women' and the 'Ethics of Business Life and National Relations', were invited to other venues such as the North London Islington Central Liberal Club and the Bethnal Green Gladstone Club.[34] Alongside a programme of Sunday lectures, by 1893 the Ethical Society of 1886 had also explored initiatives for young men and women, boys and a Kindergarten, all of which they were unable to sustain.[35] In 1890 the Ethical Society affiliated with the American Ethical Society, exchanging reports and expressing a desire to host visiting lecturers, and changed its name to the London Ethical Society. But the traces of this 1886 Ethical Society ceased in 1897 when it was absorbed into the educational provision offered by the School of Ethics and Social Philosophy which had commenced as an offshoot of the society itself. Notwithstanding its brief existence for eleven years or so, it became a prominent example for other metropolitan and provincial societies, demonstrating the growing appetite for this approach to morality and philosophy.

(c) South Place Ethical Society

Another origin of the movement comes with the South Place Ethical Society, which remained independent of the Ethical Union until 1950. Constituted as a radical chapel and supporting a sect (the Philadelphians) in the 1790s explicitly denying the doctrine of hell, it embraced Unitarianism but, under its most famous pastor William Johnson Fox, had also acquired a taste for free inquiry. This meant the 'sect' changed its name to the 'Universalists', followed by Unitarianism, dissent, and finally by the end of the century 'Religion'. In 1824 the society moved into its own chapel, and in 1864 Fox was succeeded by the American Moncure D. Conway (1832–1907) who eventually oversaw the removal of all theological teaching or doctrine from the environs of the society. His name would come with time to be a synonym for this strand of humanism when first Conway Hall (1929), then the ethical society he forged (2012), would bear his name.

Ethics beyond Christianity was also a burgeoning topic in America in the ideas of the New York academic Felix Adler and his associate Stanton Coit. These two espoused ideas which mirrored and added to metropolitan English developments. It was Moncure Conway's invitation to Stanton Coit to lecture at the South Place Religious Society in the spring of 1887 – a few months after the society had commenced its lectures – which led to Coit offering an eclectic mixture of lecture subjects which investigated 'The Death of Socrates' as well as the ethical choices evident from a prolonged study of Shakespeare. But the last cornerstone lecture of his visit was on the subject 'Ethical Culture as a Religion for the People', in which he offered a stark message and a lasting impression, beginning an argument that human surveillance of moral behaviour had supplanted that of a supreme being, largely because humans were a more obvious and discernible presence – thereby capable of exerting pressure upon the moral miscreant. If this were not a particularly optimistic message, Stanton Coit then distilled the essence of what ethicists were trying to achieve and how this had its own origin in humankind: 'Ethics is the science of good character and right conduct, and it is based on our moral experience and our moral judgement, and should be kept independent of all theology, just as the science of correct thinking is, or political economy, and all other sciences of the mind and society, and as all practical arts are.'[36] The lecture offered detail and direction to the openness and vagueness of the propositions that London ethicists had been entertaining, helping too to define themselves as rejecting the dogmatism and search for ideological purity which beset other secular organisations. But the final piece of the jigsaw proffered by Coit explained that if 'the atheist, or theist, or agnostic, or positivist does not derive his sanctions to right actions from his speculative theories', he would be welcomed in ethicism. 'We would then unite on the basis of character and conduct, and try to build up these as best we can in ourselves and others.'[37] Stanton Coit made plain that developments in the science of the mind would enable ethical views to transcend the problems that materialist philosophy posed – the unpalatable idea that the human makeup was mere matter driven by instinct. The sciences of the mind led by psychology, according to Coit, were capable of restoring an essence of humankind that was not material and that could justifiably be called 'spirit'. This he saw as an idea capable of being nurtured, making the whole ethicist project both tenable and diverse.[38] At the lecture's conclusion, the South Place Society was so impressed by Coit that they took the bold step of deciding to invite him to become their 'Minister'. Less surprising than it seemed, Coit's lecture crystallised the mutuality of thought existing between the American ethicists and the British effort to make ethics supersede and transcend dogma and ideology in Britain's religious world. Amenable and flattered, Coit saw this as an opportunity to move forward with his agenda among the like-minded. He made acceptance of this invitation conditional upon the 'South Place Religious Society' changing its name to the 'South Place Ethical Society', whereupon Moncure Conway urged the society to embrace Coit and the bright future he offered of organic and trailblazing social change:

> I hope South Place has vitality enough to grow into many more names yet, representing as it were the annual rings on the growing tree. I hope some historian will one day read the whole religious history of England in the successive names of South Place, and find in its fruit the flavour of every truth which unfolded during its time.[39]

The society accepted Coit at a special meeting convened a month later, and in its 1888 report mollified a few critics by urging all members to combine towards 'on the one hand the breaking down of superstition, and on the other of introducing higher and truer motives of action in the place of those which have disappeared.'[40]

Stanton Coit's ministry at the South Place Ethical Society cultivated a late-Victorian congregational-style life. Coit revised the Ethical Society Hymn book, provided three-quarters of the society's Sunday afternoon lecture content, and operated a class of ethical instruction, presumably aimed at adults, using the German philosopher Professor Georg von Giżycki's work (which appeared as an English textbook the following year).[41] With additional organisations for girls (conducted by one of the society's honorary secretaries, Miss E. Phipson) and a Junior Ethical Union, this was a model of how Victorian ethicists could operate without religion as an underpinning of morality, yet see their fellowship as otherwise identical to Christian congregations. London ethicists now had a strong organisation in one building under Coit, persuading them to organise and think like a religious group and nurture their principles. Moral belief was to be inspired by instruction, guidance and fellowship with recreational content aimed at heightening the ethical awareness of the individual. Coit had asked those constructing these initiatives to bear this principle in mind, and it emerged regularly in the rules and provisions of such initiatives within South Place.

Whilst audiences began to grow at South Place, and its offshoot institutions seemed to flourish, Stanton Coit's position proved problematic. He may have come from the United States with an ingrained sense of mission, and some in the society actively welcomed this, but some never quite forgave him for insisting upon the change of name. For a few members this looked like a piece of unnecessary authoritarianism, an action which was firmly at odds with the inclusive nature of the society's distinguished and proud history of searching for truth from a variety of eclectic standpoints. The situation was aggravated at the end of 1892 when Coit made his continued work as the society's minister dependent upon the membership accepting five proposals on organisation and governance, designed to give Coit greater control within the society. After a number of meetings, four of the five prescriptions were adhered to, but the fifth, a proposal for Coit to have an ex officio seat on every society committee, failed to achieve the necessary two-thirds majority. With this Coit tendered his resignation leaving the organisation's *Annual Report* to note ruefully how in future the society required 'a fusion of the traditional encouragement of unrestricted intellectual activity, and a practical earnestness.'[42] Swiftly, Moncure Conway agreed to return to South Place for an interim period. This eventually lengthened into a permanent arrangement which lasted until June 1897. The mid-1890s saw the society reforge its principles with wording which was sufficiently inclusive to indicate a distance from the Coit years, in seeking 'the cultivation of a rational religious sentiment, the study of ethical principles, and the promotion of human welfare, in harmony with advancing knowledge.'[43]

(d) The Union of Ethical Societies

On resigning from South Place, Stanton Coit established a congregation in 1892 called the West London Ethical Society. He did not become an isolated figure, but was involved in the establishment of forty ethical societies around Britain and was also the architect of the umbrella Union of Ethical Societies formed on 30 April 1896. He also founded in 1897 the Moral Instruction League that set an important and permanent element in the agenda of the British ethical and humanist movement. In large measure, he formed a national movement out of the ethical societies that were springing up in the 1890s and 1900s in many places in Britain. Those scattered within London, in the north, south, east and west of the city and environs, had, almost from their inception, sought a form of federation which would consolidate their existence and public profile, as well as acknowledge and strengthen the work done by outlying societies. At a meeting in November 1895, these four London societies, as well as South Place, the London Ethical Society and the Cambridge Ethical Society, elected delegates to form a council. This scheme was eventually realised the following April as the Ethical Union which functioned as an umbrella organisation and a more obviously regional and national forum for otherwise isolated societies.[44] The first five years saw ethical societies launched in Belfast, Portsmouth, Bristol, Edinburgh and Leicester, with others appearing in the London hinterland of Croydon, Rochester and Woking. In the immediate years after the turn of the century, societies were founded in Glasgow, Birmingham, Bolton, West Bromwich, Sheffield, Chesterfield, Liverpool, Manchester and Oxford, augmented by a flurry of societies established in Wales in Cardiff, Merthyr Tydfil, Pontypridd and Aberdare. By the end of the decade, there were societies also formed in Norwich, Stoke-on-Trent, Falkirk, Bedford, Penarth and Abertillery. The Great War of 1914–18 saw a women's group created as well as an ethical society in central London; in the years after the war came a Young People's Group and an Ethical Union at University College London. The fledgling societies in many of these smaller towns were to dissolve after five years or so, whilst those in the larger conurbations were sustained for longer.

The last years of the nineteenth century saw the Union of Ethical Societies acknowledge the existence of an average of six additional affiliated societies per year. This rose to ten in 1901–2, more than doubling again to twenty-three by 1907–8, but then fell to an average of sixteen a year.[45] The early documentarist of British humanism, Gustav Spiller, was of the opinion that the increase at the start of the twentieth century coincided with the upsurge in labour and radical unrest, indicative of the movement's long association with the social, economic and ethical claims of the Labour movement. But Spiller, in writing his history of the ethical movement, also realised that a strong and powerful pull holding this union together was the lecture circuit, a phenomenon acting likewise as the chief agent of its extension. The union actually created a Lecturers Register overseen by an Honorary Lecturing Agent who, by 1904–5, was actively offering sixteen individuals who could lecture in the provinces free of charge to local ethical societies. A year later the union expressed a wish to create a team of salaried lecturers who could be stationed in the provinces to provide more locally nuanced and cost-effective provision. In the absence of this, the union created a small library of printed and published material that could be loaned to a society where a lecturer could not be obtained for whatever reason. Many local and regional societies came to endure because of a list of charismatic lecturers from the metropolitan centre. From the UES, the lecturers included Gustav Spiller himself, Stanton Coit, Harold Johnson, Joseph McCabe, Margaret McMillan, G. E O'Dell, William Saunders and Harry Snell – the last of whom was to have a considerable influence on the fortunes of secularist ventures within British society until well into the twentieth century.[46]

From 1899, the lecture and the lecturer became the hallmark of the ethical movement. The demise of the ethical 'minister' with Coit's resignation from South Place was underway, even though he sustained his career at the West London Society for decades more. In place of the ministering leader came not so much philosophical as political ethicism, featuring the appointment of the first four 'permanent lecturers' to the South Place Ethical Society: Herbert Burrows, John MacKinnon (J.M.) Robertson, John (J.A.) Hobson and Joseph McCabe. They were different in content but rather similar in style: Hobson the theoretical economist of huge influence; Robertson the combative rationalist, literary critic, journalist, strident Liberal and staunch secularist; Burrows the retired civil servant; McCabe the ex-priest 'attack hound' of anticlericalism. Sunday discourses were now to be divided rotationally between them. One consequence of this was to make the institution less concerned with social affairs and more with intellectual and political affairs, a site for crowd-pulling giants of rationalist debate and secularist exhortation, and rather less the venue for soothing sociability and brotherhood. As Ian MacKillop says, at the turn of the century the identity of South Place became defined by its choice of permanent lecturers.[47] Hobson and Robertson were to be long-lasting stalwarts of the society, and they reflected how ethicism could both develop and voice its critiques of various contemporary issues – notably the Second South African (Anglo-Boer) War which became a significant cause celebre for the ethicist and Positivist movements (to which we return in Chapter 5). J. M. Robertson, described by one commentator as Britain's 'unknown genius',[48] was a multi-talented writer and publicist who similarly denounced the war with widely exhibited photographs that told of the British concentration camps and the devastating death toll they had wreaked on the civilian Boers.[49] Alongside the more socialist-minded Burrows and the influence of Fabian socialism and Marxism among the wider community of humanist intellectuals down to the 1930s,[50] the movement itself became for many decades best known by the lecturing work of the South Place Ethical Society.

JOHN MACKINNON ROBERTSON 1856–1933

FIGURE 6 J. M. Robertson. Picture: Artist: John Collier, Conway Hall Ethical Society/Bishopsgate Archive.

Journalist, historian and orator in the grand Victorian style, J. M. Robertson was born and raised in Scotland, leaving school at thirteen to become a clerk, then a law clerk, then a leader writer at the *Edinburgh Evening News*, followed by a move to London as assistant editor then editor for Charles Bradlaugh's *National Reformer*. Becoming a Liberal MP for Northampton in 1895, he sat on the social-justice wing of New Liberalism, championing progressive ideas, including on the elite Rainbow Circle that counted Ramsay MacDonald. Robertson was a rationalist and secularist, famed as a scholar of evidence-based argument, a prolific history writer notably of freethought and the flaws of Christian theology. But his writing was wide-ranging in field, displaying the bountiful gifts of the ferocious autodidact. In the 1890s he emerged a favourite speaker for the South Place Ethical Society, elected in 1900 as one of its first four Appointed Lecturers, and most often spoke twice a month at Sunday morning meetings with upwards of 300 hearers (with most lectures published). An opponent of the Boer War, he was an advocate of the underconsumption theory he shared with J. A. Hobson that shaped the ethicist opposition to imperialism and support for colonial nationalism. Few could match Robertson for his learning and his publishing output, and he would take on any argument of principle without concern for his reputation, being considered a brilliant debater. Indeed, Robertson and Hobson were the dazzling stars of the ethical and rationalist movement in the early twentieth century, constituting two of the most fearsome secularist minds. In death, Robertson pioneered cremation without a funeral.

Robertson and Hobson were revered at South Place as towering intellects, political speakers and observers of contemporary events and the modern condition. They were forthright debaters, undaunted by criticism, with ready answers for political and ecclesiastical opponents. Their stature led to the appointment of yet more permanent lecturers at South Place, and triggered Gustav Spiller to write in 1908 of the far-reaching ambitions of ethicism and its claim that 'the conscience has eclipsed the scriptures. . . . Democracy and Civism have shown men how to help themselves, and the Supreme test and interest of men have become Ethical, and have ceased to be Supernaturalistic.' Spiller saw this on the one hand as an unequivocal advance but equally declared that such a transition had to be carefully managed. De-coupling ethics from religion would, importantly, allow it to become autonomous, but he also noted that this process had eventually produced a belief that ethics always *was* autonomous. Another realisation was that an attachment to belief systems nullified it, thus making it emphatically *not* a species of autonomous ethics at all. From here, for Spiller and like-minded ethicists, both ethics and religion existed in separate compartments of the human mind. It then became a source of discussion as to whether this could change, whereby ethics itself gradually became invested with religious feelings and religious potential. This was acceptable provided that during this process it was also entirely purged of theological content. Spiller summarised ethics as humankind's natural antipathy to circumstances in which 'justice and desire are foiled' which enables the search for 'some theory which tends to satisfy and to reinforce justice and desire'. Spiller also noted that although ethics could be divorced from religion it could not exist without what he called 'a philosophy of life' which would evolve, in his view, into the ethical religion 'where belief in the efficacy and grandeur of moral principles is substituted for the belief in the efficacy and grandeur of a deity'.[51]

Spiller displayed a conviction that science constituted the means of achieving the quest for an ultimate morality: 'science, then, however indirectly, is working out moral problems, and the moralist must either co-operate with men of science, or else he and his work will be consigned to oblivion.' But this relationship was not new since scientific endeavour had always been the ally of ethics. This was because it revealed an ordered world, as well as one in which superstition realistically held no sway. 'Democratic effort' alongside 'dignity and self respect' were better signposts to right behaviour than 'warning and punishment'. This also meant that ethics, through scientific endeavour, scorned the pre-ordained, and instead inspired efforts to alter the environment for human benefit as a human duty.

Spiller saw such developments and attitudes as capable of creating new social sciences, such as criminology, which would encourage 'right living' far removed from a system regulated by threats and punishments. The ethical link to democratic socialism was emphasised by a conception that dialogue with the state would ensure it no longer simply protected the rich and powerful, but instead worked to abolish privilege. Ethics would further ensure that the state became a vehicle for a vast panoply of public works which included municipal provision for libraries and museums. This would be augmented with the untold benefits of town planning that would enhance the environment, aiding the messages of ethicists and social scientists who were all stakeholders in these developments. Spiller cautiously saw the ambivalence of arguing for the state to be enabling, alongside seemingly contrary statements that ethics was about cultivating the requirement for the ethical individual to undertake their undeniable duty. However, Spiller's writing also contains other slightly unresolved contradictions. A fascination with, and obvious admiration for, democracy was tempered with an equal reticence about collective mass opinion where discrimination cannot so easily be counted upon. Spiller would also seem to distance his conception of socialism from orthodox Marxist theory with a denial that the resolution of economic problems and inequality would leave 'nothing else to solve'. The descent from late-nineteenth-century Positivism was also evident in an assertion of progress moving forward through identifiable stages reaching onwards towards a 'moral ideal'.[52]

But the movement was not so ready to dispense with religion. A five-man committee of the Union of Ethical Societies in 1911, including Spiller, devoted to the promotion of ethics, pronounced the 'definite work' of ethical societies as 'ultimately [to] induce the leaders of all the churches of all denominations to modify their forms and ceremonies, their sacraments, their ritual and their preaching' until every congregation is dedicated to the cause of 'the good in the world'. But yet, in regard to ritual, the committee regarded it as 'unwise – as futile even – to think of extruding it from religion'.[53] Certainly, the ethical movement could easily persuade itself that its own moment had come, or would surely come with the peace and its aftermath. The Great War, as far as the South Place Ethical Society was concerned, had sharpened interest in its work among those prepared to 'take life more seriously'. These people were also persuaded that the great national and international problems of the period had now become ethical ones. Several Christian denominations were wrong-footed in terms of both their spiritual provision and their ability to actively provide post-war solace and solutions.[54] Ethicism appeared to offer a new conception of the world that stepped away from many of the institutions that had, perhaps unconsciously, failed individuals during the war.

4 ETHICISM TO HUMANISM

With the intellectual strength of the ethicist movement during the Edwardian period and the 1910s, it was no surprise to see numbers grow during the war that followed, fostering considerable optimism among the members. With a national following developing, publications were important to verve and unity, yet the journalistic efforts of ethicists had met with only mixed success. From its inception, the Union of Ethical Societies (which became the Ethical Union in 1920) had published a periodical *The Ethical World* which had been edited by Stanton Coit himself. This had temporary competition when *The Ethical Societies Chronicle* was launched in 1908, intended as a publicity sheet to draw audiences into lectures at Finsbury and elsewhere; however, this was suspended after it was successfully argued that the *Chronicle* was in danger of sapping energy from *Ethical World*. When this latter paper itself ceased to operate in 1916, the gap left was filled by a short-lived replacement called *The Ethical Movement*. When this ran into financial trouble, a public appeal and money to underwrite a subsequent venture allowed the union's council to launch *The Humanist* under the tutelage of the veteran publisher Charles Albert Watts to whom so much of the strategy and ammunition of the humanist movement – for his work for the Rationalist Press Association and the journal *Watts Literary Guide* (later to become the more stable and long-lasting *New Humanist*) – owed a huge debt.[1]

This chapter looks at some of the key elements that contributed towards the transition from ethicism to humanism – a sometimes indistinct changeover and one with conflicting commentary. It looks at the publishing arm of the movement so vital for the preservation of intellectual dissent from established beliefs, especially among those living away from major centres. It looks also at the feminist surge, and, first, the impulse to imagine the human self as at the heart of the movement's philosophy, its intellectual attraction and its popular appeal.

(a) From community to the self

Superficially, there are grounds for doubting the demise of ethicism before the middle of the twentieth century. One might point to considerable evidence of ethicism's vigorous survival: the Ethical Union continued to be the movement's federated body until the 1960s, whilst no major journal of the movement bore the word 'Humanist' before the mid-1950s. The period after the Great War was also one of consolidation for ethicism's prize institutions, allowing the South Place Ethical Society to realise its plans for new premises which had been peremptorily suspended in 1914. The freehold on the society's existing chapel site in Finsbury was sold for £36,000 to be followed by the purchase of a site in the north-east corner of the reasonably quiet Red Lion Square in Holborn but which also had the advantage of a frontage onto the major east–west artery of Theobald's Road. As plans were drawn up, the society stayed in temporary premises until March 1927 when the old chapel site was finally vacated. It took a year until building work commenced and a further year until the new hall was operational. This was greeted by an impressive set-piece inaugural meeting at which social psychologist and Fabian Graham Wallas (1858–1932) spoke alongside erstwhile stalwarts such as J. A. Hobson and Stanton Coit. Also present and speaking were F. J. Gould, and Charles Bradlaugh's daughter Hypatia Bradlaugh Bonner, who was now campaigning in new fields. Still, the presence of the old partisans gave credence to the concept of renewal rather than reformation.

Humanism as a separate form of non-theological position was emerging, even if not totally theorised nor epistemologically credited. As late as 1933, J.A. Hobson in his Conway Lecture acknowledged an ambiguity in 'humanism', issuing 'an earnest invitation to Rationalists to count themselves as Humanists, and to regard Ethics as the mediating principle', signalling that this was not yet an open-and-shut case.[2] There was no full-on, definitive exploration of the difference in the meaning of ethicism and humanism in regard to the nonreligious movement, and, if challenged, there might well have been hesitancy about the notion of change and contradiction between different observers. Yet humanism as a nonreligion movement was maturing in the manner of speaking about the movement, in its theorisation and in the evolving agenda for campaigning.

The nonreligious sector was speaking and imagining itself decreasingly in the exclusive senses of philosophical argument or congregational community, and instead increasingly in relation to issues of the individual – their freedoms, responsibilities, independent moral alignments and sense of self. The freedoms of ethicism had largely been inherited from secularism, and were centrally the freedoms of conscience, speech and blasphemy – of freedom to critique religion, to deploy philosophical and similar argument. The imagined congregational community had been seen as a collective, as one still governed by rules of behaviour and sentiment as if the members adhered to a church or sect, but was diminishing as the character that had been inherited from the Nonconformist tradition, embedded in the South Place Religious (later Ethical) Society, withered. In place of those two formulations of ethicist identity, the individual was coming into sharper relief as a humanist perception, being imagined as an independent moral being with choices to make and to receive tolerance from fellow members, the state and society at large. In part, this might be seen as a sharpening of secularist content dragging community ethicism out to an individual-centred humanism. But more importantly, this was moral individualism expanding into a humanist agenda: religious and spiritual individualities, gender and racial identities, colonialism and postcolonialism, sexual behaviour and identities, contraception and abortion, voluntary euthanasia and eugenics and attitudes to war and violence (pacifism, conscientious objection and disarmament). Capital and corporal punishment were a focus for some, notably in the Humanitarian Society which held many ethicists – including Hypatia Bradlaugh Bonner (1858–1935) who in 1897 published a comprehensive forty-five-page pamphlet arguing against both practices, demonstrating how executions for murder rose from nine in 1840 to sixteen in 1894, and adult floggings from eight in 1877 to sixty-five in 1894.[3] There was no central position for humanists on all of these, though most came to reflect upon each. Eugenics attracted many humanists before the Second World War and some after, including Bertrand Russell whose intellectual elitism worried over society being dominated by the ignorant, credulous and the superstitious – especially, it seems, Roman Catholics.[4] But one humanist would stand out for the vigour of his opposition to eugenics. Zoologist and statistician Lancelot Hogben (1895–1975) spoke and wrote with venom about the immorality of this spurious discipline, regarding it as 'claiming the authority of science for sentiments which are the negation of civilized decency and for doctrines which are in open contradiction of historical truth'.[5] Because humanism reflected more deeply than had ethicism upon these and other issues, all manner of moral issues were exposed to disagreement within the movement.

HYPATIA BRADLAUGH BONNER 1858–1935

FIGURE 7 Hypatia Bradlaugh Bonner Photo: from F. J. Gould, *The Pioneers of Johnson's Court* (London, Charles Watt, 1929).

Secularist, humanitarian and opponent of capital punishment and war, Hypatia was the daughter of Charles Bradlaugh, Britain's first avowed atheist member of parliament. She was brought up to the nonreligion cause, being named after the brilliant fourth-century CE Egyptian Neoplatonist philosopher and mathematician who was murdered by a Christian mob. She graduated from the University of London as a science teacher, becoming a lecturer at the Old Street Hall of Science and later for the NSS and the Rationalist Press Association (RPA), and acted as her father's secretary and biographer. Upon her marriage to Arthur Bonner, they roomed for a period with Annie Besant, mixing with London's radicals and intellectuals, she becoming a writer and editor on secularism and freethought. A popular speaker for most of her adult life, her interests found focus on the judicial system in relation to the rising blasphemy cases of the early twentieth century, to prisons and punishment, and to support for the Liberal Party and for the feminist cause. Her humanism was centred on being a humanitarian, organising campaigning against capital punishment and war (founding the Rationalist Peace Society just before the First World War). She served on the executive committee of the Humanitarian League with many other radicals, including Besant and Edward Carpenter, which from 1891 to 1919 opposed avoidable suffering among all sentient beings, reviving interest in the abolition of hanging by focussing on reducing crime rather than punishing the criminal. But she also pursued practical judicial reform, becoming a Justice of the Peace in her later years, forging a minor humanist tradition of sitting on the bench. Whilst making an original and decisive contribution to the humanist cause, especially through the RPA, much of her life's work was devoted to defending her father's secularist legacy, bestowing her with something of a Victorian air.

In the theorisation of moral issues, the range of what the thinking humanist should dwell upon widened into new content, becoming more codified and fiercely challenging. The content sometimes sprang from old issues robed in new garb, but sometimes the products of a more morally complex era. With issues like female suffrage (and how to campaign for it), the wrongs of colonialism and emerging independence movements, total war and conscription, and birth control and terminations, matters of acute debate magnified the question of how a humanist religion, without deistic authority, could now devolve decision-making to the people. The individual was now not merely listening to philosophical arguments, and being enthralled by the grandiloquence of the speakers or the mastery of the writers, but was being dared to decide. The theoretical framing of moral issues was now shifting, not just away from a biblical authority but from the assuredness of a collective position. The theorisation was moving from the abstract to the practical, in some cases to social-scientific realities, and often to first principles about the freedoms of individuals. In the evolving concept of human rights, for instance, in which the humanist cause was to become expert, pioneering and committed, new arguments had to prevail. What rights were the human to be conceived as possessing? What rights and freedoms did women and men have relative to each other? What rights was a child entitled to? These were the humanists' summons to decision-making – one found in the popular science books of Hogben and the non-fiction of Britain's most popular humanist, H. G. Wells.[6]

From this mêlée of change from congregation to individual, and from scriptural authority to moral choices, practical consequences arose. The first was a growing diversity of issues to be considered by both the movement and the individual. From this, a secondary outcome was the necessity of maintaining a moral agenda with a prioritisation, both for the individual and for the movement as a whole;

these were perennially shifting sands, susceptible to changing events which made for topsy-turviness in decision-making at management levels. A third upshot was the increasing demand for not merely adoption of a position on an issue but for active campaigning, and oftentimes considerable debate over the manner of the campaigning to be adopted. Taken together, humanism as a definer of the morality content of the movement implied the hunt for changes in politics, participation in electioneering, in pressing departments of state to consider administrative or legislative change, and, by the 1950s, for the humanist movement itself to develop the expertise to float draft bills to influence parliamentarians. Humanism represented the engagement of nonreligionists in both their own moral choices and in national and, very quickly, international moral change.

But a caveat. These trends being associated with the advent of a modern humanism did not mean absolute or final forms of change, nor binary difference between ethicism and humanism. Ethicism in the nineteenth century had contained features of individualism and political campaigning, and philosophical argumentation was in no way utterly lost to the nonreligious sector. There were features of continuity from the old to the new, and some of the arguments to be heard in the twentieth- and even twenty-first-century humanist movement were as old as the hills. We are speaking here of trends of change, of the altered prominence of certain features constituting the ethical and humanist organisations between 1896 and 2021.

(b) The Rationalist Press Association

One organisation that came quickly to represent the spirit of humanism was the RPA. Emerging from the mighty Victorian secularist tussle with religion, the RPA epitomised the fulfilment of the dream of creating a publishing outlet for the movement's ideas to reach the general public. So popular was the RPA that the hall for its monthly Wednesday London meeting proved by 1905 too small and it hired the South Place Institute in Finsbury, pointing to institutional convergence.[7] Addressing this initiative required expertise in the world of publishing as well as from the world of philosophy and ideas. The expertise came from a veteran of the secularist movement's publishing wing, Charles A. Watts (1858–1946), who had been an editor of Charles Bradlaugh's secular and republican newspaper the *National Reformer*, linking earlier radicalism to modern rationalism and suggesting even more convergence among the kindred bodies.

The idea of the RPA was the culmination of established nineteenth-century resistance to undemocratic structures and to secularist publishing and bookselling. Its manifesto ambitiously aimed at cultivating 'a critical and freely inquiring attitude of mind'.[8] Enshrining the visions of Thomas Paine, Richard Carlile and the Enlightenment, the RPA specialised in the human sciences, seeking knowledge that would benefit and enhance society and social relations. On its creation in 1899, founded upon previous secularist publishing ventures, the RPA sought to build upon the achievements of the secular movement and unbelief, characterised as one historian has remarked as the transition from 'guerrilla warfare to a full scale campaign'.[9] The association was at least partly built upon science, the universe and evolution, and of forcing religion into an ignominious retreat on these points – a task, as noted by historian Bill Cooke, perfected by Joseph McCabe.[10] The geological theories of Charles Lyell which paved the way for the evolutionary theories of Charles Darwin led onto the 'bulldog' defence mounted by T.H. Huxley, whilst the more human sciences developed their disciplines and intellectual infrastructure during this period: the foundation of anthropology, largely the work of Edward Burnett Tylor, and that of sociology assisted by Herbert Spencer, contributed to the erosion of Christianity's former confidence as the liberalising Higher Criticism of the bible questioned central tenets of the faith.[11] The fundamentals of Christianity had already been challenged: notably, by David Strauss' *Life of Jesus* (1846), the collection *Essays and Reviews* (1860), and the liberal Anglo-Catholic collection *Lux Mundi* (1889). Certainly, the RPA felt that its time had come in hastening scrutiny of Christian doctrine. Yet the apparent 'crisis of faith' created what the RPA thought was an opportunity to bridge the gap between the theologian's elevated knowledge and the grassroots Christian believer's theological ignorance, thereby gaining doubters as recruits. The RPA saw spanning this gulf as central to its mission, but the task was hard and its success is doubtful.[12]

Charles Watts provided a further connection with the past. The premises where the RPA operated from 1903 to 1955, effectively the centre of worldwide rationalism, was at Johnson's Court off Fleet Street, the former base for Austin Holyoake's publishing venture in, among other things, Charles Bradlaugh's writings. Watts himself had been an apprentice here and he learned much of what was both positive and negative about involvement in such activities.[13] When Charles Watts took over the business from his father, the younger Watts developed a magazine in 1885 to develop 'contact with readers of heretical literature', *Watts's Literary Guide*, later becoming a mainstay of humanist publishing, renamed in succession *The Literary Guide* and, in 1956, the *Humanist* and then in 1972, the *New Humanist*. From the outset, the mission was to enable readers to enter into fundamental debates of the age, with an emphasis on 'progressive thought' and scientific discoveries, and to bridge the gap between expensive, unobtainable and banned books. But the finances were always precarious. Within three years, *The Literary Guide* launched an appeal for a 'Propaganda Press Fund', run by a Propaganda Press Committee which morphed into the Rationalist Press Committee, aimed at raising £1,000 to campaign to remove the law which prevented property legacies from being used to further the ends of 'Freethought and Advanced Religious Reform'. This obstacle was eventually removed only in 1917 after a high-profile court case which delivered a landmark decision rescinding the law.[14]

THE NEW HEADQUARTERS OF THE RATIONALIST PRESS ASSOCIATION.

FIGURE 8 The Rationalist Press Association and Charles Watts' premises in Johnson's Court, off Fleet Street, in 1924. Drawing and photo: 1924 C. G. Dixon/Bishopsgate Archive.

The enthusiastic move into publishing was a late recognition that the days of the secularist lecture theatre and lecture circuit were numbered. The third quarter of the nineteenth century had seen large crowds at lectures where theological points were debated between secularist and Christian lecturers or had come to see Bradlaugh and Holyoake. But after 1900, with both figures departing, lectures became poorly attended or delivered to an audience of the converted, and lecture quality was no longer assured. George W. Foote, one of the men who made his name in the 1860s and became Bradlaugh's successor as president of the NSS, occasionally had audiences complain of his repetitiveness.[15] The association inherited the publications of its predecessor the Rationalist Press Committee, originally self-identifying as 'agnostic' like so many influential works of the 1880s and 1890s, including F. J. Gould's three-volume history of religion and works of children's moral education. As a member of the committee, Gould was a particularly strong advocate of the printed word, and agnostic seemed a more respectable term than freethinker, secularist or atheist, exposing a social-class tension within the movement. The lecture acquired a cachet for more bourgeois local patrons, as did the periodical pamphlet and longer publication whilst some platform speakers appealed more readily to middle- and upper-class patrons. Meanwhile, proletarian didacticism now relied more upon the cheap and short-format printed word, assisting the passing of platform-led secularism and working-class mass adherence – a fading characteristic called to mind as late as 1963 by a *Daily Telegraph* satirist referring to 'earnest artisans in fog-bound ethical halls'.[16]

The RPA in its early years reflected the secularist preoccupations of the nineteenth century by emphasising the challenge to religion.[17] In a sketch published in *The Literary Guide* for February 1899, it was proposed to support freedom of thought, the popularisation of science and the ongoing quest to divorce morality from religion, but then focussed upon publications on religion and biblical criticism, clearly harking back to Bradlaugh. This 'heritage' dimension of what the rationalist movement thought would win converts was reinforced by planning to produce biographies of past great rationalists. Still, the future was felt to lie in the conflict between science and religion 'with a view to disentangling the public mind from supernaturalism and mysticism'.[18] But Frederick Gould's agenda also shone through in the listing of secular education and moral instruction, plus creative works of art and poetry for inspiring humanist development, with drama portraying true morality on stage. From the inaugural meeting of the RPA on 18 September 1899, with George Jacob Holyoake in the chair, the organisation began appealing in *The Literary Guide* for suggestions of prominent contemporary rationalists to be appointed 'honorary associates' to be identified closely with the association's aims – a practice to become a permanent feature of humanist organisations – as well as for donations to promote 'truth for authority, and not authority for truth'.[19] The RPA maintained a broad front supporting scientific explanations of the universe and what it described as 'the disciplined use of knowledge'. Reflecting its politically disparate membership, the association declared it would 'eschew politics': 'our main objectives are philosophical, ethical, and educative'.[20] The emergence of socialism as an ideology adopted by some, however, would have an impact upon the association and wider secularism.

Although much was hoped for, the conclusion of the association's first year of activity resulted in the publication of only one new volume. This was *The Religion of the Twentieth Century* by Joseph McCabe who took a leading role in the development of rationalism in twentieth-century Britain, becoming prominent in the RPA as well as a permanent lecturer at South Place.[21] McCabe's relationship with the association, and indeed with other freethinking organisations, was productive, encompassing a vast journalistic output alongside a hectic lecturing schedule. Nonetheless, relationships within the association were not entirely smooth. McCabe was caustic, invoking an earlier generation and its opinions, with the RPA's publishing agenda seeking to cover old ground. Commissioning McCabe to write a biography of George Jacob Holyoake reopened debates about the different approaches to arguing for rationalism. In 1908 McCabe wrote a piece in *The Literary Guide* that, bizarrely to the modern eye, defended the blasphemy prosecution of the street orator Harry Boulter because McCabe identified him as scurrilous and in accord with all prosecutions for blasphemy in England since that brought against G. J. Holyoake in Cheltenham in 1842.[22] Such a statement offended some, such as G. W. Foote who regarded Holyoake's blasphemy prosecution as a crusade for both free speech and the honour of Charles Bradlaugh. The Bradlaugh wing of secularist campaigning was now led by his daughter Hypatia Bradlaugh Bonner who quipped back at McCabe that he and his generation had joined rationalism once the fight was largely over. Bradlaugh Bonner and her ally J. M. Robertson insisted that alterations be made to the McCabe biography of Holyoake – most unhelpfully after a significant stock had been printed.[23]

Charles Watts' personality and appetite for work kept the RPA together through rather meagre years at the start of the twentieth century. Gradually the publishing efforts gathered pace as McCabe made available a viable translation of Ernst Haeckel's classic *The Riddle of the Universe* (and a later update *The Riddle of the Universe To-day* in 1934).[24] Meanwhile, J. M. Robertson published two works under the imprint of the association, one of which was a trailblazer suggesting the entirely mythical nature of Jesus – a work that would go into several editions and spawn an industry.[25] With such barnstormers, the association's output grew in profitability, but most books were consumed by readers entering into a quasi 'book club' arrangement financed by subscriptions. This circumvented the hostility of the publishing world to 'heretical books', and the RPA was able to supply its own constituency. But Watts wanted to reach the mass market with cheap editions that were becoming popular, but initially other publishers obstructed inexpensive reprints. Success finally came when the association approached Macmillan to produce a joint reprint of T. H. Huxley's *Essays and Lectures*, the initial edition of 30,000 selling out and necessitating a follow-up 15,000 copies, instilling confidence in booksellers and effectively opening the door to RPA publishing many future reprints.

Despite this success, the move reduced the appeal of RPA as a book club, turning it to more outreach work. Watts was a careful steward, understanding the book trade and keeping true to the rationalist purpose. Aided by the author Edward Clodd, a great range of writers were drawn to RPA, witnessed by the hundreds of contract files in the RPA collection at the Bishopsgate Archive. Yet, catering to book buyers of an independent mind did not translate into a membership surge, and, in any event, many rationalist and humanist authors by the inter-war years found regular publishers willing to offer contracts. Through the 1900s and 1910s, the RPA built up a reputation as the go-to outlet on several topics, though religion and science tended to dominate, with a succession of book series, including the Cheap Reprints series of fifty-five books with about 4 million copies during 1902–12, the RPA Extra Series starting 1903 and the Inquirer's Library from 1913.[26] The enterprise finally moved into cheap pocketbooks for a mass readership in 1929 with the inauguration of one of the RPA's most visible, and ultimately famous, initiatives – the Thinker's Library. The brainchild of Frederick Watts, Charles' son, it was a further distillation of everything that the RPA had effectively learned over thirty years. Going beyond the cheap and cheerful ethos of many reprints, it comprised the 'Classics of Rationalism' augmented by a growing number of popular science works. With a distinctive livery under the term 'library', a fully grounded rationalist education was promised, stored by a specially designed bookcase. By the end of 1930, the series had reintroduced in handy high-quality pocket edition works of John Stuart Mill, H. G. Wells, Herbert Spencer, Charles Bradlaugh, Charles Darwin and T. H. Huxley. More than any other project, the Thinker's Library series seemed a springboard for popular rationalism and humanism, and within a year RPA sales trebled, on the face of it fulfilling its mission to the common reader.[27]

(c) Feminism and ethicism

Between 1887 and 1927, South Place transitioned from being a religious organisation to being one of many ethical societies that sprang up in Britain in the 1890s and 1900s. The secularist movement did have important women participants, but the movement as a whole had a very masculine character – something acknowledged by F. J. Gould in his 1900 book *Will Women Help?*, a plea for freethought to escape its unfortunately enduring reputation.[28] Given that, South Place was important in the development of feminism in the nonreligious movement.

Laura Schwartz has catalogued the Victorian interaction between suffragists and suffragettes on the one hand and 'infidel feminists' on the other, and notes the combined zeal they brought: 'Secularists active in the women's movement were motivated as much by their Freethinking beliefs as they were by a commitment to women's rights, or rather that these two intellectual currents were intertwined.'[29] Her analysis of some fifty key feminist speakers and writers demonstrates the long heritage of women fighting the secularist and freethought causes and, moreover, how their contribution has tended to be overlooked in the literature. Likewise, Madeleine Goodall has shown how women in the early ethical societies were vulnerable to close scrutiny; women were warned to beware the impact of agnosticism on the heart of feminine virtue and their supposed primary social roles in the domestic sphere.[30]

We have many reports that indicate most humanist meetings for most of their history have been strongly male. However, from the outset, women were prominent in the ethical movement. The first secretary of the Union of Ethical Societies and of the Moral Instruction League, Zona Vallance (1860–1904), was a notable feminist writer and pamphleteer. She laid out the philosophical, legal and sociological changes needed to advance women towards equality, arguing that change in 'family arrangements and traditions' was the prerequisite for change in society and, moreover: 'Ethical freedom must begin with women.'[31] Her writings in ethical-movement publications indicate that neither her audience nor the socialists she addressed wholly supported women's suffrage: there remained feminist heavy-lifting to perform within ethicism.[32] However, there is evidence that women were important leaders of other ethical societies. Florence Law (1863–1937) and Nellie Freeman (1863–1943) were secretaries at the South London Ethical Society, whilst Mary Gilliland Husband (1854–1929) was a key figure in the London Ethical Society.[33]

In the 1880s and 1890s, Leicester Secular Society discovered that secular hymn singing attracted more female members – a little to the chagrin of male members – whilst South Place Ethical Society developed a strong tradition of women musicians and hymn-writers which we look at shortly. Data are sadly short on the gender composition of early humanism. The *Daily News* census of churchgoing in London in 1902–3 found the gender balance among 970 adult attenders at nine ethical society meetings almost even, at 48:52 women to men. At South Place, however, there was a stronger male presence with 374 adult attenders split 44:56 women to men.[34] This impression was confirmed by the *South Place Magazine's* 1905–6 data on 125 subscribers due to pay their annual subscriptions, which comprised seventy-seven men (62 per cent), twenty-eight married or widowed women (22 per cent), and twenty unmarried women (16 per cent). However, a contrasting gender balance was gained from the thirty-two new members to South Place (excluding associates living at a distance) recruited from April 1905 to March 1906, of whom sixteen were single and five married women (66 per cent) and eleven (34 per cent) were men, suggesting a strong inflow of younger female members.[35] It may be that South Place was experiencing a long-term transition. In its decades of shifting from a universalist congregation to a Unitarian to an independent church, it may well have had a strong female culture shared with Christian congregations in which women averaged 60 per cent to 80 per cent of worshippers.[36] Meanwhile, the early-twentieth-century membership and subscriber lists of the Hampstead Ethical Institute and West London Ethical Society were fairly evenly split male to female, with women having majorities at times.[37] Overall, it seems that ethical groups did not have the wide female majority of Christian congregations, but, on the other hand, they were organisations accustomed to female leadership mostly missing in churches.

Moreover, there was evidence of a proto-feminist tradition from the 1830s which survived for a century at South Place. Zona Vallance came after a long string of women activists and intellectuals, including Harriet Martineau, Annie Besant, Sophia Dobson Collet, Elizabeth Cady Stanton and Hypatia Bradlaugh Bonner. Martineau (1802–76) was a celebrity of mid-Victorian writing in England, a philosopher, economist and one of the bestselling female authors of the period. In 1831 she won three essay prizes at the South Place association, leading in the 1830s to her becoming a common understudy to the chapel leader William Johnston Fox. Martineau's stature was such in literary London that the congregation had a star in the making, establishing a tradition of women's excellence in high arts. The tradition matured under Moncure Conway who, during his years of tenure between 1864 and 1897, drew the congregation further from theism towards humanism, establishing support for overt feminism and women's suffrage. But an intrinsic feminism also flourished, with Conway's wife Ellen Dana Conway and Millicent Fawcett cultivating the South Place institution as a central agency of British feminist thought and action, later introducing the American Elizabeth Cady Stanton.[38] One important figure from the congregation was Dr Alice

Drysdale Vickery (1844–1929), to be followed by Annie Besant who played a lead role in the women's movement at South Place from the 1880s to the 1920s.

Within the ethical movement as a whole, the support for women's suffrage was widespread, and many members were active, notably in the Women's Freedom League.[39] In 1913 in the West London Ethical Society, a manifesto was issued opposing the suffragettes' extreme methods, criticising the destruction of property and urging 'spiritual militancy' and persuasion for the suffragist cause. One of the leading figures in this move was Adela Coit (1863–1932), Stanton's wife, who had joined the International Women's Suffrage Alliance at its formation in Berlin in 1904; as also her daughter Margaret Wetzlar Coit who represented the League at the Alliance Congress in Budapest in 1913. Adela Coit was active in the suffrage cause from the mid-1900s, joining a move in 1908 by sixty senior Liberal women, including Millicent Fawcett, Gertrude Jekyll and Beatrice Webb, to protest a WSPU threat to silence Lloyd George in a speech on the issue.[40] In 1913 Adela Coit founded the Spiritual Militancy League for the Women's Charter of Rights and Liberty, conducting marches to Westminster Abbey and St Paul's Cathedral; when women were banned from speaking at a pro-suffrage service at the latter, a congregation of the League crowded into the nearby South Place Ethical Society to hear the speakers.[41] The League was a timely formation on the crest of middle-class suffrage campaigning, including by many women in the Church of England, its name chosen adroitly to empower women in the churches – including in April 1913 opposition to the word 'obey' in the Church of England marriage ceremony, described in the *Church Times* as a 'foolish manifesto'.[42]

Overt feminism thus had a presence within ethicism. But so too was the intrinsic feminism apparent in congregational life at South Place. As Jessica Beck has shown in her recent study, women were important to the congregation's organisation of singing, to the writing of hymns (Harriet Martineau reputedly wrote over two hundred for the congregation), and to the creation of a musical leadership of the congregation.[43] Gustav Spiller records that a typical service at South Place in the 1880s comprised a hymn, reading, announcements, instrumental music, main address, collection and a final hymn. He notes too that the West London Ethical Society included congregational singing during 1896–1901, with organ voluntaries accompanying the hymns and the Statement of Belief that was sung by the choir.[44] The Conway Hall Library contains several hymn books from various ethical societies, and Beck shows that music was a major feature of South Place Institute until it moved to Conway Hall in 1929, noting the belief in music's capacity to educate as well as to entertain – part of 'the "woman's mission" to improve societal values through traditional feminine virtues'.[45] Apart from hymns, women were participants in the musical heritage, mostly of classical music, that developed when the congregation was located in the working-class district of Finsbury between 1824 and 1927, with free, largely chamber, concerts on Sundays and Mondays for people of the district. South Place had become an emporium of majestic music intended to inspire, reform and uplift.[46] And, as Beck shows, women musicians and organisers, and, to an extent, composers were a noted feature, contributing to an intrinsic feminism in the congregation – an institution of high arts and education as well as humanism and ethicism.[47] Additionally, as in Christian congregations, women were central to many activities – including catering for tea and food, a feature emphasised by South Place owning and using its own building for round-the-week activities. There was a fully functioning sociability at South Place, serving the working-class community as well as the more middle-class congregation, ensuring a feminised space in which women catered, managed, promoted and participated in a holistic role of ethical behaviour.

However, the tenor of the institution in relation to feminism seemed to change quite noticeably. It started in 1899 when, after the South Place Society members had struggled for two years on the question of how to replace their leader Moncure Conway on his return to New York to attend to his sick wife, they decided to abandon having a minister-like figure and instead select a panel of 'Appointed Lecturers'. This set in train the tradition of the intellectual permanent lecturers, to be joined by the invited ones, again dominated by men. South Place had seven 'Ministers' over the period 1793–1897, moving thereafter to twenty-two permanent lecturers, of whom only the last – Barbara Smoker appointed in 1986 – was not a man.[48] Burrows' tender ministry-style lectureship notwithstanding, this amounted to a sharp masculinisation of the institution, now most well known for intellectual prowess and militancy, diminishing the feminine and congregational quality of the institution.

With a diminished dominance of women came challenges to feminism. On the one side, in the midst of the First World War, a UES Women's Group was founded in 1915 with the aim of providing a separate space where women could further the union's aims whilst also benefiting from (according to its 1926 constitution) 'a Social Centre for the discussion of Ethical Problems from the Women's point of view'; they also promoted a specific role for ethicist women in peacemaking.[49] A flavour of how this objective was to be achieved comes from the group's lecture list for 1930: the subjects of 'Psychology and the Child', 'The Nationality of Married Women', 'How to Handle the Adolescent', 'Birth Control', 'The Right of Married Women to engage in paid work' and 'The Homeless Women of London'. Such topics simultaneously demonstrate a desire to provide help to a wider circle of women, as well as encourage ethicist women to experiment with and adopt new life stances. Alongside this, the women's group had an extensive affiliation with a number of key reform movements. But, the longer-term tenor of the movement was not improved when the South Place Ethical Society left Finsbury in 1927 and took up residence in 1929 in the purpose-built premises in Red Lion Square. The move away from a working-class area meant that the free concerts never quite fully survived as an aesthetic mission, diminishing the outreach by women of the institution. This was arguably a distinct move upmarket, and the nature of the music events changed. Part of the cause here was the rise of Conway Hall as a humanist and secularist venue, its construction in the form of multiple meeting rooms, with a library, catering facilities as well as the main hall, meaning that it was an ideal venue for hire. With many hiring groups to be radical in politics between the wars, this reinforced the declining sense of a female-led ethical congregationalism.

(d) Moral education

In December 1897 the Moral Instruction League (MIL) was launched. Moral education was attracting interest in many European nations in the late 1890s and 1900s and would lead in 1908 to the first of six meetings of the International Moral Education Congress before 1934. It was the International Ethical Union that promoted it, and two of its greatest proponents were UK-based F. J. Gould and Gustav Spiller. This was to emerge into the longest-running campaign of the British humanist movement.

The MIL inaugural meeting in London in 1897 attracted contributors of many backgrounds – Anglican, Catholic, Unitarian and Nonconformist – and the idea of moral instruction attracted establishment support, with the Board of Education in 1906 including the injunction that moral instruction should be a part of every school curriculum. But the MIL came to represent a view that Christian education was insufficient to meet the moral demands of the age, requiring an alternative secular-based approach transcending faiths and rationalist and ethicist positions. As historian Susannah Wright makes clear, the MIL aim was not merely to transform moral education but to constitute active training for citizenship: an early MIL publication was entitled *Our Future Citizens*. The goal for secularists was a universal and synoptic morality, and this proved difficult to achieve.[50] However, much work was done to rehearse how it might be delivered.

Frederick James Gould was the key figure in moral instruction in Britain, a man whose career overlapped with many of the trends of the period, especially the transition from nineteenth-century forms of freethought to the humanist approaches of the early twentieth. Gould had a natural affinity with a considerable number of radical ideas of these years, straddling several ideologies at once. Inspired by hearing Stanton Coit lecture in 1889, he formed the East London Ethical Society, then worked with G. J. Holyoake to organise secular publishing and assisted in the foundation of the RPA in 1899. Moving to the provinces, Gould became the first full-time organiser of the Leicester Secular Society (LSS) in 1899, whose Secular Hall, which opened in 1881 on Humberstone Gate, seated 600, and unlike other national organisations had a bust of Jesus as a secular teacher. There, Gould actively lectured on what he called 'The Humanist Religion', and tried to turn the LSS from Liberal to Labour politics, making a considerable name for himself on the Leicester School Board for opposing compulsory religious education and taunting Nonconformists for their arguments about religious education. Gould tried but failed in 1908 to persuade the Leicester society to turn itself into a Positivist Church, leading him to create his own short-lived Positivist church on Leicester High Street.[51]

Gould set up a Sunday school with eleven teachers in 1900 and was elected to the Leicester School Board with some 15,699 votes. There was a constituency for his approach, and in 1901 he proposed moral instruction in all twenty-nine of the city's elementary schools, with a curriculum excluding the bible but ambitiously covering 'self-respect, self-control, truth and truthfulness, kindness, duty and honour, industry, mutual dependence of various orders of society, the nature of the social organism, the general idea of justice, the work of the State, citizenship, co-operation, international peace, and the relation of nature and art to morality'. Gould got significant agreement on moral instruction without the bible, with success also in Bradford, but attempts in 1902 failed in four other English school boards. Unfortunately for him, school board education passed in England to town councils in that year; yet, he stood repeatedly as an Independent Labour Party candidate, being elected twice, and with Labour Party support managed to get moral education part of a social-reform programme of the local authority. Moral education on Gould's model was taught for a number of years but became criticised by inspectors for lacking sufficient apparent benefit. Gould also met sustained criticism from teachers complaining of insufficient training, and the moral education without the bible had a slightly rocky outing over a decade of trial in Leicester. In 1908 he left the LSS and in 1910 departed Leicester for London.[52] But with ethical movement backing, several local authorities in England and Wales experimented or partially adopted moral instruction teaching in the late 1890s and 1900s, encouraged by UES and secularist activists for the moral education movement. Christian support was sought in Leicester, London and elsewhere to stand a better chance of getting reform proposals adopted, but criticism arose, especially during the Boer War. The dominance of secularists in the MIL left the movement open to the charge of being anti-religious or worse, and church critics ultimately exploited the moral activists' hostility to the bible and to Jesus Christ. On top of that, the MIL was internally split between those who spoke of an ethical religion or a religious spirit, and those who did not – an early manifestation of disagreements to come in the movement.

Meanwhile, the MIL also developed educational materials for schools and teacher training colleges, much of it by Gould. With a name change in 1909 to the Moral Education League, lobbying for legislation and administrative reform of the curriculum in England continued. It was also active in international liaison, and Gould himself was sent touring the United States and India during 1910–15 giving demonstration lessons, whilst moral instruction leagues were founded in a number of nations. It had further name changes – to the Civic and Moral Education League in 1916 and the Civic Education League in 1919, and in 1924 was absorbed into a civics teaching department at the home of the Sociological Society in London as emphasis shifted from moral education towards education for citizenship. More broadly, the Gould-based stress on direct moral *instruction* was becoming outmoded by the 1920s, as other practitioners argued for morality growth through children's self-development, everyday interactions and school activities. Direct teaching of what was right was no longer so acceptable in the movement.[53]

Gould's substantial legacy was to actively seek to transcend the power and ubiquity of the Christian bible and in particular its claim to be an exclusive repository of moral truth. The moral instruction lessons he had initiated in Leicester continued from 1901 until after 1912 (and possibly to 1929). The success of his efforts would be mixed with some dull failures, but his ethicism and interest in education created viable and usable moral lessons, published and widely distributed, from a vast range of cultural resources – including from Christianity. Gould sought to show that human motivation for good behaviour could be cultivated like the permeation beloved of the Fabians, using moral examples from many faiths, derived from Positivist veneration for the achievements of humankind and the benefits of studying biography. F. J. Gould is credited as being the first individual to call himself a 'humanist' in the sense that the later twentieth century would recognise, and for recognising the triangle of ethics, education and politics. The Moral Instruction League he founded was described by Gustav Spiller as one of the 'outstanding interests' of the ethical movement, offering a strategy of the limited membership being more influential by teaching large numbers of children, achieving social objectives and gaining impact as elected educationalists. That stratagem peaked during the all-too-brief reign of the directly-elected school boards in England and Wales from 1870 to 1902, followed by a much harder struggle to influence the standard local authorities which then ruled state education. Moral education might have achieved more before 1930 if the secularist cause had accepted the bible and Jesus Christ in moral teaching; so too it suffered for lack of agreement on key moral issues (like war), for lack of acceptance that this was a way to teach morality, and ultimately because church opponents held so much influence in education.

(e) The supernatural in emerging humanism

The First World War posed something of a dilemma for humanists. On the one hand, it exposed the failure of human communication alongside a catastrophic breakdown in the democratic ideal. Likewise, the challenges of war appeared to question the Whig/Liberal and Positivist arguments for a teleological narrative that spoke of humankind on an upward journey from a lower to a higher state. However, such ideas could be inverted and occasionally were. Gustav Spiller in 1916 noted that the war seemed to be a valuable argument against 'Supernaturalism', leaving the case for a benevolent god overseeing the universe as 'an empty formula'.[54] With no help from divine providence, Spiller drew on the legacy of moral instruction and ethicism to place trust in duty, endeavour and character. If ethicism had failed to prevent the war, Spiller promoted its role in reconciliation. Once the masses recognised 'the progressive Ethical Movement' as the natural replacement for religion, he argued, 'its beneficent influence [would] be soon felt among all classes and in all lands'.[55]

To that dilemma could be added the long-term issue of whether humanism, like ethicism, was a religion or not. All of the ethical societies incorporated ritual in their main meetings deemed by some as of a quasi-religious nature, notably using the singing of secular hymns. The South Place Ethical Society was typical in having Sunday 'services' or sometimes 'worship' which mimicked the Christian worship of a liberal nonconformist variety. Its Sunday services during March 1905, for instance, commenced at 11.15 a.m. and comprised a talk (in that month the four speakers were Herbert Burrows, J. M. Robertson, Graham Wallas and J. A. Hobson), two anthems and two hymns – the last including one entitled 'Arise my soul'. Further echoing church arrangements, worshippers had to pay for their sittings (known in the churches as pew renting), and this qualified them automatically as members, with those over twenty-one years also having rights to vote and hold office.[56] South Place came from Unitarianism which made up an unknown but significant element of the ethical community in the nineteenth and twentieth centuries in Britain, the United States and Canada.[57] The hymns, of course, cemented a religious character to both proceedings and to the institutions. Even though they bore no mention of god or Christ, they were open copies of the religious variety of hymns, being used to extol elevated moral values. They were not the only specie of secular hymns. The Socialist Sunday Schools, formed initially as an offshoot of the Labour Church in the 1890s, had *The Socialist Sunday School Hymnbook* that contained hymns of praise for Keir Hardie and labour values, and was still being republished at least as late as 1926.[58] Such a contextualisation is important, for it raises doubts as to whether South Place hymn singing really constitutes evidence of ethicism being a religion. We shall return to this to observe how South Place hymns came to an end.

But first, the argument that humanism was a religion has other evidence. On a straightforward level, humanists and ethicists frequently used religious vocabulary to label their ethical experiences. In 1901, when his wife was suffering a 'weak heart', Bertrand Russell was driven to contemplate 'the sense of the solitude of each human soul' by the deeply affecting mystical quality, akin to religious conversion, on hearing fellow-humanist Gilbert Murray read ancient Greek poetry.[59] It was also written about by H. G. Wells from 1908 where he laid out his 'religion of humanism' model, which he also referred to as the 'modern religion'.[60] Besides education and science, he conceived the necessity of beliefs, founded upon the order of life: 'I dismiss the idea that life is chaotic because it leaves my life ineffectual, and I cannot contemplate an ineffectual life patiently.' But, alluding to the contemporary predilection for eugenics, he asserted the demographic integration of world peoples, of intermarriage and mingling blood that will also mix the societies and the nations: 'We are all going to mingle our blood again. We cannot keep ourselves apart; the worst enemies will some day come to the Peace of Verona . . . A time will come in less than fifty generations when all the population of the world will have my blood, and I and my worst enemy will not be able to say which child is his or mine.' Inevitably, he argued, 'the solidarity of humanity' must be understood, with the removal of 'the delusion of the permanent separateness of the individual and of races and nations'. In that coming together of humanity, Wells acknowledged that 'in varying degree, I hold all religions to be in a measure true'. But they did not match the moment:

> All these religions, are true for me as Canterbury Cathedral is a true thing and as a Swiss chalet is a true thing. There they are, and they have served a purpose, they have worked. Men and women have lived in and by them. Men and women still do. Only they are not true for me to live in them. I have, I believe, to live in a new edifice of my own discovery.

The religion he advanced would need to be up to the moment of 'the organized civilized world state', a socialist one, though not one of class war and 'its doctrine of hate', but a utopian state of 'towns and cities finely built, a race of beings finely bred and taught and trained, open ways and peace and freedom from end to end of the earth. It sees beauty increasing in humanity, about humanity and through humanity'.[61]

This religion in humanism sat beside a more forceful rationalist censure of the supernatural in everyday life. The majority of leading figures (and probably members too) of the RPA, SPES and UES would have felt anxious about the organisation they adhered to being classified as constituting a religion. However, it was common for rationalists in the movement to pronounce a linguistic flip – for a 'religion of rationalism', a 'religion of the twentieth century' or a 'religion of the open mind' – as an appeal to displace supernaturalism with a faith in nature and rationality.[62] The word 'religion' was here being used flexibly to denote the wider intellectual regime of human life. Some, like J. M. Robertson, sought a conciliatory stance, writing in 1925: 'Nothing, however, is more natural than that men who have thought themselves out of a supernaturalist creed should wish to conserve the name which has connoted not merely their cosmic ideas but their ethical leanings and aspirations.'[63] Having lost his faith in 1895–96, Joseph McCabe came to London where he met with Gould and was persuaded to write up his experiences, launching the bestselling secularist book *Twelve Years in a Monastery* (1897).[64] This was merely the beginning of a prodigious writing career, totalling close to 250 books, including his survey of the state of scientific knowledge, biblical criticism and ethics in *Modern Rationalism: Being a Sketch of the Progress of the Rationalistic Spirit in the Nineteenth Century* (1909). After a spell as organiser and full-time lecturer of the Leicester Secular Society, preceding Gould, McCabe returned to London to work for Stanton Coit teaching in his School of Ethics and began a career contributing to the RPA journal, *The Literary Guide*. From this

FIGURE 9 Stanton Coit's Ethical Church in Bayswater pictured in 1913. Photogravure: W.E. Gray/Humanists UK/Bishopsgate Archive.

start, McCabe was an authoritative presence in metropolitan rationalism with an impressive lecturing workload augmented by his prolific publishing output that Bill Cooke estimates at a book written or translated every ten weeks.[65] McCabe offered a pugnacious and accosting stance towards organised religion, one delivered through his elevation in the early 1900s to a permanent lectureship at SPES, a man whose experience of the Roman Catholic Church from within gave him the attribute of knowing what he was talking about. Whilst his attitude was not typical of all the membership, he was esteemed for being the belligerent champion of rationalism in the face of religion's long record of egregious outrage.

Two cultural traditions sat side by side. One was that of the arch-secularist represented by Joseph McCabe; the second was that of the exponent of the 'religion of humanism', represented especially by Stanton Coit. In 1914 the West London Ethical Society, to which Coit repaired after his time at South Place and then in the United States, changed its name to the Ethical Church, becoming the base for his explicit attempts to redefine the terms 'religion' and 'religious' to mean reverence for, and striving towards, the concepts of the good, true and beautiful, rather than what had traditionally been viewed as being the origin of these, that is god. His adoption of the word 'church' in place of 'society' has been seen by many as a step from an evolving secular humanism back in the direction of religion.[66] Certainly, the religious tradition he represented within ethicism remained vigorous. The South Place Ethical Society had as its object from 1896 'the cultivation of a rational religious sentiment', and this was finally written into the Society's deed in 1930 (remaining its object until 2012).[67] Likewise, the general object of the Ethical Union became in 1920 'The Ethical faith', whose aim was 'To promote a Religion of Human Fellowship and Service'.[68] Most brazenly, Coit's Ethical Church building, a former Methodist Chapel, evoked the sentiment most strongly, being full of paintings, busts and shrines, accompanied by a rich ritual with Sunday lecturers and evening concerts of classical music.[69]

Coit dominated at the Ethical Church as a minister might his congregation, in a way that SPES pointedly abandoned in 1899–1900 in favour of rotating lecturers. With an affinity to Church of England ritual, Coit maintained a distinctive format, albeit moderated by the appointment of Harold J. Blackham in 1933 as first Coit's junior, then in 1935 his successor. Still, Blackham was, initially at least, devoted to Coit, publishing an ardent eulogy after his mentor's death in 1944 in the form of a 'spiritual portrait' in which he extolled his 'ethical piety' and 'his faith in eternal values'.[70] Blackham portrayed the young Coit as having been a follower of Emerson's 'ethical mysticism' and 'socialized religion' which he wished to apply to a 'secular moral task' encompassing a democratised, and even socialistic, version of Anglicanism.[71] Blackham acknowledged that Coit mixed a 'religious truth as a philosophical truth', adding 'an uncompromising dependence upon empirical sociological methods'.[72] In this way, Blackham drew from Coit a religious vocabulary for his own humanism, and, philosophical origins apart, seemed in the 1940s to profess his own thoughts in a religious epistemology. But, from being the ardent exponent of Coit's religious humanism, Blackham shifted. After his master's death in 1944, Blackham rather coyly identified Coit's 'mistake' of believing he could convert Christians to ethical idealism whilst idealising the institutional church as a mechanism for this plan (which he had laid out in detail).[73] Blackham then diverged more resolutely, in the early 1950s reverting the Ethical Church once again to the West London Ethical Society, before selling the irrevocably church-style building and, with the proceeds, acquiring a prestigious office-cum-residential building at 13 Prince of Wales Terrace, which was destined – eventually – to be given as a gift to form the headquarters of the British Humanist Association. As we shall see in Part II, Blackham changed from deputy minister in an ethical church in the early 1930s to the architect of the British and international humanist movement's secular turn. For a decade more until the 1960s, rituals – in the form of hymns, addresses and anthems – were sustained at SPES, and the language of a 'religion of humanism' continued to be unpopularly invoked by some humanist writers. But Coit's inspirational legacy at the Ethical Church might well be described as that of proposing and misjudging a *religious* humanism and exposing the need for a *secular* humanism – of which, ironically, his pupil and successor Harold Blackham was to be the mastermind between 1950 and 1980.

5 THE PAST, THE STATE AND INTERNATIONALISM

Almost as soon as it came into being, the ethicist movement started to transition into the humanist movement, edging more and more from a mainly protesting mode towards a constructionist and progressive posture. Though by no means new to the cause, utopian humanism developed three distinctive components between 1896 and 1930. The first of these was having a usable past, a history, in which humans from antiquity to the present day could be reimagined according to the agendas of the ethicist, humanist and rationalist rather than the power structures of contemporary party politics, nationalism and empires. The second component was constructing a new imagining of the state, both in its internal workings and in its moral bearing. The third element was internationalism – an ideology in which the weaknesses and immoralities revealed by the new history could be rectified by cooperation between peoples and nations, where the chauvinism of empire-building and the oppression of indigenous peoples could be halted, and in which equalities of wealth, moralities and education might be realised. In humanist drawing rooms, journals, books and pamphlets of these decades, the beginnings of plans came into view – perhaps starting to be squinted at as converging in one single grand plan.

(a) A usable past

From 1900 to as late as the early 1960s, history books for children and the general reader were dominated by narratives of kings and queens, wars, empires and patriotic heroism. The British classroom was customarily adorned by a Mercator's projection map of the world with the Greenwich meridian running north and south down through Great Britain, and with the British colonies, dependencies and territories coloured pink. Something like a third of the land surface of the planet was pink, the British Empire far exceeding the empire of any other European power (and there were seven to choose from) in extent, power and benevolence. To be patriotic was to be in awe of the imperial project, and to be thankful to God for shining upon this magnificence.

The nonreligion movement from its early origins in Enlightenment thought, and perhaps from before even that, offered a critique of this worldview. The history of science had been one of the challenges to empires secular and ecclesiastical, not the least being the Roman Catholic Church and its attempt to suppress new knowledge like that brought by Galileo Galilei in the early seventeenth century. Notwithstanding the patronage of British monarchs for science – for example, in founding or gracing royal observatories in Greenwich (1675) and Edinburgh (1822), and the Royal Society (1660), the Royal Society of Edinburgh (1783) and the Royal Dublin Society (1820) – research in the sciences, arts and social sciences was often slow to gain approval and support from state and church. Part of the progress of human knowledge involved the inquisitive pushing back against the obstruction of government and theology. By the middle of the nineteenth century, British science and philosophy had already produced major intellectual and research figures – David Hume, Joseph Priestley, James Hutton, Jeremy Bentham, Charles Darwin and T. H. Huxley – who are now seen as links in the chain of evolving human knowledge and secularist history. That pushback is not entirely over.

Humanists came to offer a mature ethical history of humankind. An influential pioneer narrative was trialled by Scottish explorer William Winwood Reade in his book *The Martyrdom of Man* (1872) that was to have an enduring impact upon the humanist and rationalist movements on both sides of the Atlantic for over a hundred years. Reade (1838–75) came from a landed background, but ended up in his mid-twenties exploring in Angola, then six years later in 1868 travelled through (and for a spell was imprisoned in) what became the Gold Coast and Sierra Leone. Unlike so many British explorers in Africa, he had no Christian scheme for conversion on his travels, but advanced in *Martyrdom* a secular understanding of a social-Darwinist evolution that would end in the triumph of science. In an echo of Auguste Comte, Reade told his secular 'universal' history of the world through four themes – war, religion, liberty and intellect – in which he explained how humankind was imprisoned by the first and second and won its freedom and advancement by the third and fourth. Reade focussed much on the ancient and medieval worlds, especially of Africa and the Middle East, and upon European colonialism and Islam. He introduced indigenous peoples very prominently into his narrative, dwelling upon the underlying moral and intellectual evolution of humanity. Of Alexander the Great, he wrote that he 'committed some criminal and despotic acts, but it was his noble idea to blot out the word "barbarian" from the vocabulary of the Greeks'. Yet, he observed that 'conquest, though effected by means of war, was preserved by means of religion, an element of history which must be analysed with scientific care'. On evolving religion, he wrote: 'There is a moral sentiment in the human breast which, like intelligence, is born of obscure instincts, and which gradually becomes developed. Since the gods of men are the reflected images of men, it is evident that as men become developed in morality the character of their gods will also be improved.'[1] This type of reasoning did not endear Reade to his religious readers. Denounced by Christian clergy and general reviewers of the high Victorian era for his various blasphemies, Reade enthused J. M. Robertson to write in the Rationalist Press Association's edition of *Martyrdom* that Reade was 'profoundly convinced that Religion, with whatever individual compensations, had been for Man a fountain of darkness and error, and with a high earnestness said so'.[2] Reade encouraged fortitude in the faithless. As well as *Martyrdom* being volume 25 in the RPA's Thinker's Library series, Reade's autobiographical novel *Outcast* was volume 38, in which he recounted being written by a bishop to revive his Christian faith: 'Return to my belief! As well might a river return to its source. My reply was respectfully, gratefully expressed; but it was conclusive.'[3] Reade influenced fellow Scot J. M. Robertson to become the most prolific of humanist historians in the 1890s and 1900s – a renowned lecturer in ancient and Enlightenment history, delivering lectures normally once per month at the Sunday morning meetings of SPES with many published in the *South Place Magazine*. His narrative drew on Reade's conception of universalist history to place 'civilisation' side by side with the experiences of diverse peoples, providing perspective on the evolution of ethical thought in present times. Notwithstanding the two secular hymns and two anthems at SPES meetings, this made for very intellectual and challenging Sunday gatherings in Finsbury, recrafting the past centre stage in the community's ethical contemplation. Reade's influence extends to modern times. Larry Hicok, long-time leader of Bay Area Atheists in San Francisco, was given *Martyrdom* to read by his father at the age of sixteen in 1965 and had his eyes opened to the ills of religion, stimulating him to bring in the American Civil Liberties Union to oppose prayers in his Oregon high school.[4]

With a little less earnestness than Reade, H. G. Wells mapped something similar in his own universal history, *The Outline of History: Being a Plain History of Life and Mankind*, which he took a year to research and write, bringing Reade's story up to date in an excoriation of the Great War. First published in 1919 in twenty-four weekly magazine instalments at one shilling and threepence each, then the following year as a two-volume book, it sold millions of copies in several languages. Lavishly illustrated, Wells drew on support from four academic historians, including humanist Gilbert Murray, professor of classics at successively Glasgow and Oxford Universities and a major proponent of the League of Nations and its successor the United Nations, and rationalist E. Ray Lankester (1847–1929), evolutionary biologist, zoologist and friend of Karl Marx.[5] The chasms in international relations and the folly of the Catholic Church's attempts to suppress scientific knowledge were major features of Wells' book, as Reade had written before him, attracting abusive criticism (and at least one entire book of intellectual attack) from Catholic writers G. K. Chesterton and Hilaire Belloc.[6] Wells had an important aim – to make Britons think less of nations and more about peoples when conceptualising history and the future. The Great War loomed large in Wells' perspective, writing in the introduction: 'There can be no peace now, we realize, but a common peace in all the world; no prosperity but a general prosperity. But *there can be no common peace and prosperity without common historical ideas.*' Disaster loomed, he said, if there was 'nothing but narrow, selfish, and conflicting nationalist traditions'.[7]

In a sense, every humanist intellectual was an historian making their own usable past. Bertrand Russell envisaged religious belief as a retreating feature which by the 1920s was 'practically confined to clergymen and maiden ladies'.[8] Wells set in train a chain of humanist writing in history and other subjects for children. He inspired humanist scientist Lancelot Hogben to start a career-long devotion to the popularisation of science and other subjects, writing *Mathematics for the Million* (1936) and *Science for the Citizen* (1938), two books of huge status in their fields. When based at the University of Aberdeen, Hogben produced a

FIGURE 10 H. G. Wells. Photo: ©NPG.

series of books entitled 'Primers of the Age of Plenty' which included a book by an Aberdeen colleague and historian Henry Hamilton with the same aims as Wells. 'The old history', wrote Hamilton, 'concerned mainly with power-politics, has been sectional and nationalist. It has stressed the elements that divide nations. It has glorified the rivalries of nation-herds. It has provoked chauvinism and has promoted flag worship, driving mankind towards self-destruction. In short, it has been a force making for war.' Hamilton wanted his history to recount the advances in science, technology, business administration and knowledge as the 'agencies which are unifying mankind'. He intended his history book 'to fire human beings with faith in themselves and in the capacity of man to establish peace and prosperity on earth'.[9] Thereby was a persistent chain of intellectual influence laid down within humanist thought, to be drawn in to stimulate and guide what became a distinctive bent of the movement – humanist internationalism, undergirded by policies of pacifism and disarmament, and forming a secular religion some termed 'the religion of humanity' that would be larger than the nation.[10] A template for a new history of humankind was set down, in which religion was cautiously opened to critique. In these narratives, glorification of empire disappears, the oppression and exploitation of native peoples emerges highlighted, the folly of war is laid bare, and the virtue of gentleness extolled. Very shortly, as we shall see, Wells' history would also revise the future.

(b) The state

Probably the most influential British political connection for ethicism was Ramsay MacDonald (1866–1937), prime minister in 1924 and 1931–5 and a Labour MP intermittently during 1906–37. On moving to London in 1886, he tried first the Unitarian Church and even led worship there, but he was then attracted to the ethical societies where he attended and spoke to meetings regularly, notably at South Place Ethical Society but also the Ethical Church, becoming friends with Stanton Coit and then intensely involved in the Union of Ethical Societies. MacDonald was a regular contributor in *Ethical World*, proving immensely popular in the movement, being often elected chair of proceedings at UES meetings. His light was rising in the Labour movement, and it is perhaps not a complete coincidence that his first political success was to be elected to London County Council as a councillor for Finsbury where SPES was not merely located but was so active as a community organisation. Things changed in 1906 after he was elected MP for Leicester and one of the leaders of the Parliamentary Labour Party. Yet, as we shall see later in the chapter, he became a prominent pacifist and anti-war campaigner in the 1910s, still linked to ethicists. A popular speaker, he might have become a great leader for ethicism but for being called to lead the Labour Party.[11]

Exerting influence in the state was always on the agenda of the nonreligion movement. In the first three-quarters of the nineteenth century, secularism was an element in much of the working-class radicalism of the times, though was not entirely uncontested by religious influences such as the short-lived Chartist churches of the 1840s and Labour churches of the 1890s. But within all of these, the movement towards freedom of religion and belief was a common theme for all who sought liberty to enter parliament, jury or witness box without facing specific exclusion or an offending oath. The last to be admitted were the atheists when Charles Bradlaugh, after being returned to parliament five times between 1880 and 1888, was allowed to take the oath as a known atheist in 1886, and then in 1888 secured an Act which allowed affirmation for entry to parliament. From this point, small but increasing numbers of atheists, secularists, rationalists, ethicists and humanists were elected to the Commons or appointed to the House of Lords. It remained the case, though, that the religious and belief orientation of members of parliament was kept discreet and not made again the object of insult there. Nonetheless, issues of ritual and of substance remained for reformers: from prayers in parliament and local authorities, to the annual Scottish practice of 'kirking the council' (the local authority) in a local church, some of which continue in the 2020s; to the monarch being 'Supreme Governor' of the Church of England for which twenty-six Anglican bishops have reserved positions in the Lords; and the state providing significant support for established churches, parish and church schools, and for other religious purposes. This left much for secularists to challenge.

Perhaps to the surprise of many, the law of blasphemy remained to harass and impede. From the perspective of the early 1890s, it was a law living upon borrowed time. It, and the government that wielded it, had suffered as a result of the Foote case of 1883–4 in which the lesson of giving blasphemous writings the oxygen of publicity had been ruefully learned. After he had triumphed in his quest to enter parliament, Charles Bradlaugh in 1889 moved a bill to remove the offences of schism, heresy, blasphemous libel and blasphemy at common law.[12] Although it reached a second reading it got no further, largely because sympathy for repeal was trumped by enthusiasm for retaining the law as a rudimentary 'safeguard'. Bradlaugh could scarcely hide his disappointment. One of his close friends noted that such a measure 'was not to be carried in a rush; that he must introduce it again and again'. For the fate of blasphemy this was to be prescient, although Charles Bradlaugh would never get another chance.[13]

Everyone in the freethought movement agreed that blasphemy laws and the potential for their application remained a grievance. In early 1908, a street orator Harry Boulter was arrested by the Metropolitan Police after delivering speeches in Islington which contained statements which Hypatia Bradlaugh Bonner classed variously as 'quite unobjectionable, . . . simply silly, and some were undoubtedly offensive'.[14] When Boulter was imprisoned, one supporter was anxious to note that opinions seemed to be the target of the prosecution and this was now unacceptable, arguing that 'it is possible for people who sincerely reject Christianity to live upright and honourable lives'.[15] Three years later reports began to arrive at the Home Office indicating the lectures of Thomas William Stewart and John Gott were becoming an issue in a number of provincial towns and cities. These preached against a number of familiar targets – the authenticity of the bible, the ambiguous character of the clergy and the nature of the almighty. These were street orations which sometimes borrowed idioms from music hall and other forms of popular culture, and sought to entertain whilst vilifying their targets; meetings were attended by the open sale of birth control literature and adverts for meetings on the subject. For local chief constables this was a blend of blasphemy and immorality which felt more dangerous because of the heightened concerns around civil and trade union unrest punctuating these years. In the cases against Gott, Stewart and their compatriot Ernest Pack, despite moments of a pyrrhic victory, all proceedings went against them.[16] This prompted the RPA to petition the Home Office seeking repeal of the blasphemy laws which could not be 'tolerated by public opinion' and as 'not a crime at all'; the petition also argued that the laws inhibited free discussion and that legal action was unfairly limited to the Christian religion.[17] J.M. Robertson reminded the home secretary that detaining the prisoners gave them publicity which could be awkward for the government.[18] The RPA petition and its wording would regularly resurface in the years following.

On the eve of the First World War in 1913, a blasphemy repeal bill entered parliament and Home Secretary Reginald Mckenna sought the advice of his close associate Sir John Simon, the Attorney General, who rejected the idea that the law was obsolete, arguing its ability to 'adapt to the times' made it viable and valuable.[19] This line of thinking seemed consistently in the mind of government into the inter-war period, for the law appeared flexible and the would-be objectors were a vocal minority. This meant that there was almost no political gain perceptible from acceding, and only potential political loss. In 1914 a similar bill came before the Commons with extremely lukewarm government support. What became obvious here was that such limited support came at the price of defending public order imperatives.[20] When the issue resurfaced in 1922, it did so in the shadow of J. W. Gott's very last offence which had secured him a prison sentence. His *Rib Ticklers* compared the entry of Christ into Jerusalem with the act of a circus clown. Justice Avory, in advising the jury, argued that Gott's publication was capable of inciting violence from the religious and he received a nine-month prison sentence.[21]

Further blasphemy repeal bills regularly referred to the case, but again foundered in 1922 and 1923, the latter introduced by Harry Snell MP (1865–1944), a frequent lecturer at Conway Hall and president of the Ethical Union in 1931–2. The government was unmoved, ironically comforted by its actions in the Gott case in which the published blasphemy seemed manifestly more serious than in previous instances. By 1924, during a subsequent attempt, a deputation met with the Home Secretary Arthur Henderson when Chapman Cohen, editor of *The Freethinker*, noted how the experience of being offended by blasphemy handed ridiculous elements of power to the victim that was unprecedented elsewhere within the English legal system.[22]

Versions of this same abolition bill were presented before parliament in each successive year up to 1929 when the bill was introduced by George Lansbury MP with the support of seven Labour members – indicating for the first time that it was potentially a class issue. In the last of these years, a further deputation went to the Home Secretary J. R. Clynes using the same arguments, augmented by the suggestion from Graham Wallas that the blasphemy laws had been retained because their active use was at least contemplated. Wallas was also instrumental in offering a solution based on the Indian Criminal Code which operated a conception of the 'public peace' in which both religious and nonreligious had a responsibility to maintain or face prosecution. Clynes replied sympathetically but noted there was no time for a government bill (even if he had been predisposed to this).[23] Nonetheless, the private member's bill of Ernest Thurtle went before the cabinet and passed the second reading, resulting in the bill going to a committee stage. Many views pulled in different directions with some lamentable results. Attempts to define religion proved futile, and even potentially offensive, whilst the Home Office's preoccupation with public order always seemed inadequately addressed by those sceptical of altering the law. Thurtle noted in an exasperated tone that some attempts to amend the bill would have left matters in a worse state, whilst others claimed the bill had been carelessly worded and would have left the Anglican Church unable to discipline its own clergy. Collapsing under the weight of problems and expectations, lessons were learned. A repeal was not tried again until 1936 and 1937, but the government was by then less indulgent and both bills were prevented by the whips from getting a second reading.[24]

The ethical movement's view on blasphemy took a broader, less strident approach than the anti-religious radicalism of the secularists. Yet, the state stood in the way of the nonreligious – as well as the religiously negligent – in an assortment of ways. It took a concerted and three-year legal challenge from the RPA, the National Secular Society and others to overturn a ruling that a person could not leave a legacy to a secularist or atheist organisation because it constituted the crimes of blasphemy and the illegal denial of Christianity. The ruling was finally adjudged false in the House of Lords in 1917, in the Bowman

v. Secular Society case, on the grounds that anti-Christian doctrines (apart from scurrility and profanity) did not constitute blasphemy, and that denial of Christianity was not an offence in law. Quite apart from opening the door to lucrative legacies (including for Conway Hall built 1927–9), many in the movement regarded this as decisive for undermining the notion that Christianity (as distinct from the Church of England) was legally established.[25] This case stood large in secularist culture, both in its making (which took many years to await the particular case to challenge) and for the in-house historiography of British secularism.[26] Meanwhile, though the law against blasphemy had been inactive in Scotland since 1844, the offence continued to exist there and to find new currency in decades to come.

Through these decades, humanists like Robertson and, even more, J. A. Hobson (as we see in the next section) were recrafting the understanding of the moral state in Britain. No longer did the ethics of nationalism and patriotism stand unchallenged, as the turn-of-the-century ethical theorists engraved onto Liberal principles and, also, socialist ones, ideas about the state's moral responsibilities – though other Liberals like Bertrand Russell did not turn to socialism in his excoriation of imperialism in the 1900s and 1910s.[27] But Hobson's friend and colleague, Leonard (L.T.) Hobhouse (1864–1929) did turn to leftist ideas. Regarded as the original professional humanist sociologist, he held the first British chair of sociology (at the University of London), and was also a journalist at the *Manchester Guardian*, helping his sister Emily expose the scandal of British concentration camps in the Anglo-Boer War. He resisted the onset of Marxist thought by holding to a Liberalism that expounded the state's role in emancipatory action on behalf of the individual and the alleviation of coercion. In social theory, Hobhouse drew on Herbert Spencer, another humanist favourite, to contribute strongly to the role of human senses to understanding the unknowability of an external reality because of the observer standpoint, and the role of language in constructing (verbalising) reality. He joined the new Sociological Society after it was formed by followers of the town planner, sexual progressive and proto-humanist Patrick Geddes, and took on the role of the first editor of *The Sociological Review*, and from that vantage point had a significant role in the development of the British discipline. Hobhouse produced a 1906 sociology of moral institutions and worked onwards to combine scientific sociology, ethical philosophy and social-reform programmes. He is noted for drawing on ideas concerning the social organism from his friends Hobson, Graham Wallas and Morris Ginsberg, his acolyte.[28] Sadly, despite Ginsberg's best efforts to publicise his sociological theory into the 1950s, Hobhouse was rather quickly and unfairly eclipsed by other theoreticians overseas.

Attitudes within the nonreligion movement towards the state were propelled from the 1880s to the 1940s by this network of high-profile theorists. At the forefront, the books and journalism of J. M. Robertson, J. A. Hobson, L. T. Hobhouse and H. N. Brailsford made the ideas prominent in Liberal and Labour circles and led them to reflect on the nature of freedom, the state, economics and poverty. Most influential of all was Hobson's famed role in exposing the ethics and economics of the British Empire, whilst it was Hobhouse as leader writer at the *Manchester Guardian* who persuaded the newspaper's editor C. P. Snow in 1899 to despatch Hobson to South Africa to report on the Anglo-Boer War, giving birth to the single most important book critique of imperialism.

(c) Internationalism

Radicals and republicans had developed international links in the nineteenth century, and indeed also during the era of correspondence societies in the 1790s. Moreover, the development of international Marxism owed a great deal to its base in England from the 1840s to the 1910s, where Marx and Engels presided intellectually over the cause, did most of their writing, and where radical political refugees fetched up from various countries in Europe including Russia. It is true that the internationalism of the humanist and atheist movements was to develop strong communist connections; as early as 1895, the anarchist Peter Kropotkin, exiled in London for his activism in Russia and elsewhere in Europe, gave a lecture in aid of the building debt fund at South Place on the use of land (chaired by noted British socialist Sidney Webb).[29] Such links to radicals were to increase, especially during the 1930s and 1940s. But in the early years of organised ethicism and humanism, the internationalism that arose and nurtured the intellectual development of the movement owed less to Marxism than to more specific, largely less radical causes.

International organisation was central to the movement from the start. In a way, internationalism came first, predating the formation in 1896 of the Union of Ethical Societies, with the foundation three years earlier in Germany of the International Ethical Union (IEU).[30] It held its first grandly termed Congress in Zurich in September 1896, with a long and ambitious range of objects to its manifesto – from solving 'the labour problem', and the 'grievous evil' of women in factory, home and domestic service, to 'establishing a universal ethical end in all education' and 'universal peace amongst nations' – and aimed to have international conferences follow every four years from 1908 to 1932.[31] The IEU was to nurture the idea of the pan-European character of ethicism in these early decades, with the British contribution much funnelled through the contacts and energy of Gustav Spiller and F. J. Gould. Whilst by no means creating total unanimity, the IEU from the outset spread common terms, objectives and practice among those societies which distinguished themselves from purely secularist and freethought organisations, acting as a conduit for internationalising ethicist publishing and speakers. It was to act as a mechanism by which humanist leaders in different nations forged projects and, above all, spread the idea of internationalism – the ideology of equality and cooperation between nations towards world organisation and government.

Britain contributed a great deal to internationalism. J. A. Hobson lectured regularly at South Place from 1892, and from the later 1890s his maturing humanism was, in the words of historian of thought Gregory Claeys, 'a well-crafted, carefully argued ideal which had three components: economic, ethical and religious'.[32] His potent foundation for the internationalism of the humanist movement was opposition to imperialism, and specifically to military subjugation of indigenous peoples. The movement attracted attention for Hobson's fierce critique of Sir Arthur Conan Doyle's defence of Britain's actions against the Boer republics, but Hobson's writings exposed the economics of empire and how gold and capital were at the heart of the Second Boer War – an opinion eventually (and infamously) to be influential upon Lenin. It has long been the consensus that Hobson established the principles of this argument in his 1902 book *Imperialism – A Study*, in which he set forth a general doctrine of underconsumption. As the famous mid-twentieth-century historian A. J. P. Taylor (himself a humanist) put it: 'The capitalists cannot spend their share of national production. Saving makes their predicament worse. They demand openings for investment outside their saturated national market; and they find these openings in the underdeveloped parts of the world. This is Imperialism . . .'[33] But whilst showing Hobson to be central to the establishment of the principles, recent research shows he constructed his line of argument upon at least thirty years of developing thought, much of it by secularists and ethicists. He moved partly in Fabian, partly in progressive circles in the 1890s as he worked out his position on imperialism; in 1899 he mooted that every 'increase of the size of Empire gives power to officials and less power to the people'. But he also exploited the journal *Ethical World* which he co-edited with Stanton Coit from 1898 onwards to float his ideas on the rise of coercion as empires increase in size. In *Imperialism*, Hobson argued that, in principle, imperial interference with a 'lower race' could be justified if it could be shown to be acting for the real benefit of the subject race. The problem, Hobson said, was defining and proving this welfare benefit. The system he defined had three stages: economic integration whose constituents he itemised in some detail; second, the logic of assimilation of many territories to an international order that would supersede imperialism; and third to a federated world of '"like-minded" nations', expanding to make up the whole of 'the civilized world'. Claeys has recently shown how the key elements of Hobson's internationalism here rested on ideas of predecessors starting with Comte, and specifically anti-imperialist Positivists and social Darwinists, notably the idea of enlightened imperialism built into this model which he extracted from sociologist Benjamin Kidd. Hobson spent the decades following developing his model, adapting to the changing international scene, including in a 1915 book *A League of Nations* in which he feared that the Great Powers would 'arrogate to themselves an undue proportion of authority in the determinant acts of international government' – a fear he saw within four years coming to pass at Versailles. Interestingly, Hobson borrowed the book's title from fellow-humanist and Cambridge academic Goldsworthy (Goldie) Lowes Dickinson (1862–1932), the founder of the discipline of international relations, who had coined the term 'League of Nations' in 1914, prior to it being adopted for real in 1919.[34] By 1929, Hobson spoke of 'the needs of and interests of humanity at large, the people of the world, must over-ride the purely national will'. Claeys identifies Hobson's debt to Fabians, Positivists and the Comte position of subordinating politics to ethics, whilst another historian, Glenda Sluga, emphasises how the 1907 Hague Peace Conference and the Subject Races International Committee absorbed the same Positivist contribution in revising internationalism. By the 1920s and 1930s, Hobson was engaging positively with H. G. Wells' conception of 'cosmopolitan humanity' (as Hobson put it), and with left-wing utopianism, writing in 1919 that 'the most profitable labour for Socialism is in the field of "humanism"'.[35]

At the forefront of Hobson's mind was the terror of nationalism that could undermine the uniting power of common humanity. Claeys contends that Hobson identified this uniting power as 'humanist', and, though he attributed it to John Ruskin, he did not acknowledge Comte. But more immediately, Claeys argues, when Hobson became a 'religious heretic' in his second year at Oxford he came to surround himself with ethicists, Positivists and Fabians: F. J. Gould, J. Ramsay MacDonald, and Patrick Geddes. In *Ethical World* in January 1902, it was written (likely by its editor Hobson) that 'Members of the Ethical Societies will recognise the identity of the Positivist ideal with our own.' Hobson aligned with the ethical movement very strongly. Yet, historian David Feldman has demonstrated that Hobson placed an anti-Semitic understanding of capitalism as underpinning British, French, German and American imperialism, wherein 'international financiers were the key agents' with supposed Jewish characteristics – a position resonating with numbers of early-twentieth-century British radicals and the left, and with long-term and still unresolved impacts upon the British Labour movement.[36] Though we as yet have no considered argument concerning the impact of antisemitism within ethicism and humanism, Hobson remained pivotal to the humanist development of internationalist theory.

Additionally, Hobson was also a main trigger to practical internationalist causes of the movement.[37] Hobson reported on the Boer War for the *Manchester Guardian*, contributing to a deep unease with the British prosecution of the war, the country's treatment of civilians and its capitalist backers. The humanist press became from that juncture routinely troubled by Britain's military conflicts, including the First World War in which, among 16,000 conscientious objectors (COs), humanists were the third-largest group after the religious group (comprising Quakers and literalist biblical Christians) and the socialist group. Pacifism was by no means popular, even among vaguely supportive Liberals, but became well-entrenched before the full horrors of the Great War entered consciousness. The Rationalist Peace Society (RPS) was founded in 1910 by Hypatia Bradlaugh Bonner[38] and J. M. Robertson following on the heels of Hobson in opposing the Boer War and imperialism, quickly making conscientious objection a strain in the rationalist movement. The RPS gave succour to ethicists and secularists opposed to killing and war, bolstering intellectual and no doubt personal commitment prior to the coming of conscription in 1916. Among humanist COs from 1916 were Fenner Brockway (1888–1988) and E.M. Forster, and anti-war intellectuals like Bertrand Russell, starting traditions that lasted through the Second World War and the Cold War. In 1915, Hobson made a plea to the Humanitarian Society for an early negotiated peace: '[I] found to my consternation that man's inhumanity to man struck no chord of sympathy in many members of my audience, who apparently confined their humanitarianism to a guarded condemnation of blood-sports and an advocacy of bird sanctuaries.'[39] Though always a minority position, what was set in train was the move to establish conscientious objection as a human right that would be included by H. G. Wells in his 1940 schema for what became the UN Declaration of Human Rights 1948 – though it did not include this right – and, more widely, established on the agenda the broader right to freedom of thought, conscience and religion, asserted from the late 1940s in many international conventions, declarations and covenants, and which continue to be processed today.[40]

An immediate manifestation of the ethical movement's lead on internationalism was its organisation in 1911 of the First Universal Races Congress, led by Gustav Spiller and American ethical cultural pioneer Felix Adler. Acclaimed for its defence of monogenism (the theory of common evolutionary human origins), the event was far from free from controversy on this and other points. With advance distribution of an Inter-Racial Lesson by F. J. Gould to schools in several countries, 2,000 attenders came to the four-day event at the University of London. Messages of support and patronage came from the good and great of fifty nations, including prime ministers, parliamentarians and most of the members of existing but still quite new international institutions – the Permanent Court of Arbitration and the Second Hague Conference. From Britain, France, Belgium and other European nations and their respective empires, intimations of support emanated, as too from virtually all of the universities of the UK and many from overseas; also from the leaders of the British Conservative and Labour parties (though not, curiously, of the Liberal Party), eight prime ministers, forty colonial bishops, and seemingly several hundred professors of law, anthropology and sociology (including Max Weber, Emile Durkheim, Joseph Rowntree, Lord Lever, Andrew Carnegie and George Cadbury). Many representatives of Black, Asian and other indigenous peoples came to the Congress, including Mohandas (later Mahatma) Gandhi and W. E. B. (William) Du Bois, with official representatives of over twenty governments.[41] Curious to the modern eye, eulogies to empire abounded; the sixth session started with a statement from the chair: 'The Crown was the symbol of the principles which bound the British Empire together, and those principles were the same which the Congress desired to extend to the whole of the civilised world.'[42] Against such a submissive culture, Congress delegates had to struggle. The leading African American figure William Du Bois (1868–1963) spoke about 'the negro' in different eras and countries, and posed the question: 'Were these people human in the same sense as white people were human? It seemed to him natural to assume it. When it came to the question of mixed races, it was curious to sit there as though one were a sort of zoological specimen.'[43] Notwithstanding, the conference was founded on the principle of one common or universal race (though Congress publications were titled 'universal races' in the plural) with common possibilities for development. Preceded by a special one-day session on the anthropology of race (including an exhibition depicting the major 'races and colour types' of the world), the event was naïve and too keen on avoiding controversy, yet evoking a political, moral and scientific urge to understand race, and to establish 'harmonious relations between the various divisions of mankind' as a prelude to diminishing warfare.[44]

Conceived as a moral high point for ethicism and liberal humanitarianism, the Congress of 1911 was built partly on the fame of Hobson's 1901 work on imperialism and the conferences of the IEU. It was organised in something of an overabundance of bonhomie and mutual backslapping, with pervading rhetoric of religious universalism – albeit with contending formats from Christianity, Confucianism and Buddhism. But controversy could not be kept out entirely, with Annie Besant attacking the treatment of Indians in India and South Africa, Du Bois doubting that the African American would avoid being crushed by prejudice in the United States, and Hobson himself attacking the bogus rationales of empire presented to the Congress by Christian humanitarians.[45] But delegates were alive to the contentious contexts – from gunboat diplomacy to imperial brutalities, and the rise of colonial nationalism and pan-Africanism, together with rising Black consciousness in the United States, and the women's and suffrage movements. As some historians have observed, the Congress came at the end of nineteenth-century illusions of progress as well as resting at the cusp of new-century movements.[46] Notably, it is attributed with triggering Du Bois to become an antagonist of empire.[47] Much was anticipated to follow by way of developing universal values, repeat congresses and multi-racial internationalism.[48] But the First World War, the League of Nations from 1920, the Pan-African Congress of 1921 and the rise of fascism all conspired to deter repeat congresses.

The First World War diverted internationalism to a new turn, with the humanist involvement in the Union for Democratic Control (UDC) set up by Ramsay MacDonald MP in 1913. This drew in leading political figures, just under a third of them Liberals – including Hobson, E. D. Morel, Bertrand Russell and C. P. Scott – to campaign for parliamentary control over British foreign policy, including negotiations with European democracies and peace terms that would not humiliate the losers. MacDonald was inspired by the Hobsonian principle that foreign policy should not be left to the secret, back-corridor negotiations of professional civil servants within Europe and elsewhere in the manner of their 1880s carve-up of Africa between imperialist powers. Morel, who became the influential UDC secretary, had previously been energetic to establish rights for native Africans in the Kongo, and, though his ideas on rights still contained essentialist elements, he argued for the extension of economic and commercial rights to Africans.[49] The leading figure in this was MacDonald who led the UDC and ILP in their cross-party campaign for a negotiated peace, and, as a well-known figure in South Place, undoubtedly influenced the ethicist and humanist movement as well.[50] In August 1914, Ramsay MacDonald wrote in *Labour Leader*: 'It is a diplomatists' war, made by about half a dozen men. Up to the moment, ambassadors were withdrawn [from the countries embarking on war] the peoples were at peace. They had no quarrel with each other, they bore each other no ill-will. A dozen men brought Europe to the brink of a precipice and Europe fell over it.'[51] The UDC was the focus of anti-war moves on the left wing, drawing in a membership of 650,000 by 1917, and was to surface more intimately in humanist affairs in the 1930s. But an interesting footnote: Morel, the UDC secretary, stood for Labour in the multi-member parliamentary constituency of Dundee in 1922 and was (along with the temperance candidate) the cause of Winston Churchill losing his House of Commons seat – in large measure because of Morel-incited sentiment hostile to Churchill's handling of the Gallipoli campaign in which many Dundee soldiers perished. More broadly, Churchill condemned Morel as one of 'that band of degenerate international intellectuals who regard the greatness of Britain and the stability and prosperity of the British Empire as a fatal obstacle to their subversive sickness'.[52]

FENNER BROCKWAY 1888–1988

FIGURE 11 Fenner Brockway. Photo: ©NPG.

Fenner Brockway earned a living mostly from journalism, but it was his humanism and socialism to which he was devoted, campaigning first in the Independent Labour Party in the 1910s, then fighting imperialism, war and the arms trade, and against racism and apartheid in South Africa. He organised the No Conscription Fellowship movement in the First World War, attracting the attention of the nascent MI5, but also the support of the large network of COs who formed a committed and principled community. Imprisoned intermittently for this during 1916–19, he became with Bertrand Russell and many humanists a promoter of Indian independence. Briefly Labour MP for Leyton in 1929–31, he eschewed both an unprincipled Labour Party and a totalitarian Communist Party. Yet, his own pacifism was compromised in the Spanish Civil War of the late 1930s when he supported the fight against Franco. In 1963, he explained:

> I am satisfied to call myself a Universalist. That is my philosophy. Its application? All that makes for human happiness and friendship,

human dignity, human equality, human co-operation across the boundaries of race, colour, language and religion, human conquest of science not for war but to end poverty and disease, human fulfilment, physically, mentally, spiritually, on earth and among the stars.

Re-elected an MP for Slough in 1950, he remained a humanitarian conscience, especially on immigration, racism and apartheid, and co-founding War on Want in 1961. Losing his seat in 1964 and elevated to the Lords, he kept protesting over nuclear weapons, bemoaning the humanist movement when it became less vocal about the bomb in the 1970s. An agnostic finding awe and fulfilment in the universe, he had no sense of a personal God, and was long an adviser to BHA, speaking at its conferences, and a statue was erected to him in Red Lion Square outside Conway Hall.

It was in large measure from this anti-imperialist spring that humanist anti-war sentiment uncoiled in the 1900s and was to flourish from 1916. The peace movement really started there in the Great War, and humanist Fenner Brockway rather more than Hobson was its energising and popular leader. In 1914, Brockway co-founded the No Conscription Fellowship, initially based in his Derbyshire home, to resist compulsory mobilisation, and even before that measure was introduced in 1916 (as the military could no longer count on volunteers) the Fellowship grew so rapidly that its London office was opened. Brockway was gaoled several times for his activities, with challenging and at times cruel experiences in Chester and Lincoln prisons. After his release in the 1920s, Fenner Brockway met and helped Mohandas Gandhi, researching material on nonviolence for him, and would go on to support conscientious objection in the Second World War whilst at the same time opposing fascism. But a strain of humanist opposition to unjust war had found a home with Bertrand Russell, who was already committed to the UDC when, in 1916, he determined to refuse conscription on the grounds that war with Germany was unwarranted, being worked hard by the No-Conscription Fellowship in which, his philosophical biographer suggests, he mixed with working-class people the most in his lifetime and found comradeship; this work led to his first interview by MI5 in 1916 and another when imprisoned in 1918.[53] Though Russell, unlike Brockway, would regard the Second War against fascism as justified, Brockway and Russell would be reunited in the 1950s in opposition to nuclear weapons, and for their stances to justify the security service's long-term surveillance.

One further engine of internationalism in these years was the initiation of the moral education movement. We noted in the last chapter its activities in England between the 1890s and 1920s, but the issues thrown up then were being felt in Europe and the United States, and there was an immediate thirst for cross-border cooperation in the field of education in moral teaching. Susannah Wright notes the importance of Felix Adler's book *The Moral Instruction of Children* (1892) which set out an educational programme and was reported as 'the seed from which our own [Moral Instruction] League has sprung'.[54] Adler (1851–1933) came from a rabbinic family in New York but founded the first Ethical Culture Society in New York in 1876, and it was through his acolyte Stanton Coit that he was introduced to ethicists in England and met many others from Germany, Austria, Italy, Switzerland and France at ethicist and moral education congresses in Eisenach in Germany in 1893 and Zurich in 1896. In addition, Adler's influence spread through existing labour educationalists who had been pioneering moral education since the 1870s. But the second spurt of international influence came in 1908 with the First International Moral Education Congress in London, reputedly attended by 1,400 people, and its two-volume *Report on Moral Instruction* published in the same year. An important figure at that Congress and in the production of the *Report* was humanist Gustav Spiller who, though based in Britain, had connections in Germany and elsewhere which, when combined with his organisational skills, led almost inevitably to his becoming the secretary of the International Moral Education Congress. As Wright observes, F. J. Gould's teaching demonstration tours in the United States and India in 1911–14, working full time for the Moral Instruction League, showed some problems in the export of the English model of direct moral instruction, but internationalist contacts were established. For the British ethicist, internationalism was put on the agenda, notably in relation to the future of British colonies. The story of its decline in the 1920s was told in the previous chapter, but it is important to observe the significance of education to the international community of humanists. Moral education was a distinguishing feature of humanism, not exclusive to it by any means, but ethicist and humanist contributions in Europe and North America were stronger than anything contributed by secularism or freethought. Moreover, as we shall see later in this book, moral education became the focus of the humanist movement in confronting the intensification of religious education and worship that developed in England and Wales after 1944.

The First World War disrupted ethicist plans for internationalist initiatives and indeed devastated those concerning race and moral education. Yet, the war also stimulated new thinking in the movement. The development of the idea (and the name) of the League of Nations has strong humanist contributions, and, as we shall see in Chapter 7, was to stimulate a longstanding humanist utopian ideal for benevolent world government. Moreover, the war contributed to the early acceleration of imperial disintegration in the British Empire, to which humanists became strongly attached as a schema for the ethical advancement of the nation during the next fifty years.

PART II

THE FIRST GILDED
AGE 1930–70

6 RENEWAL, THE YOUTH SURGE AND PARLIAMENT

In 1947, the Ethical Union (EU) commissioned a pioneering study by the social anthropology organisation Mass-Observation, *Puzzled People: A Study in popular attitudes to religion, ethics, progress and politics in a London Borough*, which examined popular religion in Hammersmith. Based on interviews of 500 people in 1944–5, the inquiry found low levels of religious practice though high but declining belief in religion – concluding, as described by one scholar, with 'an overdose of pessimism and a touch of melodrama in suggesting the very foundations of the country's Christian ethic were at risk'.[1] But the report fitted neatly into the EU's post-war analysis of the decline of religion and deference, and the need for new ethical leadership. Adding a surprisingly sharp secularist edge, Harold Blackham's preface to *Puzzled People* observed that nobody could be pleased with the results except those 'satisfied with the triumph of Roman Catholic indoctrination, or the ignorance and confusion of those who call themselves Christians, or the self-sufficient hedonism of crudely rationalist young men'.[2] The leader of the Ethical Church at the time, Blackham was nudging the British humanist movement to advance a new ethical plan for those 'puzzled' by losing their religion. This chapter opens an examination of these decades of significant development for the movement by looking at the constant tussle with religion, attempts to reorganise humanist organisations, the explosion in youth support, and the build-up of humanist lobbying in Westminster.

(a) Humanism, religion and outreach

In 1936 the veteran ethical campaigner F. J. Gould wrote a letter to the editor of *The Monthly Record* (himself as it happened): 'Humanist-Rationalist-Ethicist-Agnostic-Atheist as I am, I say plainly that I would to-day join the Anglican Church, or more likely the Roman Catholic Church, if I could not find in Ethical Religion (Religion of Humanity) a nobler and profounder basis than I find in any of the theologies.' Gould shows here the overabundance of self-identity monikers within the humanist movement, including the intrusion of 'religion' in tag with ethicism. In the same passage, he deprecated the movement's 'nineteenth-century method of protests, fault-finding and denunciation' in attacks upon 'backward churches', favouring the new method of the League of Nation's resort to persuasion.[3] Gould reveals how, in humanist rhetoric of identity, religion was no mere historical survival, but one flourishing even among atheists. But, it was between 1950 and 1970 that this humanist resort to religion was largely to disappear.

In 1944, Chapman Cohen, long-time editor of the NSS's *The Freethinker*, baulked at the term 'humanist', unclear as to its utility beyond applying it to every human being.[4] In 1958, his successor Colin McCall wrote in not dissimilar terms that 'almost anybody can now be called a Humanist'.[5] Even Hector Hawton, editor in 1957 of the RPA's newly renamed *The Humanist*, confessed that there was 'a certain ambiguity in the term'.[6] This left the opportunity for scores of definitions to appear. A significant attempt at concision was agreed at the first congress of the International Humanist and Ethical Union (IHEU) in 1952, called the Amsterdam Declaration, which, in its 532 words (including preliminaries), offered five core themes to humanism: democracy, creative science, the dignity of man, personal liberty and ethical living. But it specified that humanism was 'an alternative to the religions which claim to be based on revelation on the one hand, and totalitarian systems on the other', adding that humanism 'is not a new sect'. Yet, it did state that ethical humanism united those 'willing to base their conviction on respect for man as a spiritual and moral being', thereby introducing the 'spiritual' word and causing various ramifications – including some disagreement within the movement as to its meaning, as well as recurrent claims from religionists that humanists were, after all, 'really religious'.[7] Stanton Coit's plan to transform existing churches (mainly Christian ones) with a 'religion of humanism' or a 'scientific humanism' was important though controversial. H. G. Wells was an influential pioneer from 1908, in which he envisaged the religion of humanism would be the driver of a utopian world-state. The world-state became much written about, a dream of humanist internationalism, promoted by classicist Gilbert Murray and zoologist Julian Huxley in the cultural activities for the League of Nations in the 1930s. Huxley had also worked with Wells and his son on a four-volume *The Science of Life* (1931) and published his own book on *What I Believe: Religion without Revelation* in 1927 (and several later editions, dropping the main title in 1957) in which he spoke at length of 'the religion of humanism' – as a worldwide movement of commitment to peace, cooperation and ethical government.[8] So exuberant was Huxley that one reviewer, the dean of St Pauls W.R. Matthews, noted triumphantly the scientist's 'profound conviction of the vital importance of religion [that] breathes through its pages'.[9]

This inevitably meant that humanists were liable to disputation about the legacies of faith systems embedded in their organisations – most obviously the Sunday morning meetings at Coit's Ethical Church, South Place Ethical Society and the Hampstead Ethical Institute. At the most studied of these, SPES at Conway Hall, the Sunday meeting retained a secular hymn with operatic or instrumental classical music. As Jessica Beck has argued, the hymns were regarded in the early twentieth century as having both an ethical purpose and as being central to ethical society identity.[10] Most used was *Hymns of Modern Thought*, some two hundred secular hymns from a variety of authors, which had been in use since 1900.[11] In the last year of his life in February 1937, F. J. Gould mooted the removal of hymn singing; as a member of the SPES's general committee, he carried the proposal by 7 votes to 5. But it was agreed to put this to the membership in a questionnaire, producing a hung vote, 65 for and 65 against on a one-third turnout; given the disunity fomented, the general committee agreed to do nothing except to drop church-style names – 'congregation' and 'service' – and call the gathering a 'meeting'.[12] The consequence was continued publication of the SPES *Hymns of Modern Thought* (aka The Small Hymn Book), and the committee ordered 1,500 copies from the printers two months later.[13] The issue was raised a final time in 1961 when Percy Sowter, the convenor of the SPES development committee, pushed hard for the abolition of all 'hymns, chants and anthems' to banish 'the tyranny of the Victorian chapel', telling the membership 'it is necessary for us to bring ourselves into line with the best of modern thought and customs'. There had been sustained mockery in various quarters, he reported, including in the RPA's magazine *The Humanist*, so Sowter put it to a membership vote by postal questionnaire: 39 per cent voted for abolition, 39 per cent were indifferent (very likely because they didn't attend), and 22 per cent for retention. After Sowter noted to the annual general meeting that the Sunday audience did not sing anyway, the vote was affirmed 23-18. A Sunday morning lecture on 2 July 1961 by Scottish mathematician and one-time communist Hyman Levy on 'The degeneration of intellectual man' was the first South Place Sunday morning meeting without a hymn – though short passages of classical music continued to feature for some decades.[14] The Sunday meetings were less popular than once they were; by February 1967, attendances ranged from 44 to 72.[15] For many, humanism was perceived as evolving from the 'rationalistic religion' of Moncure Conway to agnosticism and rationalism, thence to the more positive form of humanism.[16] Members weren't always happy with the compromises en route. One woman joined SPES in the 1960s after attending several Sunday morning lectures, becoming a member 'against my better judgement in view of the Society's aim of a rational religious *sentiment*'; she was not happy with it, feeling the whole thing was 'based on a church service' extending even to 'the monetary collection!', and despite the best efforts of the general secretary, Peter Cadogan, she resigned in 1971.[17] Five years later, *Humanist News* opined that the BHA should not expend too much energy on the religion issue – a view disputed by anarchist Nicolas Walter.[18] Many minds thought this ongoing dispute pointless. Hector Hawton wrote in 1961: 'Humanism is claimed by some to be an alternative to religion and by others to be itself a religion. Neither side can win this argument.'[19]

In truth, the humanist movement had latterly relied on indirect definition, by offering in RPA's publications readings of the world and exclamations of its intellectual traditions – most notably in the expanding Thinker's Library. From 1929 to 1953 the series extended to 140 volumes by many authors, both new and reprinted books on the sciences, history, arts, religion, philosophy, thinking and ethical values, some lengthy but reduced to very small font to maintain the slimness of binding. Many were quite argumentative, didactic and confrontational, especially in regard to organised religion, the Christian bible and belief. One measure of success for RPA leaders lay in the reaction of the Church of England's *Towards the Conversion of England* report of 1945 which referred to the Thinker's Library as evidence of Christianity being excluded by science: 'We must remedy the situation in which the working man . . . always finds that the cheapest (or only) literature [on biology, economics or geology] is by an atheist.'[20] RPA's books were likely favoured by those with a committed rationalist outlook, though it was noted in the 1950s that few of them were bought by RPA members. Yet, though the Thinker's Library remained at the forefront of RPA output after 1945, the series suffered diminishing sales as many volumes, written before 1900, were densely theological or philosophical and quite challenging. Few were about the ethical transformation of contemporary society, being repetitive explanations of why religion was wrong, and few seemed appealing to women. This made the series even more out of date as paperbacks were now in vogue, pioneered especially by Penguin, and RPA was proving slow to adapt.

Many guides and anthologies appeared in the 1950s and 1960s, not always with RPA. Most traced humanism to classical Greece, placing denials of supernaturalism and of any existence after death at the core of the cause. Philosophers and rationalists tended to feature – Margaret Knight often mentioning Protagoras and Epicurus – and criticism of the Christian bible was involved to some degree, including denial of divinity, the soul and miracles. But mid-century guides started to focus on the modernity of humanism – on its recognition of rights of autonomy in divorce (denied in Anglican canon law), in sexual activity (though denying promiscuity as 'irrational'), in gender and race, abortion, upon its coda of morality without religion, but also – for most authors – its opposition to communism. Published as substantial paperbacks, guides to humanism were getting into the leading imprints whilst short pamphlets were distributed for young and old.[21] Julian Huxley edited *The Humanist Frame* in 1961, allowing twenty-six contributors, mostly academics, to explain how humanism was, or could be, influential in their own disciplines, whilst a guide to applied humanism came in A. J. Ayer's 1968 collection *The Humanist Outlook.*[22] Harold Blackham was clear in Huxley's academic collection about the ultimate need to reject Christianity,[23] but he most often wrote with a more conciliatory voice, saying in his Penguin book *Humanism* that humanist principles precluded outright hostilities with religion and concerned compromises about society. 'For', he wrote, 'humanism is about the world, not about humanism.'[24] Talks at schools and public meetings were opportunities to spread the news of humanism and humanist ways of thinking. Diane Munday was typical, delivering speeches with distilled arguments – defining truth as 'an attitude of mind rather th[a]n set of beliefs – many brands', and 'a way of looking at and interpreting evidence and making decisions between alternatives'. But uniformly, she wrote, humanism 'DOES reject absolutes – cannot envisage absolute wisdom or absolute authority or absolute GOOD.'[25] Likewise, Margaret Knight was clear that 'I am not out to destroy Christian convictions of people in whom they are deeply implanted and to whom they mean a great deal'; she merely regarded 'it as a mistake to try to impose them on children'.[26] Meanwhile, Julian Huxley continued to bring the idea of religion to his evolutionary humanism and the 'religion of humanism', acknowledging in his 1961 book 'that a purely materialistic outlook cannot provide an adequate basis for human life'.[27] As the century wore on, he was being pulled up by critics for being out of date in sustaining his call for a 'humanist faith'.[28]

A new track emerged in the mid-1960s. The relationship between the humanist movement and the churches became an issue of permanent significance, with Blackham leading humanists towards concerted rapprochement. On 6 April 1965, Pope Paul VI established the *Secretariatus Pro Non Credentibus*, or Secretariat for Dialogue with Non-Believers. Its founding president, Cardinal Franziskus Konig, wrote that 'all Christians are called to promote in every way possible this dialogue with men of all classes, as an expression of a brotherly love which respects the requirements of a humanity come of age'.[29] On hearing the news, Harold Blackham, as secretary of the International Humanist and Ethical Union, immediately contacted Cardinal Koenig and his secretary Dom Vincenzo Miano, and in July, accompanied by Dutch humanist leader and IHEU Chairman Jaap van Praag, Blackham had an evening meeting with them, followed by another encounter the following weekend with an agenda of two items: the Roman Catholic and humanist outlook on 'the present situation', and the plural or 'open society' – a Blackham fascination of the time (to which we return in Chapter 8) – with short papers of 750 words to be presented on both topics from each side.[30] Though Blackham announced with a flourish to the BHA annual conference at Keele University in August that the Papacy's Secretariat was going to discuss the open society and the place of Catholic schools and universities in it,[31] the talks drew condemnation from the NSS.[32] A second meeting, again in Brussels, was held four years later with almost identical themes, and the papers from it and commentaries were published. But this particular initiative failed to produce any clear-cut outcome, likely indicative of changing Catholic Church strategy in relation to humanists and atheists by the 1970s.[33]

But considerable humanist effort went into debates on religion, humanism and ethics in the philosophical groups of the humanist movement. In the post-war years, SPES and the Progressive League each had groups (both meeting in Conway Hall), as too did some local groups affiliated to the EU. In a sense, philosophers constituted part of the armoury of the nonreligious movements. Around a third of the Thinker's Library of 140 pocket-sized books could be described as philosophy, rather more than works on science, economics, law and religious criticism. Philosophers, most of them academics, and scientists willing to argue philosophically, were on the front-line, called upon in debating events of the 1950s and 1960s, then common in British universities. Philosophers were in demand. The British humanist movement was especially blessed in the mid-twentieth century with a constellation of philosophical and scientific star debaters – Bertrand Russell, Julian Huxley, Jacob Bronowski, A. J. Ayer, Barbara Wootton, Stephen Toulmin, Bernard Williams and Antony Flew – all frequent speakers on BBC radio and television programmes. However, they were carefully controlled by BBC policy from speaking on humanism and atheism; if they did, their contribution had to be scripted with a Christian interlocutor present to conclude with the Christian case. A Humanist Broadcasting Council was formed in 1959 to discuss with successive BBC directors general the opening of the airwaves to the discussion of nonreligion on religious and ethics programmes, but, despite intermittent meetings, little of substance flowed over ten years. One outcome was a BBC radio series on 'Enquiry into Humanism' conceded in 1965 by Lord Normanbrook, taking the form of six interviews with humanists on the Home Service: with A. J. Ayer, James Hemming, Madeleine Simms, Wendy Kaplan and David Pollock (as 'young humanists'), Lord Ted Willis, and Lord (Frank) Francis-Williams. A second was a confrontation four years later between Peter Ritchie Calder and Trevor Huddleston, in which the humanist position was rather reduced by the producers to attacking Christianity.[34] Despite Blackham's best efforts, the British humanist movement continued offering a resolutely secular and often argumentative face to the world. Attacks on religion were popular with members; the 1952 RPA annual conference took as its theme 'The Menace of Roman Catholicism', with the lead speaker Joseph McCabe arguing that Catholics committed more serious crimes than any other part of the community (a case researched internationally at that time).[35] At the second IHEU Congress in London in 1957, it was the delegates from the American Ethical Union who were labelled 'the pious Humanists'.[36] By then, it was a rationalistic humanism by which the British movement regarded itself. As we shall see later in this and the next chapter, the 1960s would then witness humanism starting to be infused through British society.

(b) Organisational consolidation

It is one of the truisms of British organised nonreligion that it has always been a multi-organisation movement with an individual able to have membership across all four main humanist and secularist organisations. In the mid-1960s, sociologist Colin Campbell calculated that, among their members, 30 per cent of the EU, 40 per cent of the National Secular Society and 58 per cent of the University Humanist Federation (UHF) also had a membership in the Rationalist Press Association, and that 17 per cent of the NSS and 34 per cent of the UHF also belonged to the BHA.[37] Such cross-organisation membership inevitably inspired dreams of consolidation.

The move to Conway Hall had been a stimulant to the South Place Ethical Society's activities and morale. Attendances increased significantly and the building reportedly buzzed with a range of activities. From 1930 a 'Conway Discussion Circle' met as an initiative between the society and the Rationalist Press Association. The society also operated a poetry reading circle and hosted Sunday afternoon 'At Homes', with a sustained – even increasing – devotion to the provision of music. The 1930–1 season of Sunday concerts was the forty-fifth in the society's history and it hosted twenty-seven concerts, plus weekday evening events including a country dance class which added to the musical provision. The participating membership was nearly 600 in number, clearly the result of a purpose-built venue. Rambling groups also used the hall as a base, whilst by the 1950s table tennis was being played on Wednesday evenings in – of all places – the library. In line with the boom, the society's expenditure doubled between 1928 and the following year, rising a further 60 per cent in 1930 to a total of £2,635.[38]

It was not just SPES that seemed to be thriving. Hopeful evidence of attracting younger adults came from University College London and Manchester University where, by 1930, there were student ethical groups. Members attempted to 'solve the problems of the day', though utopian idealism was evident in 'a reorientation in every department of life: social, political, economic and religious – a reorientation that shall have its basis in a deeper insight into the needs and aspirations of mankind that shall be humanistic through and through'.[39] Meanwhile, the Manchester University Ethical Union was prestigious enough to have the vice chancellor, Sir Ernest Simon, a close associate of Sidney and Beatrice Webb and a former mayor of Manchester, as a vice-president and had sub-groups investigating ethical issues concerning the empire and nationalism. Yet, the ethical movement had not grown significantly since the start of the century and remained atomised. Into the 1940s and 1950s, the Ethical Union was rather inward-looking, with few employees and direct members, a body mostly composed of small regional societies, though, with its funds swollen by a 1943 legacy of £40,669 (worth £1.9 million in 2021 terms),[40] it could invest in its debates, talks and lectures, dinners and a small range of publications. Some member societies had a greater presence than the Union. As well as SPES at Conway Hall, these included the West London

Ethical Church (from 1953 renamed Society) that held numerous meetings each month and used the proceeds of the sale of its building in Queensway to purchase 13 Prince of Wales Terrace in Kensington and renamed it Stanton Coit House in memory of its founder. More active than the EU was the NSS, the bulldog of the movement with the strongest roots in working-class radicalism, stridently opposing church and state connections. Even in the 1960s, it had the largest membership of all the secularist bodies outside of London and the south-east; 44 per cent of its membership lay in the north-west of England, the Midlands and Scotland, with 40 per cent also belonging to the RPA.[41] Meanwhile, the Rationalist Press Association had always led the way with vigorous public debate through publications about freedoms, and, with the early-twentieth-century publishers' boycott now largely forgotten, felt free to publish and to campaign – including during the Second World War to the extent that 1942 and 1943 saw them notch up record sales. With its offices moved out to Elstree north of London and its distribution centre remaining in Johnson's Court, and despite some losses of stock, the association emerged from the war in a better condition than many other publishers and was eager to campaign.

In the late 1940s, the nonreligion movement was buoyant. Chapman Cohen in the NSS journal *The Freethinker*, amid a weekly rant at Christianity's foibles and misdemeanours, rather gleefully chronicled church pessimism with the steady decay of attendance and 'a desperate series of moves' for a 'Conversion of England'.[42] But amid a short burst of church growth in the 1950s, humanist movement leaders concluded that times were changing. First and foremost, the names of the movement's organisations were dysfunctional. Terms such as 'rationalist', 'ethical' and 'secular' had diminishing resonance with the British public, whilst it was clear in reflections by the EU and the RPA in 1955 that 'humanist' was far more attractive. An 'enquiry committee' of the EU reported in 1956:

> Humanism is a universal, evolving religion of human fellowship and service which is based wholly and progressively on human knowledge and experience, independent of speculations and beliefs about God and the supernatural. Humanists aim by purely human means to help themselves and their fellow men to know, love and do the right in all relations of life. They believe in Humanity and its potentiality for greater nobility and enjoyment of life by the good and wise use of increasing knowledge of man and his environment.[43]

The RPA was coming to a similar conclusion, the first fruit of which was the renaming in 1956 of its main journal, *The Literary Guide and Rationalist Review*, as *The Humanist*, under the editorship of its most prolific writer, the novelist and SPES secretary Hector Hawton (1901–75). At the same time, these two organisations, EU and RPA, started to think about their shared aims, the good match of the activist arm with the publishing arm, and the possibility of cooperation. In April 1955, it was announced that they would work together on expanding groups and conferences and formed a joint development committee.[44] At the EU conference the following year, Joseph Reeves MP (1888–1969), then vice-president of the EU and chairman of the RPA, suggested they 'co-ordinate their activities and strive for the maximum measure of unification.'[45] A joint committee for closer working was set up, and by the autumn of 1956 reported 'proposals for the merging of the two organizations'. The limited company status of RPA was an obstacle likely to undermine claims to EU's charitable status, and a staged approach was envisaged, beginning in 1957 with the formation of the Humanist Association, combining representatives of the EU and RPA, which co-mounted with SPES the IHEU Congress in Conway Hall in July of that year. Yet, by 1959, this association had collapsed, due, according to Campbell, to RPA members determined to maintain its distinctive propaganda role. But a wider move for unity developed as the EU, RPA and NSS formed a Humanist Council (taking over a body dating from 1950 that linked RPA, EU and SPES primarily in campaigning work). From 1959 to 1963, the Humanist Council acquired the assets of the Society for the Abolition of Blasphemy as well as participated in the Humanist Broadcasting Council.[46] In the midst of this, a proposal was floated for the EU to change its name and start recruiting members as well as affiliated ethical societies. RPA disquiet arose over this and over the name of the 'Humanist Council' or association being effectively taken over by the EU, leading finally in the summer of 1962 to RPA agreement to cooperate and form an umbrella body called the British Humanist Association. RPA started the process of seeking charitable status, granted in March 1963, clearing the way to a possible fusion of activities, marked in May by an inaugural dinner in the House of Commons.

However, the humanist sector began to confront a constitutional crisis. In July 1965 Kensington Borough Council triggered the charity commissioners to remove charity status from the EU (because of nonreligious propagandising). The BHA was likewise removed (as it shared objects with the EU), whilst SPES trustees confronted the Attorney General's threat to their cherished 'religion' status (which, inter alia, allowed them to conduct legal weddings) by pointing to twelve registered 'atheistic' Buddhist groups.[47] In 1967, RPA withdrew from the plan for the union when its charitable status was removed by the Home Office because it was incompatible with its campaigning and propaganda activities, and in 1967, after the name 'British Humanist Association' having been used in all manner of contexts in the previous five years, the EU was formally renamed and began operating as a membership, not mainly federal, body. The plan to unite the nonreligion movement as a whole had failed. However, whilst SPES noted in 1964 the loss of members to local BHA groups, the BHA told its advisory council it was gaining new members at an average of 130 people a month, and bringing 'humanism' into the limelight as the core name of an expanding movement.[48]

Of all the groups, the RPA was faring the worst in the 1950s and 1960s. It had the strongest historic links with the Labour movement and left-wing intellectualism, and many in the Labour Party were RPA members, authors or supporters. Yet, as an organisation dedicated to publications, it had a distinct focus on its business activities. In addition, it was the only one of the British secularist bodies to have a significant non-British component; in 1955, 32 per cent of its membership resided outside the UK.[49] More than the others it was an outward-facing business, commissioning books, magazine articles, making contracts with authors, producing these outputs and organising their sales through booksellers – including a considerable deal of trade with the retail and distribution firms of WH Smith and John Menzies. As a business, though, it also had the task of trying to turn a profit and, for most of the time, spectacularly failed to do this. The perennial problem was that of reaching the younger generation – those in their late teens and twenties, and notably the ever-expanding student market. The problems were not unchanging, however. In the late 1940s and early 1950s, a large financial deficit of £16,570 was attributed by the leading figure, Lord Chorley, to the lack of a student market, and the puzzle was to publish things that might stimulate rationalist and humanist student groups, and a special committee was formed. Though the RPA was a major membership body – peaking in 1947 with 4,726 members and 284 subscribers – for the most part it did not organise indoor or outdoor lectures and meetings, only starting annual conferences in 1946, and its rules (determined by company law) for a long time prohibited members under twenty-one years of age (though a Student Rationalist Movement was underway by 1948).[50] The Watts family that ran the business side of the RPA was more phlegmatic. Frederick Watts said in 1951 that the association was never intended to make money: 'it was doing a great educational service to the masses who need not go without good reading matter at a cheap price'.[51]

But even as a publishing business, things were going awry. With the appearance of Penguin Books during 1935–9, paperbacks stopped being seen as 'smutty' titles, but the RPA was stuck in a rut with hardback books of Victorian and Edwardian conception of what rationalist readers wanted. Even its cheap series of 'Thrift books' did not sell; the contract had been given exclusively to WH Smiths (and John Menzies in Scotland), but members could not find any of the books on sale in their shops. In any event, some members criticised the Thrift books for having no rationalist content whatever. The RPA remained wedded for a very long time to its Thinker's Library, but the series stopped publishing new books in 1953, yet association members pressed continuously in the remainder of the 1950s for new titles. None was and the reasons were slowly revealed. In 1957, the membership was told the books were not selling well, with thousands in stock, and in 1959 the truth fully emerged: there were actually a staggering 225,000 books from the Thinker's Library in stock.[52] If accurate, this stock assessment revealed one of the greatest publishing mistakes of the twentieth century, encumbering the association with a huge loss on print and more on storage, raising the deficit to £22,000 in 1953 alone. The RPA was publishing items for its members, but its members were rarely buying them. Also, the membership fell sharply – by 41 per cent during 1947–56 – leading to cuts: its precious headquarters at Johnson's Court off Fleet Street was sold in 1954, twenty-six of thirty-two staff were let go and the Public Relations Office closed. However, it led to Hector Hawton being appointed managing director and general editor, bringing about a revamp of *The Literary Guide* magazine and *The Rationalist Annual*.[53] A novelist by trade, Hawton became in many ways one of the most successful communicators of the humanist movement, writing lucid and wide-ranging pieces in the *Guide*, and many books on rationalist issues as well. Yet, his target audience remained members of the movement rather than the wider literary audience suggested by the title of the *Guide*. Recognising this, Hawton in 1956 changed the title to *The Humanist*, telling the RPA annual meeting it was his 'intention to see that the Journal became the voice of those progressive forces which fight obscurantism in all its forms'.[54] Though 732 new members were enrolled in 1957, the association that year recognised that its publishing strategy of fifty years had collapsed; in the face of Penguin's success with cheap paperbacks, Watts and Co like other small publishers retreated with heavy losses. In 1959 it was reported to IHEU in Utrecht: 'The Thinker's Library may be revived, but the RPA is out of the publishing business.' Trying to be positive, it was noted that 'that the publishing aims of the Association have largely been achieved', and the task of the Association now was to 'help to build up a humanist movement'.[55] Notwithstanding that membership started to rise from 2,769 in 1956 to 4,704 in 1966 (70 per cent growth), crisis persisted with a drastic fall in new books being published; the publishing arm, CA Watts – having only been bought by the association in the early 1950s – was sold off (along with much of its copyright in the books) in 1961 at a capital loss of £5,400.[56] To save more money, the RPA took legal opinion on becoming a charity, but the membership was strongly against losing its propaganda role.

Meanwhile, the Progressive League became a 'think tank' for humanist development after 1945, evolving a social-action strategy. It increasingly worked with SPES on joint events and outings, drawing in other organisations – including the ethics-focussed London Personalist Group, set up by Jack Coates in 1945 in emulation of a Dutch movement, which by 1966 still had some seventy members supporting its strategy of tackling 'the greatest crisis of history' by personal reform.[57] The Progressive League's energies were expended mostly upon progressive social policies.[58] Forming a very influential group within the PL were the promoters of sexual education, knowledge and health, who had academic speakers give talks with titles such as 'The role of sex in an advanced civilization'. From the late 1940s, the League was a platform for advocating marriage, divorce and homosexual law reform – a topic on which E. M. Forster spoke to a PL meeting in the wake of the Wolfenden Committee report of 1957.[59] The PL was closely tied to SPES, meeting mostly at Conway Hall, sharing some social activities and combining for several decades in a Joint Philosophy Group, and tied also to the EU which in the 1950s listed the PL and its magazine as part of the humanist community.[60] With 500 members, the PL's work on sexual knowledge and freedoms from 1945 canalised progressive humanist thought that would emerge as legislative plans for the 'liberal hour' of the sixties.[61]

Though unification was failing, greater unity of purpose was emerging in British humanism through such causes. One individual stood out as the great engineer of unity. Harold J. Blackham had joined Stanton Coit at the Ethical Church in 1932, assuming its leadership in 1933, becoming chair of the EU soon after, then secretary from 1944 and also joined SPES in 1937 and the RPA board, making himself available to cross-represent interests on any organisation. Through his diplomatic and non-confrontational style, Blackham (known as H.J. to his friends) established himself as a charismatic figure standing for humanist unity, advancement of key causes in the public sphere and rapprochement with the churches. He quickly set agendas – notably in the promotion of moral education in schools, the emphasis on humanism rather than secularism or atheism, and the internationalisation of the cause. From the 1930s, Blackham's name became stamped all over the British and world humanist movement.

Still, the energy of the Progressive League notwithstanding, there was a general air of inertia in British humanism in the fifties. Organisation, activities and campaigning seemed in many regards little changed since the 1900s, the RPA remained wedded to reprints of books from as early as the 1840s, and intellectualism tended to the vintage. Admittedly, the RPA did engage in the 1950s with the intellectual challenges of the hour with books on existentialism, psychical research and advances in Christian theology. But, in truth, the popular taste had changed and the deep philosophical scholarship approach had a diminishing audience. A return to something like mass sales was hoped for with the retitled *Humanist* in 1956 (retitled again as *New Humanist* in 1972). But magazine readership was always low, with *International Humanism*, printed and published by RPA for IHEU in exchange for a reduction in fees to Utrecht, had only 322 non-paying and 283 paying subscribers in 1962. With something of a boom in other aspects of the humanist movement in the 1960s, one might have expected the number of paying subscribers worldwide by 1967 to have been higher than 318.[62] Reorganisation on its own was clearly not enough.

(c) Boom and bust

After decades of stable but low numbers, British humanism experienced a membership boom in the late 1950s and early 1960s. In the course of this, new demographics in the membership fuelled a changing character to the movement.

The boom was centred on youth. London Young Humanists was founded in October 1964, open to those under thirty-five, meeting twice a month at BHA headquarters at 13 Prince of Wales Terrace in Kensington, and within five months had a membership of fifty, half being teachers or students.[63] In the early 1960s, one in five British humanists were identified as teachers, and in 1965 a Humanist Teachers' Association was formed.[64] The source spring of growth, however, were students, radiating an intellectual yearning shown in new student groups of 1957–67. Humanist intellectuals started to tour the campuses and attracted considerable audiences. A key figure was Margaret Knight, famed in the movement for her two live lectures on 'Morality without Religion' on the BBC Home Service in January 1955 which won national attention primarily for the disparagement and misogyny of the right-wing press and some BBC Religious Affairs staff. For several weeks, Knight was hounded by journalists; she recalled the *Daily Telegraph* especially, which, in three leaders in a week, showed itself in her words 'violently hostile to Humanism and to me', making 'various near-libellous references to me'.[65] Her second broadcast was threatened with cancellation, but fellow-humanist Barbara Wootton (elevated as the first female life peer in 1959) was a member of the BBC Board and threatened to resign, raising the stakes; the BBC director general backed down, and Knight's broadcast went ahead.[66] Knight became hugely in demand among students: in six months in 1957–8, she held university debates at Cambridge, Durham, Liverpool, Edinburgh and Moray House, made two television appearances plus various public debates and humanist addresses in four more cities, the one in her home town Aberdeen attracting 340 people with many turned away. She would claim to have spoken at every British university campus in the years following her radio broadcasts, oftentimes in a debate with a clergyman.[67] In 1961, Knight proposed the motion at Sheffield University Students Union against Bishop Edward Wickham, the bishop of Middleton, that 'This House Does Not Believe in the Christian God'; the vote is not recorded. In the same year, the Cambridge Union voted by 64 to 60 for the motion 'that man created God in his own image'. The year after that, the Oxford University Union passed by 295 votes to 259 the motion 'This House Does Not Believe in God' – a result that attracted considerable press attention.[68]

Though a number of student humanist groups were underway by the late 1950s (including a town-and-gown organisation at Cambridge, founded in 1955 and within two years with over 300 members),[69] the humanist boom reached its height when the Oxford University Humanist Group (OUHG) for students was founded in 1958 by Tony Brierley. It was affiliated with all four main organisations (RPA, EU, SPES and NSS), and Brierley created the UHF. The OUHG mounted a programme of six speakers in winter and spring including Harold Blackham of the EU, Colin McCall of the NSS and mathematician Hyman Levy, and in the years following attracted leading speakers of the cause as well as local academics: Margaret Knight, Barbara Wootton, Francis Crick, Bishop John Robinson and in January 1961 former British fascist leader Oswald Mosley (a memorable income-earner at 2/6d, 12.5 new pence admission). After starting quite philosophical, the Oxford group topics from 1960 moved more towards the zeitgeist of sex and moral culture, with talks on hedonism, prostitution, sin and crime, the law, adultery, the sex war and 'the new morality of sex' (spoken to by James Hemming, later a leading figure in the BHA). The group kept attracting students without faith; a 1960 survey found

27 per cent of members called themselves agnostic, 18 per cent humanist, 14 per cent atheist and 21 per cent Christian. Numbers boomed: 338 members in 1962, peaking at 1,200 in late 1962 and falling to 900 in June 1963 – hailed as the largest undergraduate organisation at the university. It became a campaigning group, leading the 1963 victory in lobbying male students to grant full union membership rights for women. It defended an unmarried woman humanist (a student at Oxford College of Technology) who announced her pregnancy by a male humanist student in the university student newspaper *Isis*, and clashed with a priest, the warden of Keble College, over freedom of sexual codes. Publicity rose several notches in May 1963 when the OUHG opposed the Student Christian Movement's evangelising mission to Oxford, leading David Pollock, ex-president of the OUHG, to write an invited piece in *The Church of England Newspaper* on 'Why I am not a Christian', drawing many objectors' letters. The group's sustained questioning of sex code rules, and championing of widening access to the oral contraceptive pill and abortion, attracted frequent coverage in the UK press during 1962–4.[70] When he went up to Oxford in 1960, Pollock recalled that the changes of the sixties were 'on the horizon but were not spoken about in polite society, and [earlier] it was completely unheard of to be explicitly against religion': 'So,' Pollock continued,

> at that time we were at the cutting edge. The [Humanist] Group was out in the open about all those things, we were exciting. And you could join: all you had to do was to pay your half-crown on the door and you were a member for the term. . . . [W]e became a strong social group, committed. And as it changed over the years, we remained a strong unit.[71]

The OUHG was important for four reasons. First, from 1960 to 1965 humanism attracted large numbers of university students; an *Isis* survey in 1962 found 34 per cent of final-year undergraduates described themselves as humanists, atheists, agnostics or rationalists.[72] Second, the group did much to change the image of humanism – from fusty intellectual philosophising to up-to-the-moment campaigning on new moral issues of gender, sex and race (including apartheid). Third, the group attracted considerable national press publicity that put the churches and universities in the moral firing line in a way rarely seen before – turning the tables, as it were, on normative moral codes, with OUHG submitting evidence to the 1965 Franks Committee on the governance of universities concerning the regulation of sex and consent. Moreover, rising student unrest across the UK contributed much towards parliament lowering the age of consent in 1969 from twenty-one years to eighteen, thus ending the universities' role in loco parentis. By its vigour on contemporary moral issues and designing a sex guide for teenagers in 1964,[73] the Oxford group was among the first to challenge establishment morality in a way that resonated with young people. And fourth, many of those who were student humanists became in the later 1960s members of the BHA and RPA, each of which grew around a third in membership. Because of his success in founding the OUHG, Harold Blackham at the EU offered Tony Brierley a post as group organiser where he worked during 1961–4.[74] When the surge started, there were high hopes that humanism was going to become a mass movement, with the figure of 100,000 members being bandied about as a possible BHA outcome and a membership of 20,000 anticipated by 1968.[75] British humanism seemed to be abuzz, conspicuously at the BHA's 1967 annual conference in Nottingham where revamped procedures and rebranding were unveiled, with an *Observer* magazine photo-shoot article proclaiming that the movement was 'on the verge of its first real breakthrough since Bradlaugh's day'.[76] However, a shock was around the corner.

(d) Humanists and parliament[77]

From the late nineteenth century, individual humanists, rationalists and atheists were to be found in parliament. By the 1960s, Earl Bertrand Russell, Barbara Wootton and Fenner (later Lord) Brockway commanded considerable respect in intellectual circles, and in the nation at large even some right-wing newspapers adored Russell in the 1950s for leading Britain in international intellectualism. Throughout the twentieth century, humanists have always been more numerous (or at least willing to be counted) in the Lords than in the Commons, and were almost entirely Labour with a few Liberals or Liberal Democrats, but rarely including Conservatives. One member of the Commons without religion belonging to a right-wing party described himself in his unpublished memoir as a humanist; Ulster Unionist Harford Montgomery Hyde (1907–89), historian and barrister, MP for Belfast North (1950–9), affirmed rather than took the oath in the House of Commons, but was eventually deselected by his party for campaigning for homosexual law reform and the abolition of capital punishment.[78] But without a Conservative Party humanist willing to step forward, the would-be Humanist Parliamentary Group (HPG) was hamstrung from proclaiming itself to be 'All Party', a status that would have brought key privileges.

A HPG had existed in at least skeletal form since Joseph Reeves MP acted as de facto convenor in the early 1950s – then called the Parliamentary Committee for Freedom of Religious Controversy, which inter alia pressed the BBC to deal with religion as controversial and not merely for agreement.[79] Ad hoc alliances could form in the Commons and the Lords, but there was little organised humanist briefing.[80] But when the British Humanist Association was formed, a working group comprising Joseph Reeves (its first chairman), Harold Blackham and David Pollock took on the task in January 1965 of trying to form a more formal HPG with John Parker MP arranging the first meeting. Mindful of avoiding jeopardy to BHA's charitable status, seventy-one MPs and Lords were invited to meet the BHA committee for tea in the House of Commons in June 1965, but only five attended. Yet, from this small beginning, the slow work of establishing a group proceeded.[81] David Pollock took the lead, with an initial focus on opposing an

Education Bill that proposed government subsidy for voluntary-aided, mostly church schools to be raised from 75 per cent to 80 per cent. It led Dr David Kerr MP to attract seventeen Labour MPs to sign an amendment in favour of 'the right of all men and women to follow their own faith'; in moving this on 4 November 1966, Kerr referred to 'the right of some people to follow none of the recognised faiths but to adhere to a material faith which is generally described as humanism or secularism'. Though rejected by Tony Crosland, secretary of state for education, the eighteen signatories laid down the first concerted humanist action in the British Parliament.[82] From this, the BHA made contact with a wider group of Labour MPs, including new arrivals after the 1966 general election, and prepared the ground for humanist lobbying on what became the Abortion Act of 1967.

To avoid compromising any BHA claim to charitable status, David Pollock formed Humanist Lobby in 1965 as an independent organisation for lobbying parliament. Within a year, subscriber numbers for the briefings created a large mailing operation, increasing again in 1967 when all BHA members were invited to sign up, leading to a part-time clerk being employed. As a result of Humanist Lobby mailing on abortion, between 300 and 400 responses were received and passed to the Abortion Law Reform Association, thereby aiding the passage of this key progressive act.[83] Within months, contact was made with Leo Abse MP concerning humanist support for his divorce law reform proposals, with an inaugural meeting involving the NSS, though accompanied by the continued problem of finding a non-Labour MP to establish a cross-party HPG; a Marriage Law Reform Committee was also briefly formed involving Abse, A. J. Ayer, Pollock and others.[84] In early 1968, the range of issues the HPG became involved in rose, including BBC religious broadcasting, moral education and bishops in the House of Lords. Key parliamentary individuals joined in – Peter Jackson MP (the secretary of the group), David Kerr MP (its chair), Will Hamling MP and, from the House of Lords, Lord Ritchie Calder, Lord Ted Willis (already president of the Humanist Housing Association), Lord Chorley, Lord Fenner Brockway and others. The range of topics widened as the new Labour backbenchers were introduced to policies by the BHA and found common cause with radicals in the Lords – though some complained that the association presented humanism as 'a complete attitude to life, not merely a reaction to religion'.[85] With a few parliamentarians joining the group on a casual basis, this process winkled out humanists in the Commons and the Lords and led to MPs being introduced to key humanists, including at a dinner with Ayer in December 1968.[86] But with Labour losing the general election in 1970, things quickly stalled. HPG activity was reduced as key MPs were lost or retired – notably the chair and secretary David Kerr and Peter Jackson – and by mid-1971 HPG had stopped operating. In March 1973, a joint initiative to revive it by Pollock and Barbara Smoker (then representing the NSS) bore little fruit, and further loss of humanist supporters in the Commons after the 1974 general election (including Will Hamling MP, the HPG convenor until promoted in Harold Wilson's government) undermined the operation of the Humanist Parliamentary Group.

PETER RITCHIE CALDER 1906–82

FIGURE 12 Peter Ritchie Calder. Photo: ©NPG.

One of the key humanist journalists, Peter Ritchie Calder was responsible for a constant flow of articles over many decades concerning science, humanism and internationalism. Working up from Dundee's DC Thomson Press, he was invited as a member of the Tots and Quots science dining club in the late 1930s, keeping the club secret but developing a taste for science stories. Chosen as science editor of *News Chronicle*, he became a close friend to John Boyd Orr and a great publicist of the latter's ideas for a humanist future to world government and food supply. He was appointed by the wartime government as director of Plans and Campaigns in the Political Warfare Executive, in charge of much of the propaganda effort. In 1945, a keen socialist and humanist, he returned to being science editor at *News Chronicle* and joined fellow-humanist Kingsley Martin at the *New Statesman*. Like Martin, he was an ardent advocate of peace as president of the National Peace Council and a leader of CND. In 1953 he broke the news to the world of the discovery in Cambridge of the double-helix shape of DNA. Despite his lack of formal education, in 1961 he was appointed as a chair of International Relations at the University of Edinburgh; with a laid-back manner, students liked him, and he was awarded several academic honours, and considered for a university vice-chancellorship in the commonwealth. Made a life peer in 1966, he was much travelled on internationalist missions; *The Humanist* observed of him: 'He has studied the fight against famine and disease on the spot in some of the blackest areas. Indeed, trying to locate him is like tracking a human satellite. If you want to reach him on the telephone the chances are he is in the Arctic, or in the middle of the Sahara.' He was a signatory to the Humanist Manifesto II of 1973 and to the Secular Humanist Declaration of 1980.

The BHA had been enthusiastic about Pollock's initiative in Humanist Lobby and the HPG,[87] but things clearly went wrong. First, a number of progressive issues attracted new Labour MPs of the 1966 intake – abortion, marriage (and divorce) law reform, and homosexuality – but seemed exhausted by 1970, whilst other issues, like religious and moral education and the BBC, seemed less likely to succeed in parliament, narrowing effort to defending the existing gains (especially abortion) against right-wing Christian backlash. Second, the turnover of MPs was rapid during 1964–74, when there were five general elections and three changes of government, meaning little time to nurture relationships with new MPs, leaving humanists in the Lords as a more stable though less powerful group. Third, the failure to get more non-Labour MPs into the group was a difficulty, endangering BHA by appearing party-political. Fourth, the attempt to get the BHA and NSS to cooperate in parliamentary lobbying had failed – despite the fact that many of the individuals on either side were members of both organisations. There was a fundamental difference in approach, summarised in a 1967 letter from David Pollock to Peter Jackson MP: 'Relations between the BHA and the NSS have not been good in the past: we have been subject to "sniping" from them [NSS] for our willingness to cooperate with or even talk to Christians, and I think we have annoyed them more by ignoring them than any positive provocation.'[88] This was neither a new problem nor was it readily solved. But it did mean that coordination and professional organisation were both going to be needed in abundance. Part of the dispute was between attacking or compromising with religion. Reflecting how humanism should sit inside the British political system, Peter Ritchie Calder, elevated to a life peerage in 1966 and a member of the HPG, got to 'thinking aloud' in a letter in 1968:

I emphatically believe that humanism should be <u>for</u> and not <u>anti</u>. I think that it is a futile exercise to go on attacking the churches because they are debunking themselves very thoroughly. Humanism, not the churches, can provide the moral values for which the younger generation is searching in the modern world. But it cannot do so by setting up another Establishment, with the rational alternatives to the Thirty-Nine Articles. And therefore I am very chary when I see humanists trying to spell out doctrines to which humanists are supposed to subscribe. We are liberating ideas, not prescribing them. We want people to think for themselves.

'May I hastily add', Ritchie Calder wrote to avoid misunderstanding, 'that I am not backsliding into godfulness and I am not a quitter. I believe in militant humanism and I am glad that B.H.A. is vigorous.'[89] In the event, it would be more than thirty years before the HPG was to function effectively again.

7 SCIENCE, UTOPIANISM AND INTERNATIONALISM

Despite the impact of world recession and the two world wars, the middle decades of the twentieth century were a high point for humanism. Initially constructed upon the influence of scientists in national and international affairs, driving them was an updating of utopian ethicist dreams into practical, real-world solutions to a divided, nationalistic and imperialist planet. Internationalism – the drive to unify the world in benign cooperation and government – acquired realisable goals, and it was from British humanism of these years that the intellectual leadership emerged.

(a) Utopianism

H. G. Wells (1866–1946) was already a national hero of literature by the 1930s. He was a celebrity; his novels were widely read around the world and many being adapted into films. But Wells was also a major publicist for science, regarding it as a vehicle for social change. He advocated the creation of a utopia – a benevolent, science-driven world government, based on the League of Nations, transmogrified into something more powerful, more moral and humanist-inspired. Among his four books to RPA's Thinker's Library series, in *What Are We to Do with Our Lives?* (1935) he laid out a blueprint for an 'open conspiracy' that might reach the proverbial 'man in the street' and stir him to participation in creating utopia.[1] Like Julian Huxley, who shared an idea for a 'religion of humanism' to fill the gaps of both religion and the absence of religion with a sense of awe regarding nature and the universe,[2] Wells was impelled to write scores of books and essays on his ethical dream, emerging as the principal inspiration to nonreligionists from the 1920s to the 1940s. Wells was an optimist: 'As yet we are hardly in the earliest dawn of human greatness.'[3]

Wells' 'open conspiracy', first broached in a 1927 novel and then in an eponymous book of 1928,[4] was to be driven by elite professionals in science, medicine, social science and psychology, working together not as one organisation but as a 'large, loose assimilatory mass of movements, groups and societies',[5] planning the elevation of humankind to a state of perpetual peace, justice and productivity. This conspiracy would overturn religion's oppressive power against which he had railed in *The Outline of History* (1921). He publicised his idea internationally (in speeches at the Sorbonne and the Reichstag in 1929) and among British political elites (including two former prime ministers) and inspired major humanist figures Bertrand Russell, Julian Huxley and Cyril Joad. On receiving a copy of *Conspiracy*, Russell wrote to Wells that he did 'not know of anything with which I agree more entirely'.[6] He did have some detractors, including J. M. Robertson, who in 1925 critiqued Wells' tendency to romantic utopias.[7]

When the League of Nations was founded in 1920, Wells demanded a better one – a real 'world government' offering benign and principled rule. Like many humanists initially inspired by Hobson's anti-imperialism of 1902, Wells talked with independence movements emerging in the British Empire, especially in India, seeing vividly 'the tremendous failure of the British Imperial system', and leading to his excoriating contempt: 'No race is fit to have the upper hand over any other race; the possession of the upper hand leads at best to an inconsiderate self-righteousness and at the worst to an extreme contempt, injustice and cruelty'.[8] He refined domestic policies for a righteous social polity to promote human freedoms, efficiency and an end to poverty. The Ethical Union and the South Place Ethical Society became centres for discussing how to plan his fairer nation and world, with leading humanists giving talks at Conway Hall – including John Boyd Orr on food policy during the depression. And as historian Emily Robinson has noted, Wells played the role of unofficial contact for self-identified 'progressives', some of whom were part of political ventures like the New Britain Movement but also those of fascist Oswald Mosley.[9]

Rising to Wells' call, Cyril Joad and Jack Coates in 1931 initiated through the RPA journal *Literary Guide* the formation of the Federation of Progressive Societies and Individuals (FPSI) – from 1940 known as the Progressive League (PL).[10] Until the 1970s, the FPSI and PL constituted an important intellectual limb of the humanist movement, promoting a scientific humanism on the model advocated by Wells, Huxley and Russell. In 1936 the FPSI absorbed 123 people from another organisation, Cosmopolis (originally the H. G. Wells Society), but an attempt to dominate the SPES executive committee (dubbed by some as 'the Conway Hall Plot') failed.[11] The FPSI remained separate under Cyril Joad's leadership, supported by a millionaire American atheist patron, Pryns

Hopkins (1885–1970),[12] whilst Wells renewed the call for his 'Open Conspiracy' or an 'X Society' in the *New Statesman* in 1932.[13] Though one scholar thinks Wells was drifting in the 1930s from the conspiracy idea towards fascism,[14] the Progressive and human rights movements he inspired were certainly not. With around 600 members, many of them from the South Place Ethical Society, the PL played a key part, holding regular meetings at Conway Hall and annual summer conferences in the countryside where progressive academics – many Fabians like Barbara Wootton – offered perspectives on the future, with the reports appearing in the Progressives' newsletter *Plan*.[15] Throughout the 1930s and 1940s, the PL was strongly anti-fascist in sentiment, warning of the dark future for Europe: 'Over a large part of Europe the movement of decivilisation proceeds apace. The values which, in the course of centuries, man has come slowly to recognise, tolerance and humanity and the free play of the individual mind, are openly denied.'[16] At a meeting at Conway Hall in November 1937, humanist Kingsley Martin, in a talk on 'Armageddon Here and Now', analysed what he called 'the present world war', attacking (as his Special Branch surveillance observer transcribed it) the Catholic Church and the de facto support it gained from Dr Goebbels and the Nazi state: 'By reasons of its nature and organisation the papacy is bound to oppose the principles of Liberty, Equality and Fraternity promulgated in 1789.'[17] Martin was to deploy the *New Statesman* during his editorship from 1931 to 1960 as a mouthpiece for many humanist causes whilst forging humanist reformers into effective campaign networks. One inspired was Bertrand Russell who, by the early 1920s, had prioritised 'the spread of the scientific temper' – not science knowledge, but ways of researching and knowing that might regenerate humankind. Religion was larger in his sights than with some humanists, regarding its greatest crime, according to one historian, to be instilling fear.[18] He declared himself to the South Place audience in Finsbury in 1922 'a dissenter from all known religions, and I hope that every kind of religious belief will die out'. He had a 'will to doubt', and urged the benefits of having no dogmatic opinion but seeing 'a tentatively agnostic frame of mind' as the cure to nine-tenths of the evil of the world.[19]

So, old-fangled secularist rhetoric still remained as humanism started to fly in its halcyon decades.

(b) Science, the A-bomb and the humanist network

The mid-twentieth century marked a pinnacle of British intellectual attainment in the Western world. The nation played host to a very large number of scientists, philosophers and polymaths, an astonishingly high proportion of them humanists, who, until the 1970s, indulged in a ferment of intellectual networking and innovation.[20]

The humanist intellectual network was composed of around sixty individuals, the vast majority men, around two-thirds of them scientists. Largely an informal grouping, what brought the network together, and rendered the members morally active, were the South Place Ethical Society, the RPA, the Ethical Union and after it the BHA. One tiny but extraordinarily influential organisation also contributed – the Tots and Quots dining club running from 1932 to 1947, set up and managed by Dr Solly Zuckerman of the University of Birmingham, comprising not more than twenty members at a time, each nominated by an existing member and accepted by at least three-quarters of the group. Just over half were scientists, but it included a sociologist, an economist and a journalist. Meeting eight times a year usually in one of two Soho restaurants (Jardins des Gourmets or the Cafe Royal), for an evening of dining and debate with special guests upon a particular theme, the members were almost entirely left-leaning in politics. Key humanists in the club were Peter (later Lord), Ritchie Calder (science journalist), Lancelot Hogben (mathematician and biologist), J. B. S. (Jack) Haldane (geneticist), Kingsley Martin, Julian Huxley (zoologist) and Joseph Needham (biochemist and sinologist). More humanists appeared as dinner guests, including H. G. Wells and A. J. Ayer, both American and Soviet ambassadors to London, and at least one American army general.[21] Because the club allowed members to invite colleagues, it discussed new projects and the science agenda, including scientific support for the USSR when it joined the Allies in 1941.[22]

The network of humanists, beyond and inside the dining club, pivoted on six people: Julian Huxley, Bertrand Russell, H. G. Wells till his death in 1946, Kingsley Martin, nuclear physicist Joseph Rotblat, and the economist, criminologist and sociologist Barbara Wootton. In the late 1930s and 1940s Huxley became a leading proponent of science education and installing scientific advisers in governments, including in the League of Nations, and then from 1945 in UNESCO of which, when formally constituted in 1947, Huxley became the first director general. Given Huxley's earlier role as director of London Zoo, it was little surprise that UNESCO's first headquarters in the Hotel Majestic in Paris, with its babel of languages, was dubbed 'Doctor Huxley's Wonderful Zoo'. Huxley, and after him key UN and UNESCO staff, used science as the foundation for a Wellsian 'One World' culture of 'universal values', binding elites and people in common harmony – albeit a culture grounded in Huxley's Victorian conceptions of race laid out in a book *We Europeans*.[23] Huxley recruited other Tots and Quots, including Joseph Needham, who spent the war years advancing science in China, advertising it in London with talks to SPES at Conway Hall, and, when Huxley appointed him head of science at UNESCO, Needham created UN science centres around the world.[24] The humanist network scientists covered all sorts of specialisms – genetics (Haldane), biology (J.

D. Bernal), mathematics (Jacob Bronowski), nutrition (John Boyd Orr) and physics (including Patrick Blackett and Rotblat). These were world leading figures, and, from the names mentioned so far, four won Nobel prizes (Russell, Rotblat, Boyd Orr and Blackett). The network also extended overseas, where British intellectuals of the period were in much demand. But the network had its moments of viperous rejection. Having been invited by academic colleagues to the chair of philosophy at the College of the City of New York in 1940, Bertrand Russell was ejected from it by the New York Supreme Court amid a shrill cacophony of accusations – about Russell's atheism, nihilism, sexual promiscuity, lustfulness, eroto-mania, nudism, communism, anarchism and a lot else – conducted by an episcopal bishop, various Roman Catholics, press commentators and Mayor Fiorello La Guardia (who cut Russell's funds). Quoting Gibbon, this was described in *The Humanist* as 'the triumph of barbarism over civilization'.[25]

The other third of the humanist network comprised various professions. There were five journalists – Martin, Ritchie Calder, Jimmy Crowther (secretary general of the World Federation of Scientific Workers), proto-humanist C. R. (Bill) Hewitt (penname C. H. Rolph) and broadcaster Ludovic Kennedy. There were anthropologists (Tom Harrisson, Francis Huxley), a lawyer (Glanville Williams), doctors and psychologists (Dugald Baird, Eustace Chesser), several philosophers (Ayer, Bernard Williams, Cyril Joad) and writers (as well as Wells, E. M. Forster, George Bernard Shaw and J. B. Priestley). There were a few members of parliament – Ramsey MacDonald, Joseph Reeves, Douglas Houghton, Kenneth Robinson and Lena Jeger, all Labour; and Simon Wingfield Digby, a Conservative. There were capable and committed volunteers, dedicated to humanist causes – Barbara Smoker, Diane Munday, Madeleine Simms and many others. And presiding over the ensemble cast was humanist leader Harold J. Blackham, the strategist and conduit for speakers for conferences and meetings, putting people in touch with people and diverting volunteers and donations to where they were needed.

This group of the all-talents contrived to make people alive to science and rationality and to get them thinking ethically about their world. There were many successful humanist campaigns in these years (and we will come to these), but one of the most impressive did not succeed: the campaign against nuclear weapons. As early as a 1939 lecture, Bertrand Russell was attributed by astronomer Sir Fred Hoyle with having perceived what would become the doctrine of 'mutually assured destruction' – the stand-off between superpowers with technologically advanced weapons.[26] Fear of war among humanist scientists was widespread, focussed on the grave death tolls likely with 'advances' like area bombing, yet many joined the fight against fascism from the mid-1930s and were then recruited to the war effort. MI5 were so convinced that brilliant scientist, atheist and Marxist J. B. S. Haldane (1892–1964) was a Soviet agent that, when he designed a cheap and hugely effective family bomb shelter (far more effective than the Anderson shelter), the design was unaccountably blocked.[27] Others joined nuclear bomb research. One was Joseph Rotblat (1908–2005), who quit the Manhattan Project in 1944 when its Los Alamos scientists were told by the Americans (based on British intelligence) that Germany was not on a pathway to a bomb.[28] This was a moral turning point for Rotblat, who realised that the A-bomb could likely be used as a first-strike weapon against nations without it and would inevitably cause vast civilian casualties. Rotblat returned to Britain, was appointed at the University of Liverpool, then retrained in medical physics and moved to the University of London's Barts Hospital – according to his biographer, an ethical move that he felt certain could do lasting good, leading to his new research in cancer treatment.[29] But he got drawn into the impact of nuclear weapons upon the human body. His war work led him, along with Jacob Bronowski, to assess Hiroshima and Nagasaki after the A-bombs. But the British state became concerned with Rotblat's criticism of the bomb when, in 1946–8, he led the Atomic Scientists Association's 'Atom Train' that toured Britain publicising the real dangers of nuclear weapons. In 1954, newspaper accounts alerted him that the first American thermonuclear (hydrogen bomb) test at Bikini Atoll caused radiation injuries and one death in the crew of a Japanese fishing boat a long way from the explosion site. He realised that British and American nuclear establishments were understating the longevity and ferocity of nuclear fallout, and, remarkably, slipped through the security net to appear on a BBC television *Panorama* programme to explain what was going on – instigating the Ethical Union among others to lobby the government to call upon the UN to ban further production and testing of the H-bomb.[30] Rotblat wasn't the only humanist scientist to do this. The Oxford Committee for the Abolition of Nuclear Weapons organised its first public event in the autumn of 1955 with a 'Brains Trust' in the Town Hall involving four scientists: humanist Jacob Bronowski and proto-humanist Richard Doll (discoverer of the link between tobacco and cancer), evolutionist John Maynard-Smith (biologist, and student of Haldane), and atheist humanitarian Antoinette (Tony) Pirie (biochemist and ophthalmologist); the event was under MI5 surveillance.[31] In 1957 Pirie, a vigorous opponent of nuclear weapons, demonstrated conclusively with seven scientific colleagues the deceit of the UK and US governments regarding radiation fallout and its impact upon humans.

Meanwhile, Rotblat in 1954 had issued his own research work on the fallout and was approached by Bertrand Russell, who, on reading the scientific results, converted immediately to oppose nuclear weapons, dedicating his life to trumpeting this message. Together, Rotblat and Russell organised a manifesto of eleven nuclear scientists, often inaccurately called the Russell-Einstein Manifesto of July 1955, which declared that the human race was in peril and required an international meeting of scientists to advise the world. Also influential, the first Congress the International Humanist and Ethical Union (IHEU) in 1952 had called for a scientists-led conference that would confront the impending nuclear fears and oppose the big political actors of the Cold War.[32] All bar one of the 1955 Manifesto group were Nobel prize winners, and seven of the eleven were humanists: Russell, president of the RPA from 1955; Albert Einstein, honorary associate of the RPA, who signed the Manifesto just days before his death; Rotblat; Hermann Muller (1890–1967), president of the American Humanist Association 1956–8; Linus C. Pauling (1901–94) of CalTech, an extremely influential humanist scientist, co-founder of the International League of Humanists in 1974; Max Born (1882–1970), physicist based 1936–52 at the University of Edinburgh, and a British subject 1939–52, described as a 'strident atheist'; and Frederic Jolito-Curie (1900–58), a French humanist.[33] All of the humanist signatories were Nobel prize winners: Russell (1950 for Literature), Rotblat (1995, Peace), Muller (1946, Physiology or Medicine), Pauling (1954, Chemistry), Born (1952, Physics), Bridgman (1946, Physics) and Jolio-Curie (1935, Chemistry).[34] In combination, the Manifesto and Rotblat's charge of high radiation fallout against the Americans drove the move for consolidated scientific opposition to nuclear weapons.[35] This led to CND and to Pugwash.

After Britain exploded its own H-bomb in May 1957, a momentum of left-wing and humanist debate culminated in an article by J. B. Priestley in *New Statesman* advocating unilateral nuclear disarmament: 'a declaration to the world that after a certain date one power able to engage in nuclear warfare will reject the evil thing for ever.'[36] Kingsley Martin called a meeting at his house attended by four humanists (Martin, Russell, Priestley and Patrick Blackett), then another meeting at Canon John Collins' rooms near St Paul's at which the Campaign for Nuclear Disarmament (CND) was launched. The executive committee was over half humanist: Kingsley, Rotblat, Calder, Priestley and Russell (the CND president), the first three ex-members of the Tots and Quots club. Rotblat meanwhile became the moving force behind the Pugwash Science and World Affairs conferences, an international group of scientists seeking 'a world free of nuclear weapons and other weapons of mass destruction',[37] which first met in July 1957 at the home of a Canadian humanist and investment banker, Cyrus Eaton, in his Nova Scotia village of Pugwash.[38] Rotblat and the Pugwash Conference organisation went on to share (50/50) the Nobel Peace Prize in 1995 'for their efforts to diminish the part played by nuclear arms in international politics and, in the longer run, to eliminate such arms.'[39] Though less well known than Russell, Huxley or the American humanist scientist Hermann Muller, Rotblat contributed the organising zeal and ability for both the Manifesto and Pugwash, and much of the moral imperative behind the disarmament movement. On his ninetieth birthday he stated: 'My short-term goal is the abolition of nuclear weapons, and my long-term goal is the abolition of war.'[40] Pugwash became almost annual conferences (sixty-three in total by 2020) at changing venues around the world.

CND was the popular counterbalance to Pugwash elitism, and, as Nicholas Barnett has recently argued, the underrated product of a genuine mass movement.[41] It was an organisation representing a large following with its own ethical motivation, disproportionately weighted to the nonreligious. A contemporary left-wing magazine *Perspective* undertook a 10 per cent sample survey on the second major Aldermaston march of 1959, finding only 34 per cent professed a religious faith (and 90 per cent supporting the cause on moral grounds); Parkin in 1965 found that only 40 per cent claimed to be religious and 34 per cent atheist (way above the societal proportion); and Taylor and Prichard in 1980 gauged retrospectively the religious proportion at 41 per cent.[42] However, Bertrand Russell regarded CND from 1960 as stultifying under an inactive Christian formalism led by Canon Collins, leading him to create a partner body, the Committee of 100 (C100), which used civil disobedience – albeit largely symbolic 'sit-downs' in Whitehall and environs.[43] In a fourth study using an intimate life-story-based approach, Samantha Carroll found little evidence of a strong religious element in the Committee of 100: of twenty-four interviewed by Carroll, eighteen (75 per cent) had no religious direction from parents, four (17 per cent) were nominally Anglican, and one was religious in later life. After noting the absence of even a Quaker influence among her twenty-four, she concluded: 'it is clear that C100 members overall were a very irreligious group.' One of them was humanist journalist and anarchist Nicolas Walter, a member of the Spies for Peace group, imprisoned in 1966 for indecency in a church for shouting 'hypocrite' at Prime Minister Harold Wilson.[44] Carroll has also shown that CND comprised fearless campaigners, willing to take risks to expose the British government's secret nuclear war planning with its morally repugnant strategy of engineering the governing classes' survival whilst ordinary people would perish.[45]

So, British nonreligionists trooped to the cause of nuclear disarmament. Those without religion made up just under half of CND and C100, yet the awareness of this was poor at the time. Barbara Smoker explained to us that on the early Aldermaston marches she observed significant numbers of the nonreligious people she knew, but none bearing a humanist identity, instead bearing banners of the Labour movement. Accordingly, she wrote herself a banner: 'I think it was in 1962, there was an official photograph taken on CND Easter march which included my homemade banner.' Published on the cover of *The Humanist* (see next page), the editor Hector Hawton reported that it aroused opposition from some readers.[46] But Smoker felt that opposition to nuclear weapons became more widespread among humanists as time passed and vindicated her commitment.

JUNE 1962   ONE SHILLING

The Humanist

A RATIONAL APPROACH TO THE MODERN WORLD

HUMANIST AND SECULARIST CONTINGENTS IN THE ALDERMASTON MARCH

ROBERT BENDINER   **OUR RIGHT NOT TO BELIEVE**
GIANNI BARTOCCI   **BIOGRAPHY OF THE DEVIL**
REPORT OF THE UNIVERSITY HUMANIST FEDERATION CONFERENCE

FIGURE 13 Humanist Aldermaston march, 1962, featured on the cover of *The Humanist*. Photo: Rationalist Association/Bishopsgate Archive.

It was extraordinary how quickly humanist scientists came out against nuclear weapons and organised the movement on intellectual, popular and medical fronts. The medical researchers changed the name of the game by demonstrating the lethality of nuclear fallout. The security services MI5 and FBI worried from 1944 onwards whether Rotblat was a traitor and might pass knowledge to the USSR or even defect (by absconding with a plane that he had learned to fly). By deciding that the United States' lead on atomic and thermonuclear weapons between 1944 and 1955 constituted a temptation, perhaps an inevitability, to superiority in world diplomacy, Rotblat's leaving of nuclear physics was defecting to the side of the victims – a move he shared with Jacob Bronowski and Antionette Pirie. Those three led to the birth of the study of human anatomy of radiation fallout, making that medical sub-discipline and that of physiological impact (in which J. D. Bernal and Zuckerman pioneered)[47] in the eyes of MI5, state secrets.

JACOB BRONOWSKI 1908–74

FIGURE 14 Jacob Bronowski (right) with Hermann Bondi, BHA president 1980–99. Photo: Charles Edridge/Humanists UK/Bishopsgate Archive.

Jacob Bronowski was one of three humanists to be separately and coincidently tasked by the British military to visit Hiroshima and Nagasaki to assess the impact of atomic bombs. These were formative experiences, turning humanist scientists from bomb-making – especially as concerned the second-generation thermonuclear (hydrogen) bombs – to campaigning for nuclear disarmament. But Bronowski had worked during the war using his advanced mathematical skills (he was Senior Wrangler – top of his year at Cambridge) to improve the bombing of Germany, the area bombing version being now regarded by some as on the same ethical spectrum as nuclear devices. Not surprisingly, Bruno, as he was intimately known, moved after the war out of military research and into the ethics of science. He had vast choices before him, being a polymath of stupendous ability – theatre director, poet, mathematician, research organiser, physicist and biological scientist. By 1950 he was already a famous speaker on the radio and television versions of the *Brains Trust* alongside Julian Huxley and Barbara Wootton, and he made a famous radio broadcast describing the detonation of the first hydrogen bomb at Bikini Atoll. But he chose to work as research director of the National Coal Board, in which job his MI5 misclassification as a security risk reduced what technology he could see. He carried this baggage likely for the rest of his career, but, a man of ridiculous talent, he conquered the arts and sciences. Besides his later research achievements, the BBC selected him in 1969 to make a landmark documentary TV series, *The Ascent of Man*, in which he used history training acquired at MIT in 1953 to construct a complex story of how humanity distinctively overpowered religious oppression to combine science and culture. Born a Jew in Łódź, he spent the post-war decades recoiling from multiple holocausts, one of a special generation developing an ethical approach to science, and becoming a celebrated figure in Conway Hall and the British humanist movement.

The recent opening of MI5 personal files of British scientists and intellectuals, suspected between the 1930s and the late 1950s of contemplating passing scientific secrets to the USSR, reveals the extent of surveillance of humanists. One example will serve. Jacob Bronowski (1908–74), humanist, mathematician and polymath, had his MI5 file opened to the public reading in the early 2010s, and his daughter, Professor Lisa Jardine, read it first, leading to a Conway Hall lecture in which she described being flabbergasted at the branding of her father as a communist, and at the intrusiveness – the relentless pursuit by self-appointed citizen-spies and an anti-Semitic police constable, hell bent on disparaging him.[48] Her surprise was justified. A close examination of her father's two files (the second opened since Jardine's perusal) shows that there was no evidence of him being a communist.[49] First accused by an anonymous Hull teacher of being 'a skilful speaker and agitator of the "Communist intellectual" type, a disseminator of seditious doctrines' and of being a 'Red' on the basis of his book collection, MI5's head 'K' passed surveillance to Hull city police, whose constable attended a meeting where Bronowski spoke with 'quite a noticeable percentage of Jews', a Jewish Lance Corporal in battle dress, a woman of Jewish appearance, a Royal Navy officer who was a known troublemaker, plus a solitary local communist, and noted down Bronowski as saying that he was prepared to collaborate with communists on points with which he had sympathy. This led to a new MI5 file summary branding him succinctly: 'Bronowski, Jacob . . . Lecturer in Mathematics at the Hull University College. Communist'. From that point in 1942, Bronowski was clandestinely prohibited from secret work, employers were warned he might pass secrets to the USSR, he lost a 1947 post at the Atomic Energy Commission and the American embassy was advised of his 'readiness to collaborate with Communists', condemning him to be refused entry to the United States. He knew nothing of this surveillance and communist branding, which lasted throughout the 1950s. Without any evidence, this renowned polymath and a stout supporter of the humanist cause remained condemned as a communist by MI5. Bronowski was likely not the only victim of false accusation, for at least twenty, likely closer to thirty, leading humanists were under MI5 and Special Branch surveillance during 1932–58, and including in the 1950s the building at 13 Prince of Wales Terrace that then housed the offices of the Ethical Union.

Notwithstanding, the threat of nuclear war featured large in humanist campaigns. The work of CND faltered somewhat, in part because, as humanists and radicals saw it, the Christian churches lost a willingness to protest with even a modicum of pressure. The president of CND, Bertrand Russell, was persuaded by his radical friends, and notably his private secretary Ralph Schoenman, to establish the Committee of 100 as a separate radical organisation. However, Schoenman turned out to have been one of several Trotskyist entryists set to target the humanist movement around Russell with a revolutionary stratagem. One young Trotskyist was directed to infiltrate CND, taking part in the first Aldermaston march at Easter 1958, and in 1961 infiltrating C100, sitting down in Downing Street beside Russell.[50] Bertrand Russell was also targeted in the later 1960s when the International Group (IG), the Trotskyist predecessor of the International Marxist Group, recruited Russell as one of the sponsors for its bulletin sheet *The Week*, and in 1965 infiltrated two more members to work on his International War Crimes Tribunal; this, inter alia, investigated American war crimes in the Vietnam War, and intensified both CIA and MI6 interest in Russell.[51] Additionally, it is reported that Russell was recruited to support the IG-sponsored Vietnam Solidarity Campaign in 1966, with its director, Ralph Schoenman, also acting as Russell's personal secretary and executive director of the Bertrand Russell Peace Foundation.[52] By these seemingly duplicitous ruses, among others, humanism became initially exploited by Marxists in the late 1960s and then side-lined as much of moral radicalism escaped from humanist grasp in the next decade.

The best-known manifestations of the Committee of 100, formed in 1960 under Russell's leadership but Schoenman's alleged direction, were sit-downs in Whitehall and 10 Downing Street. And there Russell's work might have drawn little notice. Then, on 22 October 1961, President John F Kennedy declared a blockade of Cuba because a US aircraft had spotted missiles on the deck of a Russian freighter and missile sites on the island. It was feared that these were nuclear-tipped missiles that would easily strike the American mainland. This triggered Russell's intervention in the Cuban missile crisis. When the United States challenged the USSR over the missiles, world tension escalated, and Russell wrote a challenging statement to the press that was to have warned: 'Mankind is faced tonight with a grave crisis.' However, Schoenman scored out that sentence and replaced it with 'It seems likely that within a week you will be dead to please American madmen'. Meanwhile, Russell cabled missives urging caution to President John F Kennedy and Nikita Khrushchev, as well as appeals to UN secretary general U Thant and British prime minister Harold Macmillan. Two days later, Khrushchev replied to Russell's cable on Moscow Radio, and suddenly Russell's home at Penrhyndeudraeth in North Wales became the hub of media frenzy. The Khrushchev reply was read by Russell as a conciliatory act, and he cabled Kennedy to act accordingly and cabled Fidel Castro to get him to start dismantling the missiles; however, Russell's biographer discusses whether Schoenman was actually the author of these. With further cables for Russell, Khrushchev announced in twenty-four hours that the USSR was willing to remove its missiles from Cuba. In an exchange of letters with fellow-humanist Max Born, Russell was accused of blaming Kennedy for his 'illegal' moves in the episode. Russell was under no illusion that he had done anything to change the course of history and was probably no more than a bit player in these manoeuvres. But he publicised an ethically informed, real public fear about nuclear weapons and wondered too about being manipulated by his private secretary.[53]

Russell featured in an even more high-profile but ultimately painful undertaking. Having resigned in September 1963 from a disintegrating C100 (on which only four people remained by February 1963), he established the Bertrand Russell Peace Foundation, accepting Ralph Schoenman as its effective chief executive, despite pleas from fellow workers to Russell to fire him. The Foundation carried on some effective work for several years in third-world nations and in eastern Europe, but it was to the Vietnam War Russell turned, launching in 1966 his International War Crimes Tribunal, chaired by Jean-Paul Sartre, to try the United States for war crimes. Condemned by the right-wing press of both Britain and the USA, the tribunal was anything but neutral, sending Schoenman to North Vietnam to hunt for evidence of American atrocities, investigating only America's offences and pre-judging the verdicts. The tribunal's affairs fell into a chaos of biased rhetoric, delivering its judgement when Russell was ninety-five and falling ill. He had to withdraw from all projects and two years later finally sacked Schoenman; after his death, a battle erupted between Russell's supporters and Schoenman, and a Russell memorandum was posthumously published in which he wrote that 'Ralph must be well established in megalomania.'[54] Despite some support from American humanists, the chaos of the tribunal placed the Foundation as a whole in a very poor light, the embarrassment being, in biographer Ronald Clark's judgement, due to Schoenman. Neither Russell nor Clark knew that Schoenman was an entryist and the whole episode a Trotskyist imbroglio. On the brighter side, Russell's tribunal inaugurated a long tradition of people's tribunals in various nations – Latin America, West Germany, the United States and over Japan's military sexual slavery during the Second World War – signalling the enduring appeal of justice in the most trying circumstances.[55]

Science, nuclear weaponry and imperialism reacted together as a phenomenal stimulus to the British humanist movement. If conscientious objection inaugurated activism in many in the 1910s and 1940s, collective action to divert the world from a concatenation of world disasters elevated the stakes. But this was only one route to ethical relevance.

(c) The human rights movement

Three weeks after Britain declared war on Germany in September 1939, H. G. Wells wrote to *The Times* newspaper of the dangers of repeating the Great War's failure to deliver a better future for mankind: 'The League of Nations, we can all admit now, was a poor and ineffective outcome of that revolutionary proposal to banish armed conflict from the world and inaugurate a new life for mankind.' He advocated a new candour in discussing 'a real Federation of Mankind, a genuine attempt to realize that phase of world-wide plenty and safety that we have every reason to suppose attainable', leading to 'a profound reconstruction of the methods of human living'.[56] Widely debated and published overseas, this piece was followed by another in *The Times* a few weeks later with a detailed agenda for a declaration of the 'Rights of Man'. The rights of minority *peoples*, supported by the League of Nations and by 1940 becoming discredited, were transitioning piecemeal with superpower support (partly based on cynicism towards small nations) in the direction of human rights of the *individual*.[57] To systemise and exploit this transition, Wells ventured ten core clauses in his *Times* letter: (1) 'That every man without distinction or race or colour is entitled to nourishment, housing, covering, medical care and attention sufficient to realize his full possibilities of physical and mental development and to keep him in a state of health from his birth to death.' (2) That education should be a right 'to make him a useful and interested citizen' with his access to knowledge and that he 'enjoy the utmost freedom of discussion'. (3) That he and his personal lawful property are entitled to 'police and legal protection'; (4) that though any man might be subject to 'free criticism of his fellows', he should be protected from lying and 'secret dossiers'; (5) that there be freedom to work and to pay, and free choice to select both; (6) freedom of movement around the world, and to roam over country, moorland and mountain, but privacy within in his own house and garden; (7) freedom to buy and sell things 'compatible with the common welfare'; (8) that no man be imprisoned without charge for more than three weeks or trial for more than three months; (9) no forced mutilation or sterilisation, torture, beating or physical punishment whether by violence, light, darkness or forced feeding; (10) and that a Legal Code expand on this declaration, to make it 'the fundamental law for mankind throughout the world'.[58] Though immediately attacked by anti-communist Tories,[59] Wells' letters stimulated the formation of the Sankey Commission, chaired by judge and lawyer John Sankey (1866–1948) and promoted by the *Daily Herald* and the National Peace Council, and on which Wells sat drafting a revised set of principles that became the Sankey Declaration of the Rights of Man – published and distributed widely in 1940 in Penguin paperback. For all that it was called the Sankey Declaration, its eleven points came to be closely associated with Wells: the right to life and a living; the protection of minors; man's duty to community and community's obligation to him, including freedom of conscientious objection to military service; the right to knowledge; freedom of thought and worship; the right to work; the right to personal property; freedom of movement; personal liberty and judicial protection; freedom from violence; and the right of law-making. A nationwide debate ensued centred on Wells, but journalistically choreographed by fellow-humanist Ritchie Calder in the *Daily Herald*, which, during February 1940, devoted one page per edition to answering the question 'What are we fighting for?'.[60] With the Sankey Declaration translated into five languages, Wells and Calder had global ambition, and their exploitation of the mood of the superpowers put humanist rhetoric at international disposal, with the result, in the words of an Austrian international lawyer who in 1954 noted the decay of League of Nations minority rights protection: 'Today the well-dressed international lawyer wears "human rights".'[61]

Research on impulses towards human rights have concentrated on postcolonial nationalism, left-wing sources and religion.[62] The humanist influence in the origins of the human rights movement remains rather obscure and deserves closer attention than is possible here. Part of the story involves the National Council for Civil Liberties (NCCL, founded 1934) upon which many humanists served – including Sylvia Scaffardi (1902–2001) who co-founded it with her partner Ronald Kidd, who may qualify at least as a proto-humanist, Kingsley Martin (elected in 1944) and David Tribe (from 1961) – as well as drawing in what a confidential Foreign Office assessment of 1949 dubbed 'useful innocents', such as H. G. Wells, Julian Huxley and E. M. Forster.[63] We know that the FPSI had a civil rights committee in the 1930s in the early years of the NCCL, but the links between the two remain to be explored.[64] What has been written tends to focus on left-wing origins of the rights cause, and the Wells/Calder wartime human rights campaign is often depicted solely as liberal socialism in impulse. However, there were key humanists in this early human rights movement: Harold Laski, C. E. M. Joad, J. B. Priestley, George Bernard Shaw, J. B. S. Haldane, Kingsley Martin, John Boyd Orr and Alex Comfort, each of whom played some part in wartime moral dissent with British war strategy (especially aerial bombing).[65] Indeed, left-wing organisations, including the NCCL, remained throughout the 1940s sceptical of Wells' human rights initiative, drawing back from full support. As Christopher Moores argues, there was a failure to mobilise the left-wing cause behind human rights during the 1940s and 1950s, partly triggered by the conflict between the universalism of human rights and the Cold War framework, which, aided by recoil at Stalinism and the 1956 invasion of Hungary, led key intellectuals – including Bertrand Russell and Kingsley Martin – to jettison their prioritisation of socialist causes in favour of their humanism and rationalism.[66] So, it can be argued, the figures behind the movement that *did* launch the human rights cause were wearing distinctly humanist hats, and those names – including Boyd Orr and Calder – were to become prominent in the post-war UN battles for the same cause. Many British humanists had signed up as conscientious objectors in either world war, including Alex Comfort and Glanville Williams. For all that the Second War brought humanists into conflict with fascism, including Wells who was targeted by British fascists, it focussed attention on a humanist argument for pacifism, conscientious objection and world government rather than on a socialist mass mobilisation.[67] It is important to observe, however, that humanists were not united on pacifism in the Second World War; as early as 1920, Bertrand Russell went to the USSR and 'abominated' the communist government and 'had to break with all the people that endured my pacifism' during the first war, and held the war with fascism was justified.[68]

JOHN BOYD ORR, 1880–1971

Nutritionist and 1949 Nobel Peace Prize winner John Boyd Orr slid from the religious practice of his father, going to Glasgow University to study first for an arts degree, then a medical one, running the Rowett Food Institute in Aberdeen to emerge the world's leading nutritional scientist of the 1930s to 1960s. Becoming a regular member of the humanist movement when in London, his humanitarianism undergirded a quiet humanism, but became an ethical thorn in the flesh to the British and American governments. He proved in the 1930s that a third of British children were malnourished, and in the 1940s designed a World Food Board to stabilise the global food system to ensure flow to poor nations. For this, he was chosen in the late 1940s by his scientific peers to be the first director general of the UN's Food and Agriculture Organisation, but his Food Board plan was spiked by the US and UK governments over the embarrassment he had caused. Yet, he instigated the new nutritionist profession to adopt an ethical alignment, expressed in the Freedom from Hunger Campaign of the late 1950s and early 1960s. He was elected rector of the University of Glasgow in 1945, MP (Independent) for the Scottish Universities 1945–9, elevated Lord Boyd Orr of Brechin in 1949 and the first president of the World Academy of Art and Science in 1960. A close friend to Ritchie Calder and Bertrand Russell, Boyd Orr was

FIGURE 15 John Boyd Orr. Photo: ©NPG.

constant in his humanist ideals for benevolent world government and for 'the great powers of science' to address human want, speaking often at Conway Hall on these themes. When asked about his humanism, he answered about science: 'Humanists are also rationalists who look at things apart from the preconceived ideas and look at the facts.'

So, it was really during the Second World War that developments accelerated into a new realm that, historians agree, made for something qualitatively different from what had gone before.[69] Human rights was on the Allies' agenda during the later stages of the war, with the first UN bill submitted by Cuba, Chile and Panama at the 1945 San Francisco Conference. On 10 December 1948, the third general assembly of the UN adopted the Universal Declaration of Human Rights, in the drafting processes of which church as well as trade union and women's organisations were consulted, but, at that stage, seemingly none from the humanist and secularist traditions.[70] Then, in turn, the UN Declaration was the model for the European Convention of Human Rights (ECHR) of 1950, whose negotiation was a cornerstone of European legal integration in ensuing decades.

But the humanist influence on the 1948 Declaration cannot be glossed over. Around twenty people submitted drafts, including H. G. Wells and separately his Sankey Commission. It was his that had great influence in the realm of religion.[71] Moreover, Wells' reputation led to his pamphlet on *The Rights of Man* penetrating many parts of the British Empire, including Africa where in 1943 the Colonial Office noted its influence.[72] His original ten clauses and then his Sankey Commission's eleven clauses created paradigms for the thirty articles of the UN Declaration, the eighteen articles of the European Convention, and thence through the development of further international agreements. This is seen in the way Wells grouped ideas, notably in a communitarian strand of rights – the notion of the individual's duties to the community in which he lives and the community's responsibilities towards him (Sankey Article 3, which can be found in UDHR Article 29).[73] But Wells' influence can also be seen in the vocabulary. He appears to have been the originator of the phrase 'freedom of thought, conscience and religion', which first appeared in the Sankey Declaration, then in the 1948 Declaration in Article 18: 'Everyone has the right to freedom of thought, conscience and religion; this right includes freedom to change his religion or belief, and freedom either alone or in community with others and in public or private, to manifest religion or belief in teaching, practice, worship and observance.' This was closely copied in the European Convention and bore the underlying idea of the plurality of religious and secular ideologies, freedom of worship, freedom to not have a religion (freedom of thought) and freedom to change religion (which triggered a Saudi abstention in the UN). Also noteworthy was the avoidance anywhere in these documents of the notion of enforcing a state religion, and the absence of any mention of a god or gods – the most controversial issue in the drafting of the Declaration, much fought over by the UN Human Rights Division.[74] Some have attributed French jurist René Cassin as the main 'framer' of the Declaration (and winner of the 1968 Nobel prize for co-authoring it) ahead of the reputed 'father' Wells,[75] and the British Quaker and Labour-sympathetic Foreign Office diplomat (later Sir) Geoffrey Wilson drafted some elements (notably Article 18 – placing 'freedom of thought', a nod to an atheist's freedom, ahead of 'conscience' in a replica of Wells' wording).[76] Yet, the whole manner of prose in the Declaration – of the speaking of the human rights of an individual (man) – was copied from Wells and Sankey to the Declaration. Further, the ideas and much of the phraseology are uncannily similar, so that Wells' authorial claims may in some quarters be understated.

But if humanist influence was evident in the UN Declaration of 1948, it struggled in the Congress of Europe of May 1948. Organised by a Scottish Presbyterian Conservative, David Maxwell-Fyfe MP, the Congress' ECHR produced rhetoric that was markedly different from that of the UN Declaration. Notwithstanding that Bertrand Russell was an invited member of the Cultural Committee and argued that the Congress affirm 'the pursuit of knowledge, or scientific truth', it was Christian theologians and war veterans who argued that 'Humanism is not Christianity' and 'is anti-Christian'. The result was that the document referred to Europe's 'common heritage of Christian and other spiritual and cultural values'.[77] Still, Article 9 of the ECHR of November 1950 followed the UN Declaration almost exactly in defining freedom of thought, conscience and religion, including the right to change one's religion, though attached conditions to permit limitations 'for the protection of public order, health or morals'.[78]

In such ways, humanist influence in international human rights development faced epistemological struggles over cultural matters, though it enjoyed success in regard to defendable rights. Historian Chris Moores has shown how liberalism continued to be served after the war by Wells' creation, the Progressive League, which was observed by Special Branch surveillance battling in the NCCL to maintain an equality of treatment between the USSR and Western nations over human rights infractions.[79] However, human rights are perceived by one scholar from an American religious angle as failing on the global stage from the 1940s through to the 1990s.[80] Other researchers argue that human rights became more important between 1963 and 1975 when European empires collapsed and decolonisation and the ideal of race equality dominated in many nations, when second-wave feminism fed the women's movement and the United Nations entered its golden age. One consequence, though, was a shift from European dominance in human rights towards the developing world – from the Global North to the Global South.[81] The most ambitious attempt to bring religion within international law was the draft United Nations Convention on Elimination of All Forms of Religious

Intolerance and Discrimination Based on Religion or Belief negotiated during the 1960s, which would have protected the freedom of religious believers and atheist and secular beliefs; articles I and III contained what would have been the first explicit legal defence of atheism in international law. However, all that emerged was a Declaration that lost the explicit defence of atheism, though it remained implied.[82]

Notwithstanding, initiatives abounded. The formation of Amnesty International (AI) in 1961 was closely tracked by the humanist movement; in 1964 SPES affiliated with it, perhaps slightly self-interestedly to recruit new members, whilst by 1966 British humanists had formed nine AI groups (the idea being that each group worked on behalf of three prisoners of conscience).[83] In 1969, IHEU approached the British foreign secretary, Michael Stewart MP, seeking recognition in international law of humanist counsellors as equivalent in war to chaplains (a status already granted in the Netherlands).[84] The human rights movement may well have had a considerable way still to run, yet the chain of innovation in international law traces to H. G. Wells, who, as a by-product of his utopian internationalism, foresaw with clarity in 1940 that the concept of equality of rights for every human being could, and should, be the foundation upon which international cooperation between nations might rest.

(d) IHEU and world humanism

A defining moment for British humanism was the International Congress of the World Union of Freethinkers (WUF) in September 1938, hosted at Conway Hall by SPES, RPA and the Ethical Union. The event descended into controversy even before it started as Conservative backbench MPs branded it 'the Godless Congress', aware that some communists, both domestic freethinkers but others from the USSR and Western nations, were scheduled to speak. The government bowed to pressure, and the event was subjected to surveillance (from MI5 and Special Branch), prompting a significantly sour view of the connection with the Marxist-oriented Freethinkers organisation.[85] The WUF Freethinkers returned to London for a 1946 conference, but, despite its theme 'The Challenge of Humanism', it persuaded Harold Blackham that humanism required its own international body in which attacking religion was not the central task.

Anti-imperialism had been central to British ethicism since the Boer War, and in the post-war context of imperial decline humanists proffered their constructive internationalist agenda. The leading historian of internationalism has identified the twentieth-century peak of the ideal in 1948 at a six-week UNESCO seminar on 'world understanding' presided over by Julian Huxley.[86] Thereafter, the Cold War interfered gravely. The SPES general committee in November 1952, abandoning its thirlage to free speech, adopted by 8 votes to 7 what became known as the

'Permanent Directive' banning the hiring of Conway Hall by any of six named communist-front organisations and any society or person 'who persist in any conduct detrimental to the Society'.[87] Humanists were by no means united on this, as the SPES vote demonstrates. SPES disaffiliated from the NCCL because of its communist members, only re-joining in 1960 when it was judged no longer overtly communist; four years later, SPES was hosting the NCCL AGM in Conway Hall.[88] The 'anti-Red' strategy, though prudently applied by the movement, was widespread in the 1940s and 1950s. From the turn against the freethinkers in 1946 arose the formation of the International Humanist and Ethical Union (IHEU) in August 1952: its first congress in Amsterdam largely the brainchild of Harold Blackham, then president of the Ethical Union, Hector Hawton, editor of the RPA's *The Literary Guide*, and Jaap van Praag, chairman of the Dutch Humanist League; Blackham became IHEU's first secretary, Praag its first chairman. It was an organisation which, in its earliest decades, had a disproportionately large British involvement, with the first congress having a diet of mainly British speakers (including Julian Huxley, the organisation's first president, and Barbara Wootton). Huxley urged IHEU to work closely with the United Nations, and five UN-related resolutions were immediately passed in 1952, one of which led IHEU to apply to be a consultative member of UNESCO (of which Huxley had been the first director).[89] Blackham and Huxley were convinced that IHEU should become the organisational embodiment of humanist internationalism and be led by scientists, intellectuals and a wider artistic impulse emanating from the Second World War and the Jewish Holocaust. To impress the UK's place at the head of world humanism, the second congress in 1957 was scheduled for Conway Hall.

Not all humanists were optimists of internationalism. Commentary on the failures of international cooperation (especially the League of Nations) appeared in British freethought journals in the 1950s. But much of the movement's work took place by humanist proxies in organisations like the Movement for Colonial Freedom which, though strongly left-wing, was co-founded in 1954 by, and identified with, humanist Fenner Brockway, and from which offshoots including the Anti-Apartheid Movement and War on Want developed their own humanist associations.[90] Though some scholars emphasise American-led science in the development of the post-1945 world order,[91] the British contribution was as great for the intellectual standing of its research leaders and notable for its strong humanist leanings. However, there were troubling issues. IHEU was formed in 1952 by a monoculture of largely white Euro-centred humanist groups – from the Netherlands, the UK, Germany, Belgium, the United States, observer and consultative groups from Australia, Finland, Austria and Japan, with only Indian humanists as the exception. There was an urgency to reshaping humanism's moral purpose in the era of collapsing European empires, apartheid in South Africa and the threat of it in Rhodesia, and ongoing American segregation. This pressure built in the 1960s with new joiners to IHEU: by 1962 numbers rose to twenty-two bodies from fifteen nations, though majority-white nations would continue to dominate for two more decades.

The British influence in IHEU was not really based on numbers. In 1965 IHEU had 55,000 members mostly affiliated through its member organisations, but with 4,000 directly paying.[92] Of these, fewer than 8,200 (15 per cent) were from Britain. Yet, Britons were numerous as congress speakers and through multiple British humanist organisations (including regional, local and theme groups) affiliated to IHEU, giving the UK many voices. British humanism included one of the highest concentrations of key public intellectuals and scientists – major international figures in universities, writing, broadcasting (notably on the BBC overseas radio services) and the booming post-war business of international governmental cooperation and advising. On top of that, the union benefited from the organisational abilities of Harold Blackham, both as IHEU secretary 1952–65 and as a board member and prominent thinker, moralist and speaker on corporate strategy. The Netherlands had larger numbers of humanists paying IHEU more in affiliation fees, but Britain made the more prominent intellectual contribution.

Still, IHEU was afflicted with key problems. First, like many international bodies, the organisation generated much paperwork. A large volume of correspondence passed through the Utrecht headquarters; by 1961, in addition to circulars and publications, around 1,300 individual letters were posted per year, each logged (with Blackham the leading recipient with some 200 letters per annum) and around 700 letters received.[93] Second, IHEU strove to gain influence in international organisations but the progress was glacial. Volunteer representatives were stationed with each principal international body – in the United Nations (in New York, Geneva and Vienna), UNICEF (in New York), UNESCO (in Paris) and the Council of Europe (in Strasbourg) – and many of these were Britons.[94] For British humanists at least, the UN represented not only an insurance of peace but also linked radical visions of global organisation. One contributor to SPES's *Monthly Record* in 1946 proclaimed world governance was the 'only way of giving ourselves a chance' at maintaining the newly found peace after the Second World War; another in 1952 urged the UN to go even further in committing itself to organising a hierarchy of constituent nations.[95] Once again we see the humanist commitment to world government, like so many causes, with roots in Wells' FPSI as 'the only option for maintaining peace'.[96] World peace and disarmament were at the forefront of policy, but the expansion of international organisations in the 1970s would leave the humanists dangerously behind.

8 SOCIAL REFORM, SOCIAL WORK AND EDUCATION

The years 1930–70 witnessed many great advances in progressive social policy in Britain, including the so-called 'liberal hour' of the 1960s, drawing humanists into some of the most successful campaigning work they ever experienced and bestowing upon them an invigorated identity. In this chapter, we look first at the social-reform legislation, then humanist social work activity and lastly at the return of moral-education reform.

(a) Social reform

The winner of a British Humanist Association design competition, the 'Happy Man' was registered in April 1967[1] as a trademark of the organisation and, as it panned out, of the movement worldwide. It was part of the BHA cranking-up its operations, along with, in 1965, the appointment of Tom Vernon as the first full-time, paid press officer.[2] He brought a new currency of activity to the movement – the press release, which, used liberally, was designed to propel the BHA into the limelight in the midst of Britain's 'liberal hour'. With diverse short-form publications to hand, Vernon's task was to cope with the explosion in campaigning on social-reform issues in the years 1966–9.

There was much build-up to the 1960s. Some organisations involved in campaigns were born in the 1930s: the Abortion Law Reform Association (1936) and to which the EU affiliated in 1953;[3] the campaigns for the provision of birth control and advice on it for women and girls, sex education and ending censorship of sex advice books; the Voluntary Euthanasia Society (1937), which became a tenant in BHA HQ, and the associated movement to decriminalise suicide and attempted suicide in England and Wales; the campaigns for allowing assisted fertility (artificial insemination) and prevention (sterilisation). By the 1950s, the

Ethical Union was affiliated to a variety of campaign groups, including the Howard League for Penal Reform, the National Peace Council (which, among other things, was active in sponsoring British candidates for the Nobel Peace Prize like John Boyd Orr in 1949), the United Nations Association, the National Council against Racial and Religious Discrimination and the International League for the Rights of Man.[4] In each of these fields between the 1930s and early 1960s, the humanist network became busy, evolving into special groups which invariably presented the most radical plans to the British government. But it was in the 1960s that social issues sprouted with speed: decriminalisation of medical abortion and homosexuality, ending of censorship in the theatre and its effective collapse in book publishing, the 'legalise pot' campaign, protests against the Vietnam and Biafran wars, CND and a euthanasia bill before parliament. And in each of these, humanists were at the forefront.

But internal momentum to adopt policies could be slow. In 1963, David Pollock, lately president of the Oxford University Humanist Group, wrote in *The Humanist* deprecating the absence of policy on public affairs. 'At present', he wrote, 'the interested outsider may well ask: "What do Humanists say about abortion law reform?" "We don't have a policy", we have to reply: "we talk about it." "What about religious education and denominational schools?" "No – no policy; just talk."' Is it surprising, Pollock asked, 'that so few people have any clear idea of what a Humanist is?'[5] The following year, Pollock levelled criticism at the new British Humanist Association: 'What are we waiting for?'[6] The radical role of humanists continued into race relations. In the early 1950s, the Ethical Union had started a Thursday club for Black workers at premises in Inverness Place in Bayswater, which led a decade later to hopes of significant Afro-Caribbean recruitment among overall membership targets of 10,000 by 1967 and 20,000 by 1968: 'Make it clear', the BHA Plan of 1966 stated, 'that the coloured are welcome.'[7] Humanism's long-term links to feminism sprang into life over abortion law reform, culminating in the 1967 Act, which the humanists Diane Munday and Madeleine Simms had actively pursued, with the support of David Pollock in Humanist Lobby. By 1970, the BHA backed the Women's Liberation Movement's demands, including equal opportunities, equal pay, provision of nursery accommodation and the removal of legal distinctions between married and unmarried women. But it was a question not only of humanists having a policy but also of consulting. In 1967, both the 'legalise pot' movement and the churches' opposition to drugs emerged, and the BHA-affiliated University Humanist Federation organised a Young Humanist Conference on Drugs at Nottingham University in January 1968, with an opening talk by social anthropologist Francis Huxley (1923–2016), son of Julian, who had spent considerable time researching drug use among native peoples in Brazil.[8] The year 1968 was International Human Rights Year, and BHA mounted a surge of campaigns:[9] planning an inquiry into conditions in mother and baby homes; advocating liberal divorce law reform; and making a submission to the Home

Office opposing the right of a birth parent to determine the religious upbringing of a child given for adoption – an obligation partially awarded in 2002 and then removed in England in 2014.[10] If the list of campaign activity in the annual report is anything to go by, 1968 witnessed the widest spectrum of the greatest activism during the century. One BHA activist, Graham Kingsley, recalled abortion and homosexual law reform as the main campaigns of the time, adding: 'I suppose sex is always very attractive to young people.'[11]

The rise of student and youth protests in 1967 and 1968 led to a BHA submission in May 1969 to the Select Committee investigating disturbances, strikes and protests against the Vietnam War and other issues, in which BHA attributed the deteriorating relations between students, universities and schools to 'a wider crisis of authority', posing 'critical questioning of traditional ideas'. Universities, the BHA contended, should not 'seek to be arbiters of the politics or personal morality' of students and, in particular, should cease to be acting in loco parentis – a legal reform sorted two months later by the lowering of the age of consent from twenty-one to eighteen years.[12] The Student (formerly University) Humanist Federation, based in BHA's HQ at 13 Prince of Wales Terrace, produced a widely distributed liberal pamphlet on sexual morals in 1969, matching the liberal inclinations of the movement's sexologists. Young people and women were very much in focus in many humanist concerns in the 1960s, and were to remain there for decades to come.

In 1963, a concept was floated by Harold Blackham both to contextualise and add a new umbrella objective for British humanism: the doctrine of 'the Open Society'. This put a humanist hue upon Karl Popper's 1940s political philosophy that emphasised liberal democracy and humanitarianism over totalitarianism (whether of the right or left); Popper joined the BHA Advisory Council and became an RPA honorary associate.[13] Yet, the Popper connection to the humanist movement was slight. Instead, it was Blackham, Pollock and BHA chair Peter Draper who used open society as a guiding concept relentlessly broadcast in conferences, journals and books of the late 1960s. It became a central hearth for the movement to stare into, to engage members and see the common causes which held them together. Its promise of a diversity that might unite was intended to define the ideal society that humanists offered: it was unrealistic to expect everyone to be humanists, but society ought to have ground rules for people of varied beliefs to live together. Simultaneously, the open society concept backed Blackham's strategy, strongly mooted in the 1969 BHA annual report, of ditching any lingering 'anti-God League' approach in humanist affairs.[14] Humanism could be a wider, less brusque way to a united modernity. A two-day seminar co-organised by BHA and RPA aimed to persuade the membership on the open society concept and was daringly organised as a 10.00 a.m. to 5.00 p.m. event over a Monday and Tuesday at the Royal Festival Hall in December 1969.[15] With less than a month to go, with tickets at 5 guineas each (over £80 in 2022 values), bookings were only 'trickling' in, so a publicity blitz was mounted. The cast of twelve public intellectuals booked to speak were broadcast on circulars and newspaper advertisements: including political commentators Stuart Hood and Bernard Crick, psychiatrist Anthony Storr, Marxist and civil rights activist Dipak Nandy, politicians Tony Benn, John P. Macintosh (both Labour) and Jo Grimond (former leader of the Liberal Party).[16] Promotional material depicted Britain as a dysfunctional and possibly ungovernable place: 'Everywhere, democracy is challenged. Apathy and cynicism are widespread.'[17] Blackham and his supporters hoped that the open society concept would mature in BHA ideology; Pollock, newly elevated to the chairmanship of the BHA, repeated the vision in two substantial articles in *Humanist News* in the autumn of 1970, presenting a prospectus for the type of society to which humanists might aspire, whilst articulating an expansive view of all manner of progressive reforms, ranging from ending religious segregation of schools to the politics of the workplace.[18]

There were several motivations behind BHA's adopting the open society concept. It made wide-ranging demands for practical action by BHA members, emphasising the value of lobbying to secure individual reforms – a focus on cajoling and prodding in which Pollock had already become practised. But the democratisation of the workplace and places of learning echoed trade union and student movements of the period, whilst the open society concept was inserted notably into humanist submissions to parliament on church control of schools and compulsory religious education (in one 1969 submission calling for 'providing for all children an education which will fit them for living in a changing, open society').[19] Open society promised an intellectual structure that would shift the focus away from 'religion bashing' towards shaping a secular society guided by ethical considerations, over-optimistically contextualised by Pollock against traditional religion's 'catastrophic collapse into irrelevance'.[20]

However, not all BHA members were enamoured. Political tensions arose from time to time in the BHA, as in 1966 when the annual conference made it into the papers over a policy proposal to broaden the social base of the movement away from the middle and professional classes, drawing protest from 'roundly professional or middle-class' members as described by *The Guardian* journalist present. 'It's all very well and righteous', a delegate told his fellow humanists, 'to make an appeal to the lower orders, but there is something of an intellectual character in the very notion of humanism.' Interpreted to mean that abstract thought did not enter the working-class mind, Blackham and Tony Lambert of the University Humanist Federation rebuked the speaker.[21] But sustained criticisms emerged from inside the Association's dedicated study group, which convened in May 1969.[22] A group of Marxists, seemingly coordinated by a married couple, Jack and Patricia Knight, criticised the liberal (and hence bourgeois) conception of the open society for failing to address social and class inequalities – a vein supported by Brian Morris and Ken Jones, members from Lewes and Leeds respectively.[23] Other critics disliked the strategy of reaching a friendly accord with churches.

One was David Tribe (1931–2017), then in his final year of the presidency of the National Secular Society, who regarded the open society concept as ideologically incoherent and insufficiently secularist – a point noted by participant observer sociologist Susan Budd in 1965.[24] Tribe objected to the long-term attempt to find accommodation with churches, directly attacking Blackham's vision:

> By advancing personal freedom in accordance with some universalist ideal this movement was always much closer to the churches in its real sympathies than secularism. . . . So the heirs of the ethicist tradition believe that, 'Christians who accept the "open mind" and the "open society" as major ideals and who are ready to realistically tackle the common problems of a modern society, are surely better friends to the humanist than those who are fiddling sour old tunes'.

Blackham was criticised especially for being too sanguine about the Catholic Church as either more reasonable or rational than it had been.[25]

The open society Festival Hall seminar attracted eighty-nine paying attenders and made a loss of £662.[26] Despite its critics, it retained a presence in BHA leadership rhetoric as late as the 2000s and framed the association's submissions to the British government on human rights and democracy.[27] At the same time, the concept was transformative for some who approved the strategy of compromise and liaison with the churches. Blackham led the movement into a broad policy of inserting humanist influence into the wider body politic and the faith community organisations of Britain. Whilst the 'attack the churches' policy associated with Joseph McCabe and David Tribe graced many of the movement's magazines, Blackham offered a long-term prospect of unity and a constructive role for humanists in a more open British civil society.

(b) Sex and knowledge

Humanists were at the forefront of the struggle to spread sexual knowledge. This had come to prominence in the nineteenth century with Charles Knowlton's *The Fruits of Philosophy*, first published in 1834, which sold steadily until 1877 when secularists Charles Bradlaugh and Annie Besant published it again, leading to their trial for obscenity, eventual acquittal on a technicality and their fame and notoriety. Besant and later Marie Stopes, and many others, campaigned for wider sexual knowledge and availability of contraceptives as well as for legalisation of medical abortion. By the mid-twentieth century, censorship was on the way out, but sexual knowledge was still closely watched by the police and law officers, resulting in the prosecution of Penguin in 1960 for publishing D. H. Lawrence's novel *Lady Chatterley's Lover*. The thirty-five defence witnesses included three humanists – E. M. Forster, James Hemming and Noel Annan, whilst a fourth, *New*

Statesman journalist and proto-humanist Cecil R. Hewitt (aka C. H. Rolph), wrote the Penguin Books account of the trial.

The humanist fight for liberalisation of sexual attitudes first came to a head in the 1950s. The humanist-led campaign for decriminalising male homosexuality was apparent in the evidence to the Home Office Wolfenden Committee. Church organisations and religious medics equivocated, the supposed 'radicals' among them suggested decriminalising homosexual relations for men over twenty-one for acts in private (though sustaining the 'sin' of homosexual relations and the social ostracism of 'inverts'), whilst conservative Christians, especially those at the British Medical Association, put up the fiercest opposition to any change. By contrast, a network of humanist organisations, coordinated by the Progressive League which, though rather prematurely written off by one historian,[28] hosted a special conference in March 1954 which led to the Ethical Union, the Rationalist Press Association, the Personalist Group, the Eugenics Society, Eustace Chesser and Julian Huxley presenting the least equivocal evidence to Wolfenden, generally favouring decriminalising for over 18's and social acceptance of gay men.[29] Again in 1958, at the foundation of the Homosexual Law Reform Society, humanists were the leading and most enthusiastic responders to the call for expressions of public support; these included A. J. Ayer (the society president), Julian Huxley, Hector Hawton, Noel Annan, Bertrand Russell, Barbara Wootton, E. M. Forster, Jacob Bronowski, Eustace Chesser, Alex Comfort, Cecil R. Hewitt and the publisher Victor Gollancz. By contrast, though a handful of bishops and other clergy joined, most church leaders were negative or morally conflicted. The bishop of Manchester, William Greer, wrote to say he would sign 'if it is made quite clear that I believe such acts to be morally wrong'; Maurice Harland, the bishop of Durham, declined because of 'the probability that such action will be construed as condoning a very horrible practice'; Harold Bradfield, the bishop of Bath and Wells, declined despite 'the possible recovery of persons who are afflicted with these homosexual tendencies'; the general secretary of the Methodist Church Home Mission thought decriminalisation was good but didn't want 'to give the impression that it doesn't matter'; the Church of England Moral Welfare Council wanted no names of Council members supporting decriminalisation made public; and even anti-apartheid activist Trevor Huddleston, otherwise lauded in radical circles, considered the cause too left-wing.[30] If even sympathetic Christian clergy craved concealment, humanists generally bore no such worries, and the same names were to be found again and again adorning the literature of diverse liberalising campaigns. With few humanist abstentions from the Homosexual Law Reform Society, mostly on fine points of principle, only one humanist of note declined. Lord Ritchie Calder, a known and very public supporter of the cause, cited his difficulty in 1954 after a sympathetic speech he made in the House of Lords on homosexuality law reform: 'For some months afterward I found myself almost in the position of "running the gauntlet" with colleagues.'[31]

Heterosexual relations outside of marriage were equally regarded by most humanists in the 1950s and 1960s as necessitating the end of censorious interference. On the one hand, sexual morality was changing, notably among the young, and humanists responded with sex guides and advice from early on. The author of more than thirty volumes of sex manuals, Eustace Chesser defended his first book, *Love without Fear*, against a charge of obscenity at the Old Bailey in 1942, establishing it was not pornography but medical support for young couples with relationship problems, and was acquitted by the jury (and a sympathetic judge). The humanist movement went way out in front in advocating frank sex education in schools, in print and on film, and in opposing censorship and social silence on sexual problems. Humanist psychologists, medics and intellectuals like Chesser, G. M. Carstairs, Alex Comfort, Dora Russell, Joan Malleson[32] and, in the Progressive League's nexus of specialist sexual liberals, Alec Craig, cornered the market with these arguments, publishing sex advice and making radio and television appearances in the 1950s and 1960s to discuss sex and contraception. Craig challenged censorship and prosecution of books on sex, chronicling legal cases around the country.[33] Chesser faced censorship again in 1959 when the Independent Television Authority banned him from one broadcast on sex because he had suggested that chastity before marriage was 'outmoded'. Morris Carstairs achieved international notoriety for suggesting the same in his BBC Reith lecture of 1962.[34] These controversies were short-lived. Within five years, humanist celebrities and the RPA were applauded by liberals for justifying changing sexual taste and morality, public nudity and use of contraception, and for the beginnings of widespread sex education in schools.

Sexual prurience fought a rear-guard action. Battles over sex and nonreligion came to a head in a series of mostly private cases brought by conservative Christians, beginning with Cyril Black's prosecution of *Last Exit to Brooklyn* in 1965. Student humanist groups in the 1960s stepped into sexual morality-making, including a 1969 leaflet in which two humanists advocated that 'it is good for people, especially teenagers, to have a large quantity and variety of sexual experience'. Changing the law on male–female legal difference over work sat beside demands to eradicate sexual taboos on nudity and the enjoyment of lovemaking without 'proper purpose', together with a sceptical view of 'romantic love and its untold misery'.[35] Humanist academics and social scientists made the intellectual, medical and legal case for liberalism in sexual culture, but the young generation was crafting societal change itself.

(c) Education and social work

In the 1950s, humanists tended to follow secularist habits in dealing with the churches. Typical was the spat that arose when Gilbert Murray died in 1957 and was claimed by the Catholic newspaper *The Universe* as having made a deathbed conversion, reporting how Murray's Catholic daughter had brought a priest who administered Extreme Unction. Hector Hawton responded as editor of *The Humanist* by citing the denials of Murray's son, who told how his father had been at the time comatose with illness.[36] Similar egregious Christian propaganda of late conversions, defections and depressions among prominent atheists continued – notably about A. J. Ayer in 1988 and Christopher Hitchens in 2011.[37] Such accusations had been made for many decades, including about Charles Bradlaugh's death in 1891,[38] but, despite the deep hurt for family that could result from such claims by the clergy, many humanist leaders were willing to seek better relations with churches when they held agreeable positions on progressive issues.

In 1957, a correspondent to the RPA's *The Humanist* expressed concern with the lack of humanist action in social work and policy. But quickly, things started to change, including the formation of Humanist Group Action to facilitate it.[39] The BHA and RPA were being drawn in the 1960s into a wider range of progressive issues, foreign and domestic. In 1965 a joint working party that included the Church of England's Kathleen Bliss and BHA's Harold Blackham met to explore inserting humanism in school RE syllabuses. In the following year, the Social Morality Council (SMC) was created from the ruins of an older ecumenical moral vigilance organisation as a promoter of international justice and moral education, and Edward Oliver, its Roman Catholic organiser, invited A. J. Ayer to join. Passing this on, the result was that Blackham, Ritchie Calder and James Hemming were co-opted onto the SMC which, from the humanist perspective, increased opportunity to press for moral education in schools. From the Catholic perspective it strengthened British church opposition to apartheid and the Biafran War. But also, as Oliver said, 'at one stroke it turned [the SMC] into something unique in this country and perhaps the world: the first permanent organisation in which religious believers and non-believers have come together for joint study and action.'[40]

At the same time, membership of humanist groups was mushrooming, and, not altogether with the support of the Catholic Church, the humanist-backed moral agenda for parliamentary reform in abortion, censorship, capital punishment and homosexuality came to a spectacular head in the 'liberal hour' in 1967–9. But in addition, the humanist movement was engaging in national and international planning, evident in the 1967 production of the BHA 'General Statement of Policy', which contained a long list of agreed policies: on war and disarmament, world population and resources, the open society, political reform to create 'a genuinely democratic structure', education, arts, the environment, the law – and especially how to maximise personal freedom in relation to family, sex, divorce, legitimacy, abortion, homosexuality, censorship and many other issues.[41] The General Statement of Policy laid out the diversity of humanist concerns but made a call to the membership at the annual conference to become involved in amending it. And amend it they did, as the General Statement evolved from 1967 until 1975, being updated in 1985, reissued in 1992, and finally falling into disuse thereafter.[42] But for its time, the General Statement prescribed how the humanist movement participated in reform successes in the late 1960s, often in tandem with support from some churches. Yet, other fields produced a less immediate triumph. Broadcasting, on both BBC and ITV, was considered a priority with a new BHA Broadcasting Committee, as well as TRACK (the Television and Radio Committee), set up in 1965 with over fifty advisors and performers watching government media policy, but, despite two radio series on humanism in the 1960s, the churches on the BBC's Central Religious Advisory Committee remained obdurate in not letting humanists anywhere near religious broadcasts.[43]

Political lobbying was considered a vital area, with David Pollock's work in establishing the 'Humanist Lobby' organisation being seen from 1965 as a good start, but one that 'must be consolidated otherwise there is a real danger of this effort petering out'.[44] The membership of the BHA was regarded as too small and too narrow, and the leadership planned to 'broaden class' appeal, attract more scientists and immigrants, and to develop new buildings in part through 'judicious collaboration with South Place & R.P.A.'.[45] In the autumn of 1967, increased activity was planned for members and local groups by mobilisation

FIGURE 16 Humanism and art: the movement had a strong association with both music and art. Here, Norman Cusden is setting up the first British Humanist Association art exhibition at its Leicester conference of 1966. Photo: W. E. George/Humanists UK/ Bishopsgate Archive.

for International Year of Human Rights 1968 called by UNESCO and the UN General Assembly. To mark it, BHA appealed for the cessation of the bombing of civilians in Vietnam, created a new BHA group 'Mothers in Action' to support unmarried mothers and eliminate discrimination against women, and lobbied for local authorities' family planning services to be made mandatory.[46] On its youth work, the Student Humanist Federation hosted a 1968 conference on the case for and against legalisation of drugs, followed in 1969 by Barbara Wootton's official Home Office Committee on drugs which called for reduced criminal penalties for smoking cannabis – a recommendation rejected by Home Secretary James Callaghan as a result of pressure from the churches.[47] The BHA was stiffening its social-action programme. From 1968 it collaborated with the National Council for the Unmarried Mother and Her Child to promote the rights of the illegitimate person (resuscitating Oswald Dawson's work from the Victorian period in the Legitimation League). In the autumn of that year, BHA demanded an end to all oaths in courts of law, to be substituted for a simple promise to tell the truth, whilst the student humanists held a conference on minorities – including those who wanted pornography, and lesbians.[48] Ideas were coming thick and fast.

But most urgent for the movement was to attain some measure of advance in the realm of education. Stanton Coit had proclaimed in 1898 that 'the Ethical Movement is pre-eminently educational in character',[49] and during the early twentieth century education became an ever-growing area of humanist thought and activism. In 1940, there were already complaints that a nonreligious view was making headway in the classrooms of English council schools. *The Times* reported that Father F. Woodlock SJ of Farm Street Church in London deplored that 'the majority of teachers, both in elementary and secondary schools, were normally unattached by any vital link to any religious denomination', believing 'that their mental outlook owed more to, and had been formed by, G. B. Shaw, H. G. Wells, and Bertrand Russell than by any Christian philosophy of life'.[50] But it was after 1945 when humanist approaches crystallised into two main strands. The first was social-action humanist activity wherein education was identified as the key to promoting humanist ideals and social diversity, and thereby giving space for non-mainstream religions and nonreligion to be discussed. Education was seen as providing a platform for debates about personal freedoms, rights and responsibilities in the modern world, and humanist educationalists recognised the need to introduce children to these early in life in order to endorse a more tolerant and liberal social outlook.[51] The second strand was led by forward-thinking educationalists committed to curriculum development and reform in the classroom. The education sector became extremely important to the movement, bringing many teachers in the 1950s and 1960s to join the humanist cause. In practice, both education strands shared a joint understanding that to realise humanist objectives there must be structural reform to the school sector and a challenge to existing religious education policy.

Effective change seemed to come with the formation of the Humanist Teachers' Association in the mid-1960s. There was no automatic opportunity to discuss humanism in the classroom unless there were classes in Religious Instruction (as it was generally known before 1970) or Religious Education or Religious and Moral Education (in successive decades). The Education (Butler) Act 1944 put the place of religion in education on a new footing in England and Wales, removing a lot of local rights, rendering 'collective worship' compulsory and legislating for an 'agreed syllabus' for religious education in each education authority. With the arrival of many non-Christian children in Britain in the 1960s, the agreed syllabuses tended to become inoperable and ignored at the secondary level, though more enforced at the primary school level, leading the BHA to agree with the official Plowden report on the need for greater flexibility – though objecting to its direction that children 'should not be confused by being taught to doubt before faith is established'.[52] The BHA had used its 'open society' policy to guide its submission to Plowden, calling for 'a common educational experience as a preparation for life in a democratic, open society'.[53] Regarding collective worship, the BHA noted to the Department of Education and Science that 'worship to order' in the late 1960s was leading to a perfunctory approach, poor student understanding of religious concepts and a growing trend for the law to be plainly ignored. Humanists then, as now, were particularly incensed by the widespread non-functioning of the right of parental excusal of their children attending either worship or RI teaching, and the absence of a school alternative; parents felt that an excusal request would be seen as undermining school culture and lead their child to be isolated in a room.[54]

On its formation in 1963, Harold Blackham took the BHA on a new educational strategy – replacing the attack on the Butler Act with working on getting moral education introduced in schools as a vehicle for humanist content and for critical thinking. As the first chair of the BHA Education Committee, he oversaw a report on proposals for religious and moral education jointly produced by a group of Christians and humanists in 1965. With the Social Morality Council (SMC) formed in 1965, Blackham became its first chairman and started work for moral education in county (local-authority) schools in England and Wales. In 1967, BHA launched its campaign with two pamphlets, one by James Hemming, who became the movement's central education specialist and shared with Blackham a belief in liaising with Christian liberals for change to the system; the NSS was pushing an education policy along similar tracks.[55] But the first major breakthroughs in local education authority (LEA) work were by Harry Stopes-Roe in 1969 when he was co-opted onto Birmingham's Agreed Syllabus Conference, leading him to join BHA, and by John White when appointed as a humanist representative on the Standing Advisory Council on Religious Education (SACRE) for the Inner London Education Authority (ILEA).[56] Individual humanists in the 1960s and 1970s were being invited with increasing regularity to speak in RE classes, often at upper secondary level, about humanism. Diane Munday as 'one voice alone' felt she achieved much in 1964 in her local struggle to have St Helen's Primary School in Hertfordshire move from voluntary-aided church school to a county school.[57] By the dedication of individuals, awareness of humanism filtered through the education sector, but, without separate humanist schools, progress before 1970 remained slow.

Meanwhile, humanist influence seemed more difficult in social work, with slow-scale lobbying of government about policy, yet humanists were able to achieve much through direct social action. The first field of note was housing. In 1954, four members of the social service group of the Ethical Union – Lindsay and Mora Burnet, Ena Elkin and Beatrice Pollard – were concerned that there was little provision of housing for the elderly, and the little there was tended to be difficult for non-Christians to access since it was generally controlled by church groups, which maximised admission for Christians. Taking their cue from the Dutch Humanist League, the Ethical Union Housing Association Ltd. was formed to build and convert houses, starting with a donation of £75 from EU coffers, funds from other humanist bodies and £400 in cash raised at a single public meeting. Its first project at 8 Burgess Hill, Hampstead, opened in 1957 as Burnet House, providing fourteen small flats. The second scheme was funded by a bequest from Charles Victor Wagner, and the new block of twenty flats called Blackham House was opened at Parkhill Road. Rebranded in 1965 as the Humanist Housing Association (HHA), on the opening of a third project Rose Bush Court by the Minister for Housing Anthony Greenwood MP in 1967, the BHA produced a guide for local Humanist Groups to form housing associations, suggesting targeting specific tenants: elderly persons for whom landladies were reluctant to take responsibility; lower paid single men and women; unmarried mothers; large families; and ex-mental hospital patients. Though the Merseyside and Guildford Humanist groups expressed interest in such projects, work was concentrated on the national housing association with new developments in the later 1960s in Pembury, Tunbridge Wells and Stevenage, the last the Symonds Green project for 125 homes – giving a total by 1980 of 600 flats on 19 sites.[58] Throughout its work, the HHA accepted funds from all quarters (including a lucrative appeal on BBC Home Service by Lord Ritchie Calder) and provided housing for the religious and nonreligious alike, so long as they were over sixty years of age. Further projects came – in Cambridge, Chelmsford, Farnham, Chingford and Surbiton, with multiple developments in some places. By 1999 the HHA had 1,028 homes, 44 per cent of them in London, but management was proving increasingly difficult. Properties were in need of extensive modernisation and upgrading, and the operation – by 1995, the HHA had 129 staff – had reached a scale beyond the reach of the association. In addition, by the later decades of the century, housing associations such as the HHA were reliant upon government funding, and these stipulated that tenants had to be selected by a points-based system dominated by need, based upon deprivation, low income, local connection, occupation, age and other approved criteria, but no longer upon religious or life stance positions. This meant that not only was the HHA unable to prioritise those without church connection or religion, but that religious housing associations rarely could do so either, in effect removing the initial problem that had led to the creation of HHA. Accordingly, the later 1990s and early 2000s witnessed a search for a suitable reorganisation, and in 2003 HHA merged with St Pancras HA to become part of the Origin Group.[59] By then the needs of the nonreligion and special needs groups were being catered for, but for its time the HHA had been distinctive and energising within the humanist movement.

BARBARA WOOTTON 1897–1988

Widowed six weeks after her first wedding, Barbara Wootton emerged from Cambridge as a polymath of prodigious academic ability and commitment to social reform. Her interests in economics, town planning, crime and justice led her to social research for the Labour Party, touring the USSR to study its social experiment and developing a detailed interest in crime and punishment, especially relating to children. An academic mostly at Cambridge, she was a go-to candidate for public bodies, serving as a BBC governor, a long-time magistrate, being elevated a life peer as Baroness Wootton of Abinger, then becoming the first woman deputy speaker of the Lords. A member of four government commissions, including chairing a drugs law inquiry that proposed ending cannabis-user

FIGURE 17 Barbara Wootton. Photo: ©NPG.

penalties, she led parliament towards ending child criminal culpability and wrote critically on children's treatment by the courts. An ethicist from her teens, she was a regular speaker at the Progressive League's summer conferences and helped in its generation of new ideas. She was also a star figure in the Ethical Union/BHA and the RPA and was loudly proud of the Agnostic Adoption Society in the 1960s as an early sign of diminishing prejudice against nonreligionists. She helped fellow humanists whenever she could, notably to get in front of the microphone at the BBC, and was much in demand as a speaker on formal occasions. She ploughed a sometimes controversial furrow for her feminism, opposing humanist support for the 1967 Abortion Bill partly because she considered that it passed control over women's bodies to largely male doctors – a position now widely held among progressive abortion law campaigners. Her applied social science was a model for the humanist movement, not just for showing how principles should change practice but for emphasising that humanists should not fear modernising their principles.

Indeed, the housing initiative in the 1950s inspired diverse social action in the 1960s, especially in relation to children. The idea for the Agnostics Adoption Society (AAS), initiated in 1963 and formally founded two years later, is attributed to the epidemiologist Richard Doll after difficulties he and his wife experienced as atheists in being accepted for adoption; the Dolls part-funded the start because the first treasurer, Tony Brierley of the EU, had difficulties in raising funds.[60] Co-established with the National Secular Society, the AAS aimed initially to place 'difficult' babies – notably Black and Asian children who were not receiving attention from many existing adoption societies. Its work grew quickly, with 41 adoptions during 1966, and by September 1971 it had placed 200 children, some with Jewish, Hindu, Muslim and mixed-religion couples, leading to its change of name in 1969 from the Agnostics to the Independent Adoption Society (IAS).[61] It was pioneering not merely because of who it assisted but because of its procedures. Tom Bolton was a communist in the 1960s and, though he and his wife Roisìn were from Catholic families, they knew that a church agency would be unlikely to consider them as suitable adoptive parents. They would not anyway have been willing to promise a Catholic upbringing for a child; in addition, he did not trust religious adoption societies, in large measure because he had heard unfavourable reports about Irish Catholic homes for single mothers. A recommendation led him to the IAS, which, Tom quickly discovered, had no religious 'test' of suitability and worked on honesty and considerable openness between birth mother, adopting parents and with the child too. When Dermot was adopted as a baby by Tom and

Roisìn through the society in 1970, he was raised with constant awareness of his adoption – a policy of openness that extended to updates and letters with the birth mother via the society, with Dermot knowing much about his birth family background from quite early in his life. This was a rare if not unknown procedure in the traditional adoption societies, which generally shuttered birth parents from adopting parents. The IAS policies of openness and information sharing, along with more rigorous scrutiny of adopters' ability to cater for the needs of the child, were explored with day-trip picnics for potential adopting parents with society social workers. With expansion from 1972 into placing children likely to wait longer, the society's protocols worked a treat for the Boltons, who went on to adopt a second child in 1974, and became standard in the adoption sector by 2000 and reflected in the Adoption and Children Act 2002. One outcome was that Tom, Dermot and his family discovered the term 'humanism' and became Humanist UK members in the twenty-first century, with Dermot actively involved as a volunteer with humanism in education and speaking about humanism in schools.[62] For BHA, the adoption society was a source of much pride, with sponsors including A. J. Ayer, Francis Crick, Julian Huxley, Margaret Knight and Barbara Wootton. On the last page of her memoir, Wootton observed that IAS was one signifier of society's acceptance of humanists when other signifiers – notably those in the gift of the BBC of which she had been a governor – were so sadly lacking.[63] Wootton was much involved with children, in part through her work as a magistrate and in part because in 1962 she successfully moved in the House of Lords a resolution raising of the criminal age of responsibility in England and Wales from eight to twelve – sadly reduced on amendment in the Commons to ten.[64] Adoption was joined by other humanist initiatives: the Humanist Youth Service Committee of the mid-1960s, which informed a variety of activities, including schools overseas;[65] and the Humanist Health Council formed in 1965 by Peter Draper (1933–2016), a significant figure in public health medicine, and active for several years in issuing discussion papers, including on the impact of permissive sexual behaviour upon young people's well-being, and coordinating patient-organisation responses to NHS reforms, going on in 1975 to launch the Unit for the Study of Health Policy at Guy's Hospital Medical School.[66]

A further example of humanist initiative in child social work comes from Edinburgh. Nigel Bruce, a Foreign Office diplomat stationed in the Middle East and Central Africa during the late 1940s and 1950s, retired to Scotland in 1961 where he was directly involved in the pioneering development of new and separate judicial courts called 'children's hearings' (sometimes 'children's panels') for children facing criminal legal proceedings. Through pamphlets and letter writing in *The Scotsman* newspaper, he sought to influence the Kilbrandon Commission of 1961–4[67] which came to argue, with him, that children should be excluded from the standard courts system and be given more humane and compassionate treatment in an environment where wigs, gowns and confrontational layout should be absent, and within which decisions over facts were separated from decisions over the measures of care required. Bruce contributed to this with a book *Face to Face with Families*, which argued that the whole family was in the dock when a child was assessed, and the family should be part of the solution – not part of the accused.[68] Parallel to his campaigning, Bruce led the BHA-affiliated Edinburgh Humanist Group in an innovative social-work venture. In 1964, troubled by the courts casting misbehaving boys exclusively to residential religious homes of dubious repute, the group established family-based homes for six to eight pupils aged over eleven years of both sexes, raising £6,500 from BHA members across Britain, and pressed on to open the first school, Crescent House, in 1966 and a second, Kincraig House, in 1969. Each was run on humanist principles, substituting a stable home environment for the retributive regime then common in other establishments. Each home had a salaried married couple acting as 'houseparents', and, with regular postings in *Humanist News*, the homes were kept going by generous donations from UK humanists. There were many troubles in management policy along the way, in part because the religious-style regime was eschewed and something new had to be invented and supported by an advisory team of humanist-sympathetic psychologists. One home had to be disbanded after fire damage in 1979, and the other kept going till 1982, when resources were diverted into provision of three self-contained flats for up to nine young people. By the 1980s, with legal and social work changes, the Scottish judicial system started to treat children better, in part due to the representations of Bruce and other humanists, and, with this, humanist social-care ventures kept adapting into the late 1980s.[69] The scale of this type of humanist work reduced at the end of the century when, as in the case of adoption, the principles of humanistic treatment became state policy, with local authorities and state supervision eliminating the need for, and the desirability of, belief-defined agencies. The secular state, which humanists worked to achieve, intervened.

Social work overseas was also something to emerge in the early 1960s, following the Freedom from Hunger Campaign of the UN's Food and Agriculture Organisation inspired by John Boyd Orr's World Food Board concept (see page 137). The BHA provided support for a scheme for rural betterment conducted in Bihar by the Radical Humanist Movement of India, but one African school at Swaneng Hill in Botswana attracted both British funds and humanist involvement. It was founded in February 1963 by husband-and-wife team Patrick van Rensburg (1931–2017) and Elizabeth (Liz) Griffin (b.1938) and was dedicated to access to equality education as the basis of a more just society. Rensburg, a South African vice-consul to the Belgian Congo, was introduced to Western humanism and antiracial ideals that led him to resign in 1957 in opposition to apartheid, fleeing to London in 1960 where he helped organise the early Anti-Apartheid Movement (AAM), at their rallies meeting his wife Liz, co-founder (with David Tribe) in 1961 of Humanist Group Action. After Patrick published the influential *Guilty*

Land: The History of Apartheid in 1962, he and Liz moved to Bechuanaland (from 1966 Botswana), starting their school on a shoestring. Griffin's uncle was Harold Blackham who, at the school project's inception in 1962, organised a £500 gift from the Ethical Union as its contribution to the Freedom from Hunger Campaign and a $5,000 donation from American atheist, socialist and pacifist millionaire Dr Prynce Hopkins. British humanists, including SPES, continued to help Swaneng Hill throughout the 1960s by sponsoring a British teacher and his family, with regular financial donations (including direct from humanist branches like that at Havering), and the school became the model for two further institutions created in conjunction with the Botswana government for a wider African educational reform movement.[70]

Despite its success, social work always took second place in the humanist agenda to campaigning for social-reform legislation at home and abroad. There were perhaps seven areas of change: homosexual law reform, abortion law reform, sex education, marriage and divorce law reform, contraception, abolition of censorship (starting with the offence of blasphemy on stage in 1965) and prison and penal reform. The Progressive League claimed to have helped found the Homosexual Law Reform Association in 1958, attracting significant humanist support to it, including its president A. J. Ayer.[71] One notable example of humanist expertise came from Cambridge law professor Glanville Williams who in 1958 published *The Sanctity of Life* that showed in detail how, over centuries, the legal and theological principle of 'sanctity' had held back the development of ethical and compassionate laws concerning sterilisation, artificial insemination, abortion, suicide and euthanasia. Williams – described by David Tribe of the NSS as 'champion of every cause that might raise legal eyebrows'[72] – attained a critical role in guiding the ALRA, the Voluntary Euthanasia Society and the HLRS, and was an inspirer of humanists to join these and other groups.[73] With such professional guidance, humanist organisations drew in feminist campaigners like Diane Munday and PR specialists like Madeleine Simms. There is much more to be discovered concerning how this tight network of humanist reformers operated, but it is clear that the 1960s was an exceptional decade for the effectiveness of humanist advocacy in British domestic reform causes.

Extraordinary success followed between 1960 and 1969 for the humanist-led 'liberal hour', when, under the parliamentary coordination of Labour's Roy Jenkins MP, home secretary 1965–7, a series of key social-policy reforms were passed. Then, in the 1970s, humanists came centre stage to defend these reforms from a backlash of Christian conservative evangelicals and Roman Catholics. Many of the causes were linked by concern for the human body. Humanists took a key role in the Abortion Law Reform Association, assisting David Steel MP in 1965–7 in the design and passage of the Abortion Act through Parliament. This was a cause that prompted some division in the humanist movement, with opposition to the reform coming from Leo Abse and Baroness Barbara Wootton. The latter was so criticised by some humanists that she resigned from the vice presidency of the BHA in 1967–8. Labour MP Leo Abse resigned from the BHA Advisory Council two years later when he joined the campaign to repeal the Act.[74]

Marriage and divorce law reform had been an early and enduring concern of the ethical movement. The Divorce Law Reform Union, though headed by Arthur Conan Doyle and Lord Birkenhead, had been guided by an activist of the Ethical Union, May Seaton-Tiedeman (1862–1948), who became the Union's honorary secretary from c. 1902 to at least 1938, when she campaigned by Sunday speeches at Hyde Park Corner, letters to the press and supported proto-humanist A. P. (Alan) Herbert MP in his successful extension of the grounds for divorce in England and Wales (from adultery to desertion, cruelty and insanity) in the Matrimonial Causes Act 1937.[75] The Progressive League also had its own body on these matters, the Marriage Law Reform Society of 1947 (which started as a PL committee including Eustace Chesser and Alex Comfort), which designed legal change and made submissions to government. This issue remained long in humanist crosshairs (including in 1969 when the BHA AGM voted for the secular licensing of places of marriage in England and Wales, to end the religious monopoly of marriage outwith a registrar's office).[76] In parliament, particular changes led by humanists included the promotion of cremation – a longstanding humanist policy nurtured by Joseph Reeves MP in the 1950s – and abolition of the felony of suicide and the crime of attempted suicide – pressed for by the Voluntary Euthanasia Society and in parliament by proto-humanist Kenneth Robinson MP (who also supported the VES cause). Mental-health reform was another area in which Robinson was important in the 1950s, and again in the 1960s when he became Minister of Health under Harold Wilson's Labour government, leading to reorganisation and improvement of provisions, attracting the support of other humanists including Cecil Hewitt. As a final example, the campaign to abolish capital punishment was one in which humanists, including Hewitt and Sydney Silverman (who introduced bills to the Commons in 1956 and 1965), were prominent, side by side with many Quakers in the Howard League for Penal Reform, and attaining ultimate success in 1965 as a humanistic sense of communitarianism condemned executions.[77]

If success in education reform was elusive, the 'liberal hour' was astoundingly triumphant on autonomy rights over the human body. The humanist contribution was critical, both inside and outside parliament. The new and young Labour MPs elected in the 1966 general election are considered to have included many nonreligionists and humanists, plus older parliamentarians like Douglas Houghton MP, who agreed to join and be honoured by the BHA for his part in promoting abortion and other reforms. It might be conjectured that Roy Jenkins was a proto-humanist for his sweeping agreement with these proposals and willingness to confront religious objections – policies as home secretary described as 'liberal humanism' by his colleague Denis Healey.[78] Whilst humanists in the movement were few compared to the scale of, say, church membership, the 1960s proved that they were at the front-line of ethical evolution, bringing professional skills in medicine, law, social science, broadcasting and press relations, combined in an understanding of the moral power of human compassion, dedication and determination that delivered social work action in housing, adoption and race relations. At the same time, concern for humanists' welfare surfaced. Under Blackham's instigation, the British Humanist Association in 1965 offered its first counselling service to people without religion in an experimental scheme providing pastoral care for religious unbelievers with twelve volunteer counsellors, training for almost a year, who would – it was said – fulfil many of the functions of the parish priest, and might undertake hospital visiting. In this small way, there was a harbinger of larger-scale work in the public sphere in future decades.[79]

PART III

THE CRISIS DECADES, 1970–97

9 THE DREAM FADES, 1970–82

'The BHA had an unhappy year in 1970', the association's *Annual Report* opened in 1971. Falling membership and a £15,386 debt presented evidence of unfolding calamity: membership renewal had not worked properly for some time, instigating a 29 per cent fall in members in twelve months, whilst there had been a hopelessly inflated estimate of income.[1] In a separate blow, the Humanist Trust (set up in 1967 to handle all charitable work of the BHA) had its charitable status revoked in 1970 by the Department of Education and Science. Similar problems afflicted the RPA, whose membership of 4,704 in 1966 was close to its all-time peak, but then crashed 61 per cent in six years and lost charitable status in 1971.[2] The BHA blamed failing office systems for inability to retain members for more than a year or two; the RPA blamed new technology for ending membership-based rationalist book clubs.[3] Both associations put economy measures in place, but the humanist movement was to prove to be in a longer-term malaise, entering almost three decades of decline. What was going wrong?

(a) From boom to bust

Humanists had enjoyed a heady time in the late 1940s, 1950s and 1960s, precipitating domestic growth, contact with churchmen seemingly willing to countenance reform and admittance of humanists to the top table of civil society, and extraordinary international influence. But the 1970s brought new realities at home and overseas. After the high excitement of legislative and legal successes for humanist causes in the 'liberal hour' of the 1960s, the 1970s propagated a sense of burgeoning crisis.

Humanists were induced in the 1960s to accept negotiation with the Vatican and participation in the churches-led Social Morality Council, but the

1970s activated a different dynamic. Church attitudes to humanism distinctly hardened, promoted partly by realignments within religious organisations and partly challenged by the rise of new evangelicals and a breed of 'outsider' lay conservatives like Mary Whitehouse and Malcolm Muggeridge who deprecated the recent sway of liberal clergy. The Catholic Church became better organised and more confident. After the vacillation of the Second Vatican Council and the opening of Catholic discussions with BHA and the International Humanist and Ethical Union (IHEU) in 1966 and 1970, the door slammed shut again. At UNESCO, humanists had sat at the top table in the late 1940s and 1950s, but by the mid-1970s they were part of large outer constituency of influencers meeting in the INGO meeting – the International Non-Governmental Organisations – where humanists sensed they were outgunned by better Roman Catholic organisation. In 1986, Anne Sieve, by then working at SPES but ten years earlier representing the International Planned Parenthood Federation, recalled to Ernst van Brabel, IHEU's representative to UNESCO 1967–80, their shared 'happy memories' of fighting Catholics in these meetings over the celebration of International Women's Year in 1975. In reality, the humanists and their social-reform colleagues found their influence diluted to the point of disappearance in this outer constituency of UNESCO, outnumbered by religionists.[4] No longer were leading humanist figures of the sciences and journalism leading internationalism. By then, many were elderly: Harold Blackham retired as EU secretary in 1965 (though continued with education work), whilst Kingsley Martin died in 1969, Bertrand Russell in 1970, Boyd Orr in 1971, Bronowski in 1974 and Julian Huxley in 1975. The high humanist generation of the 1940s and 1950s was passing.

Meanwhile, the 1960s generation of young humanists was moving on. Many of the 'young Turks' of student and youth humanism of the 'liberal hour' felt that flagship objectives of legislative change had been achieved. As a result, some left the humanist movement during the 1970s. David Pollock of the Oxford University Humanist Group boom of the early 1960s became a prominent figure in the BHA in the mid-1960s, taking a major part in promoting the 'open society' ideology as well as the successful campaigns over abortion, homosexuality, divorce and censorship, but in 1975 he withdrew from the executive committee, reporting: 'towards the end of the sixties, as those reforms were won, it all became rather passé, and [people said] "we don't have to worry about these things now, we're in the clear".'[5] As Pollock's name started to disappear from committee *sederunts* in 1974 and 1975, another to go was Graham Kingsley who reflected in 2020 that his 'drifting away from humanist activity was probably caused by the feelings that key battles had been won' as well as a need to focus on his career. There was, he recalled, 'a justified feeling that important advances had been made, and that in the UK at least, these changes seemed to be secure'.[6] But, complacency quickly gave way to calamity. The Oxford University Humanist Group folded in the early 1970s, followed in 1977 by the winding up of the Student Humanist Federation. Pollock thinks the buzz of excitement had gone for the young by the 1970s:

> It became much more acceptable not to be religious – not as much as it is now, but nevertheless, it was – And they didn't attract the right people to give their time. And it did take a lot of time. So, it went into decline. I don't know when exactly it collapsed, . . . but it clearly did collapse in the early seventies.[7]

An immediate consequence was an internal wrangle over the purposes of humanism: between the 'activists' who wanted the British Humanist Association to bring about social change and the 'philosophers' who wanted it to concentrate on presenting humanism as a viable system by which to live. Each side had their own study groups – including the Humanist Stance for Living Group. A secondary crisis was among local humanist groups, which became less secure, plus the Humanist Teachers' Association and the Humanist Nurses' Organisation which both withered on the vine and closed in 1973.[8] The commitment was suffering, and less 'new blood' was coming up to provide verve. In 1972 Jack Knight told the members in *Humanist News* there were slowly declining numbers.[9] Membership had grown from 2,898 in 1965 to a peak of 4,179 in 1968, but then fell.[10] Internal analysis pointed to maladministration, with systemic failure in membership records; in the days before direct debits and digital payments, there was a lengthy and time-consuming need to post out reminders, to receive and bank cheques, followed by further reminders to catch the careless. Prolonged inefficiency may be part of the issue. Notwithstanding a BHA People First campaign in 1972 on environmental and over-population issues, a marked decline of interest set in from about that year, with membership dipping below that of the mid-1960s. Consequently, BHA's paid staff were cut in half in twenty-four months.[11]

Things got worse. In 1975 further financial crisis induced by high inflation led to a substantial increase in the subscription, which, accompanied by the BHA abandoning its normal press advertising (principally in *The Observer* newspaper), was anticipated would induce a renewed membership fall. This duly happened when a thousand members – 40 per cent of the total – were lost in two years.[12] Moreover, the work of the BHA contracted. By the late 1970s the annual reports were thin, with diminishing numbers of projects reported, committees with fewer meetings and little action; in 1977 there was a record of virtually no social events. By 1979, the association was drifting without a development plan (or even for managing decline), and the 1979 general election showed that several humanist MPs (almost all Labour) lost their seats as Margaret Thatcher swept to power.[13] The financial situation was dismal. The BHA's 1981 *Annual Report* admitted that for many years they had been reliant on the sale of investments, but this resource had been exhausted. 'During the past few years of heavy inflation', it was announced, 'our income has not kept pace with the increase in our running costs. By the end

FIGURE 18 Red Lion Square protest in 1974. In the protest anti-fascists and the National Front each marched to meetings at Conway Hall, with police intervening with horses, culminating in the death of Kevin Gately from a blow to the back of his head. Photo: ©NLA/reportdigital.co.uk.

of 1981 it was obvious that the organisation was in a severe financial crisis and that urgent action was needed.' By the following year the situation was so poor that the frequency of *Humanist News* was reduced.[14]

At Conway Hall, things were just as bad, but for some different reasons. A crisis blew up for South Place Ethical Society in June 1974 when, after four years of renting out Conway Hall to the right-wing anti-immigration party National Front (NF), an anti-fascist counter-demonstration outside in Red Lion Square by Liberation (Fenner Brockway's foundation, formerly the Movement for Colonial Freedom) led to vicious clashes. In these, a young student, Kevin Gately, died from a blow to the head by an unknown person, some alleged a police truncheon – seemingly the first violent death in a political demonstration in mainland Britain since 1919. Liberation had been allowed to book the small hall for the same time as the NF were in the large hall, and the police had permitted both groups to march to the same destination at the gardens. A public inquiry led by Lord Scarman ensued but did not attribute blame for the death.[15] Leaving aside the responsibility directed by some (including Barbara Smoker) at the Metropolitan Police, a three-way dispute broke out at SPES between those who blamed the 'Communist element' and defended the NF's right to free speech and hire of the hall, those who thought right-wing extremists should be banned, and those who blamed the failure of both parties to obey the hiring condition of no marching to meetings at Conway Hall. In any event, forgetful perhaps of SPES's 1952 ban on letting the premises to communist organisations, the general secretary, Peter Cadogan (who gave evidence to the inquiry), stated that 'the principle of free speech that applies [at Speakers Corner] applies equally in Conway Hall', meaning, he said: 'We accept no responsibility, moral or otherwise, for Kevin Gately's death.' An attempt led by Barbara Smoker to get the SPES trustees to apply 'ethical principles' to the commercial letting of rooms failed, beaten by a motion that the principle of freedom of speech must dominate all activities, so that SPES lets to the NF continued – and to other controversial organisations like the Paedophile Information Exchange.[16] Kevin Gately's death posed a clash of principles at SPES, with revelations emerging six years later of a secret and longstanding selective lettings policy. One trustee and life member averred: 'To be true to itself, an Ethical Society cannot aid the National Front by use of its reputable premises to promote racial spite and conflict.'[17] This presaged more rancour to come between right and left within the humanist movement.

But a crisis of an existential kind arose when the trustees and the general committee of SPES got themselves into a fankle over whether or not the society was a religion. During 1972–9, much consideration was given to the striving for 'rational religious sentiment', as the objects of the society stated and which allowed legal weddings under the Places of Worship Registration Act 1855, weighed against the possibility that 'worship' of a deity no longer took place – which would end weddings. In 1973, eight trustees gave the Registrar General written assurance 'that the hall was a place of religious worship', whilst the Law Commission had been told the year prior that 'by no stretch of the imagination can our ethical humanism be held to include "worship"'.[18] Thus, the trustees and general committee exposed what seemed to be deliberate misrepresentation of the 'meetings and observances' at Conway Hall. Whilst staring down the barrel of this particular gun – of massive legal expenses, feared at one point to be as high as £60,000 plus VAT (though working out at only £36,000) – and possible prosecution by the Attorney General, an air of gloom pervaded in 1978–80 as the income from hall lettings declined sharply, and there was even some talk of selling Conway Hall to developers.[19] A High Court case ensued in 1980, the upshot of which was that the society was refused religion status (losing weddings) but was allowed to start afresh with charitable educational status.[20]

Then, a new financial low was reached in March 1982 when *Humanist News* carried a *cri de coeur* for £5,000 urgently needed to re-finance the BHA: 'Critical cash-flow situation. Please, NOW!'[21] All-in-all, these were perilous times for organised British humanism. And things were only going to get worse.

(b) Changing agendas

The boom of the 1955–70 period had been associated with humanism forming a key element of the evolving moral umbrella. This had been enhanced by the 'open society' conceptual framework that played such an important part in helping radicals of the liberal and left wings come together long enough to create a powerful moral utopianism.

This could be seen in a number of ways: in the work of Young Liberals led by Peter Hain in the Anti-Apartheid Movement, including the 'Stop the Seventy Tour' against the all-white Springboks rugby team's matches in 1969–70;[22] in the housing campaign that led to the formation of Shelter in 1966; and in the rise of the Women's Liberation Movement in 1969–70. In a sense, left-wing radicalism appeared to be sidestepped during the youth-led late 1960s in Britain. The Communist Party was seen by many as a spent force, and the Labour Party lacked a powerful left-wing in that decade. And even when the Labour governments of Harold Wilson from 1964 to 1970 were radical, it appeared not on traditional class-based political lines but on social, gender and racial equality, opposing the white-majority government in Britain's former colony in Rhodesia and on the liberal moral agenda of 1967–9. Humanists had been able to play an inspirational part in the 1960s radical causes and aspired to sustain this into the 1970s. In the spirit of the times, the BHA in 1971 sought to align itself with the Women's Liberation Movement, going 'overboard for it' as one journalist put it, backing the demand for free contraception, abortion on demand, 24-hour nurseries and equal pay.[23] Notwithstanding left-wing radicals being hard at work (of which more in a moment), humanists had genuinely helped define this pliable apolitical character of 1960s radicalism.

Humanist membership decline can be contextualised in two main things. First, the agenda of the 'liberal hour' – that had given common cause for humanists with feminists, housing reformers, anti-racism and libertarianism – had attained much of its initial objectives by 1970, depriving humanism of achievable targets. Meanwhile, other aspirations such as the legalisation of assisted dying (then referred to as euthanasia) proved impossible to advance in the face of an unfavourable political climate. The opposition to liberalisation in the 1960s had been clearly comprehensible as the machinations of conservative religion, but from the early 1970s the role of religion in moral politics in Britain was thought to be on the wane. Diane Munday, a senior BHA member and a leading activist for abortion law reform, perceived in retrospect that there had been a change in campaigning style in the 1970s to which organised humanism failed to adapt. Prior to this, campaigning had been 'direct' in the sense that influence or pressure would be brought to bear on those who had the power to bring about change.[24] Indeed, whilst acknowledging the participation of humanists in mass demonstrations such as CND, Harold Blackham had conceived of the BHA as an organisation which lobbied those in the corridors of power.[25] Munday felt that the less academic and more diffuse tactics adopted by political movements in the 1970s were alien to those who envisaged campaigning as 'reasoning rather than shouting slogans'. The subsequent hiatus in the movement's campaigning was, she told us, brought about by a refusal or inability by existing members to change tactics, at the same time as an unwillingness or inability to recruit those who were attracted to a wider campaigning base.[26]

Second, come the 1970s the 'apolitical' reform umbrella underwent significant decline, effectively ending humanist-style radicalism as a major force. The 'open society' idea, promoted by Harold Blackham and David Pollock, peaked at the Festival Hall conference of December 1969, but by the time the book of the event appeared in 1971 the concept was being overtaken by the regeneration of left-wing zeal after the election of the Conservative government of Edward Heath.[27] New radicalism arose to confront burgeoning right-wing racism in the National Front and the British National Party and embodied in right-wing youth groups such as the skinheads. The coherence of the Labour Party as a centrist home of radical politics eroded quickly, opening the way to the splintering of British socialism and the collapse of the Labour government in 1979 amid recriminations. Radicalism was re-politicised in new groups, often Trotskyist in ideology. These included the International Socialists (IS), founded in 1962, renamed the Socialist Workers Party in 1977; the Anti-Nazi League it created in 1977–81 (and various factionalist revolutionary socialist offshoots); Militant Tendency, formed in 1964; the International Marxist Group, 1968–82, which arose from a split in the Communist Party of Great Britain; and Rock Against Racism of 1976–82. The moral landscape shifted. Even in CND and demonstrations at Greenham Common in the later 1970s against the installation of American cruise missiles, at which there were undoubtedly humanists, the marshalling ethic was one of feminism.[28]

Against this leftist radicalism, the years 1970–82 were framed by manifest decline in British humanism – decline in numbers, spirits and the power of its liberal moral leadership. BHA membership slid from 4,122 in 1970 to 1,126 in 1983, whilst that of the RPA fell from 2,538 in 1968 to 1,460 in 1982.[29] One nadir in fortunes came in January 1982 when the BHA executive committee wrote to the IHEU headquarters in Utrecht to confess that the association could not meet its financial commitments – mainly its annual subscriptions to the union. A deficit had been running for many years, the general secretary wrote, but the situation was now very serious. Seemingly, the BHA had run out of cash, and the only asset that the organisation possessed was its grand (though largely let out) headquarters building at 13 Prince of Wales Terrace in Kensington, renovated at great cost in 1970, which, it had been decided, could not be sold as it would achieve a very low price.[30] The following year, 1983, BHA told IHEU that it had lost 56 per cent of its paying membership in a year, and, in an act of charity, IHEU wrote off the BHA's 1981 debt – the subs for 1982 and 1983 remaining outstanding.[31] To underline its dire predicament, the BHA executive told an emergency general meeting in 1982 that it had to institute a 25 per cent hike in its subscriptions, seek charitable status and form a separate body of non-charitable status that could legally continue with its campaigning work, especially against religious interests. This was a reversal. The EGM was told: 'We have no investments left. We have a small membership of about 1300. We cannot continue to exist, let alone work and expand, while we pay in tax 40% of our income from rents, sales of books and Happy Man ware, social events and suchlike.' Sounding almost like an epitaph, charitable status was the only way to reduce tax and rates burdens and seek grants from other charities. With SPES winning its legal case in 1980 concerning charitable status, the objective of 'advancing Humanism' as an educational or charitable object was now accepted as a bone fide charitable cause.[32] So, there remained hope in 1983 that BHA could rebalance its books, resume open campaigning and rebuild its infrastructure of members and causes. For, without causes humanists had no raison d'etre.

(c) Campaigning

For all the catalogue of threats and failures, the 1970s is a curious period in British humanist development. On the one hand, it seemed like the 1960s had experienced the most incredible advance in humanist social aims. Yet, on the other hand, the campaigning opportunities seemed to be narrowing. Ironically, British society was secularising and, arguably, 'humanising' itself, leaving what role for the BHA?

One of the most remarkable developments was the growing, almost effortless, transformation in broadcasting culture in the 1970s. Even the BBC seemed to be changing, as programmes with a humanist bent were broadcast. When in December 1973 Cardinal John Heenan debated at peak 'God-slot' time (directed by the Postmaster General to be reserved for religious programmes) on BBC television over three Sundays the benefits of the Roman Catholic Church to British society, he was overpowered by two humanist and atheist debaters – abortion campaigner Madeleine Simms and philosopher Bernard Williams[33] – an extraordinary event, never to be repeated on British television. However, even when the sympathetic director general Charles Curran in the mid-1970s sought to restrict the BBC's role as a bulwark of Christianity, the outcome was more to do with letting non-Christian religions behind the microphone rather than permitting direct promotion of humanism – a view affirmed by the Annan Report of 1977. The real change came in science, cultural and wildlife programmes, starting with Jacob Bronowski's *The Ascent of Man* (1973) landmark series on science and civilisation, and on through other high-value atheist-leaning documentaries including Carl Sagan's *Cosmos* (1980) astronomy series to dominate high-value science, archaeology and history programmes. This happened, too, in much comedy programming, with many atheist comics and documentarists coming to the fore from the 1960s, perhaps most noteworthy of whom were Stephen Fry, later a distinguished supporter of the BHA, and the polymath Jonathan Miller, later to be president of the Rationalist Association.[34]

As cultural change proceeded, the purpose of humanism was an issue that humanists worried over like a dog with a bone. With constant advancement into new areas – especially in relation to sexual knowledge, internationalism and disarmament – critics within the movement argued that the primary, perhaps the only, purpose was to fight the churches' influence and, for some, their very existence. This notion of 'core purposes', if you will, resurfaced in every period of modern humanist history. When Blackham's dialogues with the Roman Catholic Church in the early 1970s petered out, some colleagues wished to distance humanism from religion. In 1973 Harry Stopes-Roe (1924–2014) used the phrase 'education in stances for living' on a BHA religion in school's project (a term criticised by James Hemming as static and lacking the dynamism children would understand), but turned in 1975 into the term 'life stance' – a moniker to envelop religion and nonreligious positions. 'The essence of the matter is', Stopes-Roe wrote, 'that "life stance" is an opening-up of the concept "religion"', and he spent considerable space in lectures and published essays refining definitions in terms of philosophy, morality, values and 'ultimate reality'.[35] Initially used on Birmingham's draft Agreed Syllabus of Education, Stopes-Roe thought it would be 'helpful for the humanist movement generally if we could clear up the confusion on "religion" [and] on the consequent anger & animosity that flow from that difference of opinion on it'.[36] Happily adopted inside the movement internationally in the later 1970s and 1980s, 'life stance' failed to catch on more widely outside of it.[37] For some members, humanist organisations should offer systems to encourage and counsel people to lose faith. For others, the humanist movement had different purposes. A writer in *Humanist News* in 1976 noted the currency of issues to do with homosexuality and abortion: 'Sir, Has the BHA gone sex mad? . . . The BHA seems to be losing sight of its main purpose which should be to fight religious influence and belief.'[38] Whilst the NSS maintained its frontal assault on religions and the RPA provided educational materials for the layperson to understand the folly of faith, the BHA had set up a study group on 'religious humanism' in the late 1960s that continued into the 1970s.[39] Added to this, Blackham had set up the Counselling Group, which was to prove very popular in the 1970s, offering one-to-one help for BHA members and others at an open-house 'Sunday Centre' in BHA headquarters. At the same time, the association's executive noted the rising demand for humanist celebrants for funeral ceremonies and organised a one-day seminar to test demand for training whilst reaching an agreement with RPA, SPES and NSS to develop a joint list of celebrants.[40] With the rising popularity of the self and well-being in the 1970s, humanists were evidently participating in fundamental culture change.

But some aspects of the movement's issues never seemed to change, resuscitating old combative instincts and slogans. Despite the occasional interest of Scotland Yard in the 1950s in pursuing complaints of blasphemy from NSS open-air speakers,[41] freedom of expression had seemed to flourish from the mid-1960s onwards and several set-piece episodes, such as the obscenity trials for *Lady Chatterley's Lover* (1960) and '*Oz*' magazine (1971), bore witness to this, providing apparent evidence that the legal system now backed freedom over prohibition. However, there were setbacks, one being the apparent victory of Sir Cyril Black MP's successful private prosecution of Hubert Selby Jr's *Last Exit to Brooklyn* (1966, but which had little effect because of being limited to the City of London, and was reversed on appeal in 1968).[42] Libertarians and writers were convinced by such precedents that the appetite of the state for prosecuting either obscenity or blasphemy, and the appetite of juries to find guilty, had evaporated.

Yet, to those not of their persuasion, they looked like a dangerous lobby. A leading sceptic of this new freedom was Mary Whitehouse, Cyril Black's friend, who questioned how far discussion of the limits of free speech had merely been establishing opportunities for people to test its boundaries.[43] This had been the impetus behind her formation of the National Viewers' and Listeners' Association (1965), a constituency Whitehouse cultivated assiduously. She was especially vocal in ensuring that the Danish filmmaker Jens Jurgen Thorsen was excluded from entering Britain in 1976 where he proposed to produce a film loosely entitled *The Sex Life of Christ*, and she galvanised opposition from the Prime Minister James Callaghan, Cardinal Basil Hume, Archbishop Robert Runcie and seemingly the Queen.[44] Then, in June 1976, Mary Whitehouse received a copy of *Gay News* in the post, containing James Kirkup's poem *The Love That Dares to Speak Its Name* that depicted promiscuity with a range of contemporaries including the Roman centurion at Christ's execution who then proceeded to have sex with Christ's corpse.[45] After investigation and legal wrangling, Whitehouse instigated a private prosecution for blasphemous libel amid considerable publicity. The high-powered lawyers John Mortimer and Geoffrey Robertson defended *Gay News*, confident of acquittal by parading literary and media establishment figures, as in the successful defence at the *Lady Chatterley* trial of 1960.[46] Archbishop Donald Coggan and Cardinal Basil Hume refused to appear for the prosecution, but this advantage was nullified by the presiding judge, Alan King-Hamilton, who many felt had a hostile attitude to the defendants. He also had a receptivity to Whitehouse's piety which, Jim Herrick said, the defence failed to take seriously, holding prayer meetings near the court. The judge summed up by noting the poem's power to inflame public order. The jury convicted by a margin of ten to two, subsequently confirmed on appeal and a Law Lords' hearing.[47] The case mobilised free speech lobbies in England and Scotland, led by Bill McIlroy, former editor of *The Freethinker* and secretary of National Secular Society, and Nicolas Walter, the editor of RPA's *New Humanist*. For Herrick, the case stiffened resolve in the Campaign for Homosexual Equality.[48] But things then took a surprising turn. The Monty Python film *Life of Brian* appeared in 1979, for some a sustained attack upon orthodox religion with the Brian figure wandering on a picaresque journey through a New Testament landscape peopled with human frailty, absurdity and idiocy. In the end, Brian met the same fate as Christ, but the crucifixion was turned into something of a comic set piece. The Python film was banned by thirty-nine local authorities but was never prosecuted or banned nationally, largely down to the film's painstaking focus on Brian and not Christ.[49] So, this meant that the Kirkup poem was the last successful prosecution for blasphemy in the UK. Yet, though McIlroy and Walter lost their battle with Mary Whitehouse, within thirty years their side was to win the war.

A notable outcome of the *Gay News* trial was the formation of the Gay Humanist Group (GHG) in 1978 – later the Gay and Lesbian Humanist Group – responding to Whitehouse's reported claim that opposition to her moral crusading was orchestrated by a 'homosexual, humanist lobby'.[50] George Broadhead (1933–2021), then a member of the Campaign for Homosexual Equality (CHE), reportedly said: 'We know there's no such thing as an organised band of humanist homosexuals – so let's make it happen!'[51] A committee of six founding members, including seasoned anti-apartheid activist and militant secularist Barry Duke (b. 1947) and Jim Herrick, was assembled to create the world's first gay humanist group.[52] Launched during the 1979 CHE conference in Brighton, Bill McIlroy warned that 'the small gains made by Britain's gay population in the last ten years could be quickly reversed if Christian reactionaries had their way'.[53] The conference was opposed by twenty-two local evangelical clergy and a menacing leaflet from the far-right National Front. Duke remembered saying to Broadhead,

'We've gotta do something' – and he said, 'What?' And I said, 'Let's pick one of the churches, . . . wait for the service to begin and then march in, stand at the back of the hall and just stand with our arms folded and say *absolutely nothing* and stare at the pastor – because there's nothing they can do us for.'[54]

A service at a Pentecostal Church duly disintegrated amid scenes of chaos, with not only a confrontation but also a concession from a pastor that he had signed the protest without having examined its contents properly.[55] Barry Duke subsequently noted with satisfaction that this church eventually shut down due to lack of custom and became a bar.[56] As popular attitudes towards gay relationships hardened in the 1980s,[57] the GHG aimed to promote an awareness of humanism among gay people, the rights of gays and humanists, and to further an understanding and awareness of gay people among humanists.[58] Author and lesbian activist Maureen Duffy (b. 1933) became the group's honorary president, giving a philosophical underpinning for the group's existence in a lecture at Conway Hall in March 1980 and a subsequent pamphlet. Duffy emphasised that the group's campaigning would make a 'contribution to the ethics of compassion' within the evolving 'fluid morality' based on common feeling and humanity. 'Coming out', she said, would 'leaven the lump of society with our visible and acknowledged presence' and help 'grasp our own existence and participate in the whole of human life'.[59]

(d) Sex and moral education

The BHA was gratified to learn in 1976 that public opinion was following its position on voluntary euthanasia, with 69 per cent of British people agreeing strongly or moderately with its availability for people with incurable illness, including 54 per cent of Catholics, 72 per cent of Anglicans, 71 per cent of Methodists, 80 per cent of atheists and 86 per cent of agnostics.[60] This seemed like evidence that it was not merely sexual matters upon which the movement attracted wide support. Certainly, with campaigners like Diane Munday and her humanist colleague Madeleine Simms remaining active in sexual-reform work in the 1970s, the humanist movement's social policy continued to lead progressive opinion. Munday continued to speak to the NSS and others in defence of abortion law reform and hung on the peg of 'Religious Opposition to Sexual Freedom'.[61] In 1976, Munday said that some churches and clergy supported issues like abortion and even divorce law change because such reform 'embodies many Humanist principles and is clearly the result of applying Humanist rather than religious criteria'. She went on: '[W]ith the growing awareness of the value of happiness on this earth, and acceptance of the fact that absolutes have no place in human relationships, a more reasonable attitude becomes possible which eventually leads to the sloughing off of old dogmas.' Many humanists regarded liberal change as a great victory for humanist ideals: 'Today, we Humanists are often told we are living on the remnants of Christian Heritage. It would I think be equally accurate to say we are thriving on the wealth of Humanist achievement before which ecclesiastical power has had to give way.'[62]

Some in the movement did not like this. They felt that social policy, plus nuclear disarmament, did not define the character of humanism, and, consequently, these policies started to fall from campaigning. So much so that in 1981 Harry Stopes-Roe and Fenner Brockway expressed disappointment that the humanist movement had not espoused for some time the pro-nuclear-disarmament cause.[63] Some thought-specific policies were being foisted upon the membership. In 1976, J. A. A. Nichols of Guildford wrote to *Humanist News*: 'Sir, Do we have to support abortion on demand to remain members of the BHA? . . . Could it be that the "leading lights" of the BHA, in supporting the lunatic fringe of pro-abortionists, have only succeeded in making us look foolish in the eyes of the public, and weakening our influence in other far more important areas?'[64] Munday and Simms responded vigorously to the criticism of abortion on demand being BHA policy, and letters continued for a few months in 1976.[65] Likewise, the decriminalisation of homosexuality divided opinion; A. A. Nichols of Guildford opposed BHA policy of support for the Campaign for Homosexual Equality.[66] At the heart of such spats was a vision of one section of the membership that the association existed to promote a secularist agenda against theocracy. Yet, the leadership resisted, and the BHA, NSS and RPA were mobilised in 1977 with a plethora of political, medical and women's groups to defend the Abortion Act from the threat of Catholic-orchestrated repeal.[67]

Heterosexual sex education came to the forefront of intellectual debate within and outwith the movement in the early 1970s. Humanists Eustace Chesser, Alex Comfort and Martin Cole were the three longstanding instigators, with a fourth, Alex Craig of the Progressive League, attacking censorship. An influential pamphlet by Maurice Hill and Michael Lloyd-Jones, *Sex Education: The Erroneous Zone* published by the NSS in 1970, gave a hilarious and ridiculing review of the howlers to be found in existing, conservative-driven sex education publications – to the extent of ridiculing Chesser's publications. A recent historian of education quipped that 'the view of modernity endorsed by the NSS was a variety of vulgar(ised), that is, ill-digested, typically leftwing or left-leaning, Freudianism'.[68] A new sexologist in the movement, Dr Martin Cole (1931–2015), a lecturer in genetics at what became Aston University, led the abortion reform campaign in Birmingham in the mid-1960s and then founded the Birmingham, later renamed British, Pregnancy Advisory Service – reputedly initially conducting consultations in his front room, with the private Calthorpe Nursing Home he co-founded being where abortions were undertaken. But he was also a promoter of sex education, becoming well known for his work on films and for being director of *Growing Up* (1971), a 23-minute film aimed at children. Scripted, narrated and directed by Cole, *Growing Up* became the target of negative press and political attention for its scenes of a naked family (man with erect penis, woman, boy and girl), the depiction of heterosexual intercourse by a clothed couple and a scene of female masturbation. Strongly supported by the humanist movement, the film premiered in Conway Hall in October 1971 with over 400 free tickets distributed by the South Place Ethical Society, including to the British commander of the Salvation Army, who ordered 20 tickets for his officers. But prior to screening, SPES was warned by the Director of Public Prosecutions that no child be admitted and let it be known they would be watching the entrants to the building; SPES trustees, fearful of legal proceedings that might bankrupt the entire society, voted 6-3 to ban the event, only for the general committee to find cancellation impossible at three days' notice.[69] No legal case resulted then or later, so that the film was widely screened to university students in the autumn of 1971, and in the later 1970s in a few schools in Scotland where the DPP's remit did not extend.[70] The furore that followed was led by Mary Whitehouse, taking various forms – including Lord Longford speaking in a Lords debate on obscenity, and the temporary suspension of schoolteacher Jennifer Muscutt, the masturbator in the film, by Birmingham Local Education Authority (which also banned the film from its schools). Though Baroness Dora

Gaitskell and a local Anglican canon came to Cole's defence, he was rebuked by a raft of politicians and the Archbishop of Canterbury, Michael Ramsey. Criticised by one historian as being 'pre-feminist' and tending to male chauvinism, *Growing Up* is credited with being the most influential sex education film for children rarely to be (legally) seen by children, and for setting a red line for British sex education material that has never been crossed.[71]

Cole's initiative regarding sexual imagery was part of wider humanist sexology. In the same vein was James Hemming, the leading humanist moral education campaigner and author, long an influential figure in the BHA.[72] The most self-assured innovation came in Alex Comfort's 1972 book *The Joy of Sex: A Gourmet Guide to Lovemaking* – famous for its explicit line-drawings of sexual positions, accompanied by textual guidance on the use of intense levels of intimacy. Already a well-known figure on BBC radio and television, Comfort found that his book propelled him to celebrity status, becoming the template for many imitators. It did well overseas, spending eleven weeks at the top of the *New York Times* bestseller list, and between 1972 and 2021 went through numerous reprints and new editions (including a pocket edition), as well as a sequel, *More Joy of Sex* (1973), with its own multiple editions. Notwithstanding, sex education did not advance evenly in British schools. Despite many interventions by state education authorities and a recent legal requirement to teach it in England (strongly promoted by Humanists UK), students in the twenty-first century report huge variation in the content and quality of sex education. In any event, the internet in the late 1990s undid secrecy about sex.

In the 1970s, the most intense of humanist movement activity concerned moral education, whose starting point was the need to reform religious education. Moral education has been a central concern of the humanist movement since F. J. Gould's work in the 1890s and 1900s, but it was in the late 1960s and 1970s that it attained its highest point of national success. Educational psychologist James Hemming and close friend Harold J. Blackham came in the early 1960s to share a vision of implementing humanism in wider society through transforming religious education into moral education. Blackham, ever the strategist, perceived this also as an arena that could bring the humanist movement into closer harmony with like-minded educationists in both state and church sectors. Meanwhile, Hemming brought a philosophical and practical educational experience, with well-worked curricula, publications and trials already undertaken. Among progressive educationalists, there was belief in moral education emerging as a by-product of the method – of classes in critical thinking (sometimes termed philosophy). This merged various groups of progressives, and the humanist movement, especially the Rationalist Press Association, perceiving the promotion of rationalism among school children (notably of the new comprehensive schools) to be a truly egalitarian and society-wide route to building an ethical society.

JAMES HEMMING, 1909–2007

The most influential thinker on what humanist-based education for children would look like, James Hemming was trained as a psychologist, cutting his teeth as advisor from 1945 on the international New Education Fellowship that promoted radical education and experimentation. Already a keen supporter of moral education as a replacement for religious education and for sex education for all children, he was one of three humanists to appear for the successful defence in the *Lady Chatterley* obscenity book trial in 1960. The NEF had links with UNESCO and internationalist ambitions like the humanist movement itself, so Hemming was already well known when, in 1963, he joined the BHA on its formation. In 1965 he sought to get the NEF on side with his plans: 'The situation we face today is that the concept of absolute and eternal morality rooted in divine revelation has for some time been breaking down. This is not because people are becoming degenerate but because the foundations of certainty have been crumbling.'[73] Hemming promoted East–West understanding in education, touring in Europe, Australia and South Africa in the late 1940s and organising an early international

FIGURE 19 James Hemming. Photo: Humanists UK/Bishopsgate Archive.

conference in 1962 with Julian Huxley. Closely associated with Harold Blackham and his strategy of accommodation with the churches, Hemming was the leading professional educationalist in the BHA and the Social Morality Council from 1965, writing many books on child psychology and sex education. He was closely associated with the BHA-sponsored *Journal for Moral Education*, becoming the first nonreligionist in the 1970s on the National Council for Religious Education. His skilled advocacy did much to reorientate educational professionals to the openness, diversity and neutrality to which much of British schooling now aspires.

The arrival in 1965 of the Social Morality Council had done much to raise Harold Blackham's stature, giving him the opportunity to chair the organisation and become the key British figure in promoting moral education. He had for some years planned moral education to be at the heart of humanist activities, starting in 1963 when a group of humanist educators, including Hemming, met at the Institute of Education in London, bringing in some Christian educators to jointly produce a report in 1965, followed in 1968 by the launch of an SMC moral education campaign. The final element to slot into place was a source of funding. They hooked up with academic educationalist John Wilson (1928–2003), nine years a schoolmaster and then a professor of religion at Trinity College, Toronto, before becoming a lecturer first in philosophy and then in educational studies at Oxford University, and also director of the Farmington Trust Research Unit.[74] The Farmington Trust was a Christian organisation, seemingly linked to a Christian school, and became the funder of the Social Morality Council between 1968 and 1972 before withdrawing, apparently because it found Blackham's proposals 'too secular'. From September 1969 the Social Morality Council itself registered as a charity (later renamed the Norham Foundation), seemingly gaining funding from May 1973 from a new charity, the Warborough Trust, set up specifically to fund the SMC and moral education.[75] The funds raised by these means oiled the wheels of the movement through to the early 1970s.

The funds were used initially by John Wilson to start a moral education curriculum project in 1968 at Oxford University which generated syllabus material in the form of books. Blackham got the SMC and Catholic Church to support the campaign after he produced a paper that won over Edward Oliver, Catholic Bishop Christopher Butler and Anglican Bishop of Durham Ian Ramsey, who published *The Fourth R*, a 1970 report on religious education that backed 'the "humanistic" function of education' and Blackham-designed radical reform.[76] Having registered as an educational charity in 1969, the SMC in 1970 produced its own report, *Moral and Religious Education in County Schools,* largely written by Blackham, and he became the executive director of the SMC in 1970. The SMC then took over a separate organisation, the Council for Moral Education, acquiring its resources and won a grant of some £5,000 in 1972 from Margaret Thatcher, as secretary of state at the Department of Education, which funded the creation of the Centre for Moral Education, initially at Goldsmith's College in London. And in 1971, the *Journal of Moral Education* was launched, published by the Rationalist Press Association.[77]

From the start, Blackham envisaged the movement would be the means to put an 'open society' in place in Britain. His sight was set upon 'a universal morality [that] would consist of rules of conduct equally binding on all in virtue of their being human'.[78] The moral education movement was to be the means to invoke this, but it was not to be a new theocratic moral system: 'From a secular and Humanist point of view, an Open Society requires universal sharing of public institutions and services, not least education, with toleration of different ways of thinking and living'.[79] By producing his own approving report on these developments, Blackham marshalled the BHA behind this work, and moral education became centre-front of association campaigning. From 1968 to the mid-1980s, Blackham was the driving force behind this, not as a vision of revolt against religions or religious education, but one of compromise. Moral education, he wrote in 1983, 'is governed by a general concept of morality shared across cultural boundaries down the ages, for which there is historical evidence'.[80]

This hopeful progress started to falter in the 1970s. Blackham's campaign was not without controversy in humanist circles with, in 1970, voices of protest raised in the NSS's *The Freethinker* against humanists being rushed into cooperative work with churches without due democratic process.[81] Thirteen years later, Harry Stopes-Roe, then chair of the BHA, told Blackham that he was surrendering too much ground to religionists and probably mixing with them too much both in the SMC and in consultations with church figures. In a letter, Stopes-Roe impressed upon Blackham that humanism should be part of a wider 'education in naturalistic life stances' rather than embedded in religious education; Blackham replied: 'Oh dear! I suspect we have different views of morality or of what is important in it.'[82] The differences were broader than that. Side by side with attempted rapprochement over moral education, the BHA education committee continued to pursue an attack policy upon church schools. In 1973 David Pollock organised an education meeting at the Labour Party Conference at Blackpool, with a project group for a Campaign Against Religion in County Schools set up with £200 BHA funding, and agreeing to leaflet delegates with a James Hemming-devised slogan: 'Social Education, not Religious Education – Give the Children something they *can* believe in.'[83] Harry Stopes-Roe fought the education corner vigorously at BHA through the 1970s and 1980s, keeping it at the forefront of committee meetings, generating articles on philosophy and morality by the score, hosting conferences (often in Birmingham), composing discursive letters and writing to members of religious and schools committees relentlessly pressing the humanist position.

Hemming and Stopes-Roe represented clashing strategies at times, with the latter being upbraided by the BHA general secretary for going beyond policy. But in September 1973, they won a dual invitation to join the National Council for Religious Education.[84] This seemed a moment of humanist breakthrough, accompanied simultaneously by admission to the Standing Conference on Inter-Faith Dialogue in Education (SCIFDE). Most hopeful of all, Stopes-Roe had been co-opted onto the Birmingham City conference modernising RE for schools, culminating in January 1974 with an innovatory 'agreed syllabus' that included teaching on humanism and communism. Birmingham led several local education authorities (LEAs) sympathetic to the inclusion of nonreligion in the syllabuses, including in Hampshire and the ILEA (inner London), which later produced a report on innovative plans for religion in school assemblies.[85] However, there was a setback in Birmingham where in late 1974 Conservative Party members on the City Council objected to the RE syllabus, including humanism and communism whilst the Church of England National Society for Promoting Religious Education opposed plans for revamping school assemblies; legal opinion was sought that concluded the syllabus was illegal. Stopes-Roe was incensed by this. He drafted an emergency motion for the BHA executive committee, put to the AGM, which burned the association's bridges with ecumenical approaches to religious education, demanding the national adoption of 'Education in Stances for Living' to replace 'Religious Education', whilst in a published statement Stopes-Roe branded the proponents of RE as universally 'bigots'.[86] The language was intense, the mood furious. Perhaps it was coincidence, but in early 1975 Harry Stopes-Roe was in effect disinvited from joining the National Council for Religious Education, whilst James Hemming was twice affirmed by the religious organisers as the favoured appointee (despite two BHA officials asking NCRE that Stopes-Roe be invited instead). Though reinstated by April 1975, Stopes-Roe's anger was sustained when, back in Birmingham, the agreed syllabus was revised to reduce nonreligious viewpoints to 'context' for understanding religion. He compelled the BHA to appoint a QC who advised that any challenge to the lawfulness of the revision to the syllabus was likely to fail and cost £4,000 – which might well have bankrupted the BHA. The mood remained febrile – both within and outwith the association. In February 1975, Barbara Smoker, supported by half the meeting, moved on the BHA executive committee that Stopes-Roe's phrase 'stance for living' be removed from an association draft Education Bill and replaced with 'belief systems'; with Stopes-Roe refusing to back down, the chairman used his casting vote to defer the matter to a sub-committee.[87] It seems that Stopes-Roe's loss on the Birmingham agreed RE syllabus so angered him in 1974 that he ever after refused to return to a policy of full-blooded compromise with the churches. His irascible rhetoric stiffened whilst his intolerance of potential allies grew – including feminists with whom he could not agree on key issues like beauty contests and pornography, even siding with arch-conservative Mary Whitehouse.[88] This would have important consequences when he was chair of the BHA in the 1980s. Meantime, ecumenism over RE was in meltdown, with various Anglican RE teachers' associations offering stiffening resistance to the humanist intrusion and worrying over the direction for the 'Agreed Syllabus'.[89] Yet, from the dust emerged in 1975 an influential BHA argument on RE, 'Objective, Fair and Balanced', co-written by Stopes-Roe and Pollock, which, from there on, guided association education policy.

Whilst direct discussion over modifying the RE syllabus collapsed in 1974–5, and despite the BHA's multiple trajectories, the moral education strategy seemed to be progressing. Harold Blackham had engineered from 1970 that it be devolved to the Social Morality Council which he chaired, perhaps in part so that it could be a charitable body (which the BHA at that time was not) designing both teaching and training for teachers, and could treat with sympathetic churches without interruption from critics like Stopes-Roe. Along with the DoE grant in 1974, the SMC found funding for the Centre for Moral Education from various sources. However, finance was intermittent and fear for the closure of the SMC was expressed in a Lords debate in November.[90] The Centre was racking up bills and ill-feeling with its university hosts and had to become peripatetic, transferring successively in the mid- and late 1970s from Goldsmiths College to the Institute of Education, both in London, thence to St Martin's College in Lancaster, and finally to the University of Leicester. Each move fostered bad feelings. The principal of St Martin's College was particularly angry at being, in his view, misled and then abandoned as the SMC moved its centre from Lancaster to Leicester without warning.[91] This was symptomatic of the organisational nightmare the centre's governing body, the Social Morality Council, became under the secretaryship of Edward Oliver. He was a past master at clever lobbying for money, camouflaging a poor bank balance, and convincing backers of signs of success in grant acquisition – in one case, when he had not yet written an application. For much of the 1970s, the humanist–Catholic coalition of Blackham, Oliver and Bishop Butler petitioned charities and government departments seeking the funds to get moral education off the ground. But just as the Stopes-Roe frenzy erupted in January 1975, SMC was declared dormant and about to go into liquidation. Somehow it kept going as a voluntary body, with appeals for funds to Archbishop Donald Coggan on the promise of a 'comprehensive support and information service for teachers and parents', and undertaking to support home-school partnership.[92] A meeting was sought with Prime Minister Harold Wilson, and, on only getting to see Fred Mulley the education secretary, Blackham and Oliver asked the Labour government for the unlikely sum of £1 million over five years; Mulley contemptuously rejected their request – perhaps because they asked him to emulate Margaret Thatcher.[93]

Between 1973 and 1978, rising ecumenical pressure and sometimes foreboding were expressed in letters to Michael Ramsey and Donald Coggan, archbishops of Canterbury, concerning the consequences if the Social Morality Council initiative between humanist and Christians on moral education was allowed to collapse. Opposing letters came from Catholic and Anglican bishops too,[94] leading to the Anglican Bishop of St Albans and a Conservative MP informing Runcie specifically that they opposed the joint moves of Harold Blackham and Bishop Butler to get state funding.[95] More letters from Anglican defenders of the status quo followed, warning that any move to end the obligation for RE and school worship 'would legalise the propagation of such atheistic ideologies as Humanism and Communism'.[96] Though Margaret Thatcher when education minister in 1974 had initially funded SMC, she seemed less than friendly when leader of the opposition in 1977, so that humanists were shut out from the two main political parties on RE and moral education. Pincered by Catholic–Anglican friction, Blackham's strategy of improving relations with the churches, seemingly the only route to humanist wider influence, was in the late 1970s on the rocks due to opposition from both conservative religionists and assertive rationalists. The Social Morality Council kept going until the early 1980s, but without Church of England backing, and with an apparent withdrawal of Catholic Church support, it had become solely a humanist body until its dissolution in 2005.

In 1980, a new member wrote in the *Humanist Newsletter* about how she joined the BHA in the hope of becoming actively involved: 'I looked forward to stimulating discussions, comradeship and a regular chance of meeting like-minded souls. Imagine my disillusionment when I encountered a declining, tired and fragmented organisation: constantly moaning about finances and no support from a local BHA Group.'[97] As it contracted, BHA narrowed to a hard-core membership which urged renewed battle with religion whilst others perceived a declining threat from that quarter. In this atmosphere, British humanism's unity and entire future was at risk.

10 THE LONG, TROUBLED EIGHTIES, 1983–97

The rising problems in the humanist movement seemed to multiply in the 1980s. Though there were important international developments, a financial and membership crisis of 1982–3 caused British humanism to shrink to a shadow of what it had been in 1968, pushing the British Humanist Association again to the constitutional predicament – to campaign or be a charity? A 1984 editorial in *New Humanist* noted that the memberships of humanist and secularist organisations and readership of its publications were estimated to be 'probably lower now than they have been since the Second if not the First World War'.[1] At the same time, internal rancour grew louder with the onset of Thatcherism.

(a) From inspiration to administration

In 1975, a young telephone engineer made his way to the headquarters of the British Humanist Association at 13 Prince of Wales Terrace, Kensington. John Leeson (b. 1947) was younger than most humanists, a product of adult education and working in communications, and giving little thought to religion until his mid-twenties. However, when he broke off from a Jewish girlfriend because her parents disapproved of her marrying outside the faith, he browsed in Foyles and found Bertrand Russell's book, *Why I am Not a Christian*, developing a humanist consciousness that took him to join London Young Humanists, swiftly rising through their depleted ranks to organise their activities.

Then in 1983, Leeson was co-opted onto the BHA's executive committee where he discovered that all was not well. The committee was 'a centre of paralysis', swamped in paperwork, troubled by clashing personalities and distracted by real estate management of the headquarters building. Leeson noted that the general secretary of the time, Maeve Denby (d. 1993), struggled in the executive committee (EC) meetings where 'she would have needed to be an amazon-type character to have resisted the atmosphere'.[2] In 1983, Denby remonstrated that 'the EC must spend more of its time on policy', including, she suggested, the humanist stances on disarmament, euthanasia, moral education and disestablishment of the church: 'But it seems to me crazy that the whole of the agenda is to do with administration.'[3] Leeson succeeded Denby in that year and noted for his four years as honorary general secretary that fractious BHA committee meetings could run late into the night. A dominating presence on the executive committee for almost two decades was Harry Stopes-Roe – as chairman 1977–83, and executive committee member until 1994. A philosopher and university lecturer preoccupied with getting humanism into moral and religious education in schools,[4] he was intellectually gifted and avuncular on a personal level, but even Stopes-Roe's friends conceded that he was a poor leader and manager. Leeson drew on his industrial-management experience and mooted a system of standing orders, seeking to improve the conduct of meetings but irritating Stopes-Roe.[5] When Richard Paterson (b. 1945), a former civil servant and humanist celebrant from South Wales, took the chair in 1995, he found the association 'virtually moribund' with new members deterred by the inactivity in the organisation. Paterson felt Harry Stopes-Roe revealed a 'genial individual on a personal level' but a 'powerful, dominant personality' who viewed dissent as a threat to his authority. Those unwilling to submit to a rather authoritarian rule simply left.[6] The new executive director, Robert Ashby, unflatteringly characterised Stopes-Roe as a 'ponderous, glasses on chin, quasi-philosopher' and also described how he drove away activists.[7] Eventually, Stopes-Roe in 1994 was counselled to withdraw from the day-to-day running of the organisation and instead become a less-active vice-president.

One of the few lasting achievements of this era was that the SPES and the BHA managed to sort out their charitable status after the Charities Act 1960 had led to decades of complications. With the BHA losing its charitable status in 1965,[8] the South Place Ethical Society won educational charity status in 1980 with the BHA following in December 1982. After fifteen years and a bill of £100,000, the BHA re-joined the tax-exempt fold, contingent upon the creation of a 'political arm', titled Humanist Campaigns, which could have been the launch-pad for all kinds of initiatives which the BHA itself was unable to pursue, but, as John Leeson remembered, it languished and eventually became defunct.[9] Still, finances were markedly improved and campaigning was to resuscitate.

But problems remained. Whilst SPES continued to enjoy its splendid Conway Hall base, the BHA experienced intensifying building problems and diminishing activity. The organisation's main asset, 13 Prince of Wales Terrace, was in the early and mid-1980s a source of vital rental income but was in a lamentable and ungovernable condition. At one juncture, Maeve Denby discovered that the BHA had been paying the electricity bills for all its tenants; when a technician

FIGURE 20 BHA headquarters, 1969–94. Expensively refurbished in 1970, the prestigious property at 13 Prince of Wales Terrace, Kensington, had been bought by West London Ethical Society in the 1950s with the proceeds from selling the Ethical Church, and acquired by BHA with paying tenants in the upper storeys. Though much liked in the movement, it caused many problems. Photo: Charles Edridge/Humanists UK/Bishopsgate Archive.

was despatched by the electricity board, he 'took one look at the fuse board and fled, saying he was not equipped to deal with it'.[10] There was an ancient lift of questionable reliability, whilst the BHA library was accommodated in a basement room afflicted by damp that made for a 'happy hunting ground for bookworms – not of the human variety'.[11] The biggest headache was the large penthouse-style flat occupied from 1974 to 1992 by Michael Brett Weinstein (1945–92), a flamboyant and eccentric American tenant, hyperbolically described by a eulogist as 'the greatest life insurance salesman in the world', who had gained a highly favourable lease arrangement.[12] An obsessive collector of antiques, Weinstein's bedroom was likened to a 'gigantic Bedouin tent' with 'Egyptian tomb style decoration'.[13] The apartment was the scene of lavish entertaining, a champagne lifestyle rather at odds with the picture that Weinstein habitually painted of himself as a long-suffering tenant. In 1975, he began complaining of water ingress from the roof that obliged him to remain awake emptying buckets, whilst in 1976 faulty wiring caused a fire in the attic. The BHA forked out considerable sums on roof repair, but the leaks continued into the 1980s and the tenant could not be removed. After threatening exposure in *Private Eye*,[14] Weinstein's legal proceedings forced BHA in 1991 to replace the roof.[15] His death the following year instigated further legal struggle when his surviving partner tried to take over the tenancy. With the association remaining dependent on tenants' rents, the BHA's problems with their building seemed intractable.[16]

In the doldrums, the BHA kept operating with a diminishing number of paid administrative staff. A larger circle of activists gave extra income and business to the central organisation, but by the early 1980s this was mainly 'fork suppers' – genteel dining events, either at Conway Hall or Prince of Wales Terrace, hosted by a committee member with paying guests listening to an expert speaker; the 1986 annual report noted with regret the host quitting.[17] Funds were so short at the BHA that the main means of communicating to its membership and the general public, *Humanist News,* had been reduced to a collection of unbound A4 pages, printed using a device kept in a member's garage.[18] Building pressures led to much emphasis being put upon issuing briefing papers – straightforward statements on moral issues on one side of A4, ranging from adoption to animal rights with a separate set of longer briefings aimed at children.[19] The building was a millstone and the executive committee considered selling it. After a period in 1990 of BHA sharing with RPA in Red Lion Passage as tenants of SPES, Barbara Smoker suggested that NSS, of which she was then president, purchase a vacant office building at 47 Theobalds Road adjoining Conway Hall, and invited BHA and RPA to share the new space to create a 'Humanist Centre'.[20] Having purchased the building, the NSS punched through the remarkably thick wall between Conway Hall and No. 47, and the BHA, having sold 13 Prince of Wales Terrace in May 1994, became the tenant of the NSS at the newly named 'Bradlaugh House', opened amid a fanfare of publicity by the veteran Labour politician Michael Foot MP and Hermann Bondi. However, two things became apparent. One was that the Theobalds Road premises were too small for the cluster of organisations. The second was that 13 Prince of Wales Terrace had been sold hastily when the property market was adverse, netting what some considered the small sum of £650,000, leading to two decades of shunting from one unsatisfactory rental office to another.[21] There was a sense that the building at No.13 had been part of the organisation's identity, having been purchased by Blackham using the proceeds of Coit's Ethical Church, whilst the fate of a bust of Pallas Athene salvaged from the Ethical Church in Bayswater remains unknown to this day.

One source of constancy in these troubled decades came from mathematician and cosmologist Professor Hermann Bondi (1919–2005), who from 1983 to 2000 was president of both the BHA and the RPA. As the longest-serving president of the BHA, he was an eloquent advocate for the humanist movement, and his position straddling the two main organisations at the same time brought stability, a calmness of spirit and a wide perspective concerning the role of humanism in a world still under the power of superstition and inequality. Through the trying years, he helped to steer the humanist ship across some stormy waters, turning up to support events and meetings and to allow the office-bearers to innovate and thrive. And reform started to take shape. The property problem apart, the new executive leaders of the 1990s were determined to reform the BHA's dysfunctional management. Richard Paterson brought experience from the civil service to bear on the creation of a strategic plan – the Patterdale Principles (a Lake District village where the committee held a strategy residential weekend in December 1992). Helped by a facilitator, they strove to develop their scheme – resulting in a plan entitled 'Making Humanism Happen'. The plan comprised raising the BHA's profile by promoting human values, gaining equal status with religion in education and public ceremonial, making BHA a flexible and dynamic charity, and seeking participation of people from all parts of British society.[22] A new executive director Robert Ashby (b. 1965) was attracted from charity administration and PR, sharing the profile of several humanist leaders as gay and an outspoken atheist, although less typically a Conservative.[23] Director from 1994 to 2000, Ashby remembered arriving at 47 Theobalds Road and finding himself surrounded by a ramshackle environment of 'glorious eccentricity', with an NSS officer pegging up used teabags to dry and reuse. But Ashby reported that the offices sparked with intellectuals and 'really contemporary, alive, political people' like Jim Herrick and the 'deliberately provocative' anarchist Nicolas Walter of the RPA, Barbara Smoker of NSS and BHA's Richard Paterson, John Leeson and Robbi Robson, the last recruited in 1997 from the Royal College of Nursing and a former civil servant. Ashby found a 'vast contrast' between them and a more moribund wider membership. 'It was all about a few people who were eccentric – rather glorious – but eccentric', Ashby mused to us.[24] He is credited with starting the professionalisation of BHA operations, getting staff and volunteers working in proper unison.

Publicity was not easy with meagre resources, but Ashby found the media retained an appetite for arguments about religion and morality which he offered as a controversialist on talk radio. By the close of 1997, he had given seventy-four radio interviews and various television appearances, principally on education and morality.[25] He took to the road, speaking to local groups around the country, finding some – like Birmingham's – more active than the national organisation with major policy objectives (including entry to local SACRE committees and officiating at humanist funerals) whilst meetings could attract audiences of sixty or more. The West Glamorgan Humanist Group reported in 1993 that 'most of all in our monthly meetings we simply enjoy the company and support of other Humanists'.[26] The resilience of humanism during its dark decades may have lain in the local branches, with the forty-four groups in England in 2003 reporting a considerable range of activities.[27] Ashby's peregrinations took him to Belfast where he was understood to be a 'culturally protestant atheist', to Edinburgh where he was served tea and to Glasgow for beer. Some local organisers he encountered led lives which told of deep currents of British counterculture: 'They had little small holdings and sheep and things, lots of them', Ashby recalled, 'and spinning wheels in some cases, I mean – [the] *curious* world of the crofter and the self-sufficient.' Some were still interested in the 'universal language', Esperanto, that accompanied mid-twentieth-century 'one world' humanism and lobbied the leadership for its promotion.[28] The new BHA management of the 1990s was often exasperated by some longstanding members seeking ideological conflict with organised religion. Warned on his appointment that running BHA was like herding cats, Ashby remembered meeting members who would 'rant about God', whilst *Humanist News* frequently contained vitriolic complaints about Christianity. Here was a demographic fascinated by argument and arcane disputes. In like sentiment, Paterson recalled how the BHA had been 'the plaything of people with a philosophical bent',[29] whilst Robbi Robson, who succeeded Paterson as chair in 1997, with an aim to establish human values held in common with religions, found 'a lot of very elderly men in particular who argued about how many angels sat on the pinhead'.[30] With a surfeit of older men raging against churches, Ashby came upon women, often their wives, relegated to domestic tasks by 'very clear gender roles' – what he called 'grumpy old chaps looking at the rostrum and wanting a grumpy old speaker' whilst women scurried round saying 'Oh, I must make the tea'.[31] Appalled by the marginalisation of women, Ashby and Robson embarked on a programme of recruiting female celebrants. And not helping matters was the continued use of the association's newsletter, *Humanist News*, later renamed *Humanity*, for long feature articles and philosophical debates which, from some of the published letters, were boring many members.

Many in the movement of the 1990s were reluctant to link humanism to longstanding radical causes. Richard Paterson told of how he tried to get BHA to affiliate with the Campaign for Nuclear Disarmament (CND), and the reaction being as if he had 'screamed an obscenity'.[32] There was distrust of the environmentalist movement and its cultural anchoring on the political left; in 1994 a woman complained that she had joined the BHA to meet others who rejected theism, and if she were 'railroaded into political arenas and campaigns such as saving the whale and the ozone layer' then she might resign.[33] Reflecting twenty years later, Paterson thought that the BHA had failed to effectively articulate how humanism could guide the individual in leading a more ethical life.[34] Conservative attitudes had become ascendant among the ordinary membership of a thinned-out humanist movement – mainly white, male, middle-aged to elderly, middle-class professionals concentrated in the south of England, uninclined to radical politics. Some of the humanist movement's intellectual heavyweights, such as philosopher Antony Flew, were articulating a rather right-wing version of humanism, whilst North American secularist Paul Kurtz (1925–2012) exalted scientific rationalism and objectivity in the face of postmodernism, multiculturalism, radical feminists and the animal rights movement, affirming that humanists should believe in equality and not egalitarianism.[35]

All the same, the BHA was abuzz with executive activity by 1994–6. Robbi Robson, then vice-chair of BHA, wrote in a memo: 'The BHA is in a transitional period. It has been a voluntary organisation which had a small administrative core staff but its functions have been run on a day-to-day basis by volunteers. . . . It is moving towards being a professionally run organisation, managed by a volunteer committee, but whose work is carried out by paid staff.'[36] Focussed by the five-year 'Making Humanism Happen' strategic plan for 1995–9, BHA generated long lists of actions, outputs, programmes and teaching packs from networks and working parties, whilst a commercial company, Human Horizons, was tasked with inserting humanist material on media.[37] A Humanist Forum comprising representatives from BHA, SPES, NSS, RPA and Gay and Lesbian Humanist Association (GALHA) slowly hammered out agreed joint campaigning, whilst unification was being talked about in small meetings and private letters.[38] More openly, ahead of a general election, anticipation was being raised for an imminent new zeitgeist and a change in government. The Humanist Parliamentary Group, after many years dormant, was revived in May 1994 with Lord (Jack) Dormand of Easington offering himself as the leader, and within a year the BHA director Robert Ashby provided a comprehensive briefing across humanist issues for the education group of the Parliamentary Labour Party.[39] Labour's victory in 1997 seemed at first to be an auspicious moment for the BHA with high hopes for humanist-friendly policy change. An editorial in *Humanist News* by Ashby argued that the Labour majority would facilitate controversial legislation, much of it 'in line with the humanist principle of social justice in an open society'.[40] This pro-Labour stance matched the BHA leadership's 'party line' and that of Richard Paterson (a Labour Party member) in particular. But Labour's return to power drew right-wing rebuke; ironically, Robert Ashby as a Conservative took a bit of flak from the membership for arguing the executive line. Certainly, by the time a Humanist Parliamentary Group was formally organised in the 1990s, its secretary Lord Dormand described the 'struggle' of maintaining it, even of more than forty members from both houses, though most from the Lords, and the inability to register as an 'All Party' group.[41] With forty-seven openly declared humanists in Parliament, and not one of them a Conservative MP, Robert Ashby told *The Independent* newspaper in 1996: 'Surely, coming out as a humanist is not such a scandal?'[42]

But ideological problems beset everything. Should BHA, like the National Secular Society, promote rationalism and engage in the age-old contest with theism and its proponents? Or should it instead work with the liberal religious and advocate a more pastoral humanism focussed on providing services and fostering community? Robert Ashby argued that BHA should 'seek an increase in rationality amongst the population', telling the truth about Feng Shui and 'other such rubbish to end its imposition upon the gullible'.[43] Other senior BHA staff felt differently. Robbi Robson stated the choice was 'our organisation . . . fighting against the religious establishment or focusing on the positive aspects of living as a humanist'.[44] New and more diverse members of the association questioned the worth of 'religion bashing' and wanted a more outward-looking and inclusive humanism. 'I am a new member and a committed humanist', wrote one correspondent to *Humanity*, 'but when I look through your magazine, I feel I have as little in common with some of your columnists and letter writers as I do with fundamentalist Christians.'[45] This sentiment was gaining ground,[46] but this shift took time. In the interim, the emphasis at BHA in the five years from 1992 to 1997 was on being busy – on returning the humanist movement to a state of activity and dismiss the sense of do-nothingness and in-fighting of the previous two decades. But, some former leaders we spoke to were despondent about the condition of the BHA in the 1990s. The organisation relied on volunteers, with long-suffering administrators working in dilapidated, poorly ventilated and heated office conditions at Bradlaugh House where the meeting room had no natural light.[47] Liaison with other organisations in the building was poor, whilst, on policy matters, the humanist response was weak to the rising Conservative dismembering of education and social services and to rising evangelical influence. 'You know', Richard Paterson reflected disconsolately, 'when you're fighting the alligators, you don't worry about draining the swamp.'[48] Management throughout the period was prone to distraction, firefighting over many seemingly trivial matters which, notwithstanding, were of existential moment.

(b) A schismatic and illiberal era

Buildings and mismanagement were not the only causes of the parlous condition of the British Humanist Association through the 1980s and 1990s. Whilst the RPA and SPES were relatively calm, the BHA seemed to suffer from all sorts of crises. A downbeat article by *The Guardian* in February 1982 on the BHA's woes was titled simply: 'Spirit of the Age Beats the Humanists.'[49]

In the 1960s, the BHA had been favoured by a benevolent political climate receptive to liberal reform, whilst even the major churches looked benignly upon Blackham's diplomatic advances. Humanists were sometimes overly optimistic about the inevitability of progressive change, so that by the later 1970s the leadership had failed to develop a compelling vision of what the movement could accomplish during reactionary, non-progressive periods. As David Pollock observed, the BHA and RPA appeared both too radical and too marginal to garner mainstream support.[50] Some commentators thought that secularisation was so far advanced that secularist opposition was no longer needed. Kenneth Furness, BHA general secretary in 1982, attributed the organisation's decay to a feeling that religion had been defeated, despite the backlash from conservative religion.[51]

A 1984 editorial in *New Humanist* by Nicolas Walter wondered whether as the 'proportion of people who live without religion or superstition was probably larger than ever before' there might now be so many humanists that it could be said that a humanist movement was redundant.[52] Some thought the expansive moral and social vision of the 1960s was no longer part of the agreed agenda. In 1985, Diana Rookledge, one-time president and chair of the Hampstead group, believed the focus should return to core issues, tackling religious privilege and promoting moral education, asserting that 'we must create more of a reason for the BHA to exist. It isn't much use if it exists only for the gratification of its few members.'[53] For some, pushing this strategy threatened to limit the humanist movement to the denial of religious claims rather than articulating a positive set of linked beliefs. Yet this was always the job better done by the National Secular Society.

In 1985 the BHA circulated a survey to members, out of which only 172 replies were received, itself a signal of poor engagement. It showed 72 per cent of members were male, most living in the south-east of England, 36 per cent aged forty to sixty, with 53 per cent over sixty years old.[54] One of the few signs of vigour came from the Gay Humanist Group, which, by the mid-1980s, had eighty members, though no branches, its president the poet and novelist Maureen Duffy, holding regular events at Conway Hall and maintaining close contact with kindred societies, including direct affiliation from 1985 to IHEU.[55] Administered with cultural awareness by an irrepressible George Broadhead from his Warwickshire home, the group's colourful banners were to be seen on numerous pride marches and demonstrations, whilst a pop-up bookstall of humanist texts was supplemented by a popular run of screen-printed T-shirts bearing slogans, including 'Lead me into Temptation – Please!'[56] Prominent speakers at Conway Hall meetings included filmmaker Derek Jarman (1942–94), critic and artist Emmanuel Cooper (1938–2012) and the first openly lesbian MP Maureen Colquhoun (1928–2021), whilst the group's name changed in 1987 to the Gay and Lesbian Humanist Association (GALHA) to refresh its image.[57] Yet, that organisation struggled to reflect diversity, with a primary appeal to older gay men, low numbers of BAME people or the young, and opposition at the 1990 AGM to the adoption of the word 'queer'.[58] So even the gay humanist branch of humanism was some way behind the moral curve.

Overall, though, the British Humanist Association in the 1980s and 1990s appears depleted and demoralised, and singularly unresponsive to the Conservative ideology of Thatcherism. There seemed, reflected John Leeson, to have been an almost total disconnect in those years between the BHA and broader social issues.[59] Some of those we spoke to found it curious in hindsight that such a connection had not been made.[60] One of the few correctives at the time was supplied by the sociologist and political theorist Bernard Crick (1929–2008), a participant in the 1969 open society conference, who wrote in 1985 that anti-religion had become a 'substitute for an adequate understanding of what we should mean by a humanistic morality and human identity. I cannot see human identity in terms of militant individualism whether of the Nietzschean or economic liberal kind. . . Humanism is not just respect for the able, but for all.'[61] Liberal Christians were the loudest opponents of Thatcher, including the unreceptive audience to her 'Sermon on the Mound' at the General Assembly of the Church of Scotland in 1985 – to which an editorial in *New Humanist* responded in classic form by complaining about the 'deplorable' spectre of theology being used to justify political positions.[62] Nostalgia and antiquarianism among the BHA's aging membership seemed obsessed with the past – a fascination with the halcyon days of the Ethical Union, the 'golden age' of the National Secular Society under Charles Bradlaugh, and a sense that the 1960s lingered on in 13 Prince of Wales Terrace. The BHA's advisory council read like a 'who's who' of the 1960s 'cultural revolution' and, as Nicolas Walter complained in 1984, fewer contemporary public figures were identifying now with the cause.[63] In 1980 only two sitting MPs were willing to have their names printed on the BHA's advisory council list – Lena Jeger (1915–2007) and Arthur Palmer (1912–94). There was an inability, even within the BHA's traditional hinterland of the Labour Party, to reach out to younger political personalities who held humanist sympathies.

The humanist movement struggled in the 1980s with its most acrimonious and schismatic period. In 1985, 40.1 per cent of those belonging to the BHA were members of one of the 'other national Humanist organisations' (understood as SPES, RPA and NSS).[64] This was both a source of movement strength and an invitation to movement-wide disputes. One blazing row seemingly started in the NSS in the early 1980s, in which some left-wingers took umbrage at what they perceived was an anti-socialist campaign within the humanist cause. Colin Mills and Terry Liddle, chairman and co-founder respectively of the Socialist Secular Association (SSA), resigned in November 1983 first from the NSS Council of Management and then the NSS entirely, after what they described as 'a malicious attack' by Bill McIlroy, editor of *The Freethinker*, who allegedly claimed the SSA was attempting to take over the NSS. Mills told their fellow members of the SSA that 'the NSS has abandoned its former vigorous radical stance and has become a timid, ineffectual outfit whereby right-wingers and "extremists of the centre" gratify their egos'. Mills complained of the NSS now containing 'Tory monarchists, advocates of Friedmanite economics and supporters of nuclear weapons and apartheid'.[65] The dispute spread to several publications, including in 1984 the SPES *Ethical Record* where Colin Mills repeated his allegation of 'an anti-socialist vendetta'. Challenging him, Barbara Smoker, fourteen years president of the NSS, retorted that the society had always attracted socialist members, and the vast majority – including, she believed, the entire executive – were socialist like herself. But, Smoker argued, there was no wish for the NSS to duplicate the Socialist Secular Association and thus tried to avoid divisive policy decisions and 'to remain an umbrella organisation for secularists of every political persuasion'. In reply,

Mills argued that the vendetta had been underway intermittently for at least thirty years in the NSS, including under the previous president Bill McIlroy.[66] The NSS controversy spread onwards to the BHA, spicing *Humanist News* columns in late 1983 and early 1984. In this way, the fume and foam of tumult in one organisation seemed inevitably to spill across others.

BARBARA SMOKER 1923–2020

There was no more vigorous and indefatigable figure in British nonreligion than Barbara Smoker. Brought up a Roman Catholic, she described herself as very religious when young, aspiring to be a nun. But she trained as a shorthand typist, saw active service in the Pacific during the Second World War and craved intellectualism and critical thinking. A voracious reader of philosophy and science, in 1949 she discovered her loss of belief in god whilst flicking through books in a public library and dedicated herself to atheism and humanism, preferring to self-identify more with the former. Acting first as organiser for the George Bernard Shaw society and editor of *The Shavian*, she was drawn to humanist and secularist meetings, inspired greatly by Harold Blackham, finding

FIGURE 21 Barbara Smoker. Photo: Humanists UK/Bishopsgate Archive.

her metier as a speaker whether from platform or floor. An early task was secretary for the first IHEU conference in London in 1957, establishing her indispensability in office-bearing, lecturing and acting as the moral and constitutional conscience of nonreligionist organisations. Identifying as a radical liberal or a socialist, she was the keenest of humanists in the Committee of 100, willing to be arrested in the cause of disarmament, and reckoning on being constantly watched for her radicalism; she claimed with pride that a telephone engineer in the 1960s found a listening device in her flat (and put it back). A supporter of gay liberation and abortion law reform, she was chair of the Voluntary Euthanasia Society 1981–5 and president of the National Secular Society 1971–96. Ever energetic, she estimated she conducted more than a thousand funerals as the NSS president. Never feeling at home as much as she did in Conway Hall, in 1986 she was the only woman ever to be made an appointed lecturer there.

Political alignments were not the only area of controversy. The issue of the humanist movement's relations with the churches reared its head every few years, often in new forms. The Harold Blackham strategy of the 1940s and 1950s, and perfected by him in both the BHA and IHEU in the 1960s and early 1970s, emerged in a new, more potentially divisive form in the 1980s. The towering figure of American humanism, Paul Kurtz believed that the Moral Majority and Fundamentalist movement were temporary aberrations and brought to his role as co-chair of IHEU from 1986 to 1994 a distinctive platform of humanists entering dialogue with American churches and thereby securing higher profile. In 1984 he organised the first-ever 'Fundamentalist/Humanist Dialogue', which brought twelve fundamentalists and evangelicals face to face with twelve humanists, including British philosopher Antony Flew.[67] This was something of a shift to the right for international humanism, playing better in an American setting than in Europe. Flew aroused even more controversy when, three years later in February 1987, an edited book on *Anti-Racism* was condemned by David Rose in *The Guardian* newspaper review, but mentioned something 'a great deal nastier' to be found in Flew's chapter. Then a vice-president of the RPA, Flew had been one of the leading humanist philosophers in Britain since the 1950s, his right-wing reputation leading him to be critical of the Anti-Apartheid Movement, an organisation that faced a motion of disaffiliation at an AGM of the National Secular Society; when it was heavily defeated, according to one account, 'Flew became enraged, denounced those present as "socialist bastards" and stormed out of the meeting'.[68] Against this background, the book reviewer Rose charged Flew with arguing that 'the disadvantages suffered by black people are essentially their own fault – either through inherent, genetic shortcomings, or through their failure to "adapt" culturally to British society'. Flew's 'evidence' was reportedly a survey supposedly showing that Black people suffered higher rates of unemployment than whites, but that Asians had a lower rate – a survey, Rose contended, superseded by newer evidence that suggested no such thing. Argument erupted, first in *The Guardian* led by the book's editor.[69] But then a furore lasting several months broke within the Rationalist Press Association, partly stoked by a campaign against Flew and his supporters, propelled by the Warwickshire Humanist Group (WHG) sending a circular letter by Roy Saich that said the WHG 'regrets that Antony Flew, Vice-President of the Rationalist Press Association, should have contributed to an apparently racialist book'. An initial letter of objection to the book was sent to RPA by Karl Heath based on a reading of *The Guardian* review but not of the book; he rectified this in a review in *Freethinker* in which he lambasted the entire book and its contributors for having 'consulted together to produce this attack, not upon racism, but upon those who condemn it', and making allegations of racism in regard to the contributors' arguments and expressions far more egregious than those by Rose in *The Guardian*. This drew a cascade of correspondence, some published, some not, involving a range of leading lights in the British humanist movement, in which some at BHA backed Flew's position but refrained from saying so publicly.[70] Copies of most of the articles and letters were sent to the headquarters of IHEU in Utrecht, leading to Walter needing to write there explaining what was going on within British humanism.[71] Attempts to calm the ill-feeling never fully worked. Flew held strong Conservative Party sympaties and came to associate with the reinforcement of religious education in state schools. RPA correspondence with him expressing disquiet continued, culminating in his resignation, seemingly to some relief, as an RPA vice-president.[72] Quite apart from its implications regarding racism, this uproar signalled that the movement did not agree with the virtues of progressive social policies. It also came at the low point in humanist-movement fortunes in the UK. But, additionally, many of those in the movement as a whole – and not just in the RPA – had come in recent decades from business and management backgrounds, and, as with the 'open society' ideology of the 1960s and 1970s, some perceived the humanist movement as having a permanent but mostly concealed political split between the left and right.

But, by the 1990s, schism seemed the least of the BHA's problems.

(c) Education and campaigns

The campaigning of the humanist movement in the 1980s did not fare much better. Indeed, in some regards it was this decade that witnessed the final end of a number of 1960s utopian dreams.

The moral education campaign that had so dominated the 1970s did seem to gain some mileage in the 1980s as the *Journal of Moral Education*, which humanists by then led through the Social Morality Council, was established in educational, psychological and related disciplines. Educationalists were fired up by a febrile atmosphere in the 1980s as radicals and liberals slugged it out with the conservative government of Margaret Thatcher for control of education, notably at the Inner London Education Authority (ILEA). Success seemed to be nudging forward at local-authority level where advisory committees, termed SACREs, on religious and moral education, persuaded many key LEAs to adopt progressive curricula, leading for the first time to significant revision in the nature of religious education. The revised RE syllabus at the ILEA appeared in 1984, and that for Brent the following year. Accompanying this, publishers scented profitability in new moral education books for schoolchildren, producing attractive textbooks in 1985–7 that contained a real leap forward in the treatment of ethnic minorities, controversial sexual issues and humanism. Blackie published *Worlds of Difference* in 1985, whilst Heinemann produced *GCSE Religious Studies: Contemporary Moral Issues* by Joe Jenkins, quoting people of different ethical positions, including pages on humanism, plus well-developed and visually exciting topics on highly controversial issues. The voluntary euthanasia extract read: 'Humanists believe that people have the right to end their own lives when they wish. They believe that death is final and inevitable, but nevertheless can be dignified, peaceful and painless with the aid of modern drugs.'[73] For the time, this seemed a radical advance in progressive education.

With the collapse of the Social Morality Council as an ecumenical promoter of moral education,[74] the infusion of a secular moral culture was weakening children's receptivity to traditional religious education. Yet, this did not bring the moral education revolution any closer. Brian Gates, director of the Moral Education Centre at St Martin's College, Lancaster, in the early 1980s, worried over moral and religious education experiencing 'the end of a beautiful relationship'.[75] Despite an IHEU-Vatican dialogue in September 1988 in which Harry Stopes-Roe participated,[76] one event installed a new obstacle in England and Wales to this particular dream – the Education Reform Act 1988. When this bill reached the House of Lords during a late-night session, a group of broadly evangelical and conservative Christian Lords led by Anglican Baroness Caroline Cox put forward several key clauses concerning state schools and ensured their passing in a thinly attended sitting – acerbically referred to in a later BHA briefing paper as 'when the Christian Right executed their notorious midnight hijacking'.[77] Section 7 required that daily acts of collective worship required since 1944 'shall be wholly or mainly of a broadly Christian character', without it being 'distinctive of any particular Christian denomination', except where a LEA standing council determined otherwise; section 8 instructed that agreed RE syllabuses 'shall reflect the fact that the religious traditions in Great Britain are in the main Christian whilst taking account of the teaching and practices of the other principal religions represented in Great Britain'; section 11 required that mandated standing advisory councils on religious education (SACREs), previously optional, should be set up by every local education authority, confining half their statutory membership to the Anglican Church and other religion representatives.[78] This last measure was reinforced by a Department of Education and Science circular of 1991 that placed some restrictions upon nonreligious representatives on SACRES.[79] With a focus upon 'shared values' in RE, Conservative promoters of the Act wanted to ensure systematic pressure upon the nature of local curricula. The BHA immediately determined to be represented on each one of these SACREs and was able to make progress with adoption of RE syllabuses that included humanism.[80] But by 1994, Baroness Cox proudly boasted to the Lords that Ofsted inspectors could not find a single primary school failing to comply with the law with regard to worship.[81] However, to balance this step backwards, the DES recognised the BHA as a body that should be routinely consulted because of the role it played in religious education development.[82] The Act shelved success in moral education in state schools in England and Wales. In Scotland, though, there was a different trajectory for moral education, built upon the statutory power of headteachers to determine much of the curriculum. Religious instruction was perceived in the 1960s to be in crisis, leading to the Miller Report of 1972 that advised religious education be shifted from being mandatory but not inspectable and often confessional (a position it had been in since 1872) to being non-confessional and taught by trained staff; however, religious worship continued often to be confusingly included in this mix, and Roman Catholic state schools continued to be subject to church control of RE.[83]

If the state of education depressed, some issues could not fail to make humanists sit up and pay attention. In 1989 the world was rocked by the Salman Rushdie affair surrounding the content of his novel *Satanic Verses*. Strident protests erupted in Bradford, and many Muslim communities were rapidly politicised, complaining that English law did not protect Islam and Muslims from blasphemies; a test case in 1991 proved that the Rushdie book was neither a blasphemous nor a seditious libel, offences only possible against the Church of England.[84] Fearful that a government might seek to create parity for all religions, the Campaign Against the Blasphemy Law, originally formed in 1977 to battle the *Gay News* trial, was reformed in May 1989 by Bill McIlroy and Nicolas Walter as secretary and press officer respectively, which took out full-page adverts of over 211 signatories, dominated by humanists and secularists but including proto-humanist Joseph Needham and members of the arts community like Beryl Bainbridge, John Cleese, Harold Pinter (a member of the BHA Advisory Council) and one clergyman Don Cupitt (inspirer in 1984 of the Sea of Faith movement that regarded religion as a human creation).[85] Meantime, also in 1989, the British Board of Film Censors became nervous about its existing policy of 'prior restraint' (asking for cuts where there 'might be blasphemous' material) and refused a certificate entirely for Nigel Wingrove's film *Visions of Ecstasy* which depicted a young Saint Theresa of Avila engaged in a spiritual, but obviously physical relationship, with the crucified Christ. The European Court of Human Rights rebuffed Wingrove's appeal by permitting member states their own unique laws around cultural issues. Further problems ensued when Michael Newman, a member of the BHA Executive Committee, was arrested for selling a copy of Wingrove's 'blasphemous' video at Birmingham Young Humanist Meeting in February 1992, and the BHA warned its officers to avoid such actions.[86] In the event, the blasphemy law remained unchanged until the new millennium.

The 1990s witnessed occasional spurts of campaigning revival at BHA – such as when a director of External Affairs was hired but subsequently dismissed for misconduct.[87] Perhaps the only genuinely positive development of the early 1990s was that there was a gradual increase in the number of ceremonies being provided by humanist celebrants (then called officiants) – especially funerals. Harriet Martineau has been acclaimed for conceptualising a secularist burial ritual in the mid-Victorian period to displace 'the dismal anxiety of Christians'; this was followed by a 1906 handbook by F. J. Gould, *Funeral Services Without Theology*, and developments at SPES and a pamphlet by RPA in 1944 in conjunction with the Cremation Society under the parliamentary leadership of Joseph Reeves MP.[88] After other funeral publications, coordinated action came from Jane Wynne Willson (b. 1933) who, having started humanist groups in Bristol and Cheltenham and serving on the BHA's executive committee from 1966 to 1972, retired from teaching in 1988 and became BHA chair from 1989 to 1992.[89] Provoked by the traumatic experience of arranging the cremation of her aunt without any ceremony which could provide emotional support and a sense of closure, she became preoccupied from the mid-1970s with the design and conduct of humanist funerals. There were few resources then: 'We used to sort of do it in my sitting room', she remembered. 'It used to be that anyone who was interested in taking up doing humanist funerals would come and spend the day and we'd have lunch and just talk. They'd ask, "What's involved?"' With no advice pack and only a few readings she decided to write a book.[90] Appearing in 1989, *Funerals without God* was a practical guide for those who wished to conduct a ceremony for a deceased relation or friend, setting out the basic format of a humanist ceremony, the simple practical measures to be taken, and suggested possible readings and phrases for different demographics of deceased persons. The BHA's office reportedly received as many as eighty orders per day, with numerous editions following, setting in train a popular undertaking of the humanist movement.[91] Other rituals in family life attracted Wynne Willson attention in a 1997 book on being a humanist parent.[92] With Nigel Collins appointed as National Ceremonies Coordinator of celebrants in 1990, BHA established a national register with eighty people on the books by 1992 operating in thirty-two areas (including Scotland at that time) with a 24-hour telephone helpline, followed by formal accreditation in 1997.[93] Funerals were by far the most popular service; starting with fewer than 100 ceremonies in 1987, by 1994 rising to over 1,500 – 85 per cent of them funerals, 13 per cent weddings and 2 per cent namings, all performed by 140 celebrants backed by a programme of training seminars.[94] With ceremonies appearing in features on television and in newspapers, the humanist movement's ritualising of life started to draw public attention.[95]

(d) Britain in world humanism

The long 1980s witnessed significant growth in the community of international humanism, and an agenda that was starting to change with speed. Where once British humanism led the way in its postcolonial approach to empire, ethnicity and equality, these years introduced a difficult time for the movement's influence.

An obvious issue concerned the numbers. The UK movement was dwindling throughout the 1970s and 1980s, with the BHA having around a quarter of the membership in 1982 that it had enjoyed at its peak in 1968, damaging its status in international circles. In 1962, the International Humanist and Ethical Union (IHEU) had 22 affiliated bodies from 15 nations, with 55,000 members. By 1982, there had been a doubling, with the number of nations rising to 46 paid-up organisations with 118,352 centrally recorded members (a figure lacking Norway, likely the largest national organisation in the world). The largest national organisations affiliated with IHEU were from the Netherlands (bodies with memberships of 30,669, 29,826, 11,709, 5,000 and 4,000) and Germany (29,703), whilst the two major US bodies were the American Ethical Union (3,500) and American Humanists (2,672). For comparison, figures from the UK were modest: BHA (1,508), SPES (549) and Scottish Humanist Council (110).[96] The Dutch, German and Norwegian humanist organisations (as well as a few others in Belgium, Germany and Austria) benefited as 'pillarised' groups which could receive public subsidies, but such benefits did not exist in Britain (nor most majority non-white nations). With the membership of the IHEU governing board being determined largely by the scale of fee-paying memberships, the Europeans controlled the organisation. British humanism remained overwhelmingly white in composition, but race was to be an ever-more important dimension. When humanist groups from Asia and Africa joined from the 1980s, accelerating after 2000, postcolonialism deeply penetrated the workings of IHEU.

Still, British humanists pulled well above their weight in key areas. One was human rights, in which the foundations laid by H. G. Wells and others in mid-century became translated into larger efforts in the 1970s and 1980s. A considerable focus of Western human rights movements fell upon the treatment of dissidents in the USSR and the Warsaw pact nations, partly led by religious groups like the

Society of Friends, but the arrival on the scene of Amnesty International (AI) in 1961 was within a decade to ramp up both objectives and capacity to handle campaigning activity. One figure upon whom considerable attention fell was nuclear scientist and humanist Andrei Sakharov who became a lightning rod for the work of organisations like Amnesty International. In 1973 Sakharov was one of 120 signatories to the Humanist Manifesto II, being consulted by American humanist leader Paul Kurtz on its wording; his case did much in the 1970s and 1980s to reshape Western and scientific attitudes to human rights, especially since some British scientists refused to steer their professional organisations (like the Royal Society) to join human rights campaigning on behalf of overseas scientists.[97] In the 1960s, there were no established systems to protest human rights abuses in foreign nations, nor was there acceptance that drafting of United Nations documents could involve non-governmental organisations. By the end of the 1980s, both were the norm, opening up the process at the UN to influence of organisations like IHEU and AI.[98] Humanists focussed upon developing a set of values to which world governments could adhere, with many meetings on this theme, and sympathetic world leaders and influencers were drawn into this work; in 1998, the former Swedish prime minister Ingmar Carlsson chaired an IHEU seminar in Stockholm on 'Shared values in global governance'.[99] In the same year, IHEU's five-year strategy made its third aim 'to promote the adoption of a Universal Declaration of Human Values by the UN as a moral charter for the world'.[100] Although in the post-war period IHEU had struggled to achieve the level of representation they desired (they remained only an 'informative' member of UNESCO until 1961), the seeds of cooperation had been sown.

Particular dimensions of human rights work were amenable to progress driven by individuals. Nigel Bruce from the 1960s had led the creation and management of two humanist homes for 'wayward boys' in Edinburgh. He subsequently became involved in the drafting conferences between 1979 and 1989 on the UN Convention on the Rights of the Child, being appointed chair of one of the committees at a Helsinki consultation. Bruce's major achievement was to contribute successfully to the right of the child to know his or her own parentage, irrespective of adoption and other legal proceedings (Articles 7.1, 22.1). Bruce told us that this was considered 'a strange idea' at the time: 'I felt very deeply and still do that you can't actually be a contented, rounded, integrated individual, unless you know, first of all, who your parents are or were, and, secondly, unless you've had a chance to relate to them.' He told us:

> In the early days, when I was reflecting on what humanism really is, I came to the conclusion that although it was based on thinking in the past, it must surely be rooted in respect for the future and commitment to the future. It seems to me that part of the humanist message is to look to the future, . . . 'to leave the world a better place than you found it'. I liked that phrase.

Bruce came to a commitment that 'part of any sensible humanist programme must be a policy of making sure that children know who they are'. To create an orphan, he said, needs just an embryo and to bring it into life, 'to me that's immoral, unethical'. The future must be about evolving humanist policy: 'I do think that the future must be a prime concern of all humanists, and anybody who thinks that humanism is fixed now is wrong.'[101]

It was hard for the humanist movement to attain and then sustain such influence in international organisations. IHEU in the 1950s and early 1960s was limited to member organisations from six main nations, of which the UK was one. But by 1998, IHEU had ninety member organisations from thirty-four nations, and UK influence was challenged. Equally, the enthusiasm the humanist cause brought to the UN and UNESCO was not rewarded with immediate success; at the establishment of IHEU in 1952, humanists failed to gain permanent category 'A' affiliated status with UNESCO. It was a constant struggle for pressure groups to keep at the forefront of international institutions. So much so that in 1984, the IHEU board considered a lengthy report on UNESCO which painted a bleak but undoubtedly realistic picture of failing humanist influence. From Julian Huxley's work with the League of Nations cultural organisation in the 1930s through his directorship of UNESCO in the late 1940s, British humanists felt a keen interest in 'one world' values and the anti-war agenda. But the structural instability in IHEU's influence at UNESCO undermined its influence, with biennial conferences of NGOs with an interest at which UNESCO selected a list of organisations to enter close consultation for the following two years. This induced frustration. One of the IHEU observers at the UN, May Weis, hosted a lunch for guests on Harold Blackham's visit and lecture at the UN in 1962, whilst another representative Theo Polet wrote sceptically of NGOs talking endlessly of getting UNESCO money whilst showing little interest in each other.[102] This was laborious, diplomatic lobbying, and it was proving hard to discern major benefits over decades of work. At the nineteenth conference of UNESCO NGOs in June 1984, 500 organisations competed for selection, and IHEU failed to be among the 102 that succeeded; of those, thirteen belonged to the Roman Catholic Church. Emblematic of its lack of status, the precise name of IHEU was repeatedly misprinted in UNESCO's own paperwork. The report concluded: 'The influence of IHEU, in the decision-making at NGO/UNESCO is hardly existing.' The reason for this, it was argued, was that 'the activities of IHEU in general, and its members in particular, are often wide away from the questions put forward by UNESCO to the NGOs'. UNESCO's concerns in the 1980s lay in disability, women, the year of youth, science and cultural connections, and IHEU was failing to address any of these in the manner UNESCO expected.

Whilst IHEU and its British representatives supported UN work on human rights, the most disappointing outcome for British humanists was the failure of the UK to adopt the European Convention on Human Rights into British law until

1998 (adopted under the Human Rights Act 1998). By the 1980s IHEU was already seeking to promote the next stage, envisaged to be a major push for a UN Charter (or Declaration) of Human Values, championed by the Indian Secular Society but enjoying support from British humanist philosophers. But the reports of isolation at UNESCO led the IHEU board to conclude that the United Nations was not the right body to draft such a declaration.[103] And during the 2010s, values remained unfulfilled on the humanist agenda.

(e) The BHA annual general meeting, 1997

Disputes arising from attempts to resuscitate the association after the Patterdale gathering of 1992 had been simmering for some time, erupting at the BHA's AGM at Conway Hall on 12 July 1997. The *Humanist News* described seventy-five members crammed into a hot and stuffy room 'filled with controversy and passion'.

The meeting did hear what it regarded as good news. First, the treasurer announced an extraordinary and likely over-optimistic reappraisal in financial fortunes; after debt, loss and the fourteen-year financial legacy of 13 Prince of Wales Terrace, vast new funds were seemingly unveiled as the BHA was absorbing the Humanist Trust – set up in the 1960s to satisfy the charity commissioners, but now permitted to reunite if BHA undertook the Trust's educational work. Together with a raised valuation of investments, a total of £304,000 was to be added almost overnight to the association's reserves. Second, the AGM welcomed the arrival of IHEU headquarters to London. Having been located in Utrecht since 1952, concern had mounted over several years with management processes, but the move to London was controversial – not least because the decision was taken at a board meeting held in India at which the existing director was not present. With an accusation of unconstitutional behaviour resounding for a year, the control of IHEU was transferred from the Utrecht-based board to a London-based executive committee. But finance remained a problem; the new committee noted difficulties in collecting some humanist dues for 1997, whilst the IHEU bank account apparently became inaccessible. The new executive officer was instructed to engage a lawyer to free the funds. Matters were settled before that became necessary, but the rancour fostered unpleasantness with claims of 'a conspiracy' and 'secret communications via internet'.[104] In the longer term, IHEU's move to London offered the opportunity to make the city the centre of world humanism, and, for the BHA after a gap since the 1950s, internationalism could once more come to the forefront of its identity.

But further matters fired up the AGM of 1997. A new constitution was overwhelmingly agreed which was widely seen as passing power from the executive to ordinary members; a further vote ruled that sub-committees need not be chaired by executive members. In addition, the education committee, a lively and ambitious group, had for some years operated – in many people's views very effectively – as an arm's length body from the BHA. But, in 1995, apparently without consulting, the executive committee took the decision to widen the education committee's scope (into philosophy of education and school curricula as a whole), and, when the committee refused, it was told that it was being wound up. This precipitated the committee continuing independently as the Humanist Education Forum. The AGM was the first occasion on which the membership heard the full story of this imbroglio, though a rapprochement was announced and a threatened censure motion was withdrawn. The AGM had lanced the boil, and from 1998 the forum ended up backing Marilyn Mason's highly effective work, as the new education officer.[105]

However, the most controversial item at the 1997 BHA AGM caused proceedings to dissolve into disorder. This was the executive committee's proposal to abandon its headquarters at Theobalds Road, triggered after the NSS announced that they were leaving but, if BHA did not buy the building, would retain control and raise the rent. The BHA committee had decided in some secrecy to jettison its office, without consultation with kindred societies, rousing angry exchanges (including a memo the previous month from Barbara Smoker accusing BHA of paying its staff 'vast salaries'),[106] and met loud opposition in the meeting. As the meeting's chair resigned and left the room, accusations flew, leading the president, Sir Hermann Bondi, to speak and adroitly gain agreement to defer matters to the executive committee.[107] Amid a surfeit of unpleasantness, the meeting established a need for open management and a chastening of the executive committee. A further five years passed until BHA found new premises, but the great experiment in trying to physically bring the administration of the British humanist movement together was over, at least for the foreseeable future.

Behind all this for the BHA lay an old yet ultimate issue, ticking away relentlessly. John Leeson observed that 'there is no role for a specifically non-religious organisation in a post-religious society'.[108] This lay at the heart of many of the fissures and failures. The BHA was still an organisation in search of returning to a stable and unifying purpose, one that could be an alternative to religion-baiting in an environment of rapid ecclesiastical contraction. That remained the movement's great challenge.

PART IV

THE SECOND GILDED AGE, 1998–2021

11 GROWTH AND MODERNISATION

At the time, many observers within the humanist movement looked upon the British Humanist Association's 1997 AGM as a turning point. Though some have, with hindsight, had cause to think it less so, there are important ways in which the 100th anniversary of the foundation of the Ethical Union introduced a new era. In the next chapter we turn to the modernisation of campaigning and the growing resonance of humanism in Britain. This chapter looks at how the late 1990s marked an organisational and character change: at the rising scale of the movement, how it started to be altered with remarkable speed, how the configuration of the movement's organisations changed and how the movement's character diversified into new roles in a rather breathless transformation.

(a) Of humanist identities, members and funds

Change was signalled by each of the three main organisations adopting name changes in rapid succession: the Rationalist Press Association became the Rationalist Association in 2002, the South Place Ethical Society became the Conway Hall Ethical Society in 2012 and the British Humanist Association became Humanists UK in 2017. In addition, the International Humanist and Ethical Union became Humanists International in 2019. But it was for the BHA that the new identity marked the most radical of alterations.

The organisations of the humanist movement entered the new century with diverging membership fortunes (see the graph on page 22). RPA was still the biggest British humanist organisation in 1984 with about 1,400 members, but this declined sharply to 551 in 2014 and 432 in 2018. RPA's book publishing activities fell in tandem, becoming episodic in the late 1970s with no outputs in some years. In the 1990s, only five books were listed, with four more in 2000–3, the last being Bill Cooke's history of the organisation, which stands also as something of an epitaph.[1] The name change of 2002 dropped the embarrassing word 'Press', leaving only the magazine *New Humanist*, the appearance of some works on the association's website from 1999 (which have now gone) and a few conferences. Even *New Humanist* declined, moving in the 2010s from monthly to quarterly publication. One explanation of this decline was that the popularity of rationalist literature meant its products were taken by mainstream publishers; another was that, unlike BHA or even SPES, RPA/RA suffered from an absence of agreed social aims and ideas, projecting only a thinking system to be admired through its publications. Meanwhile, SPES did not enter any permanent decline in numbers, remaining largely static between 300 and 450, where it had been for the best part of a century, and holding steady in 2021 with 439 members. Until the Covid-19 pandemic started in February 2020, its fortunes were less wrapped up with the scale of membership and more with the use of its premises at Conway Hall, which, in the 2010s especially, became ever-busy and buzzing with musical, artistic and community events, and boosted by improved rental income from outside hirers for all sorts of occasions. On top of that, Conway Hall remained as it had been since 1929, the meeting place of choice for humanists, rationalists and secularists of all organisations, the comfortable home for the movement, and its library continued as the venerated base of reason, incorporating the old libraries of both the RPA and the BHA.

The blossoming fortunes of BHA/Humanists UK stood apart from the others. It reversed the quite severe preceding decline, propelled from its dire predicaments of the 1970s, 1980s and 1990s into being Britain's most successful nonreligious organisation of all time. From its low point in 1984, the BHA regained its membership base in the next twenty years – in some years managing a 10 per cent growth rate, driving its numbers to 3,803 in 2001, close to equalling the BHA's late 1960s peak. Part of its growth can be attributed to a growing gender balance in the early 2000s – men making up 55 per cent, women 39 per cent and others 6 per cent. The organisation was resuming the fastidious policy coverage pioneered in the 1960s, producing issue-based information sheets on what 'most reasonable people' and philosophers would attest to as moral positions on, for example, animal welfare, genetic engineering, environmental questions and social issues.[2] This broadened the appeal, and aroused wider interest than had been customary during the 1970s and 1980s. After a brief plateau, growth resumed in 2006 – and at an increased pace with annual growth rates above 20 per cent in many years until 2012, when they stabilised at around 5 per cent per annum until the next decade. Local groups were doing as well as the national membership: the Newcastle-based north-east group had 241 members in 2008.[3] By 2021, UK membership was 21,000, an unprecedented size.

But membership growth was only part of the story. Ever since the early days of ethicism, there had been special categories of belonging to its organisations.

The central members of the South Place Ethical Society in the 1890s and 1900s were called 'subscribers' but there was a category of 'supporters' who lived outside of London and who could not attend its meetings regularly who paid a reduced fee. The RPA likewise had in the 1950s a second category, again with reduced benefits. The Union of Ethical Societies (from 1920 the Ethical Union) had not been created as a membership organisation for individuals, instead being designed as a federal body to which ethical organisations might affiliate. When the BHA was established during 1963–7, it was primarily not a federal body (though organisations could and did affiliate), instead being designed as a national body to which individuals took out membership renewed by annual fee; it also introduced 'associate membership' which by 1968 numbered 366 (representing 9 per cent of the number of full members); ten years later they were called 'supporters' and made up 38 per cent of the membership.[4] In the digital age of the 2000s and 2010s, the BHA triggered a significant growth in supporters with the rise of email and from 2005 social-media usage by the young. Paying no fees, they increasingly took to Facebook and Twitter to connect to campaign information. By 2014, the supporters had well overtaken the membership category, with around 30,000 of the former and 12,000 of the latter.[5] Under Andrew Copson's direction, the BHA endorsed this mushrooming group by sustaining the difference between fee and non-fee affiliation whilst merging the two in a united categorisation of 'members and supporters' used in the public and internal rhetoric of the body, in calls for lobbying and raising support for specific issues.[6] Moreover, though the non-paying supporter was often a recruiting opportunity for the paying member, they could also represent different constituencies – the first, the generally older humanists and, the second, the generally younger humanists; an analysis in 2005–7 showed that 74 per cent of BHA members were aged over sixty years, whilst fewer than 4 per cent were aged thirty or under.[7] Because the supporter category was designed overwhelmingly as a digital construct on social media and emails, it tended to attract the young people so missing from humanist ranks in earlier decades. Merging the two in a combined 'members and supporters' category had, by 2021, touched 100,000 people, comprising 21,000 members, 63,000 supporters and 16,000 members of Humanist Society Scotland (an allied organisation with which a partnership agreement was made in 2018).[8] This amalgamation of internal and outer constituencies of humanism was an undoubted success, for paying members kept rising in number whilst the influence of the combined category in campaigns became a vital addition for expressing the humanist view across different constituencies.

To what can we attribute this change in fortunes at the BHA/Humanists UK? First, there was a long-term trend towards strengthening the paid-up membership. The work of successive BHA leaders in the 1990s certainly built up a head of steam in national recruitment, though some forms of lucrative income generation – including bequests – remained sporadic. The late 2000s were reported as less successful in financial terms, yet there was a surge in membership with almost a doubling in numbers from 4,000 to 7,651 during 2005–8. Advance slowed after 2012, but the growth rate remained a healthy 4–6 per cent until 2021.[9] Second, the underlying trend of secularisation accelerated in the 1990s and 2000s, and was sustained into the 2010s with detrimental impact upon the perception of the religious alignment of the nation; in the 2001 census, those without religion – the 'nones' – constituted 15 per cent of the UK adult population, rising to 25 per cent in 2011, and could have reached or exceeded 35 per cent in the 2021 census for England and Wales – implicating a rising congruence between humanist and popular moral culture that we consider in Chapter 12.[10] Third, notwithstanding this cultural shift, some humanists retained a perception of continued ecclesiastical threats on liberty. Religious protesters demanded censorship of theatre plays (inter alia, 'Behzti' (Dishonour) in 2004, 'Jerry Springer – the Opera' from 2006, and 'Jesus, Queen of Heaven' in 2009) and the Conservative government's section 28 of 1988–2003 (the name given to the legislation that outlawed 'teaching' homosexuality in schools) attracted millionaire-backing, each triggering liberal resolve to sustain civil freedoms.[11] Fourth, small signs of humanism's penetration of the civil establishment in Britain were becoming more numerous, ranging between the quirky and the significant: in 1998, Dennis Cobell, humanist officiant, became the chaplain to the mayor of Lewisham in London, whilst in 2009 an officer of the BHA, Andrew Copson, gained the first seat for a humanist (or any nonreligionist) on the BBC's religious and belief consultative body.[12]

Fifth, rising parliamentary support for humanist ethics seemed to bring nearer legislative change on key issues. The slow increase of non-Labour humanists at Westminster heightened expectation. By 1998, the Humanist Parliamentary Group had forty-eight members, almost entirely comprised of Labour MPs and peers, and had been revived in the mid-1990s under the guidance of the genial Lord Dormand of Easington (1919–2003), described in *The Guardian* as 'the most insistent of atheists in the House of Lords'.[13] Prior to the 1997 election, Dormand had become disenchanted with the group and attempted to give up convening it due to the low attendance at its meetings.[14] But the huge new intake of Labour MPs led to a revival and in January 1998 twenty-five Labour MPs were listed as being members, including Rhodri Morgan (1939–2017), later first minister of Wales and leader of Welsh Labour between 2000 and 2009, and Nick Brown (b. 1950) the MP for Newcastle-upon-Tyne East and later Labour Chief Whip. Brown explicitly identified himself as being a humanist when becoming a Privy Counsellor – something which was perhaps related to his friendship with then BHA chair Richard Paterson – as was his appearance as the keynote speaker at the BHA's 1997 conference where he delivered a prospectus of Labour's vision for society that excited left-leaning association members.[15] But a backlash developed among some members, not merely of the right but among those who disliked any political engagement. Surely, one member asked, the BHA 'would welcome capitalist, even unreconstructed Thatcherite humanists. Wouldn't it?'[16] Another noted that some members the day after the election 'were weeping into their Weetabix on the morning of the 2nd May'.[17] Still, the Humanist Parliamentary Group grew significantly in the later 1990s. In 1998, it included twenty-four MPs and twenty-four members of the House of Lords, nearly all aligned with the Labour Party.[18] After the general election of 2001, the BHA watched carefully the proportion of members of the House of Lords who decided to affirm rather than take the oath of allegiance; there was a total 78 (out of 633 signed in), comprising 52 Labour, 1 Liberal Democrat, 10 independents and 3 Conservative.[19] BHA activity in harnessing the power of the HPG rose significantly in the mid-2000s, with executive director Hanne Stinson and David Pollock marshalling campaigning on a wide variety of issues.[20] An air of activity, diversity of interest and involvement of members came upon the movement in the 2000s. As it grew, the HPG acquired All Party status, being chaired 2005–10 by Labour peer Lord Gus Macdonald (who received BHA support one-day a week from Andrew Copson). But many in the humanist cause were disappointed in the Labour governments of Blair and Gordon Brown. Though BHA hopes were never high for the removal of Church of England bishops from the House of Lords, it distributed a detailed briefing paper in 2007 to the Humanist Parliamentary Group.[21] Indeed, there was constant surprise at just how sympathetic the Labour governments of 1997 to 2010 were towards religion. Tony Blair's government made much of its support for religion, leading 'unreconstructed Thatcherite' BHA members to reveal themselves.[22] Notwithstanding the dictum coined by his press secretary that 'we don't do god', Blair would later in his term announce his Christian faith and subsequently join his wife in the Roman Catholic Church.[23] With Conservative governments from 2010, there was little chance of significant improvement. Meanwhile, in Scotland and Wales, the creation of devolved elected governments and parliaments gave rise to enhanced stature for humanism, including the 'Time for Reflection' held weekly on Tuesdays at Holyrood to which humanists have contributed regularly by rotation after 1997; and the live-televised humanist funeral held in 2017 for Rhodri Morgan, the former first minister of Wales, that was conducted in the Senedd Cymru (Welsh parliament) building.[24]

Humanism was starting to acquire increased civil acknowledgement, helped no doubt by the movement's strengthening professionalism and well-made (often legal) argument. The language undergirding humanist positions – of equality, fairness and human rights – was now becoming more common in the daily discourse of the press and of democracy, whilst argument in civil society moved increasingly onto humanist territory. With the Human Rights Act of 1998, the newsletter *Humanist News* in the early 2000s lost its preoccupation with meandering repetitive debate, focussing instead on campaigning and humanist progress. With significant growth in levels of support, the fortunes of the movement were looking up.

FIGURE 22 The Humanist funeral of Rhodri Morgan (1939–2017), first minister of Wales 2000 to 2009, was held in the Senedd, the humanist celebrant being Lorraine Barrett, herself a former member of the Senedd. Photo: Matthew Horwood/matt-horwood.com.

(b) The business of management

Spectacular growth in humanist numbers framed the new century. From 1979 to 1988, BHA membership experienced almost continuous decline of between 3 and 16 per cent per annum; but between 1989 and 2001 there was steady growth of 5 to 8 per cent each year with membership reaching 3,803. Then, the pace changed. In 2001–2, membership rose 21 per cent and, after a pause in the mid-2000s, experienced a renewed surge in the late 2000s and early 2010s reaching around 12,000 members in 2011 and 21,000 members in 2021 (see graph on page 22). Really quite suddenly, BHA became adroit in management, campaigning and attracting young people.

One member of the executive committee told us that in the 1990s the BHA 'was very much an amateur organisation'. It was described as reactive rather than proactive and operating out of inadequate office accommodation in 'very much an amateuristic situation'. The executive committee met on a Friday evening which was very awkward for those living outside of London (including two from Wales). But with skilled new leaders, the association was described as getting more professional,[25] and over the following years it made a step change in management. In 1997, the total income of the BHA was £194,285; in 2019, Humanists UK's income was £2,670,651, with almost half this growth occurring after 2015. Allowing for inflation, this constituted a sevenfold rise in income at 2020 terms. With this, the organisation grew in scale. In the 1990s, there were about five full-time staff at BHA; by 2018, there were twenty-five employees (mostly situated at the headquarters which by then had relocated to 39 Moreland Street in Finsbury) plus hundreds of humanist celebrants, some working full-time whilst some others donating their fees to the association, and other volunteers scattered around the country.[26] Headquarters staff were overwhelmingly young graduates bringing a variety of organisational skills to humanist administration, outreach and recruitment. With this professional backbone, the renamed Humanists UK by 2021 not merely dominated the nonreligion sector, but, as we shall see in the next chapter, it was a considerable ethical presence in both British civil society and in international affairs.

It was a truism of the twenty-first century that the conduct of all charitable bodies acquired a new professionalism. This was demanded in large part as a result of deeper state regulation of the third sector, with the Charity Commissions for England and Wales and, separately, for Northern Ireland, and the Office for the Scottish Charity Regulator, requiring not merely annual financial reports but more detailed accounts of objectives and activities. Before 1998, humanist organisations were already tightening practices and procedures, and new leaders and administrators at the BHA during the 1990s and 2000s came with charitable sector experience in organisations like CRUSE bereavement care and the British Red Cross. This injection of expertise created new burdens, including financial ones. Despite signs of membership growth, finances were initially desperate in the new century. Expenditure was exceeding income, and the early 2000s saw intense cost-cutting. There was a five-month period in 2001 without a BHA executive director and a cancellation of the annual conference at a cost of £5,000. But things rapidly changed. The BHA's energetic new education officer, Marilyn Mason, appointed in 1998, had not only reunited the education committee to the mainstream of the association but was placing education at the forefront of what united the movement. Yet, within six years she was able to sum up the long-term frustrations of the organisation's leadership. Humanists, she said, were freethinkers and so were 'only loosely bound to humanist organisations, and though glad we are here for a funeral or for advice, feel no obligation to join or attend or to donate'. Humanism means, she reported, that they were at least as committed to 'good works' and other charities as they were to their philosophy, meaning that, with charitable millionaires looking elsewhere for good causes to support, the movement's 'most pressing immediate problems will tend to be financial'.[27]

At the turn of the century, some members' attitudes seemed stuck in the right-wing backlash of the Thatcher era. In 1998, there were loud voices resenting LGBT issues in their newsletter and, presumably, the existence of the Gay and Lesbian Humanist Association. Amid arguments about the equalisation of the age of hetero- and homosexual consent, one letter writer asked in 1998 whether the newsletter had been 'taken over by the small but vociferous gay lobby'.[28] Age was a likely factor. A survey carried out in 2001 canvassed the opinions of a sample of 395 BHA members, of whom the largest block was aged seventy to eighty with only one member in their twenties and few under fifty. Responses to the question 'What sort of problems do you tend to have doubts about?' included concerns over ethical living and the morality of euthanasia. Yet, more concerning submissions crept in too, expressing doubt over social liberalism – particularly LGBT issues.[29] But during the 2000s, anti-liberal dissent like this diminished as, it seemed, less nostalgia pervaded the association's operations. Facilitating this was the arrival of a generation of IT-savvy leaders and staff, able to exploit the digital revolution, starting with BHA using emails from 1996, and the following year launching its first website (of a mere six pages). Things did not run smoothly to begin with. A larger website appeared in 2000, but only the company which built it could update it in HTML code – for a fee.[30] Furthermore, getting online in the office at Theobalds Road adjacent to Conway Hall was a greater problem, relying on a frustrating dial-up connection for only one computer at a time.[31] In March 2003, a move to new premises at 1 Gower Street solved this, and an ever-increasing stream of press releases, comments, letters and parliamentary briefings issued forth with a new logo and visual identity on website and headed paper. A coherent and insistent BHA voice was being heard in lobbying, consultation, government submissions and press briefings. From 2003, membership renewal online became possible, with 'returners' totalling 90 per cent within a year. Though the financial deficit continued to grow in 2001,[32] income streams diversified, with humanist products on sale on Amazon and AbeBooks by 2002, plus revival of legacy income upon which the movement had long relied (bringing one bequest of £54,000 in 2003). One cost-saving option was abandoning annual conferences because support had become low; after some years, this was ultimately rejected and effort went successfully into a jazzed-up convention-style experience which characterised BHA from 2011 – though the smaller annual meeting could still hear disagreement. After the website came social media, with Facebook and Twitter from 2006 lifting the lid on the hitherto-inaccessible youth audience, engaged by the tweeting and allied expertise among staff and volunteers alike, creating an up-to-date organisation with a 'buzzy' and trendy feel. On 9 September 2004, the *BHA E-Bulletin*, the first emailed newsletter, was despatched originally as an occasional service, but it quickly became routine at twice a month sometimes, with hyperlinks to extended content on the BHA website.[33] With immediacy and cleverness, humanism started to delineate a moral identity aligning with that of the British nonreligious young.[34] This was accomplished in large part by the congruence of the essential skills-set and values of new BHA office staff with the demographic and ethical character of target supporters. A new audience was reached by speaking its language.

By the late 2000s, there is evidence that membership and support for BHA was already blossoming. But even with little short of a boom period, financial concerns still exercised management, and the selection of a new CEO was contextualised in that concern. Andrew Copson was a young man with little experience of leadership, having joined BHA in 2005 initially as part-time assistant to Marilyn Mason on the education brief, and when she retired Copson took over. With a period adding the role of policy and public affairs, he was selected in 2010 as the new chief executive officer. Joining at a time of membership boom, Copson observed that this was the moment for upscaling management operations. He introduced a drive towards vastly improved mechanisms for administration, resulting in a degree of professionalism unknown in the humanist sector before. Throughout the 2010s, office systems multiplied on the back of rising income and staffing. A major leap forward arose in governance arrangements: by 2021, trustees had access to twenty-two online management information folders and protocols, including a 34-page trustee handbook, 78-page staff handbook, 41-page safeguarding policy, 38-page guide to the 'Humanist Brand', a comprehensive 'risk register', byelaws, organisation diagram minutes and a variety of reports on management issues. Perhaps of most critical management purpose was an internal document on 'Humanists UK Policy' which, in its 2019 incarnation, laid out in 10,765 words the detailed objectives agreed for campaigning, documenting the direction of travel over decades past as they aligned with future aims, establishing the coherence of the charity's work for staff and trustees alike. One trustee described this set of material to us: 'In 2010 when Andrew took over, this sort of depth of management would have been unimaginable.'[35] With considerable additional skills in strategy and media, Copson's role has been widely seen in the movement as transformative.

After 2014 the management processes included the careful assessment of impacts achieved by management set against each area of its policy. Internal impact assessments were calculated and then summarised for members and supporters, partly on overall numbers of people signed up in those two categories, but, in a more detailed manner, by response rates to individual social-media posts. By 2020, top-performing Humanists UK tweets, for instance, attracted up to half a million impressions each, and around 30,000 follows, retweets and so forth – equalling the Church of England's 'follows'. With similar assessments on other social media, Humanists UK has been able to finesse the impact and reach of its online activities. The same assessments have been made for activities like funerals, weddings and baby namings, in humanist contributions to curriculum developments in state schools and legal missives and actions in various quarters of its work. The impact included 40 per cent of hospitals and 20 per cent of prisons having a humanist pastoral carer on the team, with 12,000 people receiving care, 45,000 pupils hearing an accredited humanist speaker, and 145,000 online views of annual humanist lectures.[36] This carefully supervised and very detailed work at times edged forward humanist positions within, most often, state organisations but also included actions concerning discrimination matters.

Management acquired a momentum towards success. Being on the crest of the digital wave undoubtedly lay at the heart of this. In 2014, the British Humanist Association co-hosted with IHEU the World Humanist Congress at Oxford, attracting over a thousand delegates from sixty countries. In the magnificence of the Examination Schools and Sheldonian Theatre at the University, British humanism was displaying a kudos to its fraternal delegates in a way not seen before – not even at the 1957 IHEU Congress in London, which, by contrast, was altogether a less embellished affair amid lingering post-war austerity. The environment of the University of Oxford in 2014 conferred an academic legitimacy emphasised by the participating intellectuals – including Jim Al-Khahili, Richard Dawkins, A. C. Grayling and Philip Pullman. The chairing of professional television journalists like Samira Ahmed and Nick Ross reflected the movement's public stature, whilst the location of events in the photogenic heart of the University's streets and lanes brought convivial conversation and appreciation of humanism's march forward. At the same time, though, the main events in Christopher Wren's grand 1660s Sheldonian Theatre, wreathed by the serenity of its interior and the discipline of its firm wooden seating in the upper gallery, were counterpointed by the modernity of the excited young humanist workers who, with lightning-speed typing on their smart devices, tweeted proceedings to the world. All of a sudden, running the humanist movement had become a young person's game.

FIGURE 23 The World Humanist Congress 2014 at University of Oxford, with delegates at the sumptuous Conference Dinner in the impressive Examination Schools. Photo: Andrew West/Humanists UK.

(c) Humanist services and pastoral care

The rise of the young in British humanist management had a significant impact, too, upon the activities conducted for members and supporters. The second gilded age of humanism was marked by the development of a diversification of services, some primarily for humanist members and supporters, whilst some services and pastoral care were aimed at members and non-members alike.

In the 2010s, the new CEO Andrew Copson commissioned two retired civil servants to scope the creation of Humanist Pastoral Care, aligning together various branches of nonreligious pastoral work into a coherent service. Harold Blackham had first pioneered counselling services on Sunday afternoons for BHA members. From 1963 Blackham learned about the American Humanist Association and its counselling activities, with a British group being set up in 1965, moving on by the 1980s to counselling for the bereaved and in prison.[37] But it was the rise of advocacy work in the current century that formed a key element in the upscaling of pastoral activities, using the Human Rights Act 1998 and the Equality Act 2010 to take legal action to advance chaplaincy, humanist marriage and equality rights. Assisting those in need of help as they tried to transit out from religion was another development. Losing religion could make for trying circumstances: family opposition and division, loss of friends and ecclesiastical opposition (including, from some churches, disfellowship or organised shunning and ostracism), much of this taking place from 2005 on social media. Faith to Faithless was founded in 2015 by two former Muslims as an organisation providing support for those leaving or having left any religion, though tending to focus on 'high control religions'; from 2017, it became part of Humanists UK. The brainchild of a young ex-Muslim activist Imtiaz Shams, it started by making presentations at universities and colleges and soon was providing support for people leaving Christian, Jewish, Jehovah's Witness and New Age religions, as well as safeguarding-training for teachers, medical staff, the Metropolitan Police and others encountering those in need. By 2019, 'Faith to Faithless' had produced a substantial report into the issues faced by those leaving religion.[38]

The pastoral ethos also lay behind Humanists UK edging into overseas work in the later 2010s. Copson was a member of Baroness Warsi's Foreign Office advisory group on Freedom of Religion or Belief formed in March 2014, from which the agenda of providing support to overseas people of faith and non-faith developed and brought the plight of the nonreligious into the wider conversation on rights.[39] From 2018, Humanists UK provided targeted support for humanist and nonreligious asylum seekers coming to Britain's shores, and within a year nineteen people (and within three years over thirty) from mainly Islamic nations were helped with letters of support for asylum applications.[40] Perhaps the most prominent of these cases was that of Hamza bin Walayat who had applied for asylum in 2017, arguing that he would face persecution in his homeland of Pakistan, a country where he felt it was simply 'impossible to be a non-religious person'.[41] After failing to answer what were widely regarded as incoherent questions about humanism (questions which the Home Office took as a test of non-religiousness, mistaking it for being a canonical religion with set texts), he was told he would be deported.[42] Humanists UK publicised his case, including coordinating an open letter signed by 150 leading intellectuals, and raised a petition to the home secretary accompanied by intense lobbying. As a result, the deportation decision was overturned in May 2019, and Humanists UK was invited to give training to Home Office caseworkers on how to better interview nonreligious claimants.[43] These efforts continued in 2020, now being understood in terms of a broader attempt to have the asylum system reformed, and twelve further claimants were successfully supported.[44] The case also gave rise to some academic contemplation of the difficulty for a person demonstrating that they held a nonreligious outlook (the eternal problem of proving a negative).[45]

At home, humanist forms of pastoral chaplaincy or support developed rapidly during this period. Though hospital chaplains in England and Wales had been for decades directly employed by the NHS (unlike Scotland, where the Church of Scotland had been paid by the NHS to run chaplaincy), the world of hospital chaplains at the end of the twentieth century was still trying to shake off being 'white, male and Christian', accompanied by inertia and reluctance by the powerful Church of England in conceding ground to multi-faith chaplaincy. The problem extended to the NHS management relying on the churches for much chaplaincy training, creating relatively slow professionalisation and some system failures in monitoring chaplains and handling patients' religious information.[46] Change was triggered by the election of the Labour government in 1997, with rebranding in 1998 as 'NHS Chaplaincy' structured to inter-faith rather than denominational working; this led to rapid professionalisation and, into this gaping field, humanist action penetrated the previously religious 'closed shop'. Ironically, the NHS enlarged its chaplaincy quite considerably (during 1948–2016, from 28 to 350 whole-time NHS chaplains), whilst Christian adherence rapidly collapsed.[47] Whilst Keith Porteous Wood of the National Secular Society argued prominently in the media in 2006 for public funds to not be spent on religious chaplaincy (broadly because of lack of discernible medical benefit),[48] humanists contrived to join the multi-faith and belief system being created in the NHS on two principles: that the nonreligious had a right to pastoral care and that, as the first head of Pastoral Support at the BHA, David Savage, argued in 2021, those without religion deserved to be seen as people with 'sincerely and seriously held non-religious beliefs'.[49] Problems were gradually overcome – one being getting the term 'humanist' on the list of belief positions patients might register on hospital admission, a second getting humanist chaplains (or pastoral carers, as generally termed from 2018) listed as 'on call'. Pastoral care in hospitals, prisons and colleges was becoming a social and therapeutic service in which nonreligious providers were being recognised. But to get this recognition, BHA had to press hard under the Human Rights Act 1998 and for comparable treatment under the Equality Act 2010, monitoring advertisements for fairness and sending off 'letters before action' to those thought to be non-compliant recruiters. The case was probably better received in university and college chaplaincies which started to expand rapidly to include humanists, whilst pressure fell upon the Home Office, later the Ministry of Justice in England and Wales, to get humanists recognised and on call for pastoral care towards nonreligious prisoners.

In most cases, especially initially, humanist chaplains had been volunteers, many of them celebrants, though in universities humanists could in some cases obtain fees for conducting marriages and funerals for students, alumni and staff. But with recognition of humanist involvement in chaplaincy came integration and professional development. The NHS in England and Wales issued guidelines in 2015 that defined chaplains as 'focused on ensuring that all people, be they religious or not have the opportunity to access pastoral, spiritual or religious support as they need it'. Part of the move was a recognition of equality rights in the field, so managerial level appointments came to disregard the belief orientation of applicants. The first UK humanist hospital chaplain in a paid post, Jane Flint, was appointed in February 2016 in Leicester, whilst Lindsay van Dijk was appointed in 2018 as the first humanist leader of an NHS chaplaincy team (in Buckinghamshire, including Stoke Mandeville Hospital). However, progress in NHS appointments was slower than Humanists UK would have wished.[50] By 2021, the nonreligious made up between 22 and 45 per cent of patients in hospitals, 32 per cent of the overall prison population and a significantly larger proportion of university students; even with more than 250 humanist chaplains in institutional settings throughout the UK in 2021, this was not meeting demand.[51] From 2011, BHA ran the Humanist Pastoral Support Volunteers at Winchester Prison, providing reception support for those without religion, discussion groups and counselling for bereavement. In 2019 two part-time pastoral carers were appointed by the Northern Ireland Humanist Group of Humanists UK to serve at Maghaberry Prison in County Antrim, which contained up to fifty New IRA and other dissident republicans and a smaller number of convicted loyalist paramilitaries. A prison inspectorate report highlighted that, after Christians, those who identified as 'no religion' made up the largest group of the prison's population.[52] In the early 2000s, it was rare to find humanist chaplains working in hospices, though their number has since increased markedly, with many humanist celebrants dedicating themselves to funerals and counselling work among the bereaved and the dying, believing that it is in that field of dying and mourning that humanist humanitarianism finds its apotheosis.[53] In reflection of the growing reach of humanism within British care activities, Humanists UK's CEO Andrew Copson was recruited to the Department of Health and Social Security's Moral and Ethical Advisory Group to advise on management of health-related incidents such as pandemic flu.[54] More broadly, as Copson noted in interview with us, the Covid-19 pandemic intensified government recognition of humanists' advice and assistance concerning ethical behaviour in pastoral care, with him in 2021 leading NHS England's national memorial ceremony for health service workers who died during the contagion.[55]

Death and illness are occasions of intense humanist sentiment. This was noticeable in 2018 in the fact that 81 per cent of Humanists UK's 9,276 ceremonies were funerals: 7,517 funerals, 1,122 weddings and 637 namings conducted in England and Wales.[56] Having become organised in the late 1980s and 1990s, celebrants' numbers continued to grow, and did so rapidly into the new century. Initially using Jane Wynne Willson's pioneering 1989 guidebooks, training expanded. In 2002, BHA had 181 accredited officiants, but their work was mostly not with weddings; the number of funerals had risen in that year by 30 per cent to make up 6,400 of the total of 7,000 ceremonies.[57] Public awareness grew of humanist ceremonies with newspaper coverage of well-known figures like pop singer Adam Faith having a humanist funeral.[58] Humanist weddings have been growing strongly in England and Wales despite their lack of legal recognition; in 2004 they numbered c. 287 (0.33 per cent of all religious marriage ceremonies and 0.12 per cent of all marriages ceremonies), and by 2015 they totalled 975 (1.56 per cent of all religious marriage ceremonies and 0.40 per cent of all marriage ceremonies). It was not just a matter of growth in activities; there was innovation by humanist celebrants. During 2016–18, funeral celebrants in England and Wales developed a pioneering online 'Funeral Tribute Archive'; the brainchild of Patsy Wallace from Somerset, it immortalises ordinary people's lives through tributes given at their funerals.[59] In keeping with innovation, training for such services improved during the 2010s, starting off wholly in-house at BHA and culminating in the creation in 2018 of a master's degree in Humanist Pastoral Support and Ceremonies in London.[60] Celebrants rose relentlessly in number, reaching 519 in 2020, of whom more than 68 per cent conducted funerals, 59 per cent conducted weddings and 30 per cent namings.[61] Marriages by humanist celebrants are the only ones growing among all the major providers in England and Wales (like the Church of England, Church in Wales, Methodists and the Roman Catholic Church).[62] However, they are not state-recognised weddings; the key to expanding the numbers sharply would be the legal recognition of weddings, which would likely then introduce more people to the possibilities of funeral and baby-naming ceremonies. Despite significant parliamentary support for this from the early 2010s, progress has been stalled; various legal actions have followed, including in 2020 when six humanist couples took a legal case seeking a ruling that the lack of legally recognised humanist marriages in England and Wales constituted unlawful discrimination against humanists. But the jurisdictions of Northern Ireland and Jersey, with legal assistance from Humanists UK, exploited equality arguments to obtain approval of humanist weddings, whilst Guernsey Assembly passed a new law to the same effect.[63] The first legal humanist wedding took place in Northern

Ireland in 2017, approved in August 2018 after the appeal court there ruled that it must be a right for a couple to have access to a humanist wedding.[64] By 2020 there had been 362 humanist legal marriages in Northern Ireland, making up almost 5 per cent of all humanist weddings, with the proportion rising rapidly.[65] It seems inconceivable that England and Wales will be far behind in instituting the same rights.

Meanwhile, Humanist Society Scotland (HSS), much to its own surprise, obtained early authorisation to conduct state-recognised weddings. After some BHA guidance in the early 1990s, and initially following Wynne Willson's guide book, HSS then used their own courses, catering for celebrants, counsellors and chaplains. Under Scotland's different legal framework, the HSS produced evidence of its worthiness to conduct legal weddings, demonstrating the high quality in celebrant training, supervision and counselling (considered unofficially as superior to anything then provided by churches or, for that matter, the state registry offices). Partly as a result of demonstrating a secular 'belief' basis equivalent to a religion, the Registrar General Scotland in 2005 unexpectedly invited the two senior office-bearers of HSS to his office, told them that he had decided that he had the power to make an administrative decision granting HSS the right to undertake legal weddings under the 'religious' category and that he was minded so to do – the first country of the UK which did this. Then, the UK Equality Act 2010 brought a fundamental change to the treatment of nonreligion and belief, in which henceforth the words 'religion' and 'belief' in legislation were required to be read as including 'non religion' and 'non-belief'. This paved the way for the Marriage and Civil Partnership (Scotland) Act 2014, which legislated 'belief' as a third category for marriage beside religious and civil, granting powers to provide legal weddings to any group which could demonstrate a membership and a belief system – a low threshold allowing pagans and a number of other belief groups on board as wedding providers. It led to a plethora of humanist groups gaining registration; in addition to the long-established Humanist Society Scotland, seven new humanist organisations appeared, instituting scepticism in some quarters about motives.[66] Notwithstanding, having eight organisations expanded the market, with the number of legal humanist weddings in Scotland rising between 2006 and 2019 from 434 to 5,879 (from 3 per cent to 44 per cent of all religious or belief weddings, or 2 per cent to 23 per cent of all weddings). From 2015, this meteoric rise outstripped every church, with religious weddings plummeting – notably those of the Church of Scotland and the Roman Catholic Church.[67] So much so that the wedding quickly became the single most well-known facet of humanism in Scotland. In a public opinion poll in 2018, HSS discovered that 68 per cent of adult Scots had attended at least one humanist wedding, funeral or naming ceremony, 26 per cent in the past year; with a total of 45,905 legal humanist weddings during 2005–19, there has been a remarkable penetration of humanist events into Scottish culture.[68]

The *rites de passage* may be an important element in the construction of a humanist presence in contemporary popular culture. But caution can be heard from some older supporters. Keith Furness, BHA press officer in 1971, told us in 2018 that he was troubled that the emphasis on ceremonies aped religions and supported instead the French model of civil weddings.[69] On another tack, the BHA's very busy education officer Marilyn Mason in 2004 observed that the association 'could work itself out of a role' if secular rites of passage were emulated by Christian clergy offering nonreligious celebrations.[70] Still, Humanist Society Scotland has been transformed by weddings. It had operated in the late 1980s and early 1990s as a relatively small body, based on local groups in the five principal cities (Glasgow, Edinburgh, Dundee, Aberdeen, Perth and later Inverness), which had emerged in earlier decades as standalone entities. But things started to change with the development of its funeral and wedding services, raising its profile, income stream and embeddedness in Scottish civic culture. Members of the Scottish Parliament (MSPs) of all political persuasions inevitably became familiar with HSS membership numbers, as well as personally attending humanist ceremonies, leading in the 2000s and 2010s to widespread MSP engagement with HSS lobbying on key legislation – including same-sex weddings granted in 2014 and the abolition of the ancient crime of blasphemy in 2021.[71] Few things in recent times have united politicians from the Scottish National Party, the Scottish Conservatives, the Scottish Labour Party, the Scottish Greens and the Scottish Liberal Democrats, but the HSS agendas on those and some other issues (including assisted dying and suicide) instigated the formation of a civic group of some significance almost overnight and, despite anxiety over the future of organised religion, found at last a rather welcoming embrace from some church leaders. It was perhaps serendipity that has led to HSS having the right to perform legal weddings before Humanists UK. But it has shown the international humanist movement that there are many routes to ethical leadership in modern society, and humanist marriages seem certainly able to contribute.

12 CAMPAIGNING IN THE NEW MILLENNIUM

One of the themes in this book has been the central position of campaigning in defining humanism (as an ideology and a movement) and providing identity to humanists (as individuals). In a sense, campaigning has been central to all branches of nonreligionism, stretching back to early-nineteenth-century secularism and freethought. Activism and politicking have, since the time of Tom Paine at least, constituted the hallmark of busyness in humanist affairs, pushing back against the state, the judicial system, the church and the prejudice of some ordinary people. We have suggested that the times of greatest advance for humanism have been when campaigning has been most vigorous and successful. In this chapter, we assess humanist action for progressive change in twenty-first-century Britain.

(a) Human rights campaigning

The establishment of coherent policy at BHA/Humanists UK from 1998 rested upon human rights. As we have seen in earlier chapters, the concept of human rights can be regarded as central to a great proportion of the work of ethicism and humanism, developing into a focus of many progressive organisations – including the National Council for Civil Liberties (formed 1934, renamed Liberty in 1989) upon which many humanists served – but it was only in the 1930s and 1940s that 'human rights' became both a unifying term and a campaigning theme. Notwithstanding a partial recognition in British law, the failure of the UK to adopt the European Convention of Human Rights of 1950 (coming into force in 1953) was deeply regretted by humanists and was a position not rectified until 1998. Humanist campaign work on the promotion of rights then took a new turn. Coinciding with the growth in membership and financial resources, BHA developed an advocacy-led strategy during the 2000s and more especially the 2010s. Human rights became not merely the umbrella concept for its work but was, in many ways, the defining motif of the contemporary humanist cause. At the same time, with better finances and an enlarged workforce, campaigning work became increasingly professionalised, undertaken more and more by skilled employees and legal teams. Though the opportunity continued for public demonstration and protest, the campaigning effort of members and supporters turned ever more to digitised lobbying by email and online petitions. In the main, progressive change in the UK via legislation characteristic of the 'liberal hour' of the 1960s did not return. Human rights became typically a legal test of principles to be applied in the courts, yet the environment did not remain uncontested. Conservative governments after 2010 threatened to alter the 1998 Act, and the threat in 2021 became one of weakening judicial review and imposing restrictions on the HRA. In response, Humanists UK took the lead and coordinated a coalition of 220 organisations from across the NGO sector committed to protecting the Act and judicial review – including Amnesty International, British Muslims for Secular Democracy, the Catholic Agency for Overseas Development, Children England, Christian Solidarity Worldwide, Disability Rights UK, Friends of the Earth, Greenpeace, Howard League for Penal Reform, the Institute of Race Relations, LGBT+ Consortium, Prison Reform Trust, Quakers in Britain, Reporters Sans Frontieres, RNIB and Samaritans.[1] The outcome remains uncertain but has the potential to alter the landscape of humanist campaigning.

Education has been a perennial topic for humanist hopes for change, in England and Wales focussed on the baleful effects of the Education (Butler) Act 1944 and the Education Reform Act 1988, which together strengthened the place of religion in state schooling. The movement sustained its century-long struggle to affirm the rights of the child to avoid religious education and religious worship in schools, as well as seeking the ending of state funding of church schools, and, as the corollary, for the development of compulsory moral education as foreseen by F. J. Gould in the 1890s and 1900s, though translated into a less instructional format. Despite constant campaign energy, education brought continuing disappointment for humanists. After the setback of the 1988 act, worse was to follow. Under the Conservative governments of 1990 to 1997, the level of public funding to voluntary-aided schools in England for building work stayed relatively flat, at around £23,000 per school; but under Labour from 1997, this figure started to rise, reaching £33,000 by 1999–2000.[2] The Tony Blair Labour government awarded a greater role for the 7,000 faith schools (28 per cent of all state schools, and all but 40 Christian) in England and Wales, and the 2001 Green Paper noted not just expansion in their number but a more distinctly Christian character to 'nourish those of the faith . . . [and] challenge those who have no faith.'[3] In 2005, Labour pledged £550 million to rebuild every faith secondary school in England with, for the first time, no requirement for church funding contributions.[4] Humanist MP Graham Allen (Nottingham North) constantly pressed the Department for Education and Skills for standardisation of syllabuses and inclusion of nonreligious stances in RE, but to little effect; for his activity, Allen was voted Backbencher of the Year by MPs in 2003.[5] Head teachers in northern England were noting in 2001 the rising social tension which faith schools were exacerbating.[6] The education minister, Estelle Morris, held a view of faith schools as part of the inclusive community strategy and led the admission of minority faith schools into the maintained sector – thirteen of them during 1997–2001.[7] BHA representatives were more hopeful after their meeting with the next education secretary Charles Clarke in late 2003, who held out the prospect of syllabus reform.[8] Yet, the Tony Blair administration was not merely failing to act on the secular schools agenda but was actively promoting the expansion of, and granting special privileges to, faith schools. Particularly disappointing was the maintenance of subsidised academies and their religious (often evangelical) management. With a third of state-funded schools in England and Wales defined as having 'a religious character' (being faith schools), it was hoped that a Labour government would have rowed back from this strategy; contrarily, the influence of religious groups increased, continuing under Conservative governments from 2010, with the 2018 tranche of 124 new school applications of which 33 were faith schools.[9] Since 2000, Humanists UK has put more and more effort into providing educational materials and guidance for teachers, as well as campaigning, as part of the coherent policy of striving 'to create a fair and equal society for all'. Yet, the humanists' aim of the inclusive classroom over the segregated one was receding, putting them more at odds with the Labour Party.

Ground-level work in education expanded to match. By 1998, there were forty humanists on local-authority Standing Advisory Committees on Religious Education (SACRE) in England and Wales, and BHA education chair Marilyn Mason pushed for more.[10] The Humanist Teachers' Network was resuscitated after it closed in the early 1970s, with a newsletter *Edlines* and an online Education Forum, as well as annual conferences for its SACRE representatives around the country, producing books and CD-ROMS, and sending speakers out to schools.[11] Inclusivist RE syllabuses were still being introduced, such as in Islington and Brent boroughs in 2002–3, bringing renewed impetus to local humanist groups on SACRE panels. Leading by example, Mason, driven by experiencing a lot of religion at school despite a nonreligious experience at home, was able to make a convincing case to a government adjudicator to refuse permission for a new church school in her own borough, leading her to disseminate extensive guidance on ways humanists could take local action.[12] Taking over from Mason in 2006 as BHA's education officer, Andrew Copson focussed some effort on the human rights of the child in the schooling system, pointing to the possibly secret world of new 'independent' trust schools where religious policy might not be so open. Pointing to the cross-party opponents of expanding faith schooling,[13] Copson led in the 2008 creation of the Accord Coalition, a wide group of organisations, teachers unions and religious and nonreligious supporters committed to making faith schools more inclusive in religion and belief; by 2021, Accord had a wide range of partners, including the National Education Union, the Runnymede Trust, Women against Fundamentalism, British Muslims for Secular Democracy and the Unitarian and Free Christian churches.[14] Many of these organisations also worked with the humanists in the Fair Admissions Campaign pressing for the end of religious favouritism in school admissions and its implications for ethnic and social selectivity.[15] Following this were several challenges to unlawful admissions policies in faith schools, including in a 2012 case in Richmond upon Thames concerning what BHA regarded as misleading statements on planning of a new faith school.[16] From 2011, BHA/Humanists UK ran a special campaign against creationism teaching in schools and promoted teaching about evolution, mobilising science organisations and leading scientists. This resulted in 2014 in creationist teaching being banned in academies and free schools and required evolution be added to the National Curriculum for primary schools in England.[17]

There were other education campaigns. One was successful opposition by BHA/ Humanists UK and the National Secular Society in 2016–18 to the government's plan to abolish the 50 per cent religious admissions cap in religious free schools, introduced in 2010.[18] Another in the early 2010s attacked separate inspectorates for religious schools, after which in 2015 Bridge Schools Inspectorate ceased to be an approved inspectorate for independent schools following manifest issues in grading some Christian and Muslim schools, leading to an Ofsted commitment to universalise its common inspection frameworks.[19] Meanwhile, also in 2015, BHA was responsible for a High Court case in which three humanist parents and their children objected to the exclusion of humanism from the curriculum content of GCSE Religious Studies delivered in schools and academies unregistered as having a religious character, with a view to nonreligious worldviews being considered on an equal footing. BHA thought the case successfully established that the law requires religious education mandated by the state to be 'objective, critical and pluralistic', but the government merely withdrew the offending assertion and avoided wider reform.[20] In 2020 Humanists UK issued a 'Manifesto for Inclusive Schools' which sought the removal of religious indoctrination from British state schools.[21] Real change was gradually embedded in the religious dimensions of school management and curricula. At the same time, the movement had specifically campaigned for fifty years for sex education to be obligatory in schools, before finally seeing the compulsory introduction of relationship and sex education (RSE) in England in September 2020.[22] Meanwhile, Wales Humanists, part of Humanists UK, applied sustained scrutiny and pressure upon the Senedd (parliament) to complete in April 2021 a rights-based approach to education that had been developing over some years, with religious education renamed religion, values and ethics (RVE) in which humanism was to be discussed on equal terms with religions, and sit alongside relationships and sexuality education – a development belligerently described as an 'atheist power-grab' by the pressure group Christian Institute.[23]

The situation in Scotland in relation to religious and moral education in state schools has been different. With considerable power held by headteachers over the curriculum, in non-denominational (broadly Protestant-heritage) state schools 'religious observance' was compulsory but loosely defined as not necessarily 'worship' but, from 1980, as 'community acts' for 'spiritual development' that celebrated 'the shared values of the school community'; RE was a separate function, though from 1982 inspectable. Piecemeal but significant change followed by the Scottish Education Department, with its replacement agency, Education Scotland, in 2011 overseeing 'religious and moral education' introduced for non-denominational schools with a country-wide curriculum in which humanism featured; state denominational schools (almost all Roman Catholic) retained 'religious education' under church supervision as prescribed by legislation dating back to 1918.[24] In all of this, Humanist Society Scotland played a significant part in lobbying and curriculum development, but combined with considerable ground-level activity with schools and teachers to place humanism and resources in the mix of classroom work. Equally, HSS pressed against the ease with which schools might opt out of sex and relationships education. Notwithstanding the Curriculum for Excellence implemented in 2010, Scottish state education has not been centred on a national curriculum, and schools (effectively meaning headteachers) and local authorities have been encouraged to develop teaching and learning in conjunction with parents, learners and the wider community in the light of 'local circumstances and community expectations', leaving most work to be done – unlike in England – outside of the legal system.[25]

Education is an area of longstanding concern to humanists and before them ethicists and secularists. Headway has been made through a concatenation of campaigning approaches, set against a background of rapidly declining student and adult religiosity. With church schools making up a third of the total in England and Wales, and with the entire state education structure in Scotland fossilised almost entirely between 'non-denominational' and 'Roman Catholic' schools, the humanist movement looks set fair for sustained activity.

A second campaigning cause, the movement for voluntary euthanasia, has also been frustrating for the humanist movement. The central focus for humanist and other reformers in England, Wales and Northern Ireland was the Suicide Act 1961, which criminalised assisted dying. Public support was strong: increasing numbers of British people from 2000 have been travelling to Switzerland for an assisted death, whilst 89 per cent of British adults in 2019 expressed support for a right to die, and many nations and regions from 2000 introduced laws permitting assisted deaths. Both BHA/Humanists UK in England and Wales and HSS in Scotland have backed two things: legal challenges of individual humanists for a right to die, incorporating medically assisted dying or assisted suicide; and parliamentary bills to legislate for specific rights in this field. In 2002, humanist A. C. Grayling helped lawyers acting for Diane Pretty, who suffered from motor neurone disease and sought freedom from various courts under the European Convention on Human Right to allow her husband to assist her death; she failed at each attempt.[26] In 2008–9, BHA became drawn into vocal support for Debbie Purdy, who suffered from multiple sclerosis, in her legal case to obtain clarification on her husband's position should he assist in her death; the Law Lords ruled that the European Convention of Human Rights did confer rights concerning the manner and quality of death, though the law itself remained unchanged.[27] Between 2012 and 2020, BHA backed court action by members Tony and Jane Nicklinson, Paul Lamb, Noel Conway and Omid T, seeking to allow the terminally ill a voice to make their case to end incurable suffering in the High Court, Appeal Court, Supreme Court and European Court of Human Rights. Assisted dying bills were put forward by Lord Falconer in 2014–15, Rob Marris MP in 2015 and Baroness Meacher in 2021. In Scotland, where there is no law regarding assisted suicide, the state prosecutors decide on a case-by-case basis if an offence has occurred – including murder and culpable homicide – and after two bills in 2010 and 2013, and a further one in 2021, the HSS became a major supporter of the cause. This included in 2015–16 supporting its former treasurer, Gordon Ross, in a bid to openly clarify the murky legal procedures, resulting in Scotland's senior judge Lord Carloway issuing a full statement on hypothetical cases to guide prosecutors and the public.[28] In each case, whether in Scotland or the rest of the UK, the concept of human rights of the individual over their own life has become central in the argument for reform, backed by humanists and by progressive opinion generally – including some theologians. Though no legislation has been attained on this issue, with every court action the moral argument became better grounded and the legal case seemingly stronger.

(b) The character of humanist protest

The movement's campaigning has become in the twenty-first century organised mainly in calm meetings, lobbying, legal argument, representations to government and liaison with other pressure groups. Sometimes, as in gay pride marches, celebration and protest seemed wrapped in one. But protests have taken place.

In early 2003 the looming Second Gulf War against Iraq and its president Saddam Hussein struck its critics, including many humanists, as unjustified. When UN weapons inspectors failed to uncover Iraqi 'weapons of mass destruction', anti-war sentiment rose not merely from pacifists but from those supporting the UN refusal to endorse an American-led invasion. Large-scale demonstrations took place in London, Glasgow and elsewhere, with in the region of two million protesters, including the giant event on Saturday, 15 March 2003. This conveniently began outside the BHA's new offices in Gower Street, where Hanne Stinson and Marilyn

Mason led BHA and RPA members from across England and Wales, under what were described as 'impeccably moderate' banners emphasising the irrationality of war.[29] Mason remembered how the BHA was welcomed by other marchers for its benign influence amid groups of less reasonable protesting tactics.[30] With opinion polling in January 2003 showed outright public opposition to war at 47 per cent,[31] humanists formed a tiny fraction and an almost unobservable element of anti-war marching, but for some of them it was a matter of some conscience and personal meaning – especially those new to demonstrating.[32] One of the war's most vocal opponents was BHA chair, Christine Butterworth, who was concerned about the influence of the Christian fundamentalist right on US foreign policy, seemingly reuniting imperialism with religion.[33] When in January 2003 Anglican bishops unanimously regarded war as not morally justified without 'compelling new evidence',[34] some humanists wished the BHA to take a firmer stand against conflict, 'the religious sectarian element' and 'the strength of the Judeo-Christian lobby in the USA'.[35] Though David Pollock expressed concern such politicking might compromise BHA's charitable status,[36] the war drew much commentary on the humanist movement's pacifist heritage – ranging from the Rationalist Peace Society and Hypatia Bradlaugh Bonner's advocacy of arbitration in the First World War through to CND, Bertrand Russell and Barbara Smoker's sustained loud voice against war.[37] Humanist conscientious objectors, including Russell, were brought to mind by an annual commemoration involving Smoker and Butterworth during the Gulf War on 15 May 2003 at the Commemorative Objectors' Stone unveiled in Tavistock Square by the Peace Pledge Union supported by nonreligionists.[38] The demonstrations were anything but violent. They were in the main, faultlessly middle class in tone, with many professionals ambling in family or in workplace groups. It was an occasion for people of many age groups, but perhaps rarely had so many of older people come from suburbs to object to a government about to declare war. It was protest firmly lodged in respectability.

Something of a contrast was evident in the character of protests concerning sexual and reproductive rights. Sexual identity, full decriminalisation of homosexuality, equal marriage for same-sex couples, abortion, contraception, and sex education and censorship – these had constituted leading issues in the humanist cause since the nineteenth century. After the significant strides in this field in the 1960s and their defence in the 1970s, challenges came during the conservative backlash of the 1980s and 1990s. Gay and lesbian rights were one of the few areas of zest in humanism in these years, with the Gay Humanist Group (later renamed the Gay and Lesbian Humanist Group) established as an independent body in 1979 drawing the humanist movement into support, and by the 2000s the humanist movement in Britain had positioned itself at the forefront of sexual politics and ecclesiastical obstructions. It was one field in which young people felt drawn to the humanist movement and were willing to take to the streets in more vigorous demonstration.

CLAIRE RAYNER 1931–2010

Nurse, agony aunt, broadcaster and humanitarian, Claire Rayner was a staunch atheist and humanist, becoming president of the British Humanist Association from 1999 to 2004 and being vice-president for six more years until she died from breast cancer in 2010. She revealed in her autobiography something of the physical and mental cruelty of her parents, and of being placed in a Canadian psychiatric hospital. On returning to the UK in 1951, she trained as a nurse, becoming first a midwife and then a nursing sister in London. From the late 1950s, she started newspaper writing on patient care and nurses' conditions, retiring ten years later from nursing to concentrate on writing, emerging as one of Britain's leading agony aunts at *Woman's Own* and *Petticoat* magazines, and *The Sun* and the *Sunday Mirror* newspapers. Her candour and forthrightness in discussing sexual issues broke new ground

FIGURE 24 Claire Rayner (1931–2010), nurse, journalist, agony aunt and BHA President 1999–2004, was much concerned with sexual and reproductive rights, and a critic of Joseph Ratzinger. Photo: @NPG

in both written and broadcast journalism, and attracted huge audiences when she moved to TV-am in the late 1980s. All the while, she was a campaigner – for the Patients' Association, for the charity Sense, for the Down's Syndrome Association and for Cancer Research UK. A prodigious writer, in addition to her journalism, she wrote over ninety books of fiction and non-fiction. Rayner was BHA president at a time when the humanist cause in Britain was emerging from crisis and division, showing how its honesty and scepticism might appeal to those less interested in philosophy but more in finding a refuge from upbringings and careers blighted by religious issues, sexual ignorance and domestic abuse. Rayner offered open criticism of church leaders whose policies hurt women, yet offered a compassionate and open culture for women to talk about distinctive medical conditions like breast cancer and to discuss death without god.

Joseph Ratzinger, the conservative theologian Pope Benedict XVI, came to Britain on a state visit in September 2010. Scottish humanists were determined not to allow Benedict's visit to pass unprotested, as he was scheduled to lead an open-air mass on Glasgow Green. Ahead of his arrival, Humanist Society Scotland debated at its annual general meeting on how to react to the event, agreeing that something needed to be done to make a public declaration of Scottish secularisation. Perhaps aware that a counter-demonstration to the mass would neither be seemly nor attract many humanists, the meeting agreed to rent an existing advertising hoarding for a four-figure sum that would be facing the pontiff's platform (albeit at some distance) and to proclaim the message: 'Two Million Scots are Good Without God.' This attained moderate media coverage. Perhaps more effective, however, was a solo demonstration by a young woman member of a Scottish secularist society. Having alerted the media and acting on her own, she conducted a one-person protest when Pope Benedict was driven in a cavalcade along Princes Street in Edinburgh. She protested about the Vatican's sexual policy and the widespread evidence of abuse of children and young people by Catholic priests, handing out condoms to disparage the church's continued opposition to birth control.[39] In a way, the depth of feeling came through this one woman's protest, rather in contrast to the passivity of a billboard making a rather anodyne point.

The next day Pope Benedict went on to London where much larger protests took place. It was Benedict's views on sexual morality and gender politics, and the church's failure to tackle sexual abuse of children by clergy, that drew special condemnation from tens of thousands of mostly young people. Protest was spearheaded by Marco Tranchino of Central London Humanists and aided by human rights campaigner Peter Tatchell, with BHA providing headquarters coordination. At a press conference at Conway Hall, Tranchino highlighted the papacy's opposition to equality for LGBT people as well as its anti-democratic nature. He contended that 'in a liberal society . . . no religious leader should have privileged, undemocratic influence upon our political leaders'.[40] On 18 September 2010, around 20,000 people of the 'Protest the Pope' movement on contraception, sex abuse and women's ordination processed to Whitehall where they were addressed by Tatchell, Terry Sanderson of the National Secular Society, Richard Dawkins and Andrew Copson. Copson spoke of the 'radical mismatch' between socially liberal values and those of Pope Benedict – one of whose associates referred to Britain as a 'moral wasteland'.[41] Copson explained that unlike Britain, the Vatican was a state that had 'concealed the sexual abuse of children and frustrated justice as a matter of national policy'. It had, he said, used its position as a state to lobby the UN against the human rights of women and LGBT people; human rights, liberal and secular democracy and the pursuit of justice were the 'real moral values to live by in the twenty-first century'.[42] To his surprise and delight, the sound of hundreds of people chanting 'BHA! BHA! BHA!' echoed around Whitehall. 'Protest the Pope' found the humanist movement in renewed campaigning vigour, confronting religious policies in public spaces – including Copson debating with a representative of the Catholic Church on Channel Four News.[43] Opinion polling showed that Benedict was even more unpopular with the public following his departure than before his arrival. A year later, a majority had forgotten about the papal visit: 91 per cent thought that it had made no difference to their moral values and 59 per cent disapproved of the Catholic Church.[44] Interestingly, the classic secularist and rationalist critique of churches was being outpaced on sexual and gender policy grounds. The London demonstrations were proof of just how far the young people of Britain could be moved to action by issues related to sexual freedom.

Humanist protest was becoming divergent in its character. Some of the issues were old and often cerebral, relating to freedom of speech and blasphemy that had been the bread and butter of the movement for a century and a half. A longstanding issue that remained into the twenty-first century was that of humanist access to broadcasting. Reflecting the changing religious and legal culture of the nation, the government agreed in 2003 to a law requiring all five terrestrial television channels to provide programmes not merely about 'religion' but about 'religion and other beliefs'. Despite some experimentation, anticipated humanist access to the iconic *Thought for The Day* on Radio 4, and other broadcasts categorised as religion and ethics and monopolised by those with a religious faith, did not, for the most part, materialise. Though diversity of radio stations, podcasts, social and online media have diminished the relevance of a single programme in British culture, *Thought for the Day* has been broadcast since 1939, and at under three minutes in length, remains an intense irritant to humanists every morning six days a week.[45] Humanists of a certain age, brought up since the Second World War on the BBC's talk radio channel, persist in placing the reform of this brief programme high on the campaigning agenda of Humanists UK.

Despite a changing pattern of protest against the churches, the early 2000s witnessed a renewed impetus to revitalise the intellectual underpinnings of the humanist movement. After the 1960s, the philosophy groups of SPES and the Progressive League diminished as a leading form of humanist outreach and featured little in the activities of the 1970s, 1980s and 1990s. But rapid and agile reaction to news stories by intellectual heavyweights of humanism was needed in the twenty-first-century digital age. Office staff had to be able to summon up experts to react to rolling-news media, the web and (after 2005) social media. So it was in 2000, BHA organised a Philosophers Group – a 'think tank', as it was termed in its early design at BHA HQ – which by 2003 was running an annual conference and designing a website.[46] The idea was to have two-hour evening meetings, five times a year, to be held in central London, at which issues could be raised by BHA staff or by thinkers to produce a written end product. The products were not envisaged as academic papers but as pamphlets, press releases, articles in serious newspapers, letters to the press and to government departments, with discussions recorded for easy transcription. With an initial list of twenty-five philosophers mostly in academic positions (usually philosophy departments, but occasionally in separate medical ethics units), the first meeting in March 2000 brought together sixteen, including Julian Baggini, Nigel Warburton, Simon Blackburn and Barry Gardner MP. Over the following five years, a variety of topics were tackled – death, creationism, toleration. In addition, in 2003 a Humanists Scientists' Group was formed, initially with fourteen members, including Sir Hermann Bondi, Richard Dawkins and Colin Blakemore, working on an anti-creationism project with the Philosophers Group.[47] However, the Philosophers Group did not sustain its initial high activity; attendances fell off, and by February 2005 only four philosophers came. Social media demanded sharper reaction, but there was still a place for the high-status lecture. As well as the annual Conway Memorial lectures with prominent philosophers, scientists and cultural figures, which have been running under the management of SPES since 1908, new annual lectures prospered from the 1990s: the NSS's Thomas Paine lecture at Conway Hall, and the BHA/Humanists UK new annual Bentham lecture instituted in 2005, attracting Jonathan Wolff first and then a succession of legal minds. There followed the Voltaire lecture, Darwin Day lecture, Rosalind Franklin Women's Day lecture and Holyoake lecture. The scholar as speaker remains a feature of humanist and atheist meetings at local and regional levels, both in Britain and in most nations where these movements operate. Besides that, though, the humanist movement always sought to spread news of humanism in a distilled form that could appeal to those who were in the position of waiting to discover that they were already humanist. Traditionally undertaken by pamphlets and books, by the 2010s it was being done mainly by the internet, and one of the new methods which Humanists UK pioneered was the MOOC – the 'massive open online courses'. In 2018, two courses, presented by Sandi Toksvig and Alice Roberts, were launched, which, within three years, over ten thousand people had taken with almost 30,000 people enrolled. CEO Andrew Copson contributed to fronting the movement's public intellectual presence with a steady output of books for general and specialist readers alike: *The Wiley Blackwell Handbook of Humanism* (2015, co-edited with A. C. Grayling); *Secularism: A Very Short Introduction* (2019); *The Little Book of Humanism* (2020, which reached the *Sunday Times* bestsellers list); and *The Little Book of Humanist Weddings* (2021), the last two co-authored with Humanists UK president Alice Roberts.

One of the big attractions in the 2000s and early 2010s was the group known as the New Atheists, each of whom became well known to the audiences of BHA, RPA and NSS, and who formed star attractions at annual conferences and other meetings. Though none was strictly a philosopher, Richard Dawkins, Christopher Hitchens, Sam Harris and Daniel Dennett became international media stars for their outspoken manner and vigorous criticism of organised religion and belief, their books selling millions of copies worldwide.[48] From interviews with supporters, it seems that rather than triggering conversions from religion, Dawkins and Hitchens conferred confidence and certainty among many nonreligious followers.[49] Yet, many other recent authors with an atheist marque to their books stood out for their non-confrontational, measured and less brash permeation of popular culture, such as Philip Pullman's (1946–) trilogy *His Dark Materials* (1995–2000) and *The Good Man Jesus and the Scoundrel Christ* (2010), Terry Pratchett (1948–2015), Iain Banks (1954–2013) and Stephen Fry (1957–). The cultural infusion of humanism into British society has long been strongly connected to the character of the humanists involved, and this appears the more so with the rise in recent decades of media consumption. Though Richard Dawkins remained a celebrated supporter of Humanists UK, chairing the Darwin Day lecture until 2018, the vociferous style of the New Atheists had been arguably outshone in affection by the 2020s by a more gentle and appealing version in the public square.

(c) We're all humanists now?

In 2018 Humanists UK, through its affiliate Defence Humanists, was represented for the first time at the national remembrance ceremony at London's Cenotaph by its CEO, Andrew Copson, whilst Lorraine Barrett represented Wales Humanists at the Cardiff ceremony; two years before, Humanist Society Scotland's CEO, Gordon MacRae, made the first official humanist wreath-laying at Edinburgh's Stone of Remembrance.[50] Humanism was starting to acquire increased civic acknowledgement. In part, perhaps, this may have been because humanism was coming to represent an underlying universalism – the shared ethical position of a people no longer united by a faith. In 1996, a BHA-commissioned MORI poll indicated that 10 per cent of the adult UK population shared humanist beliefs; by 2006 this had tripled to 36 per cent, with likely a significant increase since then.[51]

Throughout the UK, including in the churches, there was a growing acceptance – reluctantly at times – of the altered landscape in which equivalence of rights emerged to those of legitimate but different belief systems. The statistics of secularisation and church decline were of such severity in the 2000s and 2010s that some church managers were approaching new experts in the nonbelief sector for advice. In a way, the utter pessimism that has come over many British church leaders since the 1990s makes the prospect of some changes – such as to *Thought for the Day* – a red line beyond which they cannot conceive of stepping whilst still remaining part of the civic establishment. This feeling seems especially strong in the Church of England, the one remaining state church in the UK.[52] Anglican bishops were fearful mostly privately, though in Archbishop John Carey's case publicly, that something more than a change in numbers and institutions was underway. The disintegration of the Christian foundations of the country came to seem possible, and the growing success for humanist-movement activity in the UK added up to the realignment of the British people to nonreligious values. And it is the campaigning of the young and their alienation from the Christian value systems of moral reserve and deference that terrorise some church leaders. With the numbers of members and supporters of Humanist UK reaching six figures, the movement may be attaining the level of a mass-membership movement, aided by the widening humanist acculturation of British society. Most notable has been the long-term decrease of intolerance of gay people, most marked among religious people; between 1983–95 and 1998–2007, the proportion saying same-sex sexual relations was wrong fell from 75 to 52 per cent of Anglicans and from 75 to 44 per cent of Catholics.[53] This has proceeded as active church connection has declined, intensifying the degree to which church identification no longer guarantees adherence to the churches' moral standpoints. With religious decline, the moral alignment of the UK has rotated towards positions championed by humanists and other progressives. And it is through that championing that the humanist movement has attained rising stature. So it emerged that the BBC's ethical output had been (and still is) handed as a monopoly to those in churches selected to broadcast, many of whom do not reflect the moral orientation of the listenership nor, it must be suspected in some cases, fully endorse the laws of the British state (over abortion, homosexuality and sex education for example).

Through the gateway of humanism, nonreligion was assuming a place in British society with greater ease than ever before. Improved funds and innovation enabled new forms of humanist public profile, but it was the daring and determination on the part of the movement that brought this about. In 2009 the Atheist Bus campaign snowballed from modest beginnings to become something of a national, then international, publicity spectacle promoting a humanist and atheist message on a previously untried scale. The comedy writer Ariane Sherine penned an opinion piece in *The Guardian* newspaper telling of her disquiet at reading adverts containing a verse from the bible adorning the side of London buses, directing the reader to an evangelical website threatening 'an eternity in torment in hell'. Sherine, offended by its irrationality, was told by the Advertising Standards Authority that they could see no legal objection, so she resolved on an atheist advertisement that would 'distribute reassurance' rather than fear.[54] 'There's Probably No God. Now Stop Worrying and Enjoy Your Life' was adopted as the slogan by the BHA, its finances boosted when their patron, Richard Dawkins, offered to match donations up to £5,500. In practice, over £150,000 was raised, funding advertisements on the side of 800 buses across the UK, 1,000 London Underground trains and 2 animated screens on Oxford Street.[55] At the campaign's launch, BHA chief executive, Hanne Stinson, emphasised that the message was not aimed at religious people but at reinforcing and comforting the doubter; a bid by evangelical group Christian Voice to silence the campaign was rejected by the Advertising Standards Authority.[56] By February 2009, the campaign was copied by humanist, secularist and atheist groups in at least fifteen nations around the world, conferring humanism with the rarity of a global brand image. A rising public profile in the late 2000s, fuelled by several publicity coups, sustained a preoccupation with brand and image which, with the help of focus-group work among members and nonreligious people, demonstrated an outdatedness of 'British Humanist Association'; renamed Humanists UK in 2017, this reflected a deliberate appeal to the entire nonreligious population and to achieve a greater coherence. Andrew Copson, Chief Executive from 2010, considered that the rebranding reflected confidence: a 'will and self-perception of ourselves as an organisation that *should* have a message and *should* have a platform from which to appeal to wider society.'[57] The rebranding emphasised consistency and clarity as well as communicating positive values. 'The cause remains the same as ever', wrote Copson: 'a tolerant world where rational thinking and kindness prevail.'[58]

In the 2000s and 2010s, awareness of secularisation and the declining popularity of the churches was becoming evident to many. The Bible Society and the London religious think tank Theos became troubled by the dominance of 'liberal humanism' in the public sphere and the difficulty of inserting god there – and the even greater difficulty of getting people to react positively when they did.[59] In his 1999 article 'Godless in Greenwich', William Rees-Mogg wrote in *The Times* that 'We're now well into the third generation stage of the decline of religion', but, he noted, the new century was to be welcomed in by a 'Faith Zone' at the Millennium Dome in Greenwich – an 'intellectual dumbing down of our post-Christian society's attitude to religion [that] would have shocked any 19th-century agnostic.'[60] Survey after survey gathered statistics of seemingly terminal church decline under newspaper headlines that alternated between gloom and whimsy: 'Churches may "bleed to death"' (2000), 'Couples jilt the church for wacky wedding venues' (2001), 'Less is more when it comes to worshippers'

(2001), 'Dwindling Catholics put faith in buddleia' (2002), 'Anglican Church "in meltdown" as attendances fall' (2002), 'Stuck in the past, losing members and aging fast' (2002), 'Bishop warns Church that it may disappear' (2004), 'The end is nigh for Unitarians, warns minister' (2004), 'Church faces last rites, says Carey' (2005) and 'Church, old, bankrupt, empty, seeks saviour' (2005). As stories of church splits, child sex abuse and malign behaviour by priests, bishops and at least one cardinal, words like 'scandal', 'schism' and 'secularisation' frequented the columns of the daily press.[61]

The heft of human rights and equality work was such that it was not confined to that sphere nor to the BHA's links to government. Relationships with religion, for example, became in many ways more congenial, despite anti-religious voices still being heard loudly in the movement. Some new members felt ill at ease: 'Must I go out and preach anti-Christianity?' asked one.[62] The result was more agreement to pursue the Blackham strategy of accommodation with those churches and religious people sharing humanist concerns and willing to engage with the movement. Even members of the older guard, like Jim Herrick, born in 1944 and moving during his career between the main British nonreligion organisations, resigned as editor of the National Secular Society's stridently secularist magazine *The Freethinker* in 1981 because, he told us, 'I was tired of all the anti-religious stuff' – what he called 'bashing the church'. In 1984 Herrick slipped across to edit RPA's *New Humanist* magazine, remaining associated with it until retirement in 2005. His outlook had changed, he reported to us, signalling what was likely a widespread sentiment among humanists by the 1980s and 1990s.[63] Greater effectiveness and subtlety was desired.

(d) Human rights, the state and internationalism

For humanism, the Human Rights Act 1998 became a legal 'hook' upon which to hang campaigns in support of minorities of various types, and also for hanging their campaigns for the equality of the nonreligious in ways that made them a group more difficult for government to ignore.[64] The HRA incorporated the fundamental freedoms and rights set out by the European Convention on Human Rights (ECHR) in domestic law in Britain.[65] Its implications were first pointed out in the BHA in a 2001 presentation by Madeline Pym, then the association's media officer, who drew attention to four different ways in which the HRA could be used: indicating good practice, in test case litigation, third-party interventions and auditing policy, and legislation for HRA compliance.[66] She cautioned that bringing prosecutions was likely to be risky, expensive and offer no definite prospect of success. However, the other avenues were to be extremely fruitful for the BHA and were rapidly developed under Hanne Stinson's leadership; by the early months of 2003, Christine Butterworth noted how the HRA was 'proving invaluable to our campaign efforts'.[67] A favoured tactic was to point out the incompatibility of existing legislation with the HRA in the hope that government would be pressured to take action – including in June 2002 the BHA's submission to the Lords Select Committee on Religious Offences that the offence of blasphemy might breach the HRA.[68] This submission also initiated a four-year campaign against government proposals on a new crime of incitement of religious hatred by the device of extending racial hatred to religion; BHA in England (and HSS in Scotland concerning a similar bill in 2020–1) joined some religious groups in opposing this for obstructing free speech on religion. Meanwhile, Hanne Stinson was closely involved, representing the BHA on the Steering Group in government planning of the Equality and Human Rights Commission.[69] Third-party interventions rose significantly, consisting of supporting individuals using the courts to bring discrimination cases under the terms of the HRA. In 2008 an employment tribunal in Abergele, North Wales, unanimously found in favour of Mark Sheridan, a former employee of Prospects – an evangelical Christian Charity working with people with learning disabilities that took over a local-authority service funded by the Labour government's outsourcing policy; Prospects had four years previously introduced a policy restricting the recruitment to Christians and making non-Christian staff ineligible for promotion.[70] Sheridan resigned in protest, and claimed constructive dismissal, with his case supported by the BHA, who paid his legal costs.[71] Thought to be the first case of an employment tribunal determining how far a religious organisation could discriminate on the grounds of religion or belief, Sheridan won.[72]

All of this amounted to little short of a 'human-rights turn' to the toil of the British humanist movement. The appointment in 2001 of Hanne Stinson as BHA director, plucked from working at the British Red Cross, marked a considerable change in style and rhetoric. In recalling to us her 'pitch' at the BHA job interview on the day after 9/11, she told the panel she wasn't going to be anti-religious but be more a partner to those, including Muslims targeted in the febrile atmosphere, with whom she would talk and consult.[73] The HRA made the BHA a talking organisation with religious groups in a comprehensive and fraternal manner, starting with the long-running Equality and Human Rights Steering Group comprising religious and humanist representations on which Stinson carved the mould for future humanist influence across churches, government and agencies. Even the Evangelical Alliance, an unlikely friend, praised the sentiments and work of BHA leaders in joint meetings in 2005 with civil servants and a government minister, whilst Stinson and David Pollock met during 2003–7 with the representative of the Home Office Cohesion and Faiths Unit concerning detailed representations on religious discrimination by various organisations.[74] BHA became as much a partner as opponent with like-minded bodies seeking legal change and a leading talker to government.

DAVID POLLOCK, b. 1942

The first time David Pollock experienced scepticism about religion was when he was five on his first day at primary school. With children clasping hands together to pray, he decided there and then to keep his head down and just survive this irrational regime. This was the start of his lifelong project of working for rationalist and humanist causes. At Oxford University he was a leading force in the Humanist Group of the early 1960s, and from there he and colleagues, including Tony Brierley, bridged to the British Humanist Association and the Rationalist Press Association where they led pioneering initiatives. David was a strong supporter of Harold Blackham, together promoting the Open Society concept to place the humanist movement in a stronger societal position. He set up Humanist Lobby and personally ran it to unite humanist MPs in parliament. He had a good eye for business, the law and finances, chaired the BHA educational committee, and was chair of the Rationalist Association for several years. Pollock was rarely limited in what he did. A hugely energetic individual, he volunteered and led, getting initiatives off the ground, calming fiercely protesting members, and attended scores of humanist meetings overseas – meetings of IHEU and of the European Humanist Federation – becoming renowned by colleagues of diverse cultures for his clarity and fairness from the chair, always with an eye on a timely and successful conclusion. He

FIGURE 25 David Pollock. Photo: Humanists UK/Bishopsgate Archive.

chaired with aplomb mass meetings and press conferences – including that of the defendants in the Oz blasphemy case. Despite a gap in some humanist activity during 1975–90, he persisted as a trustee of the movement, and, after the crisis years, returned to help the resuscitation of the BHA in the 1990s and 2000s. As senior trustee, Pollock carried a strong sense of the past and future of the movement, always collecting paperwork to be filed in his vast archive, and promoting the project from which this book has emerged. One of his oldest colleagues said: 'I'm told by David Pollock who knows everything, as you probably realise; that's not meant to be satirical, he does.'

During 2003–21, the work for humanist-led and funded legal review grew, embedding its perspective into legal and government culture. From the early 2000s, auditing proposed legislation to ensure compliance with the HRA to increase ties between the BHA and the instruments of the state – including the influential Joint Committee on Human Rights (Commons and Lords) (JCHR), set up in 2003 to which the BHA and other interested organisations returned detailed comments and suggested amendments, which were included in JCHR reports giving them a wide readership. With the BHA also sending out press releases on many topics to the HPG and government ministers, humanists became an alert, innovative and ground-breaking human rights organisation, its interventions ranging across a wide spectrum.[75] Combining human rights and equality principles gave the BHA a potent legal basis to assist minorities of like belief and sexual groups. In this way, BHA also became the funder and guide to interventions on rights of assisted dying, LGBT and marriage ceremonies. Many cases were lost, and into the 2020s continued to be so. But the persistence of the BHA in its lines of legal work marked the underlying belief that right was on its side and that, sooner or later, UK courts would be forced into concessions to keep in line with international law and conventions. This signalled to others that human rights constituted a secular domain in which rights pertained to all, regardless of faith or institution.

Secularisation came in various guises. Whilst blasphemy was for a moment enshrined as a central part of English culture in the 1990s by both the Rushdie affair and the Wingrove film *Visions of Ecstasy* (featuring sexualised scenes involving Saint Teresa of Avila), the pressure to harmonise with European law could not be kept out forever. To this end, a House of Lords Select Committee on Religious Offences met in 2003 with the NSS's Keith Porteous Wood enlisting the historian of blasphemy, David Nash, as a source of information and expertise, whilst the British Humanist Association was represented by David Pollock and Hanne Stinson at the same meeting, with both organisations arguing for repeal of the blasphemy law. With angry evangelical protests outside the Church of St Martin-in-the-Fields and from Christian Voice members as they noisily left the gallery before secularist evidence, the arguments for repeal of the blasphemy law – little changed since the Victorian period – produced no clear steer from the Select Committee and blasphemy remained upon the statute book.[76] Eventually, a letter instigated by Liberal Democrat Evan Harris MP and signed by leading figures, including Lord Carey, a former archbishop of Canterbury, urged the abolition of the law in England and Wales. Harris tabled an amendment on 9 January 2008 to the Criminal Justice and Immigration Bill then before parliament; the government minister, Maria Eagle, clearly speaking with the authority of Prime Minister Gordon Brown, indicated immediately that subject to the outcome of consultation the government would produce its own amendment. With Rowan Williams, then archbishop of Canterbury, other consulted churches and the human rights lobby, also in favour, abolition on three main grounds was agreed, undoing: the religious discrimination in favour of Christianity and the Church of England; the danger of the law becoming the domain of private prosecutions (such as happened in the Christian Voice attempt to prosecute the BBC in respect of *Jerry Springer: The Opera*); and the violation of the right to freedom of expression. Introduced in the Lords on 5 March 2008, the government amendment abolishing the two offences of blasphemy and blasphemous libel passed by 148 votes to 87, in the Commons the following 6 May (on a 'matter of conscience' free vote for Conservative MPs) by 378 votes to 57, and, with royal assent two days later, centuries of blasphemy proceedings were brought to an end.[77] With it, *Visions of Ecstasy* was awarded in 2012 a full film certification with no cuts. The law remained different in Scotland, where there had been no prosecution since 1843 and no likelihood of one, but it remained an embarrassment to the country and its newly restored parliament in Edinburgh – especially because nations with active blasphemy laws, such as Pakistan, pointed at Scotland in response to European criticism of Islamic nations. Humanist Society Scotland led the campaign to achieve abolition, attracting cross-party support from MSPs during the early 2010s, and finally the Scottish government inserted in the Hate Crime and Public Order (Scotland) Act 2021 a blasphemy abolition clause sparingly constituted of eight words: 'The common law offence of blasphemy is abolished.'[78] The votes in both parliaments demonstrated not merely the support for the measure but the decline in animosity towards many secularist policies. Only in Northern Ireland does blasphemy remain a crime.

But despite the repeals of blasphemy laws, many in the humanist cause were disappointed in the Labour governments of Tony Blair and Gordon Brown. The failure in education that we noted earlier was replicated with the failure to endorse legal recognition for humanist weddings in England and Wales, remaining for the time being, no matter its recruitment growth, a problem for Humanists UK at the start of the 2020s. Meanwhile, Humanist Society Scotland, like everybody else, accepted the likely permanence of the structure of Scottish state education.

There are no secular state schools in Scotland; there never have been, and, in most estimations, it is doubtful that there will be any for a very long time. Nearly all Scottish state schools are either Christian (legally termed 'nondenominational') or Roman Catholic ('religious'), a segregation that both defines Scotland's religious problem *and* the mechanism that helps neutralise claims of sectarian discrimination. The result is that HSS has put its efforts into changing what happens in religious and moral education classes and school assemblies, encouraging modern moral education to be worked into the curriculum by adventurous teaching staff. Furthermore, HSS found that it had friends in each of the parties in the Holyrood Parliament in Edinburgh, so that other areas of change – such as equal marriage and abolition of the blasphemy law – were passed with notable ease and speed. In Northern Ireland, where religious influence in the state is unlikely to change radically in the short term, Humanists UK has since 2016 given priority to working through both legal and lobbying exercises to improve the position and self-confidence of the nonreligious.

If humanism's domestic influence in the British state has been slow to advance, its influence in the field of internationalism has had a considerable heritage to uphold. In the 1940s and 1950s, British humanists became not only influential in the United Nations and its agencies but in leading the international movement. In the 1990s, the European Union gave humanism a strong European base. National and international organisations of humanism flourished with the formation in 1991 of the European Humanist Federation, headquartered in Brussels, which became a strong advocate of its cause in the European Union and its agencies, with almost half of its member organisations in 2021 being founded since 1990, but oftentimes competing on a slightly unequal playing field against state-funded churches.[79] Assisting this was the transfer in 1998 of IHEU's headquarters from Utrecht to London, bringing a long-term rising stability and improved management in IHEU affairs. In 2002, it produced the Second Amsterdam Declaration, updating the first version of fifty years earlier, providing in 506 words (including preliminary and concluding passages) a re-wording of the original points, notably introducing the term 'lifestance', but demonstrating an uncharacteristic restraint in altering the fundamental descriptors of humanism. However, the second declaration's failure to specifically mention race, gender or sexuality might be regarded as a missed opportunity to explain the realities of human rights in the new century.[80] The more so since IHEU experienced a serious swing towards the non-European world, well represented by the establishment in 2014 of the *Freedom of Thought Report*, subtitled 'A Global Report on the Rights, Legal Status, and Discrimination against Humanists, Atheists, and the Non-religious'. This has produced annual reports on the state of the law and licensed populism against the position of nonbelief in every nation in the world.[81] The international organisation fell in step with the British movement: IHEU headquarters took up residence in the shared office space with BHA at Theobald's Road and then Gower Street in 2003 (though it has moved more recently to separate accommodation); and the CEO of BHA, Andrew Copson, became president of IHEU in 2014. When BHA changed its name in 2018 to Humanists UK, and the following year IHEU to Humanists International, this reaffirmed the place of internationalism and a postcolonial interest within British humanism.

On this widening landscape, IHEU became appreciably more responsive to the developing nations in Africa and south-east Asia from the late 1990s, backing the causes of individuals suffering from both legal and populist campaigns against atheists, including blasphemy prosecutions that could lead to execution and murder. At the end of the 2010s there was a growing concern with the plight of apostates in distress, with all national humanist organisations represented at the IHEU General Assembly in Malta in 2016 being encouraged in this direction. IHEU's *Freedom of Thought Reports* from 2013 established that the overwhelming majority of countries were failing to respect the rights of atheists, with laws that denied the right of atheists to exist, revoked their right to citizenship, prevented them from working for the state, obstructed their access to public education, banned them from holding public office and criminalised their expression of views on, and criticism of, religion.[82] A perception existed, supported by the information gathered by IHEU's reports, that the situation for the nonreligious was deteriorating across the world. In his forward to the 2016 edition, Ahmed Shaheed, United Nations Special Rapporteur on Freedom of Religion and Belief, expressed his distress at the 'rising intolerance related to religion or belief worldwide' with 'global trends clearly showing a resurgence of religiously motivated action in the public sphere'.[83]

Furthermore, the advice and expertise of Humanists UK regarding the nonreligious overseas was now being sought by the British government with Andrew Copson being appointed to the Foreign and Commonwealth Office (FCO)'s Freedom of Religion and Belief Advisory Group in 2014.[84] Two years later, Copson travelled as a delegate to the UN Human Rights Council where fifteen separate interventions were made on topics including the sexual and reproductive rights of women, rights to peaceful assembly and association in Saudi Arabia and Egypt, freedom of expression in Bangladesh, the rights of LGBT people in Latvia and the human rights of refugees and migrants in Europe. Wider foreign policy work included attention to the ongoing situation in Bangladesh, where a murderous campaign was being conducted by Islamists against humanist bloggers, LGBT activists, religious minorities and academics. As a result of the BHA's lobbying, the Foreign and Commonwealth Office minister condemned some of the killings.[85] International Freedom of Religion and Belief continued to be a major theme of work with the FCO and the UN during the following year.[86] Punctuating these efforts was the periodic emergence of *cause célèbres* where the plight of particular individuals and extreme cases of persecution attracted international attention. Some of these victims were directly associated with the humanist movement: in 2019, Humanists UK urgently lobbied the British government to raise the issue of

Gulalai Ismail, a human rights activist and feminist from Pakistan, who was at the time a board member of Humanists International. She had been arrested on grounds of 'sedition' after speaking out publicly about sexual assaults and disappearances allegedly carried out by the Pakistani military.[87] Whilst she was incarcerated, her father was also abducted by police and her relatives and supporters threatened and intimidated. After many months in captivity she was eventually released and subsequently escaped to safety in New York.[88] In 2021, both Humanists UK and Humanists International were engaged in the defence of Mubarak Bala, president of the Humanist Association of Nigeria. In April 2020, Bala had been arrested and detained without any formal charges on allegations of blasphemy, following the creation of a post on social media which was construed by the Nigerian authorities as 'provocative and annoying' to Muslims.[89] A year later, he remained in jail despite a ruling by the Federal High Court of Nigeria that he be released on bail and that his detention and denial of his ability to choose his own legal representation constituted gross infringements of his rights to personal liberty, freedom of thought and expression and movement. Then, in April 2022, Bala was sentenced to 24 years imprisonment for blasphemy on pleading guilty on eighteen counts. Both Humanists UK and Humanists International continue to campaign for his release.[90]

Humanists UK, as well as Humanist Society Scotland, no longer left overseas campaigning work just to the international humanist movement. Each interceded in campaigns for individuals, groups and organisations, investing in human rights representation, which might bring immediate benefits to those in perilous predicaments. More broadly, the Human Rights Act 1998 and the Equality Act 2010 made humanist rhetoric at home more legally apt and resonant, with society's moral argument moving increasingly onto humanist territory. With rising support, and with much to do, the fortunes of the movement were changing. Symbolising this was its lead role in seeking full equality for LGBTQ+ peoples, including equal (gay) marriage. Humanism as a title and movement was not in any sense *taking over* civil society, but there were growing signs of confluence between the values of the movement and those of civil culture – what many humanists regarded as the latter catching up with the former. Looking in 2021 to the future, after eleven busy years at the helm of Humanists UK, Andrew Copson reflected on the new institutional recognition of the charity's programmes on the part of government and the third sector more broadly, and spoke about closing the gap between the third of people with humanist beliefs and the 7 per cent who actually identified with humanism. 'It's trying to solve the problem of the two humanisms', he said. 'There's the humanism in society, which has never been stronger, and the background values of our society are just so in tune with the humanist approach in many ways.' Yet then, he went on, 'there's the humanism of organised humanism, which, although it's in different parts of the UK and meeting the significant needs of those people [who join], it isn't becoming the self-identified approach to life of all the people who have it as an implicit approach to life'. Getting organised humanism more recognised with implicit humanists is a future objective: 'Trying to close the gap between those two humanisms must be a future aim.'[91]

There has been a next stage envisaged by many humanists. First raised in the 1980s, some key individuals spoke of the continued need for universal values and global ethics (including UN secretary general Kofi Annan in 2003[92]). But world attention around 2000 rather seemed to be focussed on extending sets of *rights* for communities or collectives of people – the disabled, women and non-white races – whilst *values* failed to excite the responsiveness of either the UN as a whole or individual governments. Rights was a demanding field as it stood. There was mounting criticism from some quarters of the human rights agenda as too closely allied to the universalist agenda of liberalism; Islamic and Christian scholars, including Alasdair MacIntyre, condemned the notion of human or natural rights as fiction and a pseudo concept being peddled by anti-religious forces.[93] This sentiment gathered support from some unlikely bedfellows. The 1999 UN Resolution against the Defamation of Religions, promoted by Muslim interests, eventually attracted strong opposition from British and American evangelical organisations, the liberal International Centre Against Censorship and the secular International Humanist and Ethical Union, which regarded the resolution as regression from the UN Declaration of Human Rights.[94] Even though conservative religions were split, human rights law and discourse was adopted from the early 2000s onwards by the British Humanist Association as a front-line campaigning strategy, opening up productive avenues through which the charity's aims and objectives could be pursued in a legal environment. As historian of law Chris Moores has noted, though the Human Rights Act 1998 was not a universal panacea nor the dawning of a 'last utopia', yet the work of the civil liberties lobby was transformed through the integration of the language of rights and human rights, leading NCCL/Liberty to a campaigning theme of creating a culture of rights.[95] In the limelight of this culture by 2021 sat the British humanist movement, led by Humanists UK and Humanist Society Scotland, each with a booming adherence, positioning themselves as advisors to governments required to have a new regard for ethics, and constituting a moral source spring and coordinator of the third sector as a whole.

13 CONCLUSION

Nurtured in the 1880s and 1890s in fellowship groups mixing intense intellectualism with the singing of secular hymns, modern humanism in Britain started as an embryonic ethicism within a larger secularist and rationalist cause. It spent the twentieth century as a small and sometimes fragile movement, but, as its quasi-religious elements eroded, its moral influence rose through vigorous campaigning by scientists, writers and activists in national and international affairs. They achieved legendary successes in the 1940s, 1950s and 1960s, including in a 'liberal hour' of progressivist change driven by a generation of student humanists. But this was followed by a quarter of a century of declining humanist fortunes and existential threats. Only after a determined and sometimes painful strategic change in the 1990s, a regalvanised leadership set about gaining a grip on the zeitgeist of the young so that by the 2000s and 2010s, with the religiosity of the British people decaying with startling speed, it came to the threshold of being a mass movement.

This book has shown how a nonreligious movement once defined by secularism developed into a positive cause, promoting rationalistic explanation and critical thinking, freethought and free speech. However, the preceding pages have demonstrated the rising importance of an evolving ethical cause. The humanist movement's early moral audacity in Victorian Christian culture turned in the late twentieth and early twenty-first centuries into moral common sense in a largely secular one. Humanists could no longer be taken, as Susan Budd did in 1967, as having 'defined themselves as outside the wider society, because they reject an important part of its official [Christian] values'[1] – since humanist values have *become official* in all manner of legislation and international treaties, as well as converging with Britain's values of a progressive liberal society. We suggested at the outset of this book that there were four main elements to humanist moral campaigning: freedom of thought and expression; humanitarianism; the individual's autonomy over their own body; and the internationalism and human quality of 'one-world' government. Within each of these we have seen a myriad of distinct campaigns. Campaigns over censorship, sex education and the provision of platforms – even on occasion to those with repugnant policies – marked out longstanding rationalist and humanist terrain. Humanitarianism included campaigning for prison reform, better child protection and improved mental-health provisions, and the advance of counselling, and against inane and cruel penal laws on suicide, attempted suicide and assisted suicide, as well as against capital punishment and war (especially where it might cause mass civilian mortality). Advancing autonomy covered feminism and all its aims, racial equality at home and abroad, equality for homosexuality and other sexualities, birth control and freedom for religions within a secularist framework, removing theological restrictions over medicine and science, the promulgation of human rights and the right to die at a time of one's choosing. And as well as promotion of human rights, the humanist contribution to internationalism encompassed its significant part in anti-imperialism, the League of Nations (especially its 'one-world' cultural element), the United Nations and UNESCO, and the design of the one-world systems in farming and world health. Though the precise objectives and campaigns have constantly evolved from the 1890s to the 2020s, we have seen how the principles of rationalism, humanitarianism, autonomy and internationalism remained largely immutable in the humanist cause.

Since the 1890s, the place of religion and attitudes to it have endured competing currents within humanism. Justice Dillon in the High Court in 1980 criticised the word 'religious' as misleading in the South Place Ethical Society's aim of developing 'a rational religious sentiment'.[2] But it took until 2012 for the renamed Conway Hall Ethical Society to remove it. A sizeable proportion of the British humanist movement has thought that humanism has been mainly about contesting religions, theology and religious privilege, whilst others prioritised moral change. Robbi Robson, former chair and vice-chair of BHA, told us that she saw some merit in this: 'British humanists are – how can I put this? – much more positive and about values, and the National Secular Society is much more strident, and I think it's useful to have that good cop/bad cop thing going on.'[3] The movement has never been wholly united on religion, with most humanists to this day still responding to the thrill of an anti-theology argument won and a religious privilege undone. In this regard, Edward Royle may have been too narrow in his purview of secularism as only ever part of popular Victorian radicalism, rather than as emerging, refreshed and realigned, in a middle-class ethicism that then transitioned into humanism.[4] Over the piece, there was always a degree of elision of the terms 'secularist', 'rationalist', 'ethicist' and 'humanist', reflecting the joint purpose and overlapping constituencies of the organisations evolving into Humanists UK, the Rationalist Association, the Conway Hall Ethical Society and the National Secular Society. But in hindsight, the direction of travel was very marked. In 1896, secularists stood out, with tens of thousands of adhering supporters, with rationalists coming into vogue in the early twentieth century, whilst a small but vibrant ethical movement persevered through good times and bad to emerge as the leading identity of organised nonreligionism in the UK. Rationalism slipped in resonance with the British public, with the Rationalist Association diminishing in the late twentieth century, whilst the NSS maintained a high press profile but with a seeming slide in its core appeal. Though Conway Hall sustained its ethical society on an even keel, it was Humanists UK, rising by 2021 to around 100,000 members and supporters, that presented a more equable yet dynamic position. It found a place with the young only after 2000, increasingly leading with new issues – including LGBTQ+ equality and nonbelief in non-white societies in Africa and Asia. British humanism became in the twenty-first century a major attraction for scientists and journalists from BAME backgrounds who came to prominence in Humanists UK, and the work both overseas and with the Faith to Faithless group acknowledged the growing attraction of nonreligion among those from a non-Judeo-Christian heritage.

The volatility of humanism's fortunes is noteworthy. It was contraction rather than smallness that drained confidence, with young smart minds, after an exuberant 1960s, leaving the cause in the doldrums of the 1970s and 1980s. The membership and supporter success of the twenty-first century owes much to the adroitness and flexibility in management and policy, notably in BHA/Humanists UK but also at South Place/Conway Hall, which, through the social media of the former and the revived arts and crafts of the latter, have generated vibrant humanist cultures. More broadly, the rhetoric of humanism, once tarred by religionists as outlandish, dangerous and even treacherous, became – almost unseen – normalised and veined through the law and institutions of the land. The fact that Humanists UK in 2021 could lead over 200 British charities, including religious ones, in protection of the Human Rights Act was indicative of the common humanistic language of civic society. Even if its name is not always used, humanism seems unarguably a widely accepted moral compass of British society.

The fortunes of humanism have been linked to wider affairs – from world wars to changing politics (notably of the Cold War). But a most important context has been declining religiosity, oftentimes referred to as secularisation. Most notably since the 1950s, young people and the growing numbers of university students have played a major, if intermittent, part in the humanist constituency in Britain. This does not mean that secularisation has automatically brought humanist growth, but there have been links. With the highest religious adherence and conservative moral law in the UK, Northern Ireland Humanists was formed in 2016 as a branch of Humanists UK which instituted human-rights cases with rapid success in legalising same-sex marriage, access to abortion and winning political support to end the local blasphemy law. But there is considerable evidence of a very rapid turning of the religious tide in Northern Ireland. The proportion of adults with no religion has risen from 11 per cent in 2000 to 13 per cent in 2010, and then very steeply to 27 per cent in 2020.[5] This seems to point to dramatic change, likely because of many young people losing religion. But elsewhere in the UK, no religionism has been very much more advanced for decades, reaching 58 per cent in Scotland in 2017, 47.3 per cent in Wales in 2020 and 37.3 per cent in England in 2017–18.[6] The scale and rate of change make a ripening environment for the humanist movement. Furthermore, the nature of the demographic change has altered. Until late in the twentieth century, the growth in numbers of people without religion was driven by individuals *losing* religion, sometimes very painfully, and we could see this also among the leading lights of the humanist movement we examined in Chapter 2. After 2000, by contrast, the young people of Britain without religion, and young humanists also, are coming mainly from those who are second- or third-generation atheists. They are not merely without religion but, increasingly, they are also the *never-churched* and without active participation in religion. One implication of this is that they are characterised broadly as being untraumatised by religion.

This growing demographic of the never-churched could be the real game-changer for the future of the humanist movement and the moral alignment of the nation. British humanism matured into its current moral compass in tandem with a widespread secularisation of culture, the law and the individual, perhaps, as Bill Cooke suggested, aided by RPA's mass publication sales of the first half of the twentieth century undermining supernaturalism (rather than the transition being, as Church of England historian Owen Chadwick had it, a social change and not a thought change).[7] Neither proof nor falsification is easy when contemplating such grand causations. Led by bright Victorian and Edwardian minds and moral instincts about what was to be cherished as the good, humanists were able, in their very small numbers, to achieve extraordinary success during the first three-quarters of the twentieth century. Now, in the 2020s, we may be in the midst of the 'humanist turn' by which a secular rationalism is being normalised. One Jewish perception of secularisation has described the process as 'Exodus to Humanism', with a clever double meaning, but asserting secular morality, not secularism, as the replacement for 'the obsolete religion of Judaism'.[8] It was noted at the outset of this book how scholarship has identified NGOs as the locations for development of new language and political meanings, from where they have entered government, societal ethics and daily discourse. H. G. Wells and humanist supporters did much to push 'human rights' as one powerful discourse change in our culture, and whilst his utopian visions, as those also of F. J. Gould, Bertrand Russell and Julian Huxley, have been updated for sure, the kernel of what they aspired to inaugurate now underscore humanism's moral impulse rather more than secularism's anti-religionist legacy. True, judging contemporary nonreligionism by reference to the New Atheists, who slated religion in the 2000s, an observer might be forgiven for thinking the reverse – that humanism retains a narrowness of anti-religious rhetoric. But humanism is in a different place in the 2020s. For one thing, the

2010s have revealed a staggering growth in the numbers coming to be counted as humanists. The possibility of humanism as a mass movement, dreamed of in the mid-1960s, could be happening right now. And if the trends of the last 125 years are sustained, fewer of those coming to humanism are doing so after religious trauma. The numerous never-churched may be changing the character of being a humanist, so that it will be likely through inclusive good works, not divisive bad words, that the movement may enhance its claim to be at the ethical vanguard of Britain.

NOTES

Chapter 1

1 Among many other sources, see Nicolas Walter, *Humanism: What's in the Word* (London, RPA, 1997); *OED*; HET IHEU 484, letter from Harry Stopes-Roe to Brian Gates, director of the Moral Education Research and Information Centre, St Martin's College Lancaster, 12 March 1982.

2 Stephen Greenblatt, *The Swerve: How the Renaissance Began* (London, Vintage, 2012).

3 Horace J. Bridges (ed.), *The Ethical Movement: Its Principles and Aims* (London, UES, 1911); Gustav Spiller, *The Ethical Movement in Great Britain: A Documentary History* (London, Farleigh Press, 1934); A. Gowans Whyte, *The Story of the R.P.A.: 1899–1949* (London, Watts and Co., 1949); David Tribe, *100 Years of Freethought* (London Elek, 1967); Jim Herrick, *Vision and Realism: A Hundred Years of The Freethinker* (London, Foote, 1982); Bill Cooke, *The Blasphemy Depot: A Hundred Years of the Rationalist Press Association* (London, RPA, 2003); Jim Herrick, *Aspiring to the Truth: Two Hundred Years of the South Place Ethical Society* (London, CHES, 2016).

4 Ian MacKillop, *The British Ethical Societies* (Cambridge, CUP, 1986).

5 Edward Royle, *Victorian Infidels: The Origins of the British Secularist Movement 1791–1866* (Manchester, Manchester University Press, 1974); idem, *Radicals, Secularists and Republicans: Popular Freethought in Britain, 1866–1915* (Manchester, Manchester University Press, 1980); Susan Budd, *Varieties of Unbelief: Atheists and Agnostics in English Society 1850–1960* (London, Heinemann, 1977); David Nash, *Blasphemy in Modern Britain: 1789 to the Present* (London, Routledge, 1999); idem, *Blasphemy in the Christian World: A History* (Oxford, OUP, 2007); Elizabeth A. Lutgendorff, 'Slaughtering sacred cows: rebutting the narrative of decline in the British secular movement from 1890s to 1930s', PhD thesis, Oxford Brookes University, 2018.

6 Callum G. Brown, *Becoming Atheist: Humanism and the Secular West* (London, Bloomsbury, 2017); idem, *The Battle for Christian Britain: Sex, Humanism and Secularisation 1945–1980* (Cambridge, CUP, 2019).

7 Colin Campbell, *Toward a Sociology of Irreligion* (n.pl., Alcuin Academics, 1971, 2013); Matthew Engelke, 'Christianity and the anthropology of secular humanism', *Current Anthropology* v.55 (10) (2014), 292–301; Gareth Longden, 'A profile of the members of the British humanist association', *Science, Religion and Culture* v.2 (3) (2015), 91–2.

8   Laura Schwartz, *Infidel Feminism: Secularism, Religion and Women's Emancipation, England 1830-1914* (Manchester, MUP, 2013); Jessica Beck, 'The women musicians of south place ethical society 1887-1927', PhD thesis, Manchester Metropolitan University, 2018, https://heritage.humanists.uk.

9   Michael Hone, *The Bloomsbury Set: Homosexual Renaissance* (np, CreateSpace, 2017); Tanya Cheadle, *Sexual Progressives: Rethinking Intimacy in Late Victorian Scotland, 1880-1914* (Manchester, MUP, 2020).

10   Hugh McLeod, *Religion and the People of Western Europe, 1789-1989* (Oxford, OUP, 1997), 118-54.

11   David Nash, *Secularism, Art and Freedom* (London, Pinter Press, 1992).

12   Edward Royle, 'Secularists and rationalists, 1800-1940', in Sheridan Gilley and WJ Sheils (eds.), *A History of Religion in Britain* (Oxford, Blackwell, 1994), 406-22 at 416, 419, 421.

13   A term she uses three times in two pages; Budd, *Varieties*, 35-6, 150-80 esp. at 165-77.

14   Lutgendorff, 'Slaughtering sacred cows'.

15   Budd, *Varieties*, 2.

16   Susan Budd, 'The humanist societies: the consequences of a diffuse belief system', in B. R. Wilson (ed.), *Patterns of Sectarianism: Organisation and Ideology in Social and Religious Movements* (London, Heinemann, 1967), 377-405 at 380.

17   Budd, *Varieties*, 18.

18   Budd, 'The humanist societies', 382, 393.

19   Shirley Mullen, *Organised Freethought: The Religion of Unbelief in Victorian England* (New York, Garland, 1987).

20   Edward Royle, 'Freethought: the religion of irreligion', in D. G. Paz (ed.), *19th Century English Religious Traditions: Retrospect and Prospect* (London, Greenwood Press, 1995), 170-96 at 173, 196; idem, *Victorian Infidels*, 231; idem, 'Secularists and rationalists', 406-22 at 407, 416, 418, 421-2.

21   Engelke, 'Christianity and the anthropology'.

22   Matthew Engelke, 'The coffin question: death and materiality in humanist funerals', *Material Religion* v.11 (2015), 26-49.

23   Matthew Engelke, '"Good without god": happiness and pleasure among the humanists', *HAU: Journal of Ethnographic Theory* v.5 (2015), 69-91.

24   Charles Taylor, *A Secular Age* (Cambridge, MA, Belknap Press, 2007), 3.

25   Callum Brown, 'The necessity of atheism: making sense of secularisation', *Journal of Religious History* v.41 (2017), 439-56. For a further critique of Taylor, see Jon Butler, 'Disquieted history in *A Secular Age*', in Michael Warner et al. (eds), *Varieties of Secularism in a Secular Age* (Cambridge, MA, Harvard University Press, 2010), 193-216.

26   Indeed, there is an argument in archaeology that religion was *born* in death rituals in the tenth millennium BCE site at Gobekli Tepe in Turkey, which reveal 'the earliest large, settled communities, their extensive networking, and their communal understanding of their world, perhaps even the first organized religions and their symbolic representations of the cosmos'. Klaus Schmidt,

'Gobekli Tepe – the stone age sanctuaries: new results of ongoing excavations with a special focus on sculptures and high reliefs', *Documenta Praehistorica* v.37 (2010), 239–56 at 254.

27 Jeremy Carrette and Richard King, *Selling Spirituality: The Silent Takeover of Religion* (London, Taylor and Francis, 2004).

28 For these ideas, see Chris Moores, *Civil Liberties and Human Rights in Twentieth-century Britain* (Cambridge, CUP, 2017), 4–8.

29 Jon Lawrence, *Me, Me, Me: The Search for Community in Post-war England* (Oxford, OUP, 2019).

30 Dropping the preposition 'of' to become Humanist Society Scotland in 2016.

31 Historic England, *Listed Building Entry for Conway Hall* (1392343), accessed 7 April 2021.

32 Though Kevin Gately was killed in disorder outside Conway Hall in June 1974, discussed at page ???.

33 CHLA, SPES1/2/17, General Committee minutes 2 February 1965.

34 Now sadly to move online.

35 Entitled 'Donegan on stage: Lonnie Donegan at Conway hall' (Castle Music CMRCD1407).

36 *The Literary Guide* v.62 (January 1947), 11.

Chapter 2

1 Gustav Spiller, *The Ethical Movement in Great Britain* (London, Farleigh Press, 1934), 115.

2 Longden suggested the category of supporters was inflated by journalists and researchers, though this is likely a small effect. Gareth Longden, 'A profile of the members of humanists UK: an empirical study', PhD thesis University of Wales, Wrexham Glyndwr University, 2019, 12.

3 Colin Campbell, *Toward a Sociology of Irreligion* (n.pl., Alcuin Academics, 1971, 2013), esp. 17–45.

4 Edward Royle, *Victorian Infidels: The Origins of the British Secularist Movement 1791–1866* (Manchester, Manchester University Press, 1974), esp. 39–53.

5 Royle, *Victorian Infidels*, 304–5. Campbell, *Toward*, 52, cites Royle with different estimates in his thesis: 2 per cent professions, around 30 per cent newsagents, innkeepers, managers of temperance hotels and shopkeepers, 25 per cent skilled artisans (such as tailors, joiners, plumbers, hairdressers), and around 35 per cent semi-skilled and unskilled (including warehousemen weavers and labourers). Campbell viewed these data as supporting the notion that the secularist movement in the mid-nineteenth century was pan-class.

6 Edward Royle, *Radicals, Secularists and Republicans: Popular Freethought in Britain 1866–1915* (Manchester, Manchester University Press, 1980), esp. 179, 191, 299.

7 Quoted in Royle, *Radicals*, 126.

8   Ibid., 128.

9   David Nash, *Secularism, Art and Freedom* (London, Pinter, 1992), 81.

10 Laura Schwartz, *Infidel Feminism: Secularism, Religion and Women's Emancipation, England 1830–1914* (Manchester, MUP, 2013).

11 Data from or calculated from Colin B. Campbell, 'Membership composition of the British humanist association', *The Sociological Review* v.13 (3) (1965), 327–37.

12 The following data come from or are calculated from: JLA, MS BHA Questionnaire to members June 1985 (survey undertaken by Keith F. Grimson); DPA, 2001 data; BA, BHA 1/2/17, Michael Horwood, 'New direction: a strategy for the BHA' (1987) cited in Gareth Longden, 'A profile of the members of the British humanist association', *Science, Religion and Culture* v.2 (3) (2015), 87; Humanists UK Diversity Analysis for England and Wales 2020, courtesy of Andrew Copson.

13 Longden, 'A profile', 91–2; Matthew Engelke, 'Christianity and the anthropology of secular humanism', *Current Anthropology* v.55 (10) (2014), 292–301; Callum G. Brown, *Becoming Atheist: Humanism and the Secular West* (London, Bloomsbury, 2017), 169–71. There is further discussion in Campbell, 'Membership'.

14 Lawrence Marks, 'Humanists worried by falling numbers', *The Observer*, 25 July 1971, 3.

15 https://defencehumanists.org.uk/who-are-humanists/.

16 https://sundayassembly.online/

17 In *The Freethinker*, cited in Jim Herrick, *Vision and Realism: A Hundred Years of the Freethinker* (London, Foote, 1982), 39.

18 She was later a suffrage pioneer with Emmeline Pankhurst.

19 F. J. Gould, *The Life-Story of a Humanist* (London, Watts, 1923), 5, 8, 21–2, 35, 38–9.

20 Foucault 1977, in Martin A. Danahay, *Community of One: Masculine Autobiography and Autonomy in Nineteenth-century Britain* (New York, SUNY Press, 1993), 147–8.

21 Russell quoted in Barry Feinberg and Ronald Kasrils (eds), *Dear Bertrand Russell: A Selection of His Correspondence with the General Public 1950–1968* (London, George Allen and Unwin, 1969), 39.

22 Bertrand Russell, *Freethought and Official Propaganda* (London, Watts, 1922), 14–15; Bertrand Russell, *The Autobiography of Bertrand Russell One Volume Edition* (London, Unwin, 1975), 15–16, 23, 30–1, 34–6.

23 E. M. Forster, *What I Believe and Other Essays* (London, G.W. Foote, 1999), 32–3.

24 Jean Smith and Arnold Toynbee (eds), *Gilbert Murray: An Unfinished Autobiography* (London, George Allen and Unwin, 1960), 83.

25 Noel Annan, *Leslie Stephen: The Godless Victorian* (New York, Random House, 1984), 2–3, 146 *et seq*.

26 Russell, *The Autobiography*, 161, 166–7, 195.

27 Ibid., 533.

28 Hanne Stinson, interviewed by Jessica Douthwaite 9 October 2018.

29 Schwartz, *Infidel Feminism*, 15–22; Madeleine Goodall, 'Forgotten founders', *New Humanist* v.136 (Spring 2021), 60–2.

30 Yvonne Stevenson, *The Hot-House Plant: An Autobiography of a Young Girl* (London, Elek/Pemberton, 1976), ix, 9–10, 17, 19, 32, 35, 38–9, 42–4, 57, 72, 79–151, 187–9.

31 *Annie Besant: An Autobiography* (New York, Dossier Press, orig.1933, 2015).

32 Barbara Wootton, *In a World I Never Made: Autobiographical Reflections* (London, George Allen & Unwin, 1967), 52–3.

33 Frances Partridge, *Memories* (London, Phoenix, orig. 1981, 1996), 12, 38–9, 76; Frances Partridge, *Hanging on: Diaries 1960–1963* (London Phoenix, 1990), 7, 30.

34 Jane Wynne Willson, interviewed by Charlie Lynch, 13 November 2020.

35 Kathleen Nott, *The Emperor's Clothes* (London, Heinemann, 1953), esp. 253–4. On the Hoyle-Sayers episode, see *The Freethinker* v.73 (11) (September 1953), 289. Callum G Brown, "'The unholy Mrs Knight" and the BBC: secular humanism and the threat to the Christian nation, c.1945–1960', *English Historical Review* v.127 (2012), 345–76.

36 Margaret Knight, *Morals Without Religion* (London, Dennis Dobson, 1955), 14.

37 Andrew Copson, Obituary of Barbara Smoker, *The Guardian* Journal section 16 May 2020, 9.

38 Barbara Smoker, *My Godforsaken Life: Memoir of a Maverick* (London, Thornwick, 2018).

39 Diane Munday, interviewed by Jessica Douthwaite, 2 October 2018.

40 Peter Tatchell, interviewed by Charlie Lynch, 14 September 2020.

41 Joseph Needham who, though a practising Anglo-Catholic, was a sceptic and a frequent speaker at Conway Hall, writing two books on his complex relations with religion – *The Skeptical Biologist* (1929) and *The Great Amphibian* (1932). He attained the rare accolade of being elected both FRS and FBA.

42 C. H. Rolph, *Living Twice: An Autobiography* (London, Quality Book Club/Victor Gollancz, 1976), 57.

43 Conrad Keating, *Smoking Kills: The Revolutionary Life of Richard Doll* (Oxford, Signal Books, 2014), 201–2.

44 Kingsley Martin, *Father Figures: A First Volume of Autobiography 1897–1931* (Harmondsworth, Penguin, orig. 1966, 1969), 109–10, 140.

45 Christopher Hitchens, *HITCH-22: A Memoir* (London, Atlantic Books, 2010), 64–5, 82 and *passim*.

46 Peter Hitchens, *Rage Against God* (London, Bloomsbury, 2010), 1, 7, 14–19, 74, 76; Peter Hitchens, *The War We Never Fought* (London, Bloomsbury, 2012), 5.

47 Alice Roberts, in communication with Callum Brown 1 December 2021.

48 Jo Brand, *Look Back in Hunger: The Autobiography* (London, Headline, 2009), 28–9, 58–9, 70–1.

49 Shappi Khorsandi, *A Beginner's Guide to Acting English* (London, Ebury Press, 2009), 257–8; Shappi Khorsandi, 'Comic timing', *New Humanist*, January/February 2007, 6.

50 Claire Rayner, *How Did I Get Here from There?* (London, Virago, 2003), 91–2.

51 *Humanity*, August/September 1999, 5.

52 *Humanity*, October/November 1999, 7.

53 Chapman Cohen, *Almost an Autobiography: The Confessions of a Freethinker* (London, Pioneer, 1940), 28, 141.

54 Graham Kingsley, interviewed by Jessica Douthwaite, 16 October 2018.

55 Andrew Copson, interviewed by Callum Brown, 6 October 2019.

Chapter 3

1 Timothy Larsen, *Crisis of Doubt: Honest Faith in Nineteenth-Century England* (Oxford, OUP, 2006), 1–17.

2 David Nash, 'Reassessing the "crisis of faith" in the Victorian age: eclecticism and the spirit of moral inquiry', *Journal of Victorian Culture* v.16 (2011), 65–82. See also Julie Melnyk, *Victorian Religion: Faith and Life in Britain* (London, Praeger Publishers, 2008), 134–54.

3 Margaret Knight (ed.), *Humanist Anthology: From Confucius to Bertrand Russell* (London, RPA, 1961), xiii; David Tribe, *100 Years of Freethought* (London, Elek Books, 1967), 46.

4 Tim Whitmarsh, *Battling the Gods: Atheism in the Ancient World* (London, Faber and Faber, 2016).

5 Michael Hunter, *The Decline of Magic: Britain in the Enlightenment* (New Haven and London, Yale University Press, 2020), 1–27, 121–43.

6 Edward Royle, *Victorian Infidels: The Origins of the British Secularist Movement, 1791–1866* (Manchester, Rowman and Littlefield, 1974), 9–30.

7 Michael Hunter, '*Pitcairneana*: an atheist text by Archibald Pitcairne', *Historical Journal* v.59 (2016), 595–621; Gordon Pentland, 'The Freethinkers' Zetetic society: an Edinburgh radical underworld in the 1820s', *Historical Research* v.91 (2018), 314–32.

8 Patricia Hollis, *The Pauper Press: A Study in Working Class Radicalism of the 1830s* (Oxford, Clarendon Press, 1970), 28, 114–15.

9 For Carlile see David Nash, *Blasphemy in Modern Britain 1789 to the Present* (Aldershot, Ashgate, 1999), 77–99.

10 See Nash, *Blasphemy in Modern Britain*, 107–93.

11 David S. Nash, '"Look in her face and lose thy dread of dying": the ideological importance of death to the secularist community in nineteenth-century Britain', *Journal of Religious History* 19 (1995), 158–80; idem, 'Negotiating the marketplace of comfort: secularists confront new paradigms of death and dying in twentieth-century Britain', *Revue Belge de Philologie et d'Histoire* v.95 (2018), 963–88.

12 See Walter Arnstein, *The Bradlaugh Case* (Oxford, Oxford University Press, 1965); and Edward Royle, *Radicals, Secularists and Republicans: Popular Freethought in Britain, 1866–1915* (Manchester, Rowman and Littlefield, 1980), 23–32.

13 On secularism's European contrast, see Jacqueline Lalouette, *La Libre Penseé en France1848–1940* (Paris, Albin Michel, 1997); Todd Weir, *Secularism and Religion in Nineteenth-Century Germany: The Rise of the Fourth Confession* (Cambridge, CUP, 2014); Todd Weir, 'The Christian front against godlessness:

anti-secularism and the demise of the Weimar Republic, 1928–1933', *Past and Present* 229 (2015), 201–38: Lisa Dittrich, *Antikerikalismus als europäisches Phänomen: Protest und Öffentlichkeit in Frankreich, Spanien und Deutschland (1850–1914)* (Göttingen, Vandenhoeck & Ruprecht, 2014); and Tracie Matysik, *Reforming the Moral Subject: Ethics and Sexuality in Central Europe, 1890–1930* (Ithica, NY, Cornell University Press, 2008).

14 F. J. Gould, *The Life-Story of a Humanist* (London, Watts, 1923), 35–62, quote at 49.

15 Callum G. Brown, *The Battle for Christian Britain: Sex, Humanism and Secularisation 1945–1980* (Cambridge, CUP, 2019), 38.

16 Jim Herrick, *Vision and Realism: A Hundred Years of The Freethinker* (London, Foote, 1982), 9–10, 27–33.

17 David Nash, *Secularism, Art and Freedom* (London, Continuum, 1992).

18 Michael Rechtenwald, *Nineteenth Century British Secularism* (London, Palgrave, 2016).

19 T. R. Wright, *The Religion of Humanity: The Impact of Comteian Positivism on Victorian Britain* (Cambridge, CUP, 1986).

20 Ernest Belfort Bax, *Reminiscences and Reflexions of a Mid and Late Victorian* (London, Allen and Unwin, 1918), 31.

21 Ian MacKillop, *The British Ethical Societies* (Cambridge, CUP, 1986), 58.

22 Gustav Spiller, *The Ethical Movement in Great Britain: A Documentary History* (London, Farleigh Press, 1934), 100–1, 114–15.

23 James Martineau, *The Relationship Between Ethics and Religion: An Address at the Opening of the Session 1881–2* (London, Williams and Norgate, 1881), 22–3.

24 Sylvan Drey, *Herbert Spencer's Theory of Religion and Morality* (London, Williams and Norgate, 1887), 16.

25 Anon, *The Message of Man: A Book of Ethical Scriptures Gathered from many Sources and Arranged* (London Swan and Sonnenschein, 1895), 37, 198.

26 Tribe, *100 Years of Freethought*, 49.

27 Quoted in Spiller, *The Ethical Movement*, 1.

28 Ibid., 2.

29 *The Ethical Society First Report*, 1886–7, reproduced in ibid, 5.

30 Ibid.

31 Ibid., 6.

32 Stanton Coit, *Ethical Culture as a Religion for the People: Two Discourses Delivered in South Place Chapel, Finsbury, Ethical Church* (London, E.W. Allen, 1887), 156.

33 *Ethical Society Annual Report*, 1888–9 in Spiller, *The Ethical Movement*, 19.

34 *Ethical Society Annual Report*, 1895/6 in ibid., 17.

35 Ibid., 15.

36 Coit, *Ethical Culture*, 163.

37 Ibid.

38 Stanton Coit, *The Spiritual Nature of Man* (London, West London Ethical Society, 1910), 15–17, 45–52.

39 Moncure D. Conway to South Place Ethical Society, 23 November 1887, reproduced in *South Place Ethical Society Annual Report*, 1887.

40 Spiller, *The Ethical Movement*, 30.

41 Stanton Coit, *An Introduction to the Study of Ethics; Adapted from the German of G Von Gizycki Professor of Philosophy in the University of Berlin* (London, Swan and Sonnenschein, 1891). For more on this, see Matysik, *Reforming the Moral Subject*, Chapters 1 and 6.

42 *South Place Ethical Society Annual Report*, 1891/2, quoted in Spiller, *The Ethical Movement*, 33.

43 Quoted in ibid., 34.

44 Spiller, *The Ethical Movement*, 101–2.

45 Ibid., 114–5.

46 His account is in Harry Snell, *Men, Movements and Myself* (London, J.M. Dent and Sons, 1936).

47 MacKillop, *The Ethical Societies*, 60–2.

48 See Martin Richard Page, *Britain's Unknown Genius: Introduction to the Life-Work of John Mackinnon Robertson* (London, SPES, 1984).

49 *The Reformer*, January 1901, 12. For more on this and Robertson's involvement, see David S. Nash, 'Taming the god of battles: secular and moral critiques of the South African war', in A. Cuthbertson, A. Gundlingh and M.-L. Suttie (eds), *Writing a Wider War: Rethinking Gender, Race and Identity in the South African War* (Athens, Ohio University Press, 2002), 266–86.

50 On ethical socialism in its late-Victorian origins, see Mark Bevir, *The Making of British Socialism* (Princeton, Princeton University Press, 2011), esp. 215–316.

51 Gustav Spiller, *Faith in Man: The Religion of the Twentieth Century* (London, Swan and Sonnenschein, 1908), v.11, 16–17, 39.

52 Ibid., 80–3, 101–4, 139.

53 Horace J. Bridges (ed.), *The Ethical Movement: Its Principles and Aims* (London, UES, 1911), 14, 29.

54 See David S. Nash, *Christian Ideals in British History: Stories of Belief in the Twentieth Century* (London, Palgrave, 2013), 101–17.

Chapter 4

1 Gustav Spiller, *The Ethical Movement in Great Britain: A Documentary History* (London, Farleigh Press, 1934), 110.

2 J. A. Hobson, *Rationalism and Humanism* (London, Watts, 1932), 11.

3 Hypatia Bradlaugh-Bonner, *The Gallows and the Lash: An Enquiry into the Necessity for Capital and Corporal Punishments* (London, William Reeves, 1897), 42, 44.

4 Philip Ironside, *The Social and Political Thought of Bertrand Russell* (Cambridge, CUP, 1996), 75–6.

5   Lancelot Hogben, *Dangerous Thoughts* (London, George Allen & Unwin, 1939), 45.

6   David C. Smith, *H.G. Wells: Desperately Mortal: A Biography* (New Haven and London, Yale University Press, 1986), 268–314, 428–49.

7   *South Place Magazine*, March 1905, 94.

8   A. Gowans Whyte, *The Story of the R.P.A.: 1899–1949* (London, Watts and Co., 1949), vii.

9   Ibid., 2.

10 Bill Cooke, *The Blasphemy Depot: A Hundred Years of the Rationalist Press Association* (London, RPA, 2003), 30–70 at 33, 66–70.

11 Gowans Whyte, *The Story*, 5.

12 Ibid., 9.

13 Ibid., 16, 19; Cooke, *The Blasphemy*, 83–4, 146–7.

14 For material on this see https://swarb.co.uk/bowman-v-secular-society-limited-hl-1917/; https://simplestudying.com/bowman-v-secular-society-ltd-1917-a-c-406/; and http://www.uniset.ca/other/cs5/1917AC406.html.

15 David S. Nash, *Secularism, Art and Freedom* (London, Continuum, 1992), 134.

16 *Daily Telegraph*, 15 February 1963; thanks to David Pollock for this reference.

17 Gowans Whyte, *The Story*, 27.

18 Ibid., 30.

19 Company registered 26 May 1899, ibid., 32.

20 Ibid., 38–9, 41.

21 Bill Cooke, *A Rebel to His Last Breath: Joseph McCabe and Rationalism* (Amherst, New York, Prometheus Books, 2001), 39.

22 See David S. Nash, *Blasphemy in Modern Britain 1789 to the Present* (Aldershot, Ashgate, 1999), 93–5.

23 Cooke, *A Rebel*, 48.

24 Ernest Haeckel, *The Riddle of the Universe at the Close of the Nineteenth Century* (London, Watts, 1900); Joseph McCabe, *The Riddle of the Universe To-day* (London, Watts, 1934).

25 J. M. Robertson, *Christianity and Mythology* (London, Watts, 1900).

26 Cooke, *The Blasphemy*, 40–50.

27 Gowans Whyte, *The Story*, 75.

28 F. J. Gould, *Will Women Help? An Appeal to Women to Assist in Liberating Modern Thought from Theological Bonds* (London, Watts & Co, 1900); see also Edward Royle, *Radicals, Secularists and Republicans: Popular Freethought in Britain, 1866–1915* (Manchester, MUP, 1980), 250.

29 Laura Schwartz, *Infidel Feminism: Secularism, Religion and Women's Emancipation, England 1830–1914* (Manchester, MUP, 2012), 171.

30 See Goodall's entries on women unbelievers and humanists on Humanist.Heritage. uk.

31 Zona Vallance, 'Women as moral beings', *International Journal of Ethics* v.12 (1902), 173–95 at 185.

32 See a good summary of Vallance in Ian D. MacKillop, *The British Ethical Societies* (Cambridge, CUP, 1986), 152–6.

33 Madeleine Goodall, 'Heroines of freethought: women of the early humanist movement', https://humanism.org.uk. See also their entries at https://Humanist .heritage.uk.

34 Royle reports incorrectly from the *Daily News* census that women outnumbered men at South Place 'by almost two to one'. Edward Royle, 'Secularists and rationalists, 1800–1940', in Sheridan Gilley and W. J. Sheils (eds), *A History of Religion in Britain* (Oxford, Blackwell, 1994), 406–22 at 420.

35 *Daily News* census figures calculated from data in Richard Mudie-Smith (ed.), *The Religious Life of London* (London, Hodder & Stoughton, 1904), 48, 99, 111, 126, 166, 174, 236, 255; subscriber and recruitment data calculated from *The South Place Magazine*, April 1905–March 1906.

36 Hugh McLeod, *Religion and Society in England 1850–1914* (Basingstoke, Macmillan, 1996), 156–68.

37 We are grateful to Madeleine Goodall for this observation.

38 Jessica Beck, 'The women musicians of south place ethical society 1887–1927', PhD thesis, Manchester Metropolitan University, 2018, 71–3.

39 Thanks to Madeleine Goodall for this information.

40 *The Times*, 3 December 1908, 10; Elizabeth Crawford, *The Women's Suffrage Movement: A Reference Guide* (London, Routledge, 2003), online np.

41 Trevor Beeson, *The Church's Other Half: Women's Ministry* (London, SCM Press, 2011), 132.

42 *Church Times*, 12 April 1913.

43 Beck, 'The women musicians', 69.

44 Ibid., 89; Spiller, *The Ethical Movement*, 79–82.

45 Beck, 'The women musicians', 88.

46 Ibid., 19, 48–61.

47 Ibid., 19.

48 Figures calculated from the display board in the entrance lobby of Conway Hall.

49 Spiller, *The Ethical Movement*, 169, https://heritage.humanists.uk/womens-group-of -the-ethical-movement/. Thanks to Madeleine Goodall.

50 Susannah Wright, *Morality and Citizenship in English Schools: Secular Approaches 1897–1944* (London, Palgrave Macmillan, 2017), 6–7, 10.

51 For more on Gould see David S. Nash, 'F. J. Gould and the Leicester secular society: a positivist commonwealth in Edwardian politics', *Midland History* v.16 (1) (1991), 126–40. See also F. J. Gould, *The Life Story of a Humanist* (London, Watts and Company, 1923).

52 See Wright, *Morality and Citizenship*, 56, 61 (quotation), 62–4, 70–1.

53 This paragraph draws on Wright, *Morality and Citizenship*, 83–114.

54 See Gustav Spiller, *A Generation of Religious Progress* (London, Watts, 1916), 7–8.

55 Ibid., 148.

56 *South Place Magazine*, March 1905, 80.

57 Brown found this particularly in Canada when recruiting humanists for interview during 2009–17; Callum G. Brown, *Becoming Atheist: Humanism and the Secular West* (London, Bloomsbury, 2017), 8, 97–8, 106–7.

58 *The Socialist Sunday School Hymnbook* (1926), and another edition from 1917 (Jennie Lee Archive, Open University Digital Archive), published by the National Council of British Socialist Sunday School Unions.

59 Though he regarded himself as eventually triumphing over the emotion of pain; quoted in Ironside, *The Social and Political Thought*, 39–40.

60 H. G. Wells, *The Open Conspiracy: Blue Prints for a World Revolution* (London, Gollancz, 1928), 36.

61 H. G. Wells, *First and Last Things: A Confession of Faith and Rule of Life* (London, Archibald Constable & Co., 1908), 47–8, 68–9, 90, 100, 107.

62 Joseph McCabe, *Religion of the Twentieth Century* (London, Watts, 1899); Adam Gowans Whyte, *The Religion of the Open Mind* (London, Watts, orig. 1915, 1935), esp. 30.

63 J. M. Robertson, *Spoken Essays* (London, Watts, 1925), 193, quoted in Elizabeth A. Lutgendorff, 'Slaughtering sacred cows: rebutting the narrative of decline in the British secular movement from 1890s to 1930s', PhD thesis, Oxford Brookes University, 2018, 39.

64 Cooke, *A Rebel*, 35.

65 Ibid., 39.

66 Thanks to Madeleine Goodall for this description.

67 MacKillop, *The British Ethical Societies*, 58.

68 Spiller, *The Ethical Movement*, 101.

69 David Tribe, *100 Years of Freethought* (London, Elek Books, 1967), 37–8.

70 Blackham writing in H. J. Blackham (ed.), *Stanton Coit 1857–1944: Selections from His Writings* (London, privately published by the Favil Press, nd c.1945), 3–4.

71 Ibid., 14–16.

72 Ibid., 22.

73 Ibid., 24–5, 46–9.

Chapter 5

1 William Winwood Reade, *The Martyrdom of Man* (London, Watts & Co, orig. 1872, 1943), 71, 130, 138.

2 J. M. Robertson in Reade, *Martyrdom*, xv.

3 William Winwood Read, *The Outcast* (London, Watts, 1933), 60.

4 Callum G. Brown, *Becoming Atheist: Humanism and the Secular West* (London, Bloomsbury, 2017), 126.

5 Wikipedia entries on James Horrabin, the artist; Ray Lankester; Harry H. Johnston; and Ernest Barker. Julia Stapleton, 'Barker, Sir Ernest', *ODNB* (2004). Lankester was one of eight people at Karl Marx's funeral.

6 For an account of this stramash, see Michael Foot, *The History of Mr Wells* (London, Doubleday, 1995), 208–10.

7 H. G. Wells, *The Outline of History: Being a Plain History of Life and Human Kind vol. I* (London, George Newnes, nd but 1920), 1–3.

8 Philip Ironside, *The Social and Political Thought of Bertrand Russell* (Cambridge, CUP, 1996), 168.

9 Henry Hamilton, *History of the Homeland: The Story of the British Background* (London, George Allen and Unwin, 1947), 13–14.

10 One using it was French philosopher Theodore Ruyssen; Glenda Sluga, *Internationalism in the Age of Nationalism* (Philadelphia, Penn Press, 2013), 17.

11 BA, BHA/1/14/ Papers of Individual Members and Humanists, Stanton Coit, minutes; David Marquand, *Ramsay MacDonald* (London, Jonathan Cape, 1977), 24; David Marquand, 'Macdonald, (James) Ramsay 1866–1937', *ODNB* (2015); Godfrey Elton, *The Life of James Ramsay MacDonald* (London, Collins, 1939), 94.

12 The acts cited in this bill of 1889 for repeal were I Ed. VI, c. 1; I Eliz., c.2; 9 and 10 Will. III, c35; Geo. III, c49; 5 Geo. IV, c. 47.

13 Hypatia Bradlaugh Bonner, *Penalties Upon Opinion: Or Some Records of the Laws of Heresy and Blasphemy* (London, Watts & Co., 1934), 113–14.

14 Ibid., 118. The 'silly comment' was: 'If I know a man who believed in Christianity, I would kill him.'

15 TNA, HO 144 871/160552/4 Mr Alf Carrick to home secretary 9 January 1908.

16 For details of these cases see David S. Nash, *Blasphemy in Modern Britain 1789 to the Present* (Aldershot, Ashgate, 1999), 167–93.

17 Copy in TNA, HO 45 10665/216120/12.

18 TNA, HO 45 10665/216120/21 J.M. Robertson to Reginald Mckenna 5 January 1912.

19 TNA, HO 45 10665/216120/86 Memorandum from Sir John Simon to Reginald Mckenna February 1914.

20 TNA, HO 45 24619/217549/9.

21 Nash, *Blasphemy in Modern Britain*, 189–90.

22 TNA, HO 45 24619/217549/21, *The Blasphemy Laws Verbatim Report of the Deputation to the Home Secretary on April 16, 1924* (London, Johnson's Court).

23 TNA, HO 45 24619/217549/32, *The Blasphemy Laws Verbatim Report of the Deputation to the Home Secretary, J. R. Clynes on Thursday November 7th, 1929 Issued by the Society for the Abolition of the Blasphemy Laws* (London, Johnson's Court), 12.

24 Nash, *Blasphemy in Modern Britain*, 209–10.

25 House of Lords, Bowman and Others, Appellants; Secular Society, Limited, Respondents [1917] A.C. 406; Harry Small, 'This is not a Christian country', *Lawyers' Secular Society Blog Online*, 21 April 2014.

26 Several accounts of the case have appeared, including Lutgendorff, 'Slaughtering sacred cows', 12–21; and Chapman Cohen, *A Fight for Right: The Decision of the House of Lords in Re Bowman and Others v. The Secular Society, Limited* (London: Pioneer Press, 1917).

27 Ironside, *The Social and Political Thought*, 61, 66.

28 This paragraph draws heavily upon John Scott, 'Leonard Hobhouse as a social theorist', *Journal of Classical Sociology* v.16 (2016), 349–68; and Morris Ginsberg, 'A humanist view of progress', in Julian Huxley (ed.), *The Humanist Frame* (New York, Harper & Brothers, 1961), 113–28.

29 *The South Place Magazine*, no. 1, April 1895, 14–15. His lecture appeared in the May 1895 issue, 20–2.

30 Also known as the International Union of Ethical Societies.

31 Gustav Spiller, *The Ethical Movement in Great Britain: A Documentary History* (London, Farleigh Press, 1934), 186–7; Howard B. Radest, *Toward Common Ground: The Story of the Ethical Societies in the United States* (New York, Bloomsbury, 1969), 274.

32 Gregory Claeys, *Imperial Sceptics: British Critics of Empire, 1850–1920* (Cambridge, CUP, 2010), 277.

33 Quoted in ibid., 235.

34 Dickinson was a pacifist and would later become close to fellow-humanist E. M. Forster; Wikipedia entry 3 February 2021; English Heritage blue plaques, Dickson, G. W., https://www.english-heritage.org.uk/visit/blue-plaques/goldsworthy-lowes-dickinson/, accessed 3 February 2021.

35 All quotations in this paragraph are from Claeys, *Imperial Sceptics*, 43, 235–70. Sluga, *Internationalism*, 26–7, 30.

36 David Feldman, 'Jeremy Corbyn, "imperialism", and labour's antisemitism problem', *History Workshop Online*, June 2019, https://www.historyworkshop.org.uk/imperialism-and-labours-antisemitism-problem/.

37 For a review of Hobson's wider contribution to social and economic theory, see Michael Freeden (ed.), *Reappraising J.A. Hobson: Humanism and Welfare* (London, Routledge, 1990).

38 Edward Royle, 'Bonner, Hypatia Bradlaugh (1858–1935)', *ODNB* (2006).

39 J. A. Hobson, *Rationalism and Humanism* (London, Watts, 1932), 12.

40 A useful account of evolving rights prior to 1990 is in Marie-France Major, 'Conscientious objection and international law: a human right', *Case Western Reserve Journal of International Law* v.24 (1992), 349–78.

41 An excellent review of the paradigm influences shaping the Congress is in Susan D. Pennybacker, 'The Universal Races Congress, London political culture, and imperial dissent, 1900–1939', *Radical History Review* v.92 (2005), 103–17.

42 Sir Charles Bruce (former governor of Windward Islands, Mauritius, British Guiana, and colonial secretary of New Zealand), in *Record of the Proceedings of the First Universal Races Congress* (London, PS King and Son, 1911), 58.

43 *Record of the Proceedings*, 62.

44 Ibid., 2–5, 8.

45 Michael D. Biddiss, 'The Universal Races Congress of 1911', *Races* v.13 (1971), 37–46.

46 Ian Christopher Fletcher, 'Introduction: new historical perspectives on the First Universal Races Congress of 1911', *Radical History Review* v.92 (2005), 99–102; R. J. Holton, 'Cosmopolitanism or cosmopolitanisms? The Universal Races Congress of 1911', *Global Networks* v.2 (2002), 153–70.

47 Robert Gregg and Madhavi Kale, '*The Negro* and the *Dark Princess*: two legacies of the Universal Races Congress', *Radical History Review* v.92 (2005), 133–52 at 134.

48 Mansour Bonakdarian, 'Negotiating universal values and cultural and national parameters at the First Universal Races Congress', *Radical History Review* v.92 (2005), 118–32.

49 Morel was strongly influenced on imperial and African policy by ethnographer and African explorer Mary Kingsley (1862–1900). E. D. Morel, Wikipedia entry, accessed 1 February 2021. Nathan G. Alexander, 'E.D. Morel (1873–1924), the Congo Reform Association, and the history of human rights', *Britain and the World* v.9 (2016), 213–35.

50 Marquand, 'Macdonald, (James) Ramsay 1866–1937'.

51 Ramsay MacDonald, *Labour Leader* cited on https://menwhosaidno.org/PPU/people/N_brockway_fenner.html.

52 Churchill, quoted in Jim Tomlinson, 'Winston Churchill versus E.D. Morel, Dundee, 1922 and the split in the Liberal party', unpublished paper.

53 Russell voluntarily turned up at the War Office in September 1916 to be questioned by Brigadier-General George Cockerill, the head of a 'sub-directorate for Special Intelligence' that included what became MI5, who had transcripts of his pacifist speeches to Welsh miners and ordered him to desist. *The Autobiography of Bertrand Russell* (London, Unwin Books, 1975), 300–1; Nicholas Hiley, 'Counter-espionage and security in Great Britain during the First World War', *English Historical Review* v.101 (1986), 635–70 at 643; Ironside, *The Social and Political Thought*, 87, 127; Romney Wheeler, 'A conversation with Bertrand Russell', (1952), YouTube.

54 *Moral Instruction League Quarterly* v.9 (1907), 6, quoted in Susannah Wright, '"There is something universal in our movement which appeals not only to one country, but to all": International Communication and Moral Education 1892–1914', *Journal of the History of Education Society* v.37 (2008), 807–24 at 812.

Chapter 6

1 Clive D. Field, 'Puzzled people revisited: religious believing and belonging in wartime Britain, 1939–45', *Twentieth Century British History* v.19 (2008), 446–79 at 476.

2 Mass-Observation [Bob Willcock?], *Puzzled People: A Study in Popular Attitudes to Religion, Ethics, Progress and Politics in a London Borough* (London, Victor Gollancz, 1947), 7.

3 *The Monthly Record*, August 1936, 7–8.

4 Jim Herrick, *Vision and Realism: A Hundred Years of The Freethinker* (London, Foote, 1982), 98–9.

5 *The Freethinker* v.78 (26 September 1958), 308.

6 *The Humanist* v.72 (April 1957), 4.

7 https://humanists.international/policy/amsterdam-declaration-1952/.

8 H. G. Wells, G. P. Wells, and Julian Huxley, *The Science of Life*, 4 vols. (London, Waverley, 1929–31); Julian Huxley, *Religion Without Revelation* (London, Watts, 1927, 1945, 1957).

9 W. R. Matthews, book review, *Theology* v.17 (1928), 319.

10 Jessica C. Beck, 'The women musicians of south place ethical society, 1887–1927', PhD thesis, Manchester Metropolitan University, 2018, 89–90, 277–85.

11 [E. Josephine Troup (ed.)], *Hymns of Modern Thought* (London, Houghton & Co, 1900), which can be viewed online at www.leicestersecularsociety.org.uk/PHP _redirected/hymns.php. Troup left the copyright of the book to Hampstead Ethical Society.

12 CHLA, SPES/5/2/3 General Committee Minutes, 3 February and 3 November 1937.

13 CHLA, SPES/5/2/3 General Committee Minutes, [nd] January 1938.

14 *Ethical Record* v.66 (July 1961), 2–4, 17; CHLA, SPES/1/1/4 Annual General Meeting Minutes 1961, 3.

15 CHLA, SPES/1/2/17 General Committee minutes 1 March 1967.

16 *Ethical Record* v.66 (June 1961, October 1961), 7–8.

17 CH, SPES/5/2/3 (10) Correspondence of Gen Secy, letter from anon to Peter Cadogan, 10 May 1971; letter from Cadogan to anon 5 April 1971.

18 *Humanist News*, January 1976, 4. See also Sidney Hook, 'Is secular humanism a religion?' *Humanist* (1976).

19 *The Humanist* v.76 (January 1961), 3.

20 A. Gowans Whyte, *The Story of the R.P.A. 1899–1949* (London, Watts, 1949), 75–7.

21 Popular guidebooks included Hector Hawton, *The Humanist Revolution* (London, Pemberton, 1963); H. J. Blackham, *Humanism* (Harmondsworth, Penguin, 1967); Barbara Smoker, *Humanism* (London, Ward Lock Educational, 1973).

22 Julian Huxley (ed.), *The Humanist Frame* (London, George Allen & Unwin, 1961); A. J. Ayer (ed.), *The Humanist Outlook* (London, Pemberton, 1968).

23 One such is H. J. Blackham, 'The human programme', in Huxley (ed.), *Humanist Frame*, 129–43.

24 Blackham, *Humanism*, vii.

25 BA, Munday/1/2, notes for lecture on 'Humanism and social reform', card 3, *c.* 1967.

26 Margaret Knight, *Morals Without Religion* (London, Dennis Dobson, 1955), 29.

27 Julian Huxley, 'The humanist frame', in idem (ed.), *The Humanist Frame*, 13–48 at 13.

28 R. J. Mostyn, 'The religion of Julian Huxley', *The Humanist* v.72 (July 1957), 14–15; May 1957, 28; June 1957, 28.

29 Franziskus Card. Konig, 'Dialogue with non-believers', *L'Osservatore Romano Weekly Edition in English*, 10 October 1968, 6, https://web.archive.org/web/20000614101645/ http://www.ewtn.com/library/CURIA/PCIDNONB.HTM

30 HET 1733, IHEU 1, Board of Directors, Executive Committee 17 & 18 July 1965; *The Times*, 30 August 1965, 5.

31 *The Times*, 30 August 1965, 5.

32 Herrick, *Vision and Realism*, 120–1.

33 Paul Kurtz and Albert Dondeyne (eds), *A Catholic|Humanist Dialogue: Humanists and Roman Catholics in a Common World* (London, Pemberton, 1972). We are grateful to David Pollock for drawing our attention to this book.

34 Published as *An Inquiry into Humanism* (London, BBC, 1966); BBC Genome website, entries under 'Enquiry into humanism', programmes broadcast Saturdays, 10.30 am, 6 October to 13 November 1965; BA BHA/1/5/2 BHA *2nd Annual Report*, June 1965, np 2; *7th Report*, 1970, para 17.

35 *The Literary Guide* v.67 (October 1952), 153–8, 166–70; Knight's attribution of high criminality to Catholics is to be found in her papers, Aberdeen University Archive MS3133/6/4.

36 Les Sputter, quoted in HET 1733, IHEU 75, magazine cutting of Howard Radest, 'Ethical culture and humanism', *Religious Humanism* (1982), 8–12 at 9.

37 Colin Campbell, 'Humanism and the culture of the professions: a study of the rise of the British humanist movement, 1954–63', PhD thesis, University of London, 1967, British Library EThOS depository, 235.

38 Gustav Spiller, *The Ethical Movement in Great Britain: A Documentary History* (London, Farleigh Press, 1934), 40.

39 Alexander F. Dawn quoted in ibid., 171.

40 From Mr C.H.W. Bush; BA, BHA/1/5/1 *EU Annual Report*, 1953, 12.

41 Campbell, 'Humanism and the culture of the professions', 238–9.

42 *The Freethinker*, 8 February 1948, 52.

43 Quoted by Robert Ashby, former BHA director, in BA, DPA email to David Pollock 17 August 2000.

44 Campbell, 'Humanism and the culture of the professions', 209.

45 Quoted in ibid., 210.

46 SABL had been largely an inter-war joint venture of EU, NSS and RPA activists, including Chapman Cohen and Mary Seton-Tiedeman. On the Humanist Broadcasting Council, see Callum G. Brown, *The Battle for Christian Britain: Sex, Humanism and Secularisation, 1945–1980* (Cambridge, CUP, 2019), 138–43.

47 BA, BHA1/5/2 *BHA Third Annual Report*, July 1966, 2; CHLA, SPES/1/1/4 Trustee Minutes 23 July 1969, 4.

48 CHLA, SPES/1/2/17 General Committee minutes 1 April 1964; BA, BHA/1/8/7 Advisory Council 1962–92, *2nd Annual Report*, 23 June 1965.

49 *RPA Annual Report*, 1955, 8, quoted in Campbell, 'Humanism and the culture of the professions', 238.

50 *The Literary Guide* v.63 (September 1948), 134.

51 BA, RA/1/4/1 Minutes of the AGM, 13 June 1950, 20 June 1951.

52 Ibid., Minutes of the AGM, 30 July 1957, 8 August 1959.

53 Ibid., Minutes of the AGM, 12 June 1953, 24 July 1954. For other examples, see Bill Cooke, *The Blasphemy Depot: A Hundred Years of the Rationalist Press Association* (London, RPA, 2003), 146–7.

54 BA, RA/1/4/1, AGM 2 August 1955, 11 August 1956.

55 *The International Humanist and Ethical Union and its Member Organizations* (Utrecht, 1959), 46–7.

56 BA, RA/1/4/1 AGM 5 August 1961.

57 *IHEU 1966: The International Humanist and Ethical Union and Its Member Organizations* (Utrecht), 15. Warwick University Modern Records Centre, Personalist Group Papers MSS.151/3/PE/1/21, letter Jack Coates to Victor Gollancz 25 July 1961.

58 This case was first laid out by Lesley Hall, '"A city that we shall never find?" The search for a community of fellow progressive spirits in the UK between the wars', *Family and Community History* v.18 (2015), 24–36.

59 LSEA, HCA/DYSON/1, Letter from E.M. Forster to Anthony E. Dyson, 18 March 1958.

60 *The International Humanist and Ethical Union and Its Member Organisations 1957* (Utrecht), 16.

61 Organisational machinations are given in Hall, 'A city'; and in David Tribe, *100 Years of Freethought* (London, Elek, 1967), 49–52. Membership figure from IHEU, *The International Humanist and Ethical Union and Its Member Organizations* (Utrecht, n.d. *c.* 1967), 15.

62 HET 1733 IHEU 214, Board meeting 1 August 1962, Annex 251; IHEU 2, *Annual Report*, 1968.

63 HET 1733 IHEU 312, Received Questionnaires on Youth organisations worldwide, response for London Young Humanists, 1 March 1965.

64 BA, BHA1/5/2, *BHA Annual Report*, 1965, 2; Campbell, 'Humanism and the culture of the professions'.

65 OUHGA, Hilary 1960, letter Margaret Knight to AFM Brierley 18 March 1960.

66 Brown, *The Battle*, 134; idem, '"The Unholy Mrs Knight" and the BBC: secular humanism and the threat to the Christian nation, c.1945–1960', *English Historical Review* v.127 (2012), 345–76.

67 BA, BHA/1/5/1 *EU Annual Report*, 1958, 2; *The Freethinker* v.78 (11 April 1958), 119.

68 *The Times*, 11 May 1960, 9; Brown, *The Battle*, 100.

69 *The Humanist* v.72 (September 1957), 30; BA, BHA/1/5/1 *EU Annual Report*, 1958, 1; Graham Kingsley, interviewed by Jessica Douthwaite, 16 October 2018.

70 OUHGA online, letter Hector Hawton to AFM Brierley 23 January 1958; Group Card Michaelmas Term 1958; Group Card Hilary 1961; Trinity 1962 Survey; Michaelmas 1960 Survey; Trinity 1962 Posters; cutting from *The Humanist*, 1963; clipping, 'Faith in humanism by mother-to-be', *Oxford Mail*, 14 February 1963; Trinity 1963 – Article in *The Church of England Newspaper*; all at ouhg.org.uk accessed; *The Humanist*, January 1963.

71 David Pollock, interviewed by Callum Brown, 1 September 2014.

72 OUHGA, cutting *Daily Telegraph*, 6 February 1964.

73 OUHGA, cutting *The Guardian*, 26 October 1964.

74 BA, BRIERLEY/3/1, letter from Blackham to Brierley 1961; letter from BHA to Brierley August 1964.

75 BA, BHA/1/17/1 Press Releases, BHA Plan – Activities, 3 October 1966(?).

76 Colin Cross, 'Living without god', *The Observer Magazine*, 16 July 1967.

77 This section has benefited from David Pollock's advice and access to his personal archive (hereafter DPA), now held in Bishopsgate Archive.

78 Jeffrey Dudgeon, *H. Montgomery Hyde: Ulster Unionist MP, Gay Law Reform Campaigner and Prodigious Author* (Belfast, Belfast Press, 2018), 14, 49–50; Patrick Maume, 'Hyde, Harford Montgomery', *Dictionary of Irish Biography* (2009); correspondence with Jeffrey Dudgeon.

79 BA, RA/1/4/1 RPA AGM, 12 June 1952.

80 A short-lived Humanist Association of 1957 agreed some political objectives but there is no indication of any work; Cooke, *The Blasphemy*, 157.

81 BA, DPA, Joint BHA Committee of the Humanist Parliamentary Group, minutes 11 May, 15 June 1965.

82 The amendment signatories were Sydney Bidwell, Albert Booth, James Dickens, Andrew Faulds, Edward (Ted) Fletcher, Michael Foot, Hugh Gray, Bill Hilton, Denis Hobden, Peter Jackson, Lena Jeger, Russell Kerr, John Lee, Joan Lestor, Arthur Palmer, John Parker and John Ryan, https://api.parliament.uk/historic-hansard/commons/1966/nov/04/education-bill.

83 BA, DPA, Humanist Parliamentary Group file [HPG], copy of letter from David Pollock to David Kerr, 12 June 1967.

84 BA, DPA, HPG, correspondence between David Pollock and Leo Abse MP 5 July 1967, 2 August 1967; minutes of meeting of HPG 8 November 1967; Pollock note to Callum Brown, 8 May 2021.

85 BA, DPA, HPG, correspondence between David Pollock, Peter Draper, Tom Vernon and Michael Lines, with MPs David Kerr, John Parker, Peter Jackson, Edward Fletcher, Douglas Houghton and others, and Lord Boothby, 7 November 1967 to 7 August 1968.

86 BA, DPA, HPG, copies of correspondence between Lines and Ritchie Calder, 28 July and 30 July 1968. A dinner was planned but never happened with John Mortimer in March 1970.

87 BA, BHA/1/17/1 Press Releases etc., 'BHA Plan – Activities', 3 October [1966?].

88 BA, DPA HPG, copy of letter from David Pollock to Peter Jackson MP, 26 October 1967.

89 BA, DPA HPG, copy of letter from Peter Ritchie Calder to Michael Lines, 28 July 1968.

Chapter 7

1 H. G. Wells, *First and Last Things: A Confession of Faith and Rule of Life* (London, Watts & Co, [orig. 1908] 1929); idem., *A Short History of the World (1929)*; idem., *What Are We to Do with Our Lives?* (1935); idem., *The Conquest of Time* (1942).

2   Paul T. Phillips, *Contesting the Moral High Ground: Popular Moralists in Mid-Twentieth-Century Britain* (Montreal, McGill-Queen's University Press, 2013), 50–73 at 57–8.

3   Wells, *A Short History*, 302.

4   H. G. Wells, *The Open Conspiracy: Blue Prints for a World Revolution* (London, Gollancz, 1928).

5   Wells quoted in Philip Coupland, 'H.G. Wells's "liberal fascism"', *Journal of Contemporary History* v.35 (2000), 541–58, at 544.

6   Quoted in Philip Ironside, *The Social and Political Thought of Bertrand Russell* (Cambridge, Cambridge University Press, 1996), 179.

7   Chris R. Tame, 'The critical liberal', in G. A. Wells (ed.), *J.M. Robertson (1856–1933): Liberal, Rationalist, and Scholar* (London, Pemberton, 1987), 106.

8   Wells quoted in Foot, *Mr Wells*, 195.

9   Emily Robinson, *The Language of Progressive Politics in Modern Britain* (London, Palgrave Macmillan, 2017), 126.

10 For these developments, see Bill Cooke, *The Blasphemy Depot: A Hundred Years of the Rationalist Press Association* (London, RPA, 2003), 99–105; C. E. M. Joad, *The Book of Joad: A Belligerent Autobiography* (London, Faber & Faber, 1935), 96–7; Wikipedia entry on The Open Conspiracy.

11 LSEA, Progressive League/2/1, *Plan*, 5th Annual Report of FPSI, 36; Lesley Hall, '"A city that we shall never find?" The search for a community of fellow progressive spirits in the UK between the wars', *Family & Community History* v.18 (2016), 24–36 at 29.

12 Later in life he adopted the form Prynce.

13 David Tribe, *100 Years of Freethought* (London, Elek, 1967), 50; H. G. Wells, 'Project of a world society', *New Statesman*, 20 August 1932, 197–8.

14 Coupland, 'H.G. Wells's "liberal fascism"', 541–58, at 543–4.

15 Emphasising the left-wing credentials, but not finding its humanist ones, is R. A. Wilford, 'Federation of progressive societies and individuals', *Journal of Contemporary History* v.11 (2017), 49–82.

16 CHLA, NSS/4/4/20 Poster for FPSI lectures n.d., *c*. 1935–6.

17 TNA, KV2/2093 Kingsley Martin [MI5 PF file], 19 November 1937, SB transcript of speech to FPSI conference at Conway Hall.

18 Phillips, *Contesting*, 75–99 at 77, 83.

19 Bertrand Russell, *Free Thought and Official Propaganda* (London, Watts, 1922), 10, 17–19, 44–5.

20 The humanist network is the subject of a Leverhulme Research Fellowship being held by Callum Brown during 2021–3.

21 They planned greater Anglo-Soviet scientific exchange; see UEAA, SZ/TQ/1/7, minute of meeting at Cafe Royal on 13 August 1941.

22 Ralph J. Desmarais, 'Tots and Quots (act[ive] 1931–1946)', *ODNB* (2007).

23 Glenda Sluga, 'UNESCO and the (one) world of Julian Huxley', *Journal of World History* v.21 (2010), 393–418; idem., *Internationalism in the Age of Nationalism*

(Philadelphia, Penn Press, 2013), 104–5, 116–17; Julian Huxley and A. C. Haddon, *We Europeans: A Survey of 'Racial Problems'* (London, Jonathan Cape, 1935).

24 Gregory Blue, 'Needham (Noël) Joseph Terence Montgomery (1900–1995)', *ODNB* (2008).

25 See appendix by Paul Edwards in Bertrand Russell, *Why I am not a Christian* (London, Routledge, orig. 1957, 1996), 166–212; R. J. Mostyn in *The Humanist* v.72 1957, 25.

26 Fred Hoyle, *The Small World Of* (London, Michael Joseph, 1986), 162.

27 Samanth Subramanian, *A Dominant Character: The Radical Science and Restless Politics of J.B.S. Haldane* (London, Atlantic, 2019), 231–72.

28 Rotblat has been accused by a recent historian of science that his account of his leaving of the Manhattan Project contained falsehoods revealed by his own archive; Martin C. Underwood, 'Joseph Rotblat, the bomb and anomalies from his archive', *Science and Engineering Ethics* v.19 (2013), 487–90.

29 Brian Cathcart, 'Rotblat, Sir Joseph' (1908–2005), *ODNB* (2011).

30 Christopher T. Hill, *Peace and Power in Cold War Britain: Media, Movements and Democracy c.1945–68* (London, Bloomsbury, 2018), 64–77; BA, BHA/1/5/1 *EU Annual Report*, 1954, 2.

31 Antionette Pirie (ed.), *Fall Out: Nuclear Hazards from Nuclear Explosions* (London, MacGibbon & Kee, 1957). This book contained a contribution from Eric Burhop, revealed in 2019 to have been surveilled intensely in 1940–58 by MI5 and other agencies as a likely, though never proven, Soviet agent, https://edition.cnn.com/2019 /04/05/uk/uk-atomic-spy-australia-intl-gbr/index.html.

32 Hans Van Deukeren, 'From theory to practice – a history of IHEU 1952–2002', in Bert Gasenbeek, and Babu Gogineni (eds), *International Humanist and Ethical Union, 1952–2002: Past, Present and Future* (Utrecht, De Tijdstroom, 2002), 26; Cooke, *The Blasphemy Depot*, 322.

33 Percy W. Bridgman (1882–1961), American physicist, atheist, at 'Past AHA Presidents', https://americanhumanist.org/about/past-aha-presidents/ [accessed 18 January]; 'Founders', https://web.archive.org/web/20150611040404/http://www.intlh .com/index_enu.html, accessed 25 January 2020.

34 Plus Powell (1950, Physics), and Yukawa (1949, Physics).

35 Alison Kraft, 'Dissenting scientists in early cold war Britain: the "fallout" controversy and the origins of Pugwash, 1954–1957', *Journal of Cold War Studies* v.20 (1) (2018), 57–100. Martin Clifford Underwood, 'Joseph Rotblat and the moral responsibilities of the scientist', *Science and Engineering Ethics* v.15 (2) (2009), 130. See also Greta Jones, 'The Mushroom-shaped cloud: British scientists' opposition to nuclear weapons policy, 1945–57', *Annals of Science* v.43 (2005), 1–26; Christoph Laucht, *Elemental Germans: Klaus Fuchs, Rudolf Peirls and the Making of British Nuclear Culture 1939–1959* (Basingstoke: Palgrave Macmillan, 2012).

36 J. B. Priestley, 'Britain and the nuclear bombs', *New Statesman*, 2 November 1957, 554–6 at 566.

37 Full information is at pugwash.org.

38 Eaton was a frequent correspondent with Julian Huxley. Papers are held at Rice University Archives (Houston TX), Julian Sorell Huxley Papers, Series III.

39 See the citation at https://www.nobelprize.org/prizes/peace/1995/summary/, accessed 27 December 2019.

40 Rotblat, quoted in Lucy Veys, 'Joseph Rotblat: moral dilemmas and the Manhattan Project', *Physics Perspectives* v.15 (2013), 451–69 at 465.

41 Nicholas J. Barnett, *Britain's Cold War: Culture, Modernity and the Soviet Threat* (London, IB Taurus, 2018), 47–9.

42 Christopher Driver, *The Disarmers: A Study in Protest* (London, Hodder and Stoughton, 1964), 59–60; Frank Parkin, *Middle Class Radicalism* (Manchester, Manchester University Press, 1968), 27; Richard R. Taylor and C. Pritchard, *The Protest Makers* (London, Pergamon, 1980); J. Matausch, *A Commitment to Campaign: A Sociological Study of CND* (MUP, 1989).

43 Ronald W. Clark, *The Life of Bertrand Russell* (London, Jonathan Cape, 1975), 573–601.

44 Samantha Carroll, '"Fill the jails"': identity, structure and method in the committee of 100, 1960–1968', DPhil thesis University of Sussex, 2010. 85–7, 119. See also Sam Carroll, '"I was arrested at Greenham common in 1962": investigating the oral narratives of women in the anti-nuclear Committee of 100', *Oral History* v.31 (2004); Natasha Walter, 'How my father spied for peace', *New Statesman*, 20 May 2002.

45 Samantha Carroll, 'Danger! official secret: the spies for peace: discretion and disclosure in the Committee of 100', *History Workshop Journal* v.69 (Spring 2010), 158–76.

46 Barbara Smoker, interviewed by Jessica Douthwaite 9 June 2018.

47 John Peyton, *Solly Zuckerman: A Scientist Out of the Ordinary* (London, John Murray, 2001), 29–37.

48 Lisa Jardine, 'Things I never knew about my father', *Conway Memorial Lecture*, 26 June 2014, https://conwayhall.org.uk, accessed 3 March 2021.

49 All materials cited in this paragraph are from TNA, KV2/3523 and /3524 Jacob Bronowski.

50 The infiltrator became in the 1990s a committed humanist; Terry Martin interviewed by Callum Brown 21 July 2009.

51 The infiltrators are named online as Ernie Tate and Pat Brain. Wikipedia, 'International Marxist Group', 'Ernie Tait' and 'Russell Tribunal', accessed 23 February 2021.

52 Wikipedia, 'Vietnam Solidarity Campaign' and 'Ralph Schoenman', accessed 23 February 2021.

53 Clark, *The Life of Bertrand Russell*, 595–6.

54 Ibid., 604–51.

55 Tor Krever, 'Remembering the Russell tribunal', *London Review of International Law* v.5 (2017), 48–9 at 489.

56 *The Times*, 26 September 1939, 4.

57 Mark Mazower, 'The strange triumph of human rights, 1933–1950', *Historical Journal* v.47 (2004), 379–98 at 388–9.

58 *The Times*, 25 October 1939, 6.

59 Notably Guy M. Kindersley, former MP for Hitchin; *The Times*, 28 September 1939, 6.

60 Andrew Clapham, *Human Rights: A Very Short Introduction*, 2nd edn (Oxford, OUP, 2015), 34–8; Christopher Moores, 'From civil liberties to human rights? British civil liberties activism and universal human rights', *Contemporary European History* vol. 21 (2012), 169–92 at 170–1.

61 Joseph Kunz quoted in Mazower, 'The strange triumph', 398.

62 On the last of these, see Bastiaan Bouwman, 'From religious freedom to social justice: the human rights engagement of the ecumenical movement from the 1940s to the 1970s', *Journal of Global History* v.13 (2018), 252–73.

63 https://heritage.humanists.uk/sylvia-scaffardi/; TNA KV2/2093 Kingsley Martin, 58a SB Report on NCCL 13 July 1944; Tribe, *100 Years of Freethought*, back flap; Chris Moores, *Civil Liberties and Human Rights in Twentieth-Century Britain* (Cambridge, CUP, 2017), 23, 33.

64 Moores, *Civil Liberties*, 15.

65 See the exploration of this in Eric Laursen, *The Duty to Stand Aside: Nineteen Eighty-Four and the Wartime Quarrel of George Orwell and Alex Comfort* (Edinburgh, AKPress, 2018), 82–5.

66 Moores, 'From civil liberties', 174–8, 187; Moores, *Civil Liberties*, 85.

67 *The Times* 13 March 1940, 5.

68 Russell speaking in Romney Wheeler, 'A conversation with Bertrand Russell' (1952), YouTube.

69 Tony Judt, *Post-War: A History of Europe since 1945* (London, Pimlico, 2007), 565; Paul Kennedy, *The Parliament of Man: The United Nations and the Quest for World Government* (London, Penguin, 2006), 178–9; Moores, 'From civil liberties', 169–70.

70 Johannes Morsink, *The Universal Declaration of Human Rights: Origins, Drafting, and Intent* (Philadelphia, University of Pennsylvania Press, 1999), 1–3, 9.

71 'The Memoirs of John P. Humphrey, the first Director of the United Nations Division of Humans Rights', in *Human Rights Quarterly* vol. 5 (1983), 387–439 at 406.

72 TNA, CO 847/23/17 Universal Rights of Man, pamphlet by H. G. Wells.

73 See discussion of these in Morsink, *The Universal Declaration*, 335–6.

74 'The Memoirs of John P Humphrey', at 427–8, 435.

75 Sluga, *Internationalism in the Age*, 83–4. On Cassin, see https://www.nobelprize.org /prizes/peace/1968/cassin/facts/; Thomas M. Krapf and Stéphane F. Hessel, 'The last witness to the drafting process of the Universal Declaration of Human Rights', *Human Rights Quarterly* vol. 35 (2013), 753–68 at 761–2.

76 Morsink, *The Universal Declaration*, 259–60, 333. Raymond John Goodman, 'Wilson, Sir Geoffrey Masterman (1910–2004)', *ODNB* 2008.

77 The War veteran quoted here was RAF Captain Leonard Cheshire; ibid., 114.

78 European Convention of Human Rights, Wikipedia entry.

79 Moores, *Civil Liberties*, 91.

80 On this failure in internationalism, lacking a secular-humanist gaze, see Samuel Moyn, *The Last Utopia: Human Rights in History* (Cambridge MA, Belknap Press, 2010), 1–2, 44–175, esp. at 53.

81 Steven L. B. Jensen, *The Making of International Human Rights: The 1960s, Decolonisation and the Reconstruction of Global Values* (Cambridge, CUP, 2016), esp. 1–17.

82 John Claydon, 'The treaty protection of religious rights: UN draft convention on the elimination of all forms of intolerance and of discrimination based on religion or belief', *Santa Clara Law Review* v.12 (1972), 403–23 at 410. The 1981 text is at https://www.un.org/en/genocideprevention/documents/atrocity-crimes/Doc.12_declaration%20elimination%20intolerance%20and%20discrimination.pdf.

83 CHLA, SPES/1/2/17 general committee minutes 1 April 1964; BA, BHA 1/5/2 *BHA Third Annual Report*, 1966.

84 HET 483 letter from Michael Lines (Gen. Secy.) to Michael Stewart MP FCO 11 September 1969.

85 Ben Edwards, 'The Godless Congress of 1938: Christian fears about communism in Great Britain', *Journal of Religious History* v.37 (2013), 1–19.

86 Sluga, *Internationalism*, 1.

87 CHLA, SPES/1/2/13 General Committee minute book, 8 November 1952. The organisations were the British-Soviet, British-Russian, British-Hungarian, British-Polish and Britain-China Friendship societies and the International Brigade.

88 CHLA, SPES/1/2/16–17, General Committee, minutes 4 May 1960; 1 April 1964.

89 Deukeren, 'From theory to practice – a history of IHEU 1952–2002', 19, 56.

90 Stephen Howe, *Anticolonialism in British Politics: The Left and the End of Empire 1918–1964* (Oxford, Oxford University Press, 1993), 231–68 at 239–40. The MCF treasurer was Labour MP Jennie Lee; Patricia Hollis, *Jennie Lee: A Life* (Oxford, OUP, 1997), 145.

91 Sunil Amrith and Glenda Sluga, 'New histories of the United Nations', *Journal of World History*, vol. 19, (2008), 251–74; Kennedy, *The Parliament of Man*.

92 HET IHEU 1733, 1 Board papers July 1966, Annex 231 C, Report on Year 1965.

93 Calculated by Callum Brown from HET IHEU 1733–81, Record of Outgoing Correspondence 1961; 1733–88 Record of Received Correspondence 1957.

94 HET 1733–238 Documents of Board of Directors, *IHEU Annual Report*, 1998, typescript, np.

95 W. E. B. Curry, 'War, peace and human nature – A letter to John citizen', *The Monthly Record* (December 1946), 2–3; idem, 'Seeds of a united world', *The Literary Guide* (January 1952), 17.

96 Hall, 'A city that we shall never find?', 30.

Chapter 8

1 *The Trade Marks Journal* v.4632 (25 October 1967).

2 BA, BHA/1/5/1 Ethical Union, *BHA Annual Report*, 1965, 2.

3 BA, BHA1/5/1 *EU Annual Report*, 1953, 4.

4   *IHEU 1959: The International Humanist and Ethical Union and Its Member Organizations* (Utrecht), 15.

5   David Pollock, *The Humanist*, December 1963.

6   The editor of the magazine, Hector Hawton, had significant reservations on the article; correspondence from Hawton to Pollock, DPA, Leonard Evans and David Pollock, 'What are we waiting for?', *The Humanist*, April 1964, 115–16.

7   BA, BHA/1/17/5 Cuttings, 'Club for coloured workers', n.d.; BHA/1/17/1 Press Releases, BHA Plan – Activities 3 October 1966(?).

8   Francis Huxley, *Affable Savages: An Anthropologist Among the Urubu Indians of Brazil* (New York, Viking, 1957).

9   Jim Herrick, *Vision and Realism: A Hundred Years of The Freethinker* (London, Foote, 1982), 30–1.

10 Children and Families Act 2014 (c.6), ss.3(1+2).

11 Graham Kingsley, interviewed by Jessica Douthwaite, 16 October 2018.

12 HET IHEU 483, BHA Submission to Select Committee on Education and Science, May 1969, 1–2; Family Law Reform Act 1969, Part1.1(1).

13 Karl Popper, *The Open Society and Its Enemies*, 2 vols. (London, George Routledge, 1945).

14 '[T]he "anti-God League" approach appeals only to the fringe of a fringe.' BA, BHA/1/5/2 *6th Annual Report*, 1969, para 1.

15 BA, DPA Box 8, letter Kenneth Furness to executive committee 13 November 1969.

16 BHA advertisement, *The Guardian*, 1 December 1969, 4a.

17 BA, DPA Box 8 'Is democracy worth two days?' Promotional Letter from BHA, 13 November 1969.

18 These articles are now at www.thinkingabouthumanism.org/secularism/the-open -society-as-seen-in-1970.

19 HET IHEU 483, *Preliminary Submission to the Department of Education and Science Concerning Proposed Education Bill* (1969), 1.

20 David Nash, 'Humanism in Britain', in Niels De Nutte and Bert Gasenbeek (eds), *Looking Back to Look Forward: Organised Humanism in the World: Belgium, Great Britain, the Netherlands and the United States of America, 1945–2005* (Brussels: Uitgeverij Vupress, 2019), 100.

21 *The Guardian*, 30 August 1966, 2.

22 BA, DPA Box 3, 'Report of first meeting – BHA study group – democracy and the open society', 9 June 1969.

23 BA, DPA Box 3, Pat Knight and Brian Morris in 'Democracy and the open society' (June 1971 and 30ᵗʰ August 1970); DPA Box 8, Copy of letter Ken Jones to *Humanist News.*

24 Susan Budd, 'The humanist societies: the consequences of a diffuse belief system', in B. R. Wilson (ed.), *Patterns of Sectarianism: Organisation and Ideology in Social and Religious Movements* (London, Heinemann, 1967), 377–405 at 401, https://www .secularism.org.uk/news/2017/06/nss-mourns-the-loss-of-former-president-david -tribe.

25 Harold Blackham, *Humanism* (London, Penguin Books, 1968), 166; David Tribe, *The Open Society and Its Friends* (London: National Secular Society, 1971), 3, 6.

26 BA, DPA Box 8, memo Kenneth Furness to executive committee, 11 February 1970.

27 Andrew Copson and David Pollock, 'Religion and the state in an open society' (2006), https://humanism.org.uk/wp-content/uploads/BHA-Article-on-Church -and-State.pdf.

28 Who suggested that after the 1930s the PL 'lingered on until the end of the century'. Bill Cooke, *The Blasphemy Depot: A Hundred Years of the Rationalist Press Association* (London, RPA, 2003), 104.

29 Brian Lewis (ed.), *Wolfenden's Witnesses: Homosexuality in Postwar Britain* (Basingstoke, Palgrave, 2016), 104, 106–26, 142–3, 165–7, 195–8, 236–7, 245 et seq.

30 LSEA, HCA/Dyson/1–2, letters from these individuals March to May 1958; and typescript note of Honorary Committee to date 8 May 1958.

31 Ibid., HCA/Dyson/1, letter from Lord Ritchie Calder, 3 May 1958.

32 Malleson was the referring doctor who triggered the famous Bourne abortion case in 1937. *The Literary Guide* v.63 (September 1948), 142–5.

33 Alec Craig, 'Writing about sex', *The Humanist* v.72 (February 1957), 6–8.

34 Callum G. Brown, *The Battle for Christian Britain: Sex, Humanists and Secularisation, 1945–1980* (Cambridge, CUP, 2019), 238–46; Lesley Hall, *Sex, Gender and Social Change* (London, Palgrave Macmillan, 2013), 119–21, 136–8.

35 Connaire Kensit and Ruth Buchanan, *Sexual Morals – A Humanist View* (Student Humanist Federation, n.d. *c.* 1966/7).

36 *The Humanist*, v.72 (August 1957), 5.

37 For which, see A. J. Ayer, 'What I saw when I was dead', *Sunday Telegraph*, 28 August 1988; idem, 'Postscript to a postmortem', *The Spectator*, 5 October 1988, both widely reprinted online. See Christian claims upon Ayer at William Cash, 'Did atheist philosopher see God when he "died"?', *National Post*, 3 March 2001, also online.

38 For other examples, see Cooke, *Blasphemy*, 140–3.

39 *The Humanist*, v.72 (January 1957), 26.

40 NLS Peter Ritchie Calder Papers Acc10318/9: Speech by Edward Oliver, Secretary General of the SMC, AGM 2 July 1969.

41 BA, BHA/1/17/1, ms BHA General Statement of Policy (as amended by Conference), n.d. but *c.* 1967.

42 *Humanist News*, January 1992, 3.

43 BA, DPA box 8, 'People currently connected with TRACK', *c.* 1966. For the CRAC story, see Brown, *Battle*, 116–45, 256–83.

44 BA, BHA/1/17/1 Press statements, ms "BHA Plan – Activities" *c.* 1966, 1.

45 Ibid., 3–4.

46 Ibid., BHA Press Release on Humanism and Human Rights Year 20 December 1967; BHA Press Release on Family Planning 20 July 1970; *Humanist News*, August/ September 1970, 1.

47 Ibid., BHA Press Release, 'Young humanist conference on drugs 29 December 1967'; 'Home Office, The Wootton report [advisory committee on drug dependence sub-committee on hallucinogens] 1967'. For a critical account of Wootton on drugs, see Peter Hitchens, *The War We Never Fought* (London, Bloomsbury, 2012).

48 BA, BHA/1/17/1, memo to local Humanist Groups, 2 February 1968; 'Abolish the Oath', joint Humanist and Civil Liberties letter, 15 October 1968; Is it a sin to be different?, 31 December 1968. Herrick, *Vision and Realism*, 30–1.

49 Quoted in Ian MacKillop, *The British Ethical Societies*, 162; the original quotation was from Coit's first editorial for *The Ethical World*.

50 Quoted in *The Times*, 26 February 1940, 9.

51 See for example, James Hemming, 'Morality after myth', *Journal of Moral Education* v.25 (1) (1996), 39–45 at 44–5.

52 The Plowden Report, paras 562, 572; HET IHEU 483, *Preliminary [BHA] Submission to the Department of Education and Science Concerning Proposed Education Bill* (1969), 5.

53 Ibid., 1–2.

54 Ibid., 4.

55 James Hemming and Howard Marratt, *Humanism and Christianity: The Common Ground of Moral Education* (London, BHA, 1969). For the story of humanist-Christian discussions over moral education, see Rob Freathy and Stephen G. Parker, 'Secularists, humanists and religious education: religious crisis and curriculum change in England 1963–1975', *History of Education* v.42 (2013), 222–56. It should be read alongside an amended narrative in Brown, *Battle*, 246–50.

56 *Moral and Religious Education in County Schools* (London, SMC, 1970).

57 Diane Munday in *News and Notes*, 6 February 1964.

58 *Humanist News*, June/July 1994, 10. Critical initial support came from RPA (£2,500), SPES (£500), UES (£4,500) and the Progressive League (sum unknown). The president of the HHA was writer and playwright Lord Ted Willis. BA, BHA/1/11/1 Humanist Housing Association, *Ninth Annual report of EUHHA 1963*; A New Project: an appeal for £8,000 (HHA, nd); BHA, Homes for People (June 1967), typescript Report; 25 Years of Humanist Housing Association (*c*. 1980).

59 Jim Herrick, *Humanist Housing: A History of the Association* (London, Origin Housing, nd but *c*. 2013); BHA/1/11/2 HHA Papers, Board Report and Financial Statements March 1999, 7.

60 BA, BHA1/17/5 *The Times*, 5 November 1963; Conrad Keating, *Smoking Kills: The Revolutionary Life of Richard Doll* (Oxford, Signal Books, 1014), 201–2. Keating's foundation date of 1965 seems refuted by the *Times* article.

61 BA, BHA 1/5/2 BHA *4th Annual Report*, 1967; Agnostic Adoption Society Press Release 16 June 1969; DPA, Box 6A, Agnostics Adoption Society 1963–71, publicity literature.

62 This account is based on separate interviews with Dermot Bolton (b. 1970) and Tom Bolton (b. 1943) by Callum Brown, 8 July 2021; and on material collated by

Madeleine Goodall at https://heritage.humanists.uk/agnostics-adoption-society/. Advice on agency practice from Rhian Beynon, adoption manager. See also https://www.legislation.gov.uk/ukpga/2002/38/contents.

63 Barbara Wootton, *In a World I Never Made* (London, George Allen & Unwin, 1967), 164.

64 Barbara Wootton, *Crime and Penal Policy: Reflections on Fifty Years' Experience* (London, George Allen & Unwin, 1978), 161–2.

65 *The International Humanist and Ethical Union and Its member Organizations* (Utrecht, 1966), 14.

66 *Humanist News*, October 1970, 2; Peter Draper, 'Consumers and the green-paper: participation in the health services', *The Lancet* v.292 (1968), 1131–3; obituary, *The Guardian*, 22 August 2016.

67 Children and Young Persons Scotland Report April 1964, HMSO Cmnd 2306.

68 Nigel Bruce, 'Children's hearings: a retrospect', *British Journal of Criminology* v.15 (1975), 333–44.

69 Nigel Bruce, interviewed by Callum Brown 21 April 2010; *Humanist News*, November 1976, 1–2; Elizabeth Jogee, *Edinburgh Youth Homes: The First Fifteen Years* (Edinburgh, n.pub., n.d. but 1988).

70 Griffin is now known as Liz van Rensburg. This paragraph based on: https://theswanengstory.files.wordpress.com/2015/09/dab_van-rensburg_vol-6-tom.pdf; and ibid. /2015/04/swaneng-early-years.pdf, 2. The Right Livelihood Foundation at https://www.rightlivelihoodaward.org/media/remembering-apartheid-critic-and-educator-patrick-van-rensburg/, accessed 3 April 2020; *The International Humanist and Ethical Union and Its Member Organizations* (Utrecht, 1966), 15; *The Ethical Record* v. 73 (February 1968), 17; v.74 (June 1969), 18; Colin B. Campbell, 'Humanism and the culture of the professions: a study of the rise of the British Humanist Movement, 1954–63', PhD thesis, University of London, 1967, British Library EThOS depository, 215–6; David Tribe, *100 Years of Freethought* (London, Elek, 1967), 53. The EU/BHA donation is put at £750 in Kevin Shillington, *Patrick Van Rensburg: Rebel, Visionary and Radical Educationist* (Johannesburg, Wits University Press, 2020), 107, 136, 147, 157; Jim Herrick, *Aspiring to the Truth: Two Hundred Years of the South Place Ethical Society* (London, Conway Hall, Ethical Society, 2016), 210.

71 LSEA, Progressive League /2/1, *Plan* vol 37 (1967), 1.

72 Tribe, *100 Years of Freethought*, 201.

73 Glanville Williams, *The Sanctity of Life and the Criminal Law* (London, Faber and Faber, 1958).

74 BA, BHA1/5/2 *5th Annual Report*, 1968; ibid. *7th Annual Report*, 1970, para 14.

75 Cordelia Moyse, 'Tiedeman, May Louise Seaton-', *ODNB* (2020); May Seaton-Tiedeman, Wikipedia; A. P. Herbert, *The Ayes Have It: The Story of the Marriage Bill* (London, Methuen, 1937).

76 *Humanist News*, April 1969, 6, https://heritage.humanists.uk/may-seaton-tiedeman/.

77 Lizzie Seal, 'Imagined communities and the death penalty in Britain, 1930–65', *British Journal of Criminology* v.54 (2014), 908–27 at 923.

78 Quoted in John Simkin, 'Roy Jenkins', https://spartacus-educational.com/PRjenkinsR
.htm, accessed 28 July 2021.

79 *The Times*, 30 August 1965, 5.

Chapter 9

1 From 3,814 to 2,712. BA, BHA/1/5/2 *BHA 8th Annual Report*, 1971, paras 1–5, 74; *9th Annual Report*, para 53; DPA Box 3 *Evening Standard*, 26 July 1971.

2 From 4,704 in 1966 to 1,842 in 1972. BA, RPA *Annual Reports*.

3 BA, BHA/1/17/5 *The Observer*, 25 July 1971.

4 HET 1733 IHEU 486 letter from Anne Sieve to Ernst van Brabel, 18 September 1986.

5 David Pollock, interviewed by Callum Brown, 1 September 2014.

6 DPA, email Graham Kingsley to David Pollock, 9 November 2020.

7 David Pollock interview with Callum Brown, 1 September 2014.

8 BA, /BHA/1/5/2 *10th Annual Report*, 1973, paras 1–2, 52–3, 59; *11th Annual Report*, 1974, para 55; BHA Education Committee minutes, 24 July 1973.

9 *Humanist News*, Spring 1972, 3.

10 Data from BA, BHA 1/5/2 BHA 1st and 5th Annual Reports.

11 BA, BHA/1/5/2 *BHA 9th Annual Report*, 1972, para 11.

12 Ibid., *13th Annual Report*, 1976, para 1.

13 Ibid., *16th Annual Report*, 1979, para 7.

14 BA, BHA/1/5/3, *19th Annual Report*, 1981.

15 Lord Justice Scarman, *The Red Lion Square Disorders of 15 June 1974: Report of Inquiry* (London, HMSO Cmnd 5919, 1975).

16 Wikipedia entries, 'Death of Kevin Gately' and 'Red Lion Square', *Ethical Record*, Cadogan at v.79 (July/August 1974), 20; (November/December 1974), 20, and v.80 (January 1975), 18; (May 1975), 17–18; Smoker at June 1975, 16–18; CHLA SPES/1/2/17 General Committee minutes 1 March 1967; May/June 1970. CHLA, SPES/1/1/14 Trustee Minutes, 29 October 1975. On PIE, Chris Moores, *Civil Liberties and Human Rights in Twentieth-Century Britain* (Cambridge, CUP, 2017), 196.

17 A. Lovecy, *Ethical Record* v.85 (September 1980), 13.

18 CHLA, SPES/1/1/4 Trustees Minutes 27 September 1978, quotes from A. Lovecy's letter to the chairman, and memo to general committee, 1977.

19 Ibid., it.2; 31 October 1969, it.(h); 27 November 1981, its.(e) and (f). True court costs at *Ethical Record* v.86 (July August 1981), 6.

20 *Ethical Record* v.85 (July/August 1980), 1; (September 1980), 8–9, 12–13. For the case's legal context, see Russell Sandberg, 'Clarifying the definition of religion under English law: the need for a universal definition', *Ecclesiastical Law Journal* v.20 (2018), 132–57 at 136–7.

21 BA, BHA/1/17/2 Humanist Newsletter 1968–2001, *HN*, March 1982, 1.

22 See the history of the British Anti-Apartheid Movement at https://www.aamarchives .org

23 Agreed at the two-day BHA AGM; BHA/1/17/5 *The Guardian*, 26 July 1971.

24 DPA, Diane Munday email to David Pollock, 15 November 2020.

25 Harold J. Blackham, *Humanism* (London, Harvester Press, Revised Edition, 1976), 178–9.

26 DPA, Diane Munday to David Pollock, 15 November 2020.

27 Peter Draper, preface, *Towards an Open Society: Ends and Means in British Politics* (London, Pemberton Books, 1971).

28 Jill Liddington, *The Long Road to Greenham* (London, Virago, 1989), 264–92.

29 Data from BA, BHA/1/5/1–3 Annual Reports and RR/2/2 Annual Reports.

30 HET IHEU 484, letter from Kenneth Furness (BHA Gen.l Secy.) to Bert Schwartz (IHEU) 12 January 1982.

31 A drop from 1,999 to 998 members; HET 484 BHA Annual Return for 1983; letter Bert Schwartz to BHA, 6 September 1982.

32 HET IHEU 484, Notes for BHA EGM, 23 October 1982. *Re South Place Ethical Society* [1980] 1 W.L.R. 1565.

33 Quoted in Callum Brown, *The Battle for Christian Britain: Sex, Humanism and Secularisation 1945-1980* (Cambridge, CUP, 2019), 269.

34 A fuller story of Humanism at the BBC is told in Brown, *The Battle*, 116–45, 256–83.

35 BA BHA Stopes-Roe temp file 5 Education committee minutes, 24 July 1973.

36 HET IHEU 484, letter from Harry Stopes-Roe to Nettie Klein IHEU, 7 January 1987 (incorrectly dated 1986); Harry Stopes-Roe, 'Humanism as a life stance', *Free Inquiry*, November 1987 ms copy.

37 'Life stance' appeared only four times in *The Times* 1975–85 – twice used by Mary Whitehouse.

38 Letter from James Peyton of Nantwich, in *Humanist News*, May 1976, 4.

39 BA, BHA/1/5/2 *9th Annual Report*, 1972, para 12.

40 Ibid., paras 43–5.

41 One such episode at Tower Hill in August 1958; *The Freethinker* v.78 (3 October 1958), 315.

42 Wikipedia on *Last Exit to Brooklyn*, accessed 20 July 2021.

43 For an account of this from Whitehouse herself, see Mary Whitehouse, *Quite Contrary* (London, Pan, 1988); and see also Ben Thompson, *Ban this Filth! Letters from the Mary Whitehouse Archive* (London, Faber and Faber, 2013).

44 Whitehouse, *Quite*, 41–6.

45 David Nash, *Blasphemy in Modern Britain 1789 to the Present* (Aldershot, Ashgate, 1999), 242–3.

46 For Robertson's own thoughts on the episode, see Geoffrey Robertson, *The Justice Game* (London, Vintage, 1999), 147 *et seq.*

47 Nash, *Blasphemy*, 254–5.

48 Jim Herrick b.1944, interviewed by Jessica Douthwaite, 1 November 2018.

49 See David Nash, *Blasphemy in the Christian World: A History* (Oxford, OUP, 2007), 211–19; George Perry, *The Life of Python* (New York, Running Books, 1994).

50 *The Gay Humanist: Newsletter of the Gay Humanist Group* v.4 (1) (September 1984– November 1985), 3–4.

51 Barry Duke, interviewed by Charlie Lynch, 16 May 2021.

52 https://www.patheos.com/blogs/thefreethinker/2021/05/veteran-lgbt-humanist -activist-george-broadhead-dies-aged-87.

53 *Gay Humanist Group Newsletter*, no. 1, November 1979, 1.

54 Barry Duke, interviewed by Charlie Lynch, 16 May 2021.

55 *Gay Humanist Group Newsletter*, no. 1, November 1979, 1.

56 https://www.patheos.com/blogs/thefreethinker/2021/05/veteran-lgbt-humanist -activist-george-broadhead-dies-aged-87.

57 Matt Cook, 'Sexual revolution(s) in Britain', in Gert Hekma and Alain Giami (eds), *Sexual Revolutions* (London, Palgrave, 2014), 131.

58 BA, GALHA/4/4 Gay Humanist Group, 'Constitution'.

59 Maureen Duffy, *Separate Development? Out of the Closet and Into the Ghetto* (London, Gay Humanist Group, 1980), 1–4.

60 National Opinion Poll, cited in *BHA Humanist Newsletter*, November 1976, n.p.

61 BA, Munday/1/2, lecture notes for 'Religious opposition to sexual freedom', NSS Caxton Hall meeting, 7 May 1976.

62 Ibid.

63 HET IHEU 484 letter from Harry Stopes-Roe to Ernest van Brakel, 13 August 1981.

64 *Humanist News*, February 1976, 3.

65 Ibid., March 1976, 5 and April 1976, 7–8.

66 Ibid., July/August 1976, 6.

67 CHLA, NSS/4/4/14 Co-ordinating Committee Press Release February 1977.

68 David Limond, 'Frequently but naturally: William Michael Duane, Kenneth Charles Barnes and teachers as innovators on sex(uality) education in English adolescent schooling: c.1945–1965', *Sex Education* 5 (2005), 107–18 at 111.

69 CHLA, SPES/1/1/4 Trustees Minutes 6 October 1971 with letters J Glasson [solicitors] to Peter Cadogan [SPES General Secretary], 5 and 18 October 1971.

70 Callum Brown saw the film at the Student FilmSoc at University of St Andrews six weeks later.

71 CHLA, SPES/6/2/25, Growing Up 1971, passim; DVD, *The Joy of Sex Education* ([London], BFI, 2009), 'Growing Up' Disc 2, and enclosed booklet 36; David Limond, '"I never imagined that the time would come"': Martin Cole, 'The growing up controversy and the limits of school sex education in 1970s England', *History of Education* 37 (2008), 409–29; idem, '"I hope someone castrates you, you perverted bastard": Martin Cole's sex education film, growing up', *Sex Education* v.9 (4) (2009), 409–19.

72 Ibid., 417fn12; James Hemming, *Teenage Loving and Living* (London, British Medical Association, 1976).

73 Quoted in Christopher Clews, 'The new education fellowship and the reconstruction of education 1945–1966', PhD thesis, Institute of Education, University of London, 2009, 110–11.

74 CHLA, BLA/7/1/2/38, TS CV by John Wilson. *c.* 1972; obituary, *Oxford Review of Education* v.29 (2003), 421–2.

75 The Warborough Trust Ltd, 266156, registered as a charity on 4 September 1973, ceased to exist on 15 January 1997. Norham Foundation, registered as a charity on 24 July 1969, ceased to operate on 19 August 2009. Listed on Charities Register at https://register-of-charities.charitycommission.gov.uk/. Rob Freathy and Stephen G Parker, 'Secularists, humanists and religious education: religious crisis and curriculum change in England, 1963–1975', *History of Education* v.42 (2013), 222–56. The provenance of Warborough Trust funds is unknown.

76 I. T. Ramsey, *The Fourth R: The Report of the Commission on Religious Education in Schools* (London, National Society/SPCK, 1970), 50, 74–93 at 82.

77 The account in this paragraph is based on Blackham's brief history, at CHLA, BLA/7/1/2/27, TS Harold Blackham, 'Moral education in the UK', *c.* 1972–3.

78 CHLA, BLA/7/1/2/9a TS 'Relations between ME & RE', *c.* 1983.

79 CHLA, BLA/7/1/2/11 TS 'Muslim Schools in England' undated. Ahead of his time, Popper accepted an invitation from Blackham to join the Advisory Council of the British Humanist Association so long as meetings were smoke-free. BA, BHA1/8/8 Advisory Council, letter from Karl Popper to Harold Blackham, 14 February 1967.

80 CHLA, BLA/7/1/2/2 TS, 'Rationale of the relation between moral and religious education', *c.*1983.

81 See the critical letter in WA, MSP, SA/ALR/G79: Press cuttings 1960s–80s: *The Freethinker*, 25 April 1970.

82 CHLA, BLA/7/1/7, letter from Harry Stopes-Roe to Harold Blackham, 3 May 1983; letter from Blackham to Stopes-Roe, 9 May 1983.

83 BHA Stopes-Roe Temporary file, BHA Education Committee minutes 24 July 1973.

84 An example of his dominance of committee meetings (certainly of the minutes) is BHA Stopes-Roe Temporary File, Education Committee minutes, 26 September 1973; 19 March 1974. The upbraiding was in a letter Kenneth Furness to Stopes-Roe, 14 June 1974.

85 *Assemblies in County Schools* (London ILEA SACRE, 1978); *Religious Education in Hampshire Schools* (Hampshire CC, 1978). See also Freathy and Parker, 'Secularists'; idem, 'Context, complexity and contestation: Birmingham's agreed syllabuses for religious education since the 1970s', *Journal of Beliefs & Values* v.32 (2011), 247–63.

86 BA, BHA1/5/2 *12th Annual Report*, 1975, para 12–13; BA, BHA Stopes-Roe, Temp Education File 1973–78, Education, *Birmingham Post*, 10 June 1974; *Birmingham Evening Mail*, 11 June 1974; handwritten and typescript versions of Emergency Motion to 1974 Conference, with Supporting Statement; Executive and Education Committee joint meeting minutes, 15 July 1974; BHA AGM 1974 Emergency Motion 2 with Supporting Statement; Education Committee minutes, 17 April 1975.

87 BA, BHA Stopes-Roe, Temp Education File 1973–78, Education Committee minutes, 10 February 1975; Draft Education Committee report for Annual Report 1974; Education Committee minutes, 19 May 1975.

88 See a notable speech, CHLA, NSS/4/4/14, Harry Stopes-Roe, 'The BHA and commitment', 9 January 1978.

89 *What Future for the Agreed Syllabus?* (London, RE Council, 1976).

90 BA, BHA Stopes-Roe Temp File Education, Education Committee minutes, December 1974.

91 The convoluted story, including the never-ending funding crisis and the unhappiness of SMC staff with Oliver's apparently off-hand management style, is to be found in CHLA, BLA/7/1/3.

92 LPA, Coggan Papers 43 f.5 Note for the Archbishop, 19 January 1976.

93 Ibid, 43 f.1, note to Coggan, 13 January 1976; f.17, note 26 January 1976.

94 LPA, Ramsey 263, 22 & 23 letter from Butler to Ramsey, 30 March 1973; 26 letter Ramsay to McGeorge Bundy, secretary of Ford Foundation, 3 April 1973; Ramsey 273, 149 letter Robert Bishop of St Albans to Lambeth Palace, 29 November 1974.

95 LPA, Coggan 31, 285 letter Patrick Wall MP to Lambeth Place, 25 April 1976; 304 letter Bishop of St Albans to Lambeth Palace, 11 February 1975.

96 Ibid, 31 f.231, letter from Charles Oxley to Coggan, 15 January 1976. See also f.285, letter from Patrick Wall MP to Coggan, 25 April 1976. A lengthy correspondence is at f.231–337.

97 Julia Winter from Cheshunt, *Humanist News*, June 1980, 4.

Chapter 10

1 *New Humanist*, v.99 (1) (Summer 1984), 3.

2 John Leeson, interviewed by Charlie Lynch, 23 October 2020; 'Maeve Denby: obituary', *Humanist News* v.64 (November/December 1993), 3.

3 JLA, *Secretary's Report*, 1 November 1983.

4 https://www.theguardian.com/education/2014/may/20/harry-stopes-roe.

5 John Leeson, interviewed by Charlie Lynch, 23 October 2020.

6 Richard Paterson, interviewed by Charlie Lynch, 13 December 2020.

7 Robert Ashby, interviewed by Charlie Lynch, 9 December 2020.

8 BA, BHA, *Third Annual Report*, July 1966, 1.

9 *The Times*, 15 February 1983, 14; BA, BHA/1/5/3 *Twentieth Annual Report*, 1982, 1.

10 JLA, *Secretary's Report*, 1 November 1983.

11 John Leeson interviewed by Charlie Lynch, 23 October 2020.

12 BA, BHA/1/7/4 BHA vs Weinstein 174.

13 Ibid., Leeson, email to Charlie Lynch.

14 Ibid.

15 BA, BHA/1/5/3 *Annual Report*, 1991, 7.

16 Ibid., *Annual Report*, 1994, 5.

17 Ibid., *Annual Report*, 1986, 5.

18 Ibid., 1; Jane Wynne Willson interviewed by Charlie Lynch, 12 November 2020.

19 BA, BHA/1/17/51 Ethics and Humanism: Briefing Papers 1987–1996; *Animal Rights: A Humanist View* (n.d.); *Humanist Views on Divorce* (n.d.).

20 Smoker, *My Godforsaken Life*, 110.

21 *Humanist News*, No. 68, August September 1994, 2. David Pollock email to Charlie Lynch, 9 February 2021.

22 BHA/1/5/3 *Annual Report*, 1995, 3.

23 Robert Ashby, interviewed by Charlie Lynch, 16 October 2020.

24 Ibid.

25 BHA/1/5/3, *Annual Report*, 1997, 6.

26 *Humanist News Wales*, No. 1, February 1993.

27 *Humanist News*, Autumn 2003, 19–20.

28 Robert Ashby, interviewed by Charlie Lynch, 16 October 2020.

29 Richard Paterson, interviewed by Charlie Lynch, 13 December 2020.

30 Robbi Robson, interviewed by Charlie Lynch, 16 October 2020.

31 Robert Ashby, interviewed by Charlie Lynch, 16 October 2020.

32 Richard Paterson, interviewed by Charlie Lynch, 13 December 2020.

33 *Humanist News*, No. 66 April/May 1994, 9.

34 Richard Paterson, interviewed by Charlie Lynch, 13 December 2020.

35 Paul Kurtz, 'The future course of humanism', *New Humanist*, June 1996, 2–5.

36 JLA, Robbi Robson, 'New ways of working', faxed memo to executive committee, 29 June 1995.

37 JLA, BHA executive committee, miscellaneous documents 1995–96.

38 JLA, email memoir of the mid-1990s.

39 *Humanist News*, August/September 1994, 3; BA, BHA/1/18/3 BHA Briefing for the PLP Education Group, 28 February 1996.

40 *Humanist News*, no. 84, April/May 1997, 1.

41 BA, BHA/1/18/3, letter Lord Dormand of Easington to Robert Ashby, 18 July 1995.

42 Robert Ashby, quoted in Paul Routledge, 'God may be dead – but not if you're a conservative MP', *The Independent*, 14 April 1996.

43 *Humanity*, October/November 1999, 9.

44 Robbi Robson, 'My vision of a strong humanism', *Humanity*, April/May 1999, 11.

45 *Humanity*, February/March 1999.

46 Robert Ashby, interviewed by Charlie Lynch, 16 October 2020.

47 *Humanist News*, no. 86, September 1997, 3.

48 Richard Paterson, interviewed by Charlie Lynch, 13 December 2020.

49 *The Guardian*, 12 February 1982, 4.

50 DPA, David Pollock to Jim Herrick and Graham Kingsley, 8 November 2020.

51 *The Guardian*, 12 February 1982, 4.

52 *New Humanist*, v.99 (1) (Summer 1984), 3.

53 JLA, 'Development of the BHA', memorandum from Diana Rookledge to EC members, 14 April 1985.

54 Ibid.

55 HET 1733 IHEU 75 Application form from [British] Gay Humanist Group, January 1985.

56 *Gay and Lesbian Humanist: Magazine of the Gay and Lesbian Humanist Group*, 10th Anniversary Issue, v.9 (1) (Autumn 1989), 18.

57 BA, GALHA/1/11 'Gay humanist group special general meeting 11th November 1987'; Barry Duke interviewed by Charlie Lynch, 16 May 2021.

58 BA, GALHA/1/2, Minutes of the Annual General Meeting of the Gay and Lesbian Humanist Association, 13 September 1990.

59 John Leeson email to Charlie Lynch, 15 November 2020.

60 Jane Wynne Willson interviewed by Charlie Lynch, 13 November 2020.

61 *New Humanist*, Autumn 1985, 22–3.

62 https://www.scotsman.com/news/uk-news/margaret-thatchers-sermon-mound -1580740; *New Humanist* v.103 (2) (June 1988), 3.

63 *New Humanist* v.9 (1) (Summer 1984), 3.

64 Though only 29.1 per cent were members of a local humanist group (usually based in a town). The survey achieved a disappointingly low return rate of 172. JLA, MS BHA Questionnaire to members June 1985.

65 HET 1733 IHEU 486, Colin Mills and Terry Liddle, 'Why we have left the NSS', circular from Socialist Secular Association undated but *c.* November 1983. The SSA was originally the Socialist Humanist Association.

66 *The Ethical Record*, March 1984, 11.

67 See Nettie Klein's criticism in CHLA, NSS/4/4/14, *International Humanist Newsletter* v.17 (December 1981), 1; HET1733 IHEU 75, Report of Committee on Growth and Development, by Paul Kurtz, 4 April 1984.

68 *The Freethinker*, April 1987, unsigned 'News and Notes' column likely written by editor William McIlroy.

69 *The Guardian*, 6 February 1987; 4 March 1967; *The Freethinker*, March 1987, 42–3.

70 HET 484 letter to Alfons Nederkoorn, 17 May 1987, describing Flew's chapter 'racially neutral'.

71 HET 1733 482 RPA Ltd GB 1966–1995, Circular letter from Roy Saich of WHG, 19 February 1987; copy of letter Karl Heath to RPA, 9 February 1987; copy letter Nicholas Walter to Saich, 8 April 1987; letter Walter to Saich, 15 April 1987; letter Walter to Alfons Nederkoorn at IHEU, 21 April 1987.

72 Bill Cooke, *The Blasphemy Depot: A Hundred Years of the Rationalist Press Association* (London, Rationalist Press Association, 2003), 242–3.

73 *Humanist Dipper* quoted in Joe Jenkins, *GCSE Religious Studies: Contemporary Moral Issues* (London, Heinnemann Educational Books, 1987), 47, 62.

74 Rob Freathy and Stephen G. Parker, 'Secularists, humanists and religious education: religious crisis and curriculum change in England 1963–1975', *History of Education* v.42 (2013), 222–256.

75 Brian Gates, 'Religious education and moral education: the end of a beautiful relationship?', *Religion & Public Education* v.12 (1985), 162–5.

76 BA, BHA STOPES-ROE 139, Vatican and Moscow 1988–9.

77 JLA, John White et al., 'The work of the BHA Education Committee 1965–1996' (typescript briefing paper, 1996).

78 Education Reform Act 1988 at www.legislation.gov.uk. J. D. C. Harte, 'The religious dimension of the Education Reform Act 1988', *Ecclesiastical Law Journal* v.1 (1989), 32–52.

79 *Humanist News*, November 1991, 11.

80 HET IHEU 483 BHA *Annual Report*, 1989; Hounslow did this in 1994; *Humanist News*, March 1992, 5.

81 BA BHA1/18/3 Lord Dormand to Robert Ashby 24 July 1995, attached Hansard extract.

82 *Humanist News*, May/June 1992, 1.

83 Callum Brown, Jane Mair and Thomas Green, *Religion in Scots Law: Report of an Audit at the University of Glasgow* (Edinburgh, HSS, 2016), 137–91.

84 Marcus Tregilgas-Davey, 'Ex parte Choudhury: an opportunity missed', *The Modern Law Review* v.54 (2) (March 1991), 294–9; David S. Nash, *Blasphemy in Modern Britain: 1789 to the Present* (London, Routledge, 1999), 260.

85 BA, press cutting 'Statement against blasphemy law', May 1989.

86 See David S. Nash, *Blasphemy in the Christian World: A History* (Oxford, OUP, 2007), 226–30; *Humanist News*, May/June 1992, 4.

87 Jane Wynne Willson, interviewed by Charlie Lynch, 13 November 2020. *The Observer*, Sunday 30 October 1988, 73; BA, BHA/1/5/3 *Annual Report*, 1992, 8.

88 Information from Nigel Collins, who ran the BHA ceremonies network in the 1990s.

89 https://humanism.org.uk/about/our-people/patrons/jane-wynne-willson, accessed 9 February 2021.

90 Jane Wynne Willson interviewed by Charlie Lynch, 13 November 2020.

91 BA, BHA/1/5/3 *Annual Report*, 1990, 6.

92 Jane Wynne Willson, *Parenting Without God: Experiences of a Humanist Mother* (Nottingham, Education Heretics Press, 1997).

93 BHA, *Annual Report*, 1992, 5; information from Nigel Collins.

94 BHA, *Annual Report*, 1994, 6.

95 Nigel Collins, 'BHA ceremonies timeline'.

96 Data from and calculated from card index of IHEU member organisations 1980s, in HET 1733 311 Membership organisations worldwide, 1957–82.

97 One was Sir Andrew Huxley, then president of the Royal Society. Paul Kurtz, 'Sakharov: a humanist Galileo', *Free Inquiry* v.10 (1990), 46–7; Charles Rhéume, 'Western scientists' reactions to Andrei Sakharov's Human Rights Struggle in the Soviet Union, 1968–1989', *Human Rights Quarterly* v.30 (2008), 1–20 at 8.

98   Ann Marie Clark, *Diplomacy of Conscience: Amnesty International and Changing Human Rights Norms* (2010, available online), 3–15.

99   HET 1733 238 Documents of Board of Directors, *IHEU Annual Report*, 1998, typescript, np.

100 Ibid., IHEU Draft Strategy Plan 1998–2003.

101 Nigel Bruce, interviewed by Callum Brown, 21 April 2010.

102 Hans van Deukeen, 'Past', in Bert Gasenbeek and Babu Gogineni (eds), *International Humanist and Ethical Union 1952–2002: Past, Present and Future* (Utrecht, De Tijdstroom, 2002), 56.

103 HET 1733 75, Documents of a General Character, Report on UNESCO, paper to IHEU Board July 1984; IHEU Board paper on ISS proposal for a Universal Declaration of Human Values', July 1984.

104 This paragraph based on HET 1733 238 Documents of Board of Directors, *IHEU Annual Report*, 1998, typescript, np; letter from Rob Tielman (Utrecht) to IHEU Executive Committee (London), 11 May 1998; letter from Rob Tielman to Levi Fragell, IHEU President, 8 November 1998; IHEU Executive Committee minutes, 11 September 1999 at EC/98/12.4. Important details in the story are to be found in Bert Gasenbeek and Babu Gogineni (eds), *International Humanist and Ethical Union 1952–2002: Past, Present and Future* (Utrecht, De Tijdstroom, 2002), 84–7.

105 Several recollections given us inform this account.

106 BA, BHA/1/4/4 Don Liversedge papers, Barbara Smoker memo, 1 June 1997.

107 *Humanist News*, July 1997, 1–2; September 1997, 2.

108 DPA, John Leeson memoir.

Chapter 11

1   Bill Cooke, *The Blasphemy Depot: A Hundred Years of the Rationalist Press Association* (London, RPA, 2003), 302–4, 332–3.

2   BA, BHA/1/17/25 BHA *Issues* 2002.

3   BA, BHA/3/14 Circular letter, 3 March 2008.

4   Information on membership categories taken from annual reports of BHA, RPA, SPES and their successors 1930–2020.

5   Gareth Longden, 'A profile of the members of the British Humanist Association', *Science, Religion & Culture* v.2 (2015), 86–95 at 86.

6   Andrew Copson, interviewed by Charlie Lynch, 10 September 2021.

7   DPA, Age Analysis of BHA members, 2006–7.

8   Data from Humanists UK.

9   Figures produced from analysis of data used in Graph 1, page 22.

10 Data from Census 2001 and 2011.

11 See websites of Christian Voice, Christian Institute, and 'Keep the clause campaign' on Wikipedia.

12 *Humanity*, October/November 1998, 1; *Church Times*, 23 April 2009.

13 *The Guardian*, 20 December 2003, Lord Dormand of Easington: Obituary. https://www.theguardian.com/news/2003/dec/20/guardianobituaries.politics, accessed 15 December 2020.

14 BA, BHA/1/18/3 Lord Dormand of Easington to Robert Ashby, 14 May 1997.

15 *Humanity*, No. 1, December–January 1998, 6; Robert Ashby interviewed by Charlie Lynch, 16 October 2020.

16 *Humanist News*, no. 85, July 1997, 13.

17 Ibid., no. 86, September 1997, 10.

18 BA, BHA/1/18/3 Humanist Parliamentary Group, list, undated but *c.* 1998.

19 Ibid., House of Lords Affirmers on 16 July 2001.

20 *Humanist News*, Summer 2003, 14.

21 BA, BHA/1/17/80 Bishops in the HOL, BHA Briefing Paper to APPHG, January 2007.

22 Ibid., no. 85, July 1997, 13.

23 Chris Allen, 'We don't do god: A critical retrospective of new labour's approaches to "religion or belief" and "faith"', *Culture and Religion* v.12 (3) (September 2011), 259–75.

24 https://www.humanism.scot/what-we-do/humanitie/custom_tag/time-for-reflection/; https://www.bbc.co.uk/news/uk-wales-politics-40099436.

25 Paula Templeton (pseud.), interviewed by Charlie Lynch, 16 October 2020.

26 Data from Charity Commission website for BHA charity number 285987. In 2020 terms on CPI Inflation Calculator, the 1997 figure = £355,936; 2019 figure = £2,710,710. Information on volunteer celebrancy from Paula Templeton (pseud.).

27 Marilyn Mason, 'A fog of uncertainty – a humanist peers into the future', *Shap Journal* v.xxvii (2004), 25–7 at 27.

28 *Humanity*, November 1998, 13.

29 DPA, 2001 BHA Survey, Research into Humanist's Needs.

30 'Trustees Annual Review 2000', *Humanist News*, Autumn 2000, 12.

31 DPA, Hanne Stinson, Memoir, 2.

32 *Humanist News*, Autumn 2002, 14.

33 *BHA E-Bulletin*, 9 September 2004.

34 *Humanist News*, Autumn 2003, 7–8.

35 A Trustee speaking to us confidentially in 2021.

36 *Humanists UK Impact Report 2020*, 3.

37 BA, BHA/1/10/1–3 Humanist Counselling Group, 1963–1993.

38 *Humanists UK News*, September 2018, 25; March 2019, 27. Humanists UK, Annual Report and Financial Statements, 2019, 11, https://www.faithtofaithless.com.

39 https://www.gov.uk/government/news/foreign-office-advisory-group-on-freedom-of-religion-or-beliefw.gov.uk); Andrew Copson, interviewed by Charlie Lynch, 10 September 2021.

40 DPA, *Humanists UK, Annual Report and Financial Statements*, 2018, 8; *Humanists UK News*, September 2021; and Rachel Taggart-Ryan.

41 *New Humanist*, 6 August 2019, https://newhumanist.org.uk/articles/5488/asylum-for
-pakistani-humanist-rejected-over-failure-to-identify-plato-and-aristotle, accessed 22
June 2021.

42 DPA, *Humanists UK, Annual Report and Financial Statements*, 2018, 8.

43 *The Guardian*, 26 January 2018; *The Times*, 15 May 2019; *New Humanist*, 6 August
2019; DPA, *Humanists UK Annual Report 2019*.

44 DPA, *Humanists UK Annual Report*, 2019, 2.

45 Lois Lee, 'The conundrum of how to prove you hold a nonreligious worldview',
The Conversation, 26 January 2018.

46 A study by Beckworth and Gilliat discussed in Christopher Swift, *Hospital
Chaplaincy in the Twenty-First Century: The Crisis of Spiritual Care on the NHS*
(London, Taylor & Francis, 2016), 48–57.

47 Ibid., 132.

48 Ibid., 87–9.

49 David Savage, 'Inclusivity in UK pastoral, spiritual, and religious care: a
humanist perspective', *Health and Social Care Chaplaincy* v.9 (2021), 11–26 at
11; idem, *Non-religious Pastoral Care: A Practical Guide* (Abingdon, Routledge,
2019).

50 *The Guardian*, 22 February 2016, 15 July 2018.

51 https://humanism.org.uk/community/humanist-pastoral-support/.

52 *The Guardian*, 26 December 2019, 19c.

53 Two interviewees expressed these sentiments directly: Robin Wood and Gillian
Stewart, interviewed by Callum Brown, 18 August 2009 and 16 July 2009,
respectively.

54 https://www.gov.uk/government/groups/moral-and-ethical-advisory-group
#membership.

55 Andrew Copson, interviewed by Charlie Lynch, 10 September 2021, https://
www.politics.co.uk/opinion-former/press-release/2021/07/05/humanists-uk
-chief-exec-leads-nhs-england-national-memorial-to-workers-who-died-during
-pandemic/.

56 Charity Commission, *Humanists UK Annual Report and Financial Statements
2018*, 8. This is the last annual report displayed by the Charity Commission.

57 *Humanist News*, Autumn 2003, 7.

58 Ibid., 9.

59 The archive is at https://humanism.org.uk/ceremonies/funeral-tribute-archive/

60 At the New School of Psychotherapy and Counselling in London.

61 Humanists UK supplied information.

62 Figures from and calculated from data at https://docs.google.com/spreadsheets
/d/1DxfMf_wRUJFg-SWyxoKHYbFB6J9U1T5o-NafAA29r2U/edit#gid
=1699515432.

63 *Humanists UK Impact Report 2020*, 14.

64 https://humanism.org.uk/2018/08/22/first-legal-humanist-marriages-in
-northern-ireland-since-court-ruling-to-occur-this-weekend/.

65 Data from NISRA/GRONI, via Richy Thompson at Humanists UK.

66 Humanist Society Scotland (providing 3,276 weddings in 2019) began under EU guidance with a Scottish Humanist Council in 1961, reformed 1977, with the Society formed in 1989. The others, dating seemingly from no earlier than 2014 and devoted to ceremonies, were Caledonian Humanist Association (374 weddings), Fuze Foundation (573), Humanist Association of Scotland (134), Humanist Fellowship Scotland (145), Humanism in Scotland (62), Independent Humanist Ceremonies (1,270) and The Scottish Humanists (45). These data are from or calculated from tables 7.05 and 7.07 of https://www.nrscotland .gov.uk/statistics-and-data/statistics/statistics-by-theme/vital-events/general -publications/vital-events-reference-tables/2018/section-7-marriages.

67 Data from Ibid.

68 Survation, *Humanist Scotland Poll 12 July 2018*, Table 55, courtesy of Fraser Sutherland, HSS CEO.

69 Kenneth Furness b.1931, interviewed by Jessica Douthwaite, 23 October 2018.

70 Mason, 'A fog of uncertainty', 25–7. There may be some plausibility to this. Callum Brown attended a religion-free funeral in 2017 at which the officiant was a Church of Scotland minister without clerical garb.

71 As part of the Hate Crime and Public Order (Scotland) Act 2021.

Chapter 12

1 *The Guardian*, 22 July 2021, https://humanrightsact.org.uk/.

2 BA, BHA/1/17/21 Religious schools PQ Written Answer *c*. 2001.

3 Quoted in BA BHA 1/17/25, Marilyn Mason, 'The iceberg cometh', 2001.

4 BA, BHA/1/17/25, Marilyn Mason, cutting from TES, 6 May 2005.

5 *Humanist News*, Spring 2003, 4.

6 BA, BHA/1/17/25 BHA annotations to National Association of Governors and Managers' responses to Education White paper, Schools Achieving Success, November 2001.

7 BA, BHA/1/17/21, 'Faith schools', DES Background Briefing for Labour MPs, 2001.

8 With Marilyn Mason and David Pollock. *Humanist News*, Autumn 2003, 1.

9 https://humanism.org.uk/2018/11/13/more-religious-groups-apply-to-open-free -schools-in-england/

10 *Humanity*, December/January 1998–99, 8.

11 *Humanist News*, Autumn 2003, 4–5.

12 Marilyn Mason, interviewed by Linda Fleming, 8 August 2019; *Humanist News*, Autumn 2003, 13–14.

13 Andrew Copson, 'Losing faith', *New Humanist*, March/April 2006, 13.

14 https://accordcoalition.org.uk.

15 https://fairadmissions.org.uk.

16   https://humanism.org.uk/2012/12/14/full-judgement-published-in-richmond
     -catholic-schools-judicial-review/.

17   *Huffpost,* 20 June 2014, https://humanism.org.uk/campaigns/schools-and-education/
     school-curriculum/science-evolution-and-creationism/

18   Stephen Evans, 'Facilitating more religious segregation . . ', *Huffpost,* 10 September
     2017; Jonathan Romain, 'At a time when social cohesion is needed . . ', *The
     Independent,* 3 June 2017, https://fairadmissions.org.uk

19   Letter from Sir Michael Wilshaw (Ofsted) to Nicky Morgan MP [Education
     Secretary], 24 November 2015, https://assets.publishing.service.gov.uk/government/
     uploads/system/uploads/attachment_data/file/479122/HMCI__advice_note_BSI.pdf;
     https://humanism.org.uk/2015/11/24/ofsted-finds-serious-failings-at-faith-schools
     -previously-inspected-by-controversial-bridge-schools-inspectorate/.

20   Jeremy Fox and others v. the Secretary of State for Education, *Approved Judgment* [by
     Justice Warby] 25 November 2015, https://www.judiciary.uk/wp-content/uploads
     /2015/11/r-fox-v-ssfe.pdf.

21   https://humanism.org.uk/2020/11/05/humanists-uk-launches-manifesto-for-the
     -future-of-education-in-the-uk/.

22   See Department for Education guidance at https://www.gov.uk/government/
     publications/relationships-education-relationships-and-sex-education-rse-and-health
     -education; https://humanism.org.uk/2020/09/01/success-humanists-uk-celebrates
     -introduction-of-compulsory-relationships-and-sex-education-after-more-than-50
     -years-campaigning/.

23   The Curriculum and Assessment (Wales) Act 2021 came into force in September
     2022, https://www.politics.co.uk/opinion-former/press-release/2021/04/30/welsh
     -act-makes-curriculum-fully-inclusive-of-humanism/; https://humanism.org.uk
     /2021/03/03/senedd-votes-to-require-schools-to-promote-childrens-rights/; https://
     www.christian.org.uk/press_release/christians-decry-atheist-power-grab-in-welsh
     -schools/.

24   Callum Brown, Jane Mair and Thomas Green, *Religion in Scots Law: Report of an
     Audit at the University of Glasgow* (Edinburgh, HSS, 2016), 137–91.

25   See Scottish government advice on religious and moral education at https://www.gov
     .scot/publications/curriculum-for-excellence-religious-and-moral-education/.

26   https://humanism.org.uk/about/our-people/patrons/professor-a-c-grayling./

27   https://www.politics.co.uk/opinion-former/press-release/2009/07/31/british
     -humanist-association-welcomes-human-rights-ruling-in-purdy-case/.

28   https://www.humanism.scot/what-we-do/previous-campaigns/assisted-dying/.

29   *Humanist News,* Summer 2003, 4.

30   Marylin Mason b.1946, interviewed by Linda Fleming, 8 August 2019.

31   https://www.theguardian.com/politics/2003/jan/21/uk.iraq2.

32   See the coverage in *Humanist News,* Summer 2003, 4–5.

33   *Humanist News,* Spring 2003, 19; Summer 2003, 5.

34   *The Times,* 16 January 2003.

35   DPA, Vaughan Evans (BHA member) post to BHA members' forum, 21 May 2002.

36   DPA, David Pollock post on BHA membership online forum, 26 May 2002.

37 *Humanist News*, Summer 2003, 5. David Tribe, *A 100 Years of Freethought* (London, Elek, 1967), 236.

38 'The conscientious objector's stone in Tavistock square – and how it came about', https://for.org.uk/2018/08/17/co-stone-3/; *Humanist News*, Summer 2003, 4.

39 Brown witnessed the Humanist Society of Scotland AGM at the University of Stirling; *The Independent*, 23 October 2011.

40 https://www.politics.co.uk/opinion-former/2010/09/13/bha-protest-the-pope -campaign.

41 Andrew Copson, interviewed by Charlie Lynch, 15 April 2021; 'Papal visit: thousands protest against pope in London', https://www.bbc.co.uk/news/uk-11355258.

42 Andrew Copson, text of speech given to Protest the Pope rally, 18 September 2010, given to us.

43 Andrew Copson, interviewed by Charlie Lynch, 15 April 2021.

44 'The questions the Catholic Church wishes it had never asked', https://www .secularism.org.uk/the-questions-that-the-catholic.html; 'Taxpayers should not fund pope's visit, says survey', https://www.bbc.co.uk/news/uk-11180862.

45 *Humanist News*, Autumn 2003, 12.

46 Ibid., 5.

47 Ibid., Spring 2003, 3.

48 For an academic philosophy assessment of new atheism, see Whitley Kaufman, 'New atheism and its critics', *Philosophy Compass* v.14 (1) (January 2019), downloadable free.

49 Callum G. Brown, *Becoming Atheist: Humanism and the Secular West* (London, Bloomsbury, 2017), 127.

50 https://humanism.org.uk/2018/11/11/humanists-mark-historic-day-as-first-takes -part-in-national-remembrance-day-at-the-cenotaph/; https://www.humanism .scot/what-we-do/news/humanists-join-tributes-at-national-remembrance-day -ceremony/.

51 *Humanist News*, June–July 1996, 1, https://www.ipsos.com/ipsos-mori/en-uk/ humanist-beliefs.

52 The Church of Ireland disestablished in 1869; the Church in Wales in 1920, and the Church of Scotland, though persisting to self-style as 'the national church', was de facto disestablished in 1925.

53 Ben Clement, *Religion and Public Opinion in Britain: Continuity and Change* (Basingstoke, Palgrave Macmillan, 2015), 170.

54 https://www.theguardian.com/commentisfree/2008/jun/20/transport.religion.

55 https://humanism.org.uk/campaigns/successful-campaigns/atheist-bus-campaign.

56 Ibid., https://www.theguardian.com/world/2009/jan/06/atheist-bus-campaign -nationwide.

57 Andrew Copson, interviewed by Charlie Lynch, 12 February 2021.

58 *Humanists UK News*, August 2017, 3.

59 Matthew Engelke, *God's Agents: Biblical Publicity in Contemporary England* (Berkeley CA, University of California Press, 2013), 141–7.

60 *The Times*, 6 December 1999, 18.

61 *The Times*, 12 January 2000, 8; 11 January 2001, 5; 17 May 2001, 10; 9 August 2002, 9; 30 October 2002, 12; 1 November 2002; 20 March 2004, 5; 24 May 2004, 10; 12 October 2005, 4; 13 October 2005, 21, 2 April 2010, 8.

62 *Humanity*, June/July 1998, 13.

63 He was editor from 1977 to 1981. Jim Herrick b. 1944, interviewed by Jessica Douthwaite, 1 November 2018.

64 *BHA News*, September/October 2009, 1.

65 https://www.equalityhumanrights.com/en/human-rights/human-rights-act.

66 DPA, Madeline Pym, 'Implications for the BHA of the human rights act', 8 December 2001, 4.

67 *Humanist News*, Spring 2003, 19.

68 *Humanist News*, Autumn 2002, 15.

69 BA, BHA/1/17/58–60, 64, 65, 67, 68, 106, 152, 162, 163, CEHR.

70 https://humanism.org.uk/2008/05/16/news-104.

71 http://news.bbc.co.uk/1/hi/wales/7406419.stm.

72 *New Law Journal*, 22 May 2008.

73 Hanne Stinson, interviewed by Jessica Douthwaite, 9 October 2018.

74 BA, BHA/1/17/67, letter from Don Horrocks of Evangelical Alliance to Hanne Stinson of BHA, 22 March 2005; Note of meeting at Home Office on Equality Bill, Part 2, Religious Discrimination 15 February 2005.

75 DPA, E-data, Hanne Stinson, Memoir, 5.

76 The evidence offered by all contributors is available online https://publications .parliament.uk/pa/ld200203/ldselect/ldrelof/95/2071803.htm. This link also provides access to the written evidence as well and the Committee's final report.

77 House of Commons Library, SN/PC/04597, Lucinda Maer, *The Abolition of the Blasphemy Offences* (9 May 2008) House of Commons Briefing Note; David S. Nash, *Acts Against God* (London, Reaktion Books, 2020).

78 Hate Crime and Public Order (Scotland) Act 2021, s.16.

79 Twenty-seven out of fifty-six national bodies. See the review of church finances in David Pollock, 'The privileged position of the churches in Europe', *International Humanist News*, November 2007, 28.

80 https://humanists.international/what-is-humanism/the-amsterdam-declaration/.

81 The Reports are online: https://humanists.international/what-we-do/freedom-of-thought-report/.

82 *Freedom of Thought 2014: A Global Report on the Rights, Legal Status and Discrimination Against Humanists, Atheists and the Non-Religious* (London: IHEU, 2014), 11 (available online at Humanists International).

83 *The Freedom of Thought Report, 2016: Key Countries Edition. A Global Report on the Rights, Legal Status and Discrimination Against Humanists, Atheists, and the Non-Religious* (London: IHEU, 2016), 9.

84 Andrew Copson email to Charlie Lynch, 22 July 2021.

85 BHA, *Annual Report and Financial Statements for the Year Ended 31 December 2016*, 11.

86 Humanists UK, *Annual Report and Financial Statements for the Year Ended 31 December 2017*, 19.

87 https://humanists.international/2021/03/gulalai-ismail-announced-as-first-ever-ambassador-for-humanists-international.

88 'Gulalai Ismail escapes Pakistan, flees to safety', *Humanists UK News*, December 2019, 16; *Humanists UK Annual Report*, 2019, 13.

89 'Humanists come together to call for Mubarak Bala's release on first anniversary of arrest', https://humanism.org.uk/2021/04/28/humanists-come-together-to-call-for-mubarak-balas-release-on-first-anniversary-of-arrest; https://humanists.international/case-of-concern/mubarak-bala.

90 'One year after: authorities must comply with Federal High Court decision to release Mubarak Bala on bail', https://www.ohchr.org/EN/NewsEvents/Pages/DisplayNews.aspx?NewsID=27033&LangID=E. BBC News website, 5 April 2022.

91 Andrew Copson, interviewed by Charlie Lynch, 10 September 2021.

92 UN Press Release, 12 December 2003, https://www.un.org/press/en/2003/sgsm9076.doc.htm.

93 Johannes Morsink, *The Universal Declaration of Human Rights: Origins, Drafting, and Intent* (Philadelphia, University of Pennsylvania Press, 1999), x–xi.

94 Turan Kayaoglu, 'Giving an inch only to lose a mile: Muslim states, liberalism, and Human Rights in the United Nations', *Human Rights Quarterly* v. 36 (2014), 61–9 at 81.

95 Chris Moores, *Civil Liberties and Human Rights in Twentieth-Century Britain* (Cambridge, Cambridge University Press, 2017), 18–19.

Chapter 13

1 Susan Budd, 'The humanist societies: the consequences of a diffuse belief system', in Bryan R. Wilson (ed.), *Patterns of Sectarianism* (London, Heinemann, 1967), 377–405 at 399.

2 *Humanist Newsletter*, June 1980, 1.

3 Robbi Robson, interviewed by Charlie Lynch, 16 October 2020.

4 Notably as summarised succinctly in his argument at Edward Royle, *Radicals, Secularists and Republicans: Popular Freethought in Britain 1866–1915* (Manchester, MUP, 1980), 329.

5 Data from Northern Ireland Life and Times survey datasets for 2000, 2010 and 2020, at https://www.ark.ac.uk/nilt.

6 In annual surveys. Data for Scotland from https://www.scotcen.org.uk/news-media/press-releases/2017/july/scots-with-no-religion-at-record-level/, and calculated for Wales by Callum Brown from data at https://statswales.gov.wales/Catalogue/Equality

-and-Diversity/Religion/religion-by-region and for England from data, https://www
.ons.gov.uk/peoplepopulationandcommunity/culturalidentity/religion/adhocs/009760r
eligioningreatbritainbyregionoctober2017toseptember2018.

7 Bill Cooke, *The Blasphemy Depot: A Hundred Years of the Rationalist Press Association*
(London, RPA, 2003), 6–7; Owen Chadwick, *The Secularisation of the European Mind*
(Cambridge, CUP, 1975), 5–7.

8 David Ibry (ed.), *Exodus to Humanism: Jewish Identity Without Religion* (Amherst,
Prometheus, 1999), 130.

SOURCES

Links to websites are given in footnotes and may not be repeated here. All urls were correct in 2021.

Oral history interviews (transcribed)

Ashby, Robert b.1965, interviewed by Charlie Lynch, 16 October 2020
Bolton, Dermot b.1970, interviewed by Callum Brown, 18 July 2021
Bolton, Tom b.1943, interviewed by Callum Brown, 18 July 2021
Brierley, Tony b.1936, interviewed by Charlie Lynch, 26 January 2021
Bruce, Nigel b.1921, interviewed by Callum Brown, 21 April 2010
Copson, Andrew b.1980, interviewed by Callum Brown, 6 October 2019, and by
    Charlie Lynch 12 February, 15 April and 10 September 2021
Duke, Barry b.1947, interviewed by Charlie Lynch, 16 May 2021
Furness, Kenneth b.1931, interviewed by Jessica Douthwaite, 23 October 2018
Herrick, Jim b.1944, interviewed by Jessica Douthwaite, 1 November 2018
Kingsley, Graham b.1939, interviewed by Jessica Douthwaite, 16 October 2018
Leeson, John b.1947, interviewed by Charlie Lynch, 23 October 2020
Martin, Terry b.1941, interviewed by Callum Brown, 21 July 2009
Mason, Marilyn b.1946, interviewed by Linda Fleming, 8 August 2019
Munday, Diane b.1931, interviewed by Jessica Douthwaite, 2 October 2018
Paterson, Richard b.1945, interviewed by Charlie Lynch, 13 December 2020
Pollock, David b.1944, interviewed by Callum Brown, 1 September 2014 and 2019.
Robson, Robbi b.1946, interviewed by Charlie Lynch, 16 October 2020
Smoker, Barbara 1923–2020, interviewed by Callum Brown, 17 July 2018, and by
    Jessica Douthwaite, 27 September 2018
Stewart, Gillian b.1960, interviewed by Callum Brown, 16 July 2009
Stinson, Hanne b.1948, interviewed by Jessica Douthwaite, 9 October 2018

Tatchell, Peter b.1952, interviewed by Charlie Lynch, 14 September 2020
Templeton, Paula (pseud.), interviewed by Charlie Lynch, 7 November 2020
Wood, Robin b.1941, interviewed by Callum Brown, 18 August 2009
Wynne Willson, Jane b.1933, interviewed by Charlie Lynch, 13 November 2020

Documentary archives

Aberdeen University Archive

Margaret Knight Papers MS3133/6/4 Roman Catholicism and Delinquency

Bishopsgate Archive (BA)

BHA/1/2/17 Papers of the Executive Committee
BHA/1/4/4 Don Liversedge papers
BHA/1/5/1–3 EU and BHA Annual Reports
BHA/1/7/4 Weinstein vs. British Humanist Association 1989–90
BHA/1/8/7–8 Advisory Council
BHA/1/10/1–3 Humanist Counselling Group, 1963–93
BHA/1/11/1–2 Humanist Housing Association
BHA/1/14/ Papers of Individual Members and Humanists
BHA/1/17/1 Press Releases 1967–70
BHA/1/17/2 Humanist Newsletter 1968–2001
BHA/1/17/5 Cuttings
BHA/1/17/21 Religious schools
BHA/1/17/25 Marilyn Mason papers
BHA/1/17/51 Ethics and Humanism
BHA/1/17/67 Commission for Equality and Humans Rights
BHA/1/17/80 Religious Representatives in the House of Lords 2007
BHA/1/18/3 Education
BRIERLEY/3/1 Miscellaneous papers
GALHA/1/2 Annual General Meetings
GALHA/1/11 Special General Meeting
GALHA/4/4 Gay Humanist Group
MUNDAY/1/2 Lecture notes
RA/1/4/1 RPA Minute Book 1950–74

Conway Hall Library and Archive (CHLA)

BLA/7/1/2–3 Blackham
NSS/4/4/14 Press releases

NSS/4/4/20 Posters etc.
SPES/1/1/4 Annual General Meeting Minutes
SPES/1/1/14 Trustee minutes
SPES/1/2/13 General Committee minutes
SPES/1/2/16–17 General Committee minutes
SPES/5/2/3 General Committee minutes
SPES/6/2/25 Growing Up 1971

David Pollock Archive (DPA)

(Now deposited in Bishopsgate Archive, excluding e-data.)
Box 1 EU, BHA meetings and correspondence 1963–70
Box 2 BHA Executive Committee 1970–76 and Conferences 1963–8
Box 3 BHA Conferences 1969–77, Annual Reports, Education Committee
Box 4 and 5 BHA Education
Box 6 and 6A Political Committee, Humanist Lobby, HPG, AAS
Box 8 BHA Open Society
E-data: undeposited digital material sent to the authors (as itemised in footnotes)

Hertfordshire Archives (HA)

D/EWW/219 – Diane Munday's papers

Lambeth Palace Archive (LPA)

Coggan Papers 31, 43
Ramsey Papers 263, 273

John Leeson Archive (JLA)

'Secretary's Report'. 1 November 1983
MS BHA Questionnaire to members June 1985, by Keith F. Grimson
'Development of the BHA'
BHA executive committee, miscellaneous documents 1995–6.

LSE Archive (LSEA)

HCA/DYSON/1–2, Anthony E Dyson [HLRA] correspondence
PROGRESSIVE LEAGUE/2/1, *Plan*, Annual Reports

Oxford University Humanist Group online archive (OUHGA)

Hilary 1957/58 to Trinity1969/70.

National Library of Scotland (NLS)

Acc.10318 Peter Ritchie Calder Papers.
Acc.6545 John Boyd Orr Papers

The National Archive (TNA)

CO 847/23/17 Universal Rights of Man, pamphlet by HG Wells
HO 45 10665/216120/12 J.M. Robertson to Reginald Mckenna, 5 January 1912
HO 45 10665/216120/86 Memorandum from Sir John Simon to Reginald Mckenna, February 1914.
HO 45 24619/217549/9
HO 45 24619/217549/21.
HO 45 24619/217549/32
HO 144 871/160552/4 Alf Carrick to Home Secretary, 9 January 1908
[MI5 files:] KV2/2093 Kingsley Martin
KV2/3523 and 3524 Jacob Bronowski

University of East Anglia Archive (UEAA) – Solly Zuckerman collection

SZ/TQ/1/1-7 Tots and Quots Dining Society

Utrecht Municipal Archive (HET)

IHEU 1733 (by box)
1 Board of Directors
2 Annual Reports
75 Organising Committee 1984
81–87 Outgoing Correspondence
88–98 Received Correspondence
191–192 IHEU Directories
205–211 Youth Organisation 1966–2004
214 Board meeting papers 1998–2000
238 Documents of Board of Directors
284–285 Head Office move to London 1997–2003
291–300 Membership correspondence 1980–9
311 Membership organisations worldwide 1957–82
312 Questionnaires pre-1965
325 Membership payments 1969–85
482–487 Organisations' memberships, Great Britain 1963–95

663–667 1st World Congress 1951–3
668 2nd World Congress 1957

Warwick University Modern Records Centre

Personalist Group Papers MSS.151/3/PE/1/21

Primary published sources

An Inquiry into Humanism (London, BBC, 1966).
Annie Besant: An Autobiography (New York, Dossier Press, orig.1933, 2015).
Ayer, A. J. (ed.). *The Humanist Outlook* (London, Pemberton, 1968).
Blackham, H. J. *Humanism* (Harmondsworth, Penguin, 1967).
Bonner, Hypatia Bradlaugh. *The Gallows and the Lash: An Enquiry into the Necessity for Capital and Corporal Punishments* (London, William Reeves, 1897).
Idem. *Penalties Upon Opinion: Or Some Records of the Laws of Heresy and Blasphemy* (London, Watts & Co., 1934).
Boyd Orr, John. *As I Recall* (London, Macgibbon and Kee, 1966, FAO website facsimile).
Brand, Jo. *Look Back in Hunger: The Autobiography* (London, Headline, 2009).
Bridges, Horace J (ed.). *The Ethical Movement: Its Principles and Aims* (London, UES, 1911).
Bruce, Nigel. 'Children's hearings: a retrospect'. *British Journal of Criminology* v.15 (1975), 333–44.
Children and Young Persons Scotland Report, April 1964, HMSO Cmnd 2306.
Clark, Ann Marie. *Diplomacy of Conscience: Amnesty International and Changing Human Rights Norms* (2010, available online).
Cohen, Chapman. *A Fight for Right: The Decision of the House of Lords in Re Bowman and Others v. The Secular Society, Limited* (London, Pioneer Press, 1917).
Idem. *Almost an Autobiography: The Confessions of a Freethinker* (London, Pioneer, 1940).
Coit, Stanton. *Ethical Culture as a Religion for the People: Two Discourses Delivered in South Place Chapel, Finsbury, Ethical Church* (London, E.W. Allen, 1887).
Idem. *An Introduction to the Study of Ethics; Adapted from the German of G Von Gizycki Professor of Philosophy in the University of Berlin* (London, Swan and Sonnenschein, 1891).
Idem. *The Spiritual Nature of Man* (London, West London Ethical Society, 1910).
Copson, Andrew and Pollock, David, 'Religion and the state in an open society', 2006, https://humanism.org.uk/wp-content/uploads/BHA-Article-on-Church-and-State.pdf
Craig, Alec. 'Writing about sex'. *The Humanist* v.72 (February 1957), 6–8.
Curry, W. E. B. 'War, peace and human nature – a letter to John citizen'. *The Monthly Record* (December 1946), 2–3.
Draper Peter (preface). *Towards an Open Society: Ends and Means in British Politics* (London, Pemberton Books, 1971).
Drey, Sylvan. *Herbert Spencer's Theory of Religion and Morality* (London, Williams and Norgate, 1887).
Duffy, Maureen. *Separate Development? Out of the Closet and Into the Ghetto* (London, Gay Humanist Group, 1980).

Forster, E. M. *What I Believe and Other Essays* (London, G.W. Foote, 1999).

The Freedom of Thought Report, 2014-2019 (London, IHEU, 2014–2019).

Gates, Brian. 'Religious education and moral education: the end of a beautiful relationship?'. *Religion & Public Education* v.12 (1985), 162–5.

Gould, F. J. *Will Women Help? An Appeal to Women to Assist in Liberating Modern Thought from Theological Bonds* (London, Watts & Co, 1900).

Idem. *The Life-Story of a Humanist* (London, Watts, 1923).

Haeckel, Ernest. *The Riddle of the Universe at the Close of the Nineteenth Century* (London, Watts, 1900).

Hamilton, Henry. *History of the Homeland: The Story of the British Background* (London, George Allen and Unwin, 1947).

Harte, J. D. C. 'The religious dimension of the Education Reform Act 1988'. *Ecclesiastical Law Journal* v.1 (1989), 32–52.

Hawton, Hector. *The Humanist Revolution* (London, Pemberton,1963).

Hemming, James. *Teenage Loving and Living* (London, British Medical Association, 1976).

Idem. 'Morality after myth'. *Journal of Moral Education* v.25 (1) (1996), 39–45.

Hemming, James and Marratt, Howard. *Humanism and Christianity: The Common Ground of Moral Education* (London, BHA, 1969).

Hitchens, Christopher. *HITCH-22: A Memoir* (London, Atlantic Books, 2010).

Hitchens, Peter. *Rage Against God* (London, Bloomsbury, 2010).

Idem. *The War We Never Fought* (London, Bloomsbury, 2012).

Hobson, JA. *Rationalism and Humanism* (London, Watts, 1932).

Hogben, Lancelot. *Dangerous Thoughts* (London, George Allen & Unwin, 1939).

Home Office. *The Wootton Report [Advisory Committee on Drug Dependence Sub-committee on Hallucinogens]* 1967.

House of Commons Library, SN/PC/04597. Lucinda Maer, *The Abolition of the Blasphemy Offences* (9 May 2008), Briefing Note.

House of Lords. Bowman and Others, Appellants; Secular Society, Limited, Respondents [1917] A.C. 406.

Hoyle, Fred. *The Small World of* (London, Michael Joseph, 1986).

Humphrey, John P. 'Memoirs of, the first director of the united nations division of human rights'. *Human Rights Quarterly* v.5 (1983), 387–439.

Huxley, Francis. *Affable Savages: An Anthropologist Among the Urubu Indians of Brazil* (New York, Viking, 1957).

Huxley, Julian. *Religion without Revelation* (London, Watts, 1927, 1945, 1957).

Idem (ed.). *The Humanist Frame* (London, George Allen & Unwin, 1961).

Huxley, Julian, and Haddon, A. C. *We Europeans: A Survey of 'Racial Problems'* (London, Jonathan Cape, 1935).

IHEU 1959, 1966, 1967: The International Humanist and Ethical Union and Its Member Organizations (Utrecht).

Jenkins, Joe. *GCSE Religious Studies: Contemporary Moral Issues* (London, Heinemann Educational Books, 1987).

Jeremy Fox and others v. the Secretary of State for Education, *Approved Judgment* [by Justice Warby] 25 November 2015.

Joad, C. E. M. *The Book of Joad: A Belligerent Autobiography* (London, Faber & Faber, 1935).

Jogee, Elizabeth. *Edinburgh Youth Homes: The First Fifteen Years* (Edinburgh, n.pub., c.1988).

Khorsandi, Shappi. 'Comic timing'. *New Humanist*, January/February 2007, 6.

Idem. *A Beginner's Guide to Acting English* (London, Ebury Press, 2009).

Knight, Margaret. *Morals Without Religion* (London, Dennis Dobson, 1955).

Idem (ed.). *Humanist Anthology: From Confucius to Bertrand Russell* (London, RPA, 1961).

Konig, Card. Franziskus. 'Dialogue with Non-believers'. *L'Osservatore Romano Weekly Edition in English*, 10 October 1968, 6, online.

Kurtz, Paul. 'Sakharov: a humanist Galileo'. *Free Inquiry* v.10 (1990), 46–7.

Idem. 'The future course of humanism'. *New Humanist*, June 1996, 2–5.

Kurtz, Paul and Dondeyne, Albert (eds.). *A Catholic/Humanist Dialogue: Humanists and Roman Catholics in a Common World* (London, Pemberton, 1972).

Martin, Kingsley. *Father Figures: A First Volume of Autobiography 1897–1931* (Harmondsworth, Penguin, orig.1966, 1969).

Martineau, James. *The Relationship Between Ethics and Religion: An Address at the Opening of the Session 1881–2* (London, Williams and Norgate, 1881).

Mason, Marilyn. 'A fog of uncertainty – a humanist peers into the future'. *Shap Journal* xxvii (2004) 25–7.

Mass-Observation [Bob Willcock?]. *Puzzled People: A Study in Popular Attitudes to Religion, Ethics, Progress and Politics in a London Borough* (London, Victor Gollancz, 1947).

Matthews, W. R. 'Book review', *Theology* v.17 (1928), 319.

McCabe, Joseph. *Religion of the Twentieth Century* (London, Watts, 1899).

Idem. *The Riddle of the Universe To-day* (London, Watts, 1934).

Moral and Religious Education in County Schools (London, SMC, 1970).

Mudie-Smith, Richard (ed.). *The Religious Life of London* (London, Hodder & Stoughton, 1904).

Needham, Joseph. *The Skeptical Biologist*, 1929.

Idem. *The Great Amphibian*, 1932.

Nott, Kathleen. *The Emperor's Clothes* (London, Heinemann, 1953).

Page, Martin Richard. *Britain's Unknown Genius: Introduction to the Life-Work of John Mackinnon Robertson* (London, SPES, 1984).

Partridge, Frances. *Memories* (London, Phoenix, orig.1981, 1996).

Idem. *Hanging on: Diaries 1960–1963* (London Phoenix, 1990).

Pirie, Antionette (ed.). *Fall Out: Nuclear Hazards from Nuclear Explosions* (London, MacGibbon & Kee, 1957).

Popper, Karl. *The Open Society and Its Enemies* 2 vols. (London, George Routledge, 1945).

Priestley, J. B. 'Britain and the nuclear bombs'. *New Statesman*, 2 November 1957, 554–6.

Rayner, Claire. *How Did I Get Here from There?* (London, Virago, 2003).

Reade, William Winwood. *The Martyrdom of Man* (London, Watts, 1872, 1943).

Idem. *The Outcast* (London, Watts, 1933).

Record of the Proceedings of the First Universal Races Congress (London, PS King and Son, 1911).

Rhéume, Charles. 'Western scientists' reactions to Andrei Sakharov's human rights struggle in the Soviet Union, 1968–1989'. *Human Rights Quarterly* v.30 (2008), 1–20.

Robertson, J. M. *Christianity and Mythology* (London, Watts, 1900).

Robson, Robbi. 'My vision of a strong humanism'. *Humanity*, April/May 1999, 11.

Rolph, C. H. *Living Twice: An Autobiography* (London, Quality Book Club/Victor Gollancz, 1976).

Russell, Bertrand. *Free Thought and Official Propaganda* (London, Watts, 1922).

Idem. *Why I am Not a Christian* (London, Routledge, orig. 1957, 1996)

Russell, Bertrand. *The Autobiography of Bertrand Russell One Volume Edition* (London, Unwin, 1975).

Scarman, Lord Justice. *The Red Lion Square Disorders of 15 June 1974: Report of Inquiry* (London, HMSO Cmnd 5919), 1975.

Smith, Jean, and Toynbee, Arnold (eds.). *Gilbert Murray: An Unfinished Autobiography* (London, George Allen and Unwin, 1960).

Smoker, Barbara. *Humanism* (London, Ward Lock Educational, 1973).

Idem. *My Godforsaken Life: Memoir of a Maverick* (London, Thornwick, 2018).

Snell, Harry. *Men, Movements and Myself* (London, J.M. Dent and Sons, 1936).

The Socialist Sunday School Hymnbook, 1926.

South Place Ethical Society Annual Report, 1887.

Spiller, Gustav. *Faith in Man: The Religion of the Twentieth Century* (London, Swan and Sonnenschein, 1908).

Idem. *A Generation of Religious Progress* (London, Watts, 1916).

Idem. *The Ethical Movement in Great Britain: A Documentary History* (London, Farleigh Press, 1934).

Stevenson, Yvonne *The Hot-House Plant: An autobiography of a young girl* (London, Elek/Pemberton, 1976).

Survation, *Humanist Scotland Poll 12 July 2018*.

Tribe, David. *The Open Society and its Friends* (London: National Secular Society, 1971).

[Troup, E. Josephine (ed.)], *Hymns of Modern Thought* (London, Houghton & Co, 1900), online at www.leicestersecularsociety.org.uk/PHP_redirected/hymns.php.

Vallance, Zona. 'Women as moral beings'. *International Journal of Ethics* v.12 (1902), 173–95.

Wells, H. G. *First and Last Things: A Confession of Faith and Rule of Life* (London, Archibald Constable & Co., 1908).

Idem. *The Outline of History: Being a Plain History of Life and Human Kind vol. I* (London, George Newnes, nd but 1920).

Idem. *The Open Conspiracy: Blue Prints for a World Revolution* (London, Gollancz, 1928).

Idem. *A Short History of the World* (London, Watts, 1929).

Idem. 'Project of a world society'. *New Statesman*, 20 August 1932, 197–8.

Idem. *What Are We To Do With Our Lives?* (London, Watts, 1935).

Idem. *The Conquest of Time* (London, Watts, 1942).

Wells, H. G., Wells, G. P., and Huxley, Julian. *The Science of Life*, 4 volumes (London, Waverley, 1929–31).

Wheeler, Romney. 'A conversation with Bertrand Russell', YouTube, 1952.

Whitehouse, Mary. *Quite Contrary* (London, Pan, 1988).

Whyte, Adam Gowans. *The Religion of the Open Mind* (London, Watts, orig. 1915, 1935).

Williams, Glanville. *The Sanctity of Life and the Criminal Law* (London, Faber and Faber, 1958).

Willson, Jane Wynne. *Parenting Without God: Experiences of a Humanist Mother* (Nottingham, Education Heretics Press, 1997).

Wootton, Barbara. *In a World I Never Made: Autobiographical Reflections* (London, George Allen & Unwin, 1967).

Idem. *Crime and Penal Policy: Reflections on Fifty Years' Experience* (London, George Allen & Unwin, 1978).

Primary source newspapers and magazines

Ethical Record, 1961,1974–75, 1980–81, 1984.
Humanist News, 1970–2003.
Humanists UK News, 2018–2019.
Humanist News Wales, 1993.
Humanity, 1998–99.
Issues, 2002.
New Humanist, online archive
South Place Magazine, 1895, 1905–1906.
The Freethinker, 1948, 1953, 1958, 1987.
The Gay Humanist: Newsletter of the Gay Humanist Group (later *Gay and Lesbian Humanist: Magazine of the Gay and Lesbian Humanist Group*), 1979, 1984–85, 1989.
The Guardian, 2018–2020.
The Humanist, 1957, 1961.
The Literary Guide, 1947–48, 1952.
The Monthly Record, 1936.
The Observer Magazine, Colin Cross, 'Living Without God'. 16 July 1967.
The Times, 1908, 1939–40, 1960, 1965, 1975–85.
The Trade Marks Journal no. 4632 (25 October 1967).

Secondary published sources (including online)

Alexander, Nathan G. 'E.D. Morel (1873–1924), the Congo Reform Association, and the history of human rights'. *Britain and the World* v.9 (2016), 213–35.

Allen, Chris. 'We don't do God: a critical retrospective of New Labour's approaches to "religion or belief" and "faith"'. *Culture and Religion* v.12 (3) (2011), 259–75.

Amrith, Sunil, and Sluga, Glenda. 'New histories of the United Nations'. *Journal of World History* v.19 (2008), 251–74.

Annan, Noel. *Leslie Stephen: The Godless Victorian* (New York, Random House, 1984).

Arnstein, Walter. *The Bradlaugh Case* (Oxford, Oxford University Press, 1965).

Barnett, Nicholas J. *Britain's Cold War: Culture, Modernity and the Soviet Threat* (London, IB Taurus, 2018).

Beck, Jessica. 'The women musicians of south place ethical society 1887–1927'. PhD thesis, Manchester Metropolitan University, 2018.

Bevir, Mark. *The Making of British Socialism* (Princeton, Princeton University Press, 2011).

Biddiss, Michael D. 'The Universal Races Congress of 1911'. *Races* v.13 (1971), 37–46.

Blue, Gregory. 'Needham (Noël) Joseph Terence Montgomery (1900–1995)'. *ODNB* (2008).

Bonakdarian, Mansour. 'Negotiating universal values and cultural and national parameters at the First Universal Races Congress'. *Radical History Review* v.92 (2005) 118–32.

Bouwman, Bastiaan. 'From religious freedom to social justice: the human rights engagement of the ecumenical movement from the 1940s to the 1970s'. *Journal of Global History* v.13 (2018), 252–73.

Brown, Callum. '"The Unholy Mrs Knight" and the BBC: secular humanism and the threat to the Christian nation, c.1945–1960'. *English Historical Review* v.127 (2012), 345–76.

Idem. *Becoming Atheist: Humanism and the Secular West* (London, Bloomsbury, 2017).

Idem. 'The necessity of atheism: making sense of secularisation'. *Journal of Religious History* v.41 (2017), 439–56.

Idem. *The Battle for Christian Britain: Sex, Humanism and Secularisation 1945–1980* (Cambridge, CUP, 2019).

Brown, Callum, Mair, Jane and Green, Thomas. *Religion in Scots Law: Report of an Audit at the University of Glasgow* (Edinburgh, HSS, 2016).

Budd, Susan. 'The humanist societies: the consequences of a diffuse belief system'. In B. R. Wilson (ed.), *Patterns of Sectarianism: Organisation and Ideology in Social and Religious Movements* (London, Heinemann, 1967), 377–405.

Budd, Susan. *Varieties of Unbelief: Atheists and Agnostics in English Society 1850–1960* (London, Heinemann, 1977).

Butler, Jon. 'Disquieted history in *A Secular Age*'. In Michael Warner et al (eds.), *Varieties of Secularism in a Secular Age* (Cambridge MA, Harvard University Press, 2010), 193–216.

Campbell, Colin B. 'Membership composition of the British Humanist Association'. *The Sociological Review* v.13 (3) (1965), 327–37.

Idem. 'Humanism and the culture of the professions: a study of the rise of the British humanist movement, 1954–63'. PhD thesis, University of London, 1967, British Library EThOS depository.

Idem. *Toward a Sociology of Irreligion* (n.pl., Alcuin Academics, 1971, 2013).

Carrette, Jeremy and King, Richard. *Selling Spirituality: The Silent Takeover of Religion* (London, Taylor and Francis, 2004).

Carroll, Samantha. '"I was arrested at Greenham Common in 1962": investigating the oral narratives of women in the anti-nuclear Committee of 100'. *Oral History* v.32 (2004), 35–48.

Idem. '"Fill the jails": identity, structure and method in the committee of 100, 1960–1968'. DPhil thesis University of Sussex, 2010.

Idem. 'Danger! official secret: the spies for peace: discretion and disclosure in the Committee of 100'. *History Workshop Journal* v.69 (Spring 2010), 158–76.

Cathcart, Brian. 'Rotblat, Sir Joseph (1908–2005)'. *ODNB* (2004).

Census 2001 & 2011.

Chadwick, Owen. *The Secularisation of the European Mind* (Cambridge, CUP, 1975).

Charity Commission, entry for BHA Charity 285987.

Cheadle, Tanya. *Sexual Progressives: Rethinking Intimacy in Late Victorian Scotland, 1880–1914* (Manchester, MUP, 2020).

Claeys, Gregory. *Imperial Sceptics: British Critics of Empire, 1850–1920* (Cambridge, CUP, 2010).

Clapham, Andrew. *Human Rights: A Very Short Introduction*, 2nd edn. (Oxford, OUP, 2015).

Clark, Ronald W. *The Life of Bertrand Russell* (London, Jonathan Cape, 1975).

Claydon, John. 'The treaty protection of religious rights: UN draft convention on the elimination of all forms of intolerance and of discrimination based on religion or belief'. *Santa Clara Law Review* v.12 (1972) 403–23.

Cole, Martin. 'The growing up controversy and the limits of school sex education in 1970s England'. *History of Education* v.37 (2008), 409–29.

Idem. "'I hope someone castrates you, you perverted bastard'": Martin Cole's sex education film, *Growing Up*'. *Sex Education* v.9 (4) (2009), 409–19.

Cook, Matt. 'Sexual revolution(s) in Britain'. In Gert Hekma and Alain Giami (eds.), *Sexual Revolutions* (London, Palgrave, 2014).

Cooke, Bill. *A Rebel to His Last Breath: Joseph McCabe and Rationalism* (Amherst, NY, Prometheus Books, 2001).

Idem. *The Blasphemy Depot: A Hundred Years of the Rationalist Press Association* (London, RPA, 2003).

Coupland, Philip 'H.G. Wells's "liberal fascism"'. *Journal of Contemporary History* v.35 (2000), 541–58.

Danahay, Martin A. *Community of One: Masculine Autobiography and Autonomy in Nineteenth-century Britain* (New York, SUNY Press, 1993).

De Nutte, Niels, and Gasenbeek, Bert (eds.). *Looking Back to Look Forward: Organised Humanism in the World: Belgium, Great Britain, the Netherlands and the United States of America, 1945–2005* (Brussels, VUB Press, 2019).

Desmarais, Ralph J. 'Tots and Quots (act[ive] 1931–1946)'. *ODNB* (2007).

Dittrich, Lisa. *Antikerikalismus als europäisches Phänomen: Protest und Öffentlichkeit in Frankreich, Spanien und Deutschland (1850–1914)* (Göttingen, Vandenhoeck & Ruprecht, 2014).

Driver, Christopher. *The Disarmers: A Study in Protest* (London, Hodder and Stoughton, 1964).

Dudgeon, Jeffrey. *H. Montgomery Hyde: Ulster Unionist MP, Gay Law Reform Campaigner and Prodigious Author* (Belfast, Belfast Press, 2018).

Edwards, Ben. 'The Godless Congress of 1938: Christian fears about communism in Great Britain'. *Journal of Religious History* v.37 (2013), 1–19.

Elton, Godfrey. *The Life of James Ramsay MacDonald* (London, Collins, 1939).

Engelke, Matthew. *God's Agents: Biblical Publicity in Contemporary England* (Berkeley CA, University of California Press, 2013).

Idem. 'Christianity and the anthropology of secular humanism'. *Current Anthropology* v.55 (10) (2014), 292–301.

Idem. 'The coffin question: death and materiality in humanist funerals'. *Material Religion* v.11 (2015), 26–49.

Feinberg, Barry and Kasrils Ronald (eds.). *Dear Bertrand Russell: A Selection of His Correspondence With the General Public 1950–1968* (London, George Allen and Unwin,1969).

Feldman, David. 'Jeremy corbyn, "imperialism". and labour's antisemitism problem'. *History Workshop Online*, June 2019, https://www.historyworkshop.org.uk/imperialism -and-labours-antisemitism-problem/.

Fletcher, Ian Christopher. 'Introduction: new historical perspectives on the first universal races congress of 1911'. *Radical History Review* v.92 (2005), 99–102.

Foot, Michael. *The History of Mr Wells* (London, Doubleday, 1995).

Freathy, Rob and Parker, Stephen G. 'Context, complexity and contestation: Birmingham's Agreed Syllabuses for Religious Education since the 1970s'. *Journal of Beliefs & Values* v.32 (2011), 247–63.

Idem. 'Secularists, humanists and religious education: religious crisis and curriculum change in England 1963–1975'. *History of Education* v.42 (2013), 222–56.

Freeden, Michael (ed.). *Reappraising J.A. Hobson: Humanism and Welfare* (London, Routledge, 1990).

Field, Clive D. 'Puzzled people revisited: religious believing and belonging in wartime Britain, 1939–45'. *Twentieth Century British History* v.19 (2008), 446–79.

Gasenbeek, Bert, and Gogineni, Babu (eds.). *International Humanist and Ethical Union, 1952-2002: Past, Present and Future* (Utrecht, De Tijdstroom, 2002).

Ginsberg, Morris. 'A humanist view of progress'. In Julian Huxley (ed.) *The Humanist Frame* (New York, Harper & Brothers, 1961), 113–28.

Goodall, Madeleine. 'Forgotten founders'. *New Humanist* (Spring 2021), 60–2.

Idem. 'Heroines of freethought: women of the early humanist movement'. https://humanism.org.uk.

Goodman, Raymond John. 'Wilson, Sir Geoffrey Masterman (1910–2004) '. *ODNB* (2008).

Gregg, Robert and Kale, Madhavi. '*The Negro* and the *Dark Princess*: two legacies of the Universal Races Congress'. *Radical History Review* v.92 (2005) 133–52.

Hall, Lesley. *Sex, Gender and Social Change* (London, Palgrave Macmillan, 2013).

Idem. '"A city that we shall never find?" The search for a community of fellow progressive spirits in the UK between the wars'. *Family and Community History* v.18 (2015), 24–36.

Herrick, Jim. *Vision and Realism: A Hundred Years of The Freethinker* (London, Foote, 1982).

Idem. *Aspiring to the Truth: Two Hundred Years of the South Place Ethical Society* (London, CHES, 2016).

Hiley, Nicholas. 'Counter-espionage and security in Great Britain during the First World War'. *English Historical Review* v.101 (1986), 635–70.

Hill, Christopher T. *Peace and Power in Cold War Britain: Media, Movements and Democracy c.1945-68* (London, Bloomsbury, 2018).

Historic England. *Listed building entry for Conway Hall* (1392343).

Hollis, Patricia. *The Pauper Press: A Study in Working Class Radicalism of the 1830s* (Oxford, Clarendon Press, 1970).

Idem. *Jennie Lee: A Life* (Oxford, OUP, 1997).

Holton, R. J. 'Cosmopolitanism or cosmopolitanisms? The Universal Races Congress of 1911'. *Global Networks* v.2 (2002) 153–70.

Hone, Michael. *The Bloomsbury Set: Homosexual Renaissance* (np, CreateSpace, 2017).

Howe, Stephen. *Anticolonialism in British Politics: The Left and the End of Empire 1918–1964* (Oxford, Oxford University Press, 1993).

Hunter, Michael. '*Pitcairneana*: an atheist text by Archibald Pitcairne'. *Historical Journal* v.59 (2016), 595–621.

Idem. *The Decline of Magic: Britain in the Enlightenment* (New Haven and London, Yale University Press, 2020).

Ibry, David (ed.). *Exodus to Humanism: Jewish Identity Without Religion* (Amherst, Prometheus, 1999).

Ironside, Philip. *The Social and Political Thought of Bertrand Russell* (Cambridge, CUP, 1996).

Jardine, Lisa. 'Things I never knew about my father'. Conway Memorial Lecture 26 June 2014, https://conwayhall.org.uk.

Jensen, Steven L. B. *The Making of International Human Rights: the 1960s, decolonisation and the reconstruction of global values* (Cambridge, CUP, 2016).

Jones, Greta 'The mushroom-shaped cloud: British scientists' opposition to nuclear weapons policy, 1945–57'. *Annals of Science* v.43 (2005), 1–26.

Judt, Tony. *Post-War: A History of Europe since 1945* (London, Pimlico, 2007).

Kayaoglu, Turan. 'Giving an inch only to lose a mile: Muslim states, liberalism, and Human Rights in the United Nations'. *Human Rights Quarterly* v.36 (2014), 61–9.

Keating, Conrad. *Smoking Kills: The Revolutionary Life of Richard Doll* (Oxford, Signal Books, 2014).

'Keep the Clause Campaign'. Wikipedia entry access, 2 August 2021.

Kennedy, Paul. *The Parliament of Man: The United Nations and the Quest for World Government* (London, Penguin, 2006).

Idem. *The Parliament of Man: The Past, Present and Future of the United Nations* (New York, Vintage Books, 2006).

Kensit, Connaire and Buchanan, Ruth. *Sexual Morals – a Humanist View* (Student Humanist Federation, n.d. c. 1966/7).

Kraft, Alison. 'Dissenting scientists in early cold war Britain: the "fallout" controversy and the origins of Pugwash, 1954–1957'. *Journal of Cold War Studies* v.20 (1) (2018), 57–100.

Krapf, Thomas M. and Hessel, Stéphane F. 'The last witness to the drafting process of the Universal Declaration of Human Rights'. *Human Rights Quarterly* v.35 (2013), 753–68.

Krever, Tor. 'Remembering the Russell tribunal'. *London Review of International Law* v.5 (2017), 483–49.

Lalouette, Jacqueline. *La Libre Penseé en France 1848–1940* (Paris, Albin Michel, 1997).

Larsen, Timothy. *Crisis of Doubt: Honest Faith in Nineteenth-Century England* (Oxford, Oxford University Press, 2006).

Laucht, Christoph. *Elemental Germans: Klaus Fuchs, Rudolf Peirls and the Making of British Nuclear Culture 1939–1959* (Basingstoke: Palgrave Macmillan, 2012).

Laursen, Eric. *The Duty to Stand Aside: Nineteen Eighty-Four and the Wartime Quarrel of George Orwell and Alex Comfort* (Edinburgh, AK Press, 2018).

Lawrence, Jon. *Me, Me, Me: The Search for Community in Post-war England* (Oxford, OUP, 2019).

Liddington, Jill. *The Long Road to Greenham* (London, Virago, 1989).

Limond, David. 'Frequently but naturally: William Michael Duane, Kenneth Charles Barnes and teachers as innovators on sex(uality) education in English adolescent schooling: c.1945–1965'. *Sex Education* 5 (2005), 107–18.

Longden, Gareth. 'A profile of the members of the British humanist association'. *Science, Religion and Culture* v.2 (3) (2015), 91–2.

Idem. 'A profile of the members of humanists UK: an empirical study'. PhD thesis, University of Wales (Wrexham Glyndwr University), 2019.

Lewis, Brian (ed.). *Wolfenden's Witnesses: Homosexuality in Postwar Britain* (Basingstoke, Palgrave, 2016).

Lutgendorff, Elizabeth A. 'Slaughtering sacred cows: rebutting the narrative of decline in the British secular movement from 1890s to 1930s'. PhD thesis, Oxford Brookes University, 2018).

MacKillop, Ian. *The British Ethical Societies* (Cambridge, CUP, 1986).

McLeod, Hugh. *Religion and Society in England 1850–1914* (Basingstoke, Macmillan, 1996).

Idem. *Religion and the People of Western Europe, 1789–1989* (Oxford, OUP, 1997)

McSmith, Andy. *No Such Thing as Society: A History of Britain in the 1980s* (London: Constable, 2011).

Major, Marie-France. 'Conscientious objection and international law: a human right'. *Case Western Reserve Journal of International Law* 24 (1992), 349–78.

Marquand, David. *Ramsay MacDonald* (London, Jonathan Cape, 1977).

Idem. 'Macdonald (James) Ramsay 1866–1937'. *ODNB* (2015).

Matausch, J. *A Commitment to Campaign: A Sociological Study of CND* (Manchester, MUP, 1989).

Matysik, Tracie. *Reforming the Moral Subject: Ethics and Sexuality in Central Europe, 1890–1930* (Ithaca, NY, Cornell University Press, 2008).

Maume, Patrick. 'Hyde, Harford Montgomery'. *Dictionary of Irish Biography* (2009).

Mazower, Mark. 'The strange triumph of human rights, 1933–1950'. *Historical Journal* v.47 (2004), 379–98.

Melnyk, Julie. *Victorian Religion: Faith and Life in Britain* (London, Praeger Publishers, 2008).

Moores, Christopher. 'From civil liberties to human rights? British civil liberties activism and universal human rights'. *Contemporary European History* v.21 (2012), 169–92.

Moores, Chris. *Civil Liberties and Human Rights in Twentieth-century Britain* (Cambridge, CUP, 2017).

Morsink, Johannes. *The Universal Declaration of Human Rights: Origins, Drafting, and Intent* (Philadelphia, University of Pennsylvania Press, 1999).

Moyn, Samuel. *The Last Utopia: Human Rights in History* (Cambridge, MA, Belknap Press, 2010).

Moyse, Cordelia. 'Tiedeman, May Louise Seaton'. *ODNB* (2020).

Mullen, Shirley. *Organised Freethought: The Religion of Unbelief in Victorian England* (New York, Garland, 1987).

Nash, David S. 'F. J. Gould and the Leicester secular society: a positivist commonwealth in Edwardian politics'. *Midland History* v.16 (1) (1991), 126–40.

Idem. *Secularism, Art and Freedom* (London, Pinter Press, 1992).

Idem. '"Look in her face and lose thy dread of dying": the ideological importance of death to the Secularist community in nineteenth-century Britain'. *Journal of Religious History* v.19 (1995) 158–80.

Idem. *Blasphemy in Modern Britain: 1789 to the Present* (London, Routledge, 1999).

Idem. 'Taming the god of battles: secular and moral critiques of the South African war'. In A. Cuthbertson, A. Gundlingh and M-L Suttie (eds.), *Writing a Wider War: Rethinking Gender, Race and Identity in the South African War* (Athens, Ohio University Press, 2002), 266–86.

Idem. 'Reassessing the "crisis of faith" in the Victorian age: eclecticism and the spirit of moral inquiry'. *Journal of Victorian Culture* v.16 (2011), 65–82.

Idem. *Christian Ideals in British History: Stories of Belief in the Twentieth Century*. (London, Palgrave, 2013).

Idem. 'Negotiating the marketplace of comfort: secularists confront new paradigms of death and dying in twentieth-century Britain'. *Revue Belge de Philologie et d'Histoire* v.95 (2018) 963–88.

Parkin, Frank *Middle Class Radicalism* (Manchester, Manchester University Press, 1968).

Pennybacker, Susan D. 'The Universal Races Congress, London political culture, and imperial dissent, 1900–1939'. *Radical History Review* v.92 (2005) 103–17.

Pentland, Gordon. 'The Freethinkers' Zetetic society: an Edinburgh radical underworld in the 1820s'. *Historical Research* v.91 (2018), 314–32.

Perry, George. *The Life of Python* (New York, Running Books, 1994).

Peyton, John. *Solly Zuckerman: A Scientist Out of the Ordinary* (London, John Murray, 2001).

Phillips, Paul T. *Contesting the Moral High Ground: Popular Moralists in Mid-Twentieth-Century Britain* (Montreal, McGill-Queen's University Press, 2013).

Radest, Howard B. *Toward Common Ground: The Story of the Ethical Societies in the United States* (New York, Bloomsbury, 1969).

Rechtenwald, Michael. *Nineteenth Century British Secularism* (London, Palgrave, 2016).

Robertson, Geoffrey. *The Justice Game* (London, Vintage, 1999).

Robinson, Emily. *The Language of Progressive Politics in Modern Britain* (London, Palgrave Macmillan, 2017).

Royle, Edward *Victorian Infidels: The Origins of the British Secularist Movement 1791–1866* (Manchester, Manchester University Press, 1974).

Idem. *Radicals, Secularists and Republicans: Popular Freethought in Britain, 1866–1915* (Manchester, Manchester University Press, 1980).

Idem. 'Secularists and Rationalists, 1800–1940'. In Sheridan Gilley and W. J. Sheils (eds.), *A History of Religion in Britain* (Oxford, Blackwell, 1994), 406–22.

Idem. 'Freethought: the religion of irreligion'. In D. G. Paz, *19ᵗʰ Century English Religious Traditions: Retrospect and Prospect* (Greenwood Press, 1995), 170–96.

Idem. 'Bonner, Hypatia Bradlaugh (1858–1935)'. *ODNB* (2006).

Idem. *Internationalism in the Age of Nationalism* (Philadelphia, Penn Press, 2013).

Savage, David. *Non-religious Pastoral Care: A Practical Guide* (Abingdon, Routledge, 2019).

Idem. 'Inclusivity in UK pastoral, spiritual, and religious care: a humanist perspective'. *Health and Social Care Chaplaincy* v.9 (2021), 11–26.

Schmidt, Klaus. 'Gobekli Tepe – the stone age sanctuaries: new results of ongoing excavations with a special focus on sculptures and high reliefs'. *Documenta Praehistorica* v.37 (2010), 239–56.

Schwartz, Laura. *Infidel Feminism: Secularism, Religion and Women's Emancipation, England 1830–1914* (Manchester, MUP, 2013).

Scott, John. 'Leonard Hobhouse as a social theorist'. *Journal of Classical Sociology* 16 (2016), 349–68.

Seal, Lizzie. 'Imagined communities and the death penalty in Britain, 1930–65'. *British Journal of Criminology* v.54 (2014), 908–27.

Shillington, Kevin. *Patrick Van Rensburg: Rebel, Visionary and Radical Educationist* (Johannesburg, Wits University Press, 2020).

Simkin, John. 'Roy Jenkins'. https://spartacus-educational.com/PRjenkinsR.htm, accessed 28 July 2021.

Sluga, Glenda. 'UNESCO and the (one) world of Julian Huxley'. *Journal of World History* v.21 (2010), 393–418.

Small, Harry. 'This is not a Christian country'. *Lawyers' Secular Society blog* online, 21 April 2014.

Smith, David C. *H.G. Wells: Desperately Mortal: A Biography* (New Haven and London, Yale University Press, 1986).

Stapleton, Julia. 'Barker, Sir Ernest'. *ODNB* (2004).

Subramanian, Samanth. *A Dominant Character: The Radical Science and Restless Politics of JBS Haldane* (London, Atlantic, 2019).

Swift, Christopher. *Hospital Chaplaincy in the Twenty-First Century: The Crisis of Spiritual Care on the NHS* (London, Taylor & Francis, 2016).

Taylor, Charles. *A Secular Age* (Cambridge, MA, Belknap Press, 2007).

Taylor, Richard R. and Pritchard, C. *The Protest Makers* (London, Pergamon, 1980).

Thompson, Ben. *Ban this Filth! Letters from the Mary Whitehouse Archive* (London, Faber and Faber, 2013).

Tomlinson, Jim. 'Winston Churchill versus E.D. Morel, Dundee, 1922 and the split in the liberal party'. *Journal of British Studies*, forthcoming.

Tregilgas-Davey, Marcus. 'Ex parte Choudhury: an opportunity missed'. *The Modern Law Review* v.54 (2) (Mar., 1991), 294–9.

Tribe, David. *100 Years of Freethought* (London, Elek, 1967).

Underwood, Martin Clifford. 'Joseph Rotblat and the moral responsibilities of the scientist'. *Science and Engineering Ethics* v.15 (2009), 2.

Idem. 'Joseph Rotblat, the bomb and anomalies from his archive'. *Science and Engineering Ethics* v.19 (2013), 487–90.

Vernon, James. *Modern Britain, 1750 to the Present* (Cambridge, CUP, 2017).

Veys, Lucy. 'Joseph Rotblat: moral dilemmas and the Manhattan project'. *Physics Perspectives* v.15 (2013), 451–69.

Weir, Todd. *Secularism and Religion in Nineteenth-Century Germany: The Rise of the Fourth Confession* (Cambridge, CUP, 2014).

Idem. 'The Christian front against godlessness: anti-secularism and the demise of the Weimar republic, 1928–1933'. *Past and Present* 229 (2015), 201–38.

Wells, G. A. (ed.), *J.M. Robertson (1856–1933): Liberal, Rationalist, and Scholar* (London, Pemberton, 1987).

Whitmarsh, Tim. *Battling the Gods: Atheism in the Ancient World* (London, Faber and Faber, 2016).

Whyte, Adam Gowans. *The Story of the R.P.A.: 1899–1949* (London, Watts and Co., 1949).

Wilford, R. A. 'Federation of progressive societies and individuals'. *Journal of Contemporary History* v.11 (2017), 49–82.

Wright, Susannah. '"There is something universal in our movement which appeals not only to one country, but to all": international communication and moral education 1892–1914'. *Journal of the History of Education Society* 37 (2008): 807–24.

Idem. *Morality and Citizenship in English Schools: Secular Approaches 1897–1944* (London, Palgrave Macmillan, 2017).

Wright, T. R. *The Religion of Humanity: The Impact of Comtean Positivism on Victorian Britain* (Cambridge, CUP, 1986).

Websites cited regularly

Humanist Heritage
Humanism.org
https://www.legislation.gov.uk/ukpga/
Wikipedia

INDEX

Russell, Bertrand   14, 20, 31–3, 37, 63, 86, 91, 95, 97–9, 108, 117, 123–9, 133–4, 136–7, 139, 148, 152, 166, 231, 251
   Why I Am Not a Christian (1957)   185
Russell, Dora   149
Russell-Einstein manifesto (1955)   127–8
Ryan, Ronald   38

Sankey Commission Declaration (1942)   135–8
Saunders, William   57
Savage, David   220
Sayers, Dorothy L.   37
Scarman Inquiry (Red Lion Square riot   1974)   168
Schoenman, Ralph   133–4
School of Ethics and Social Philosophy   53, 80
Schwartz, Laura   6, 26–7, 71
Scott, C.P.   97
Scottish Humanist Council   15, 201, 291 n.66
Seaton-Tiedeman, May   160
Second World War. *See* World War Two
Secretariatus Pro Non Credentibus   107
secularisation   1, 7, 32, 40, 192, 212, 237–8, 242, 250–1
secularism   2–4, 7, 10–11, 30, 51, 62, 64, 69, 88, 91, 100, 114, 118, 147, 225, 236, 248–9, 251. *See also* National Secular Society
   regional location of   26, 47
   in Scotland   47
   social composition of   26–7
Secular Review   49
sex education   18, 143, 159, 177–80, 228, 231, 237, 248–9
Shams, Imtiaz   219
Shaw, George Bernard   126, 136, 152, 195
Shelley, Percy Byshe   32
Silverman MP, Sydney   160
Simms, Madeleine   14, 108, 126, 144, 159, 172, 176
Sluga, Glenda   94
Smoker, Barbara   14, 19, 37, 74, 118, 126, 129, 168–9, 182, 188–9, 194–6, 205, 231
Snell, Harry   57, 90

Snow, C.P.   92
Socialist Secular Association   194–5
Social Morality Council   14, 153, 165, 180, 183–4, 198
Society of Friends. *See* Quakers
Sociological Review   91
South Place Ethical Society   3, 7–8, 16–17, 19, 23, 53–5, 57, 60–1, 63, 71–5, 78–9, 81–2, 85, 87, 92–3, 105, 108–11, 113–15, 123, 125, 140–2, 159, 166–9, 172–3, 177, 186, 188, 191–2, 194, 200–1, 209–11, 235, 249. *See also* Conway Hall Ethical Society; South Place Religious Society
   Hymn Book   55
   Junior Ethical Union   55
South Place Magazine   72, 85
South Place Religious Society   50, 53–4, 63
Sowter, Percy   105
Spanish Civil War   98–9
Speaker's Corner. *See* Hyde Park
Special Branch   18, 124, 132, 139. *See also* MI5
Spencer, Herbert   32–3, 51, 67, 71, 91
Spiller, Gustav   5, 14, 23, 56–7, 59–60, 73, 75, 77–8, 92, 95, 100
Spiritual Militancy League   73
Stanton, Elizabeth Cady   72
Stanton Coit House   110
statistics of humanists. *See* demographics of humanism
Steel MP, David   159
Stevenson, Yvonne   34
Stewart, Thomas William   89
Stewart MP, Michael   140
Stinson, Hanne   34, 213, 230, 238, 240, 242
Stopes-Roe, Harry   153, 173, 176, 181–3, 186
Strauss, David
   Life of Jesus   67
Student Humanist Federation   152
Student Rationalist Movement   112, 167
Subject Races International Committee   94
suicide and attempted suicide, abolition as crimes   3, 143, 159–60, 224, 229–30, 249. *See also* assisted dying